today we study the day before yesterday,

in order that yesterday may not paralyse today,

and today may not paralyse tomorrow.

....

Survey of the Century
by
F W Maitland

The Other
without fear, favour or prejudice

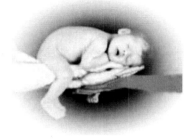

by
Chris N Greenland

An ordinary life becomes extraordinary

when you seek truth

setting your face against deception and lies.
Find it. Defend it.

Then your life will have meaning to others.
It will make a difference; howsoever small.
And the world will change; for the better.
Yes we can.

Dedication

I dedicate my story
a story like so many stories
of those who are "the other"
to

Sister Rocha, Sister Leonora, Sister Dagoberta, Sister Didyma,
Sister Radigoon, Sister Bronisflower, Sister Emmenfried, Sister
Obama,, Sister Acquilina and Sister Benedictus,
Sisters of the Order of The Precious Blood

who came from so far away and most of whom now forever lie side
by side under a tree in front of Sacred Heart Home, Bushtick,
Zimbabwe

Home for children in need of love

Acknowledgment
The author acknowledges, with gratitude, that some images appearing on
the front cover are sourced from http://www.fotosearch.com .

And to Virginia Macebo for correcting isiNdebele text.

Foreword

This book comprises a story, told by my husband, a former High Court Judge, spanning the southern African region during momentous change. Zimbabwe, Namibia, Zambia and South Africa, in particular, underwent revolutionary change as their people were liberated from the yoke of oppression.

As always, the question that arises is - what has all this meant to ordinary human beings? Have their lives been transformed for the better?

This story traces the life of one such person, who starts life in Zimbabwe and later has experience of all the countries in the region. It includes some hitherto unknown facts of significant historical interest such as the inside story of the trial of Edgar Tekere, President of the victorious Zimbabwe African National Union and why Ian Smith declared UDI.

It is a very unique biography, interesting, engaging and thought provoking. The beauty and magic that is Africa is an ever present backdrop and its animals easily come through as stars. There is also notable human drama, especially in the justice system.

However from start to finish the reader is kept challenged, on a plethora of real issues, arising on account of authentic experiences. There are no sacred cows. As intimated by the subset in the title "- without fear, force or prejudice -" political correctness is discarded as *"inconvenient truths"* and *"convenient untruths"* are thrown up for keen consideration.

The range of real issues is wide. Racism, ethnicity, xenophobia, human rights, systemic corruption, functional integrity, patronage, justice and their subsets, such as capital punishment, rape, infanticide, hypocrisy, affirmative action and systemic alienation are brought into focus on account of real life experiences.

There is an insistence that issues that affect human beings be resolved in simple truth. Your author believes that his story will not leave you untouched.

For that reason it is a story that has to be known ... because, at a certain point, it is the same story of so many whose lives are dependent, not on what they have in common with their kind, but because of what is different about them.

It should be of special interest to historians, academics, social scientists, political analysts, judges, advocates, lawyers, jurists and especially all those who know in their hearts that they are treated as different.

Palmira Rozaria Greenland

PS: The 1st publication was in early 2010.

By the year's end, and early, 2011, the impact statement of this book, that *ordinary* people can make their lives *extraordinary* by insisting on truth, so as to make a difference, was already vindicated in Tunisia, Jordan, the Yemen and Egypt ... and now in Libya.

....

....

.

On the morning of 19 October 2008, I am seated on a pavilion at the truly grand Twelve Apostles Hotel and Spa, Cape Town, described in the website brochure *as "standing at the edge of the world. On one side, a line of majestic mountains - The Twelve Apostles - reaches towards the heavens; on the other, the sun rises on breeching whales, playful dolphins, and crashing Atlantic rollers."*

I see no whales and dolphins, but my senses are imbued with all that is a beautiful morning, overseeing an enrapturing scene. Wispy clouds hang delicately in a clear blue sky, over a greenish blue sea, stretching to a distant horizon that appears so far and yet so near. The Atlantic is an immense expanse before me, quiet but surging, with long stretching rollers, almost still, but moving; moving relentlessly from far away to elapse on a beach whose sand seems to wink and glint in the rays of an early sun. I am in deep and quiet reflection, my thoughts going down the corridor of my life. Like the sea before me, my thoughts seem to come from afar to arrive in quiet surges that roll in and out of my mind's eye, sometimes as still pictures, sometimes as scenes playing out and then fading away. As I murmur a silent prayer those thoughts gently well up and then sink back into the sands of time, reappearing as footprints, footprints that start from so far away and yet so near ... ...

1. A Stranger Calls

It is 1943, in the district of Filabusi, Southern Rhodesia [now Zimbabwe]. Darkness is rapidly settling over a little cottage surrounded by trees, bushes and shrubs, infused with new life by the onset of the summer rains. Moira Williams is preoccupied with settling down for the night. She shoos the brood of chickens into their wire mesh run and, having secured the makeshift latch of the door, she goes inside just as night overtakes dusk. After preparing supper for her still absent husband, she retires to her bedroom. The room is small but cozy, lit up by flickering candlelight.

Gently she picks up her baby daughter from the bed and, cradling her in her arms, allows the child to suckle. It gives her a feeling of comfort and inner joy that counters the tiny heart wrench she feels at her husband not having returned home as yet. It helps too as regards the fact that she is feeling so unwell, feverish, cold, hot, sweaty and generally lethargic. She knows there is something wrong but resolves, as always, to beat it and resume normality. But this problem is different, stronger; debilating, and slowly making her feel quite ill. She suppresses the anxiety building up inside her. She assures herself that it will pass. The concoction of Dutch medicines and influenza potions she has taken will overcome the problem.

At the foot of the bed is a baby's cot. In it is another infant, a baby boy, gurgling and cooing as babies are wont to do. She is happy that her charges who, unlike her, seem well and happy. It is a relief. Whatever is attacking her has spared her most precious ones. When Viola, her baby daughter, seems to have had her fill, she puts her down and, having tucked her in, goes to pick up the child in the cot. He too is tenderly suckled. Three months older than Viola, he is stronger and able to draw sustenance with little difficulty. This brings feelings of warm comfort to her. It keeps the feeling of slight wooziness at bay. The ritual is completed by her burping both babies. She has been worried about the little boy. She feels so good that he is fine, wildly punching little fist, feet, arms and knees into the air with happy exuberance. She caresses, fondles and plays with her charges, giggling, cooing and sing-songing as only a mother can. That the babies are perceptibly different, Viola is pinky white and the other baby is a tingy golden-brown is an irrelevance to her. Her heart is simply bursting with love.

Having tucked them both in, Viola in the bed with her and the boy child in the cot, she is then able to lie down and await the return of her husband. It is not unusual for him to be late. It is part of a now established routine in his life as a contractual bricklayer whilst on short leave from service in the North Africa Campaign, part of World War II. It is part of their life in a struggle to survive as a young family. As long as he works their struggle has hope of success. In the heart-felt pang she feels at his absence also reposes hope and some confidence about their future as a family. She is also sustained by the presence of her little ones. As tiny and helpless as they are; in some mysterious way they give her so much strength, contentment and inner serenity.

This soon changes just as she hears the hoot of an owl outside. Ever so slowly she feels an almost imperceptible chilly stillness all around her, in the air, in the room. At first she thinks this is further manifestation of the illness that has taken hold of her, but No there is something else, something she associates with presence, the presence of someone or something. She opens her eyes wider and scans the room instinctively. Her vision picks up only the dancing interplay between light and shadow that candle light is. Suddenly this light, that she is so accustomed to, seems much too inadequate. She needs more light. Instead there seems less. She needs to see more. She is seeing too little. At the same time the feeling that something or someone is there is growing, growing strongly.

And then she sees it, the figure of an adult male, emerging from the shadows of the outer room, starting to enter the doorway to her room, then through the doorway, gliding forward towards her. It is a man, or rather the figure of a man, clearly outlined in a greyish hue. But it is a headless man ... a headless man gliding towards her. Completely absorbed by what she is seeing, she sits up and pins her eyes on him. Time stands still. She feels no fear, only a very distinct twinge in her heart, but not the twinge of fear, something quite different. The figure stops at the cot in which the baby boy is ... at the foot of her bed ... just three paces from her ... time is still ... and just a moment later ... he bends forward so that the whole of his headless upper torso dips into the cot ... and after what seems to be an eternity he straightens up ... pauses ... slowly retreating to whence he had come ... then fades away and is gone.

The spell is broken by the room being flooded by the lights of her husband's car, as it makes its final turn to park at their little home. The joy and relief she feels at his arrival are submerged by what she has seen, and yet she still feels no fear, no anguish, not even surprise at all that has just happened ... only a deep, quiet, strong inner feeling of calmness and reassurance. The next day she is found to be suffering from rheumatic fever from which thankfully she soon recovers, or so it seemed for some 60 years.

....

Sixty years later, it is the morning of 29 July 2003. Moira is now 82 years of age. She is with her youngest daughter Helen in her home in Brisbane, Queensland, Australia. The two women are engaged in conversation. Helen notices that her mother is somewhat pensive.

"Common mum, stop worrying yourself about Zimbabwe. It is only going to get worse. That's why we left or have you forgotten? Maagabee[1] is doing a good job of buggerring up the country, good and proper. Every day the news about our Zim is just so bad. Apparently there are millions of Zimbos like us who have run away from Zim. They say we are like oxygen ... everywhere ... and you still want to dream about going back".

Helen is referring to Robert Gabriel Mugabe, President of Zimbabwe, the country of their birth, from which they had fled on account of Mugabe's new found madness.

"You know that you can stay here with Lawrie and I as long as you like. Don't think it's because we love you" she says tongue in cheek. Lawrie is Helen's husband. *"We n..e..e..d you"* she adds in a tone of exaggerated reassurance.

"No, my child", Moira replies in an unusually quiet tone of seriousness *"Of course I love you ..."* she adds with a twinkle in her eye. *"No, I have someone else on my mind. Today is the 29th of July. It is Vavie's[2] birthday. Do you know that when he was a baby we used to often have him with us at Filabusi? Viola and he were babies. Nellie, his mother, was having such a bad time. I don't know why she just would not let me adopt him. But what is really on my mind is what happened one night when your father was on leave from the war and late coming home."*

Helen sits down noticing that her mother is deadly serious. She is unaware that her mother is reflecting on the incident in which the figure of a headless man stooped into the cot of the baby. Her mother had described it in such detail and intensity that it had sent a shiver down her spine.

Moira had told her ... *"At that time I felt a twinge in my heart. Vavie has always been in my heart ... so special to me ... and I have never forgiven Nellie for not letting me adopt him".*

"Oh, yes Mum, there we go again, your favourite" Helen had said protesting and feigning jealousy had gone on *"but really Mum, don't you think you just*

---

[1] **Maagabee** – a play on pronouncing "Mugabe" (pronounced "Moo gaa bee)

[2] **Vavie** – a contraction of Navavie

imagined it ... especially as you had rheumatic fever?" she had enquired insistently.

Her mother had replied ... *"No my child ... what I saw was real, and it has never left me. The rheumatic fever was not bad. I was up and about in two days. I have never had rheumatic fever again. I wonder how my child is to-day. He married such a nice girl, Pam. You know I stayed with them in Cape Town in 1997. It was wonderful. We sat on Table Mountain and looked at Robben Island where Mandela was kept for all those years. We agreed that with Mandela there was so much hope ... hope for everyone. We spoke about ubuntu[1] ... South Africa is truly blessed ... not like ..."*she trails off with a sigh.

A short while later Moira Williams leaves to check on the laundry. Her

daughter hears the sound of her collapsing and her body hitting the floor. She rushes over.

Her mother is dead. Death has been instantaneous.

The pathologist says she was dead by the time she hit the floor. He diagnoses that her death was due to a heart defect induced by rheumatic fever sometime earlier in her life. When Helen informs him that her mother had only suffered rheumatic fever in 1943 he shakes his head disbelievingly and opines that it was a miracle that she had lived so long ... some 60 years, with this heart defect.

The other baby in the cot was me, Christopher Navavie Greenland, nephew to my beloved Aunt Moira Williams, née Leith, and first cousin to her eldest daughter Viola Anne.

Throughout my life my Aunt Moira was to prove wonderfully supportive, loving, caring and unduly generous in her regard for me. When she visited us in 1997 we sat on Table Mountain and she once again told me the story of their early life, including the incident of the headless visitation[2].

---

[1] **ubuntu** – African behavioral code, characterized by acceptance, kindness and consideration
[2] **Picture is of my Aunt Moira and me - 1997**

2. In the beginning

This story, therefore, starts a little bit earlier. Soon after the turn of the 20th century Henry Hugefson Leith, son of Frederick Leith Esquire of Liverpool House, Walmer Estates, Kent, left England to settle in Rhodesia, a land then full of promise. His birth certificate records him as having been born on 27 April 1874 at Liverpool House, Upper Walmer, Kent. His father is recorded as Frederick Leith Esquire[1], his mother as Jane Ball Leith née Bradley[2].

This member of English aristocracy joined a large community of settlers who shipped out from somewhat cold damp England to seek a warm bright future in Africa with its sun, wide open spaces, wild animals, forests, minerals and other magic. He acquired a ranch in the Kezi area, near Antelope Mine, in the district of Gwanda. He named and registered it as Walmer Estates after the Leith family estate in Kent, England. He settled down well and relative prosperity followed.

Late one afternoon he received a visit by a man who arrived on horseback. The man was William Black. He greeted the man, not in English, but in isiNdebele[3], in which local dialect both men were now fluent *"Sawubona Machisela"*. [Good day Machisela!] Machisela was the nickname given to Black by the local people. The two men sat down in heavy chairs on the verandah of the estate house and conversed for a short while on trivialities like the weather and the state of the realm. Black then turned serious. *"I notice that you now have three huts at the gate"*.

He was referring to three recently constructed circular huts with pole and dagga [dry mud] walls, thatched roof and resplendent in murals according to Ndebele custom.

"Mafulela insisted that we do it this way" Leith explained.

"So you have decided to take this woman" Black enquired.

"Yes ... and she wanted her huts. She says the madlozis [ancestral spirits] have spoken and that's that! The Chief has given his approval. It cost me ten

---

[1] **Frederick William** Leith lived at Walmer Court and Liverpool House, Walmer, Kent.http://www.thepeerage.com/p27215.htm#i272147

[2] **See – thePeerage.com.** "A genealogical survey of the peerage of Britain as well as the royal families of Europe Person Page – 27215

[3] **isiNdebele** – language of the Ndebele or Matabele people

head of cattle in lobola[1]. The celebration is this Saturday. Hope you will stay and be there"

Mafulela Thebe was a Black woman of the Abezansi class of the Mzilikazi Ndebele clan that escaped from King Shaka Zulu of what is now the Natal Province of South Africa. In the western province of Rhodesia the Matabele, or rather Amandebele, were the descendants of the Zulus who trekked under the leadership of the famous Mosilikatze, commonly known also as Mzilikazi, up through the Transvaal, from whence they were driven by the Boers. Mosilikatze died in 1868, and his son Lobengula, after a fight with a brother, assumed sway in 1870. His people were divided into three main sections: the Abezansi [who were the aristocrats], the Abenhla [middle class] and the Amaholi. The Amaholi or Holi were the inhabitants of the land at the time of the invasion and thereafter were practically in the position of bondsmen and rarely allowed to possess cattle.

Mzilikazi [meaning The Great Road] [ca. 1790 - 9 September 1868], also sometimes called Mosilikatze, was a Southern African king who founded the Matabele kingdom [Mthwakazi], Matabeleland, in what became Rhodesia and is now Zimbabwe. He was born the son of Matshobana near Mkuze, Zululand [now part of South Africa] and died at Ingama, Matabeleland [near Bulawayo, Zimbabwe]. Many consider him to be the greatest Southern African military leader after the Zulu King Shaka. In his autobiography, David Livingstone referred to him as the second most impressive leader he encountered on the African Continent[2].

In the ensuing conversation, Leith met Black's concerns on the issue of a White man openly taking a Black woman as a wife. Black became convinced and comfortable with developments. He was happy to accept the invitation to the marriage ceremony. He had been agonizing over the issue himself.

At the time it was by no means common for a White man to marry a Black woman or formalize the union in any way. In Appendix F of his book "Matabele Thompson"[3], this is what Thompson, a revered expert on indigenous people, who played very important roles during the colonization

---

[1] **Lobola** – isiNdebele name for bride-price
[2] per Love To Know Classic Encyclopedia – Rhodesia -
http://www.1911encyclopedia.org/Rhodesia
[3] Matabele Thompson, HIS AUTOBIOGRAPHY AND STORY OF RHODESIA edited by his daughter Nancy Rouillard

of Southern Rhodesia, has to say in recounting a conversation with a Ndebele Nduna[1] named Intumbo –

> "Friday. Intumbo has been visiting us. During the tête-à-tête Intumbo wanted to know if I would give him my daughter for a wife, and asked how it was that the Kaffirs[2] could not get our daughters when white men who came to these parts married Kaffir women. I told him that it was only the scum of the whites who did that. He said. 'Are we only fit for your scum?' He laughed and said it was true."

Rhodesia was still in the colonial era and undoubtedly there was a relative shortage of White woman. This shortage did little to induce inter racial marriages. Instead it was something of a norm for White men to have opportunistic, predatory and clandestine sexual relationships with Black woman. Prostitution was relatively rare and condemned by both Black and White. Sexual interaction occurred in terms of an admixture of biological need and mutual attraction. So, although the taking of a Black woman as a wife was relatively rare, many White men were fairly open about their liaisons. In the result generations of brown skinned children were born who were acknowledged, in many instances, by their White fathers and materially provided for. Almost without exception these children received Christian names and the surname of their fathers. These were recorded in the offices of district commissioners, in the register of births and deaths.

As regards the union between Henry Hugefson Leith and Mafulela Thebe there was a marriage ceremony, central to which was payment of the bride price, and the union openly formalized. They had three daughters. Naomi Elizabeth was the eldest. Nellie Helen, my mother, born in 1917, was the second born. Moira was the youngest.

[Picture is of my grandfather Henry Hugefson Leith Esq and Grandmother Mafulela Thebe]

---

[1] **Nduna** – a Ndebele leader of chieftain status

[2] **Kaffir** – racist derogatory term still used in referencing black folk

Walmer Estates in Kezi, Rhodesia, comprised a large cattle ranch with some crops, such as maize, millet and sugar cane, also grown mainly for home consumption. The main house was quite an imposing edifice for the time. My grandmother, Mafulela, however preferred to live in her huts in accordance with the tradition of her people.

The three Leith girls, Naomi, Nellie and Moira were therefore relatively fortunate in that their father was in a formal union with their mother, and that the family lived together as a cohesive unit. They would spend their time gravitating between the main house and their mother's huts, spending more time with her especially as their father was often away. Their early childhood was a very happy time as they were in a settled and secure environment.

They however did not attend school even though the colonial government guaranteed education to all White children who could not afford to pay. In this respect, Coloured children were classified as White under education statutes. Why Henry Leith did not send the girls to one of the schools designated for Coloured children by the colonial government is a mystery. In the result their education consisted of learning English, history, geography ... etc. ... from their father and everything else from their mother and her people

Fluency in both English and isiNdebele was achieved at an extremely high level. Whilst not being able to write that well the girls were taught to read by their father. They were also indoctrinated about every aspect of British Royalty to the extent of knowing incredible detail about the Royal House, its composition, family relationships and even the personal foibles of its various members. What set them apart however as Coloured children was their command of English which they all spoke without local intonation. This undoubtedly was a most valuable asset when they later entered the racially discriminatory world that Rhodesia was.

It set them apart from other Coloured folk many of whom were hampered by speaking English with a "Coloured accent", i.e., with African intonation.

3. A mother and father

My grandmother was a good and loving mother to her children. Modern society professes to be intolerant of racism and other forms of race based attitudes. It is somewhat bemusing that many Black spokespersons ascribe racial and ethnic antipathy exclusively to White people. There is an incessant accusation leveled at White people that they are both a manifestation of and proponents of racial and ethnic prejudices. The reality however, and undoubtedly most Black folk know this, is that racial, ethnic and tribal antipathy, even prejudice, is not exceptional amongst Black people. Having spent much time with my grandmother and her people in my earliest years I can safely confirm that these accusations against White folk are certainly well founded but also unfair in postulating this as their exclusive preserve.

My grandmother was a very good person, rigorous in adherence to what was right and that there be no blurring of the difference between right and wrong and that conduct be principled. However, the realty was that, as much as she treated others honestly and fairly, nobody, other than fellow Ndebeles, were regarded as equal. She was proud and regal. For instance she did not eat chicken as fowls ate human excrement. Neither would she touch fish as she related fish to snake. Even as regards Ndebeles it was only members of the abeZansi class who were regarded as equals. All others were ranked on a table of lowliness.

For instance; as regards White folk, only English and Germans were accepted as equals and accorded high respect. The reason ... they were seen as the chief protagonist in two recent world wars. This seeming predisposition to violent conflict, causing untold human suffering and death, was hardly deserving of any form of opprobrium in my grandmother's book. Such people were great warriors and were to be highly respected and honoured. Pacifists were not revered. Gandhi on the other hand, enjoyed a very special place in her heart. For him to have wrested India from the British Empire, without so much as a fight, was proof of how incredibly favoured he was by the ancestral spirits as intercessionists with God Almighty.

It is hardly surprising therefore that we find that in the Walmer estate setting there was systemic manifestation of her attitude. Her huts were in close proximity to the gates providing access to the estate. These were always kept locked. She was, in effect, the gate-keeper and in possession of the keys. Typically, my mother or one of her sisters would approach her running and excitedly blurt out ... *"Mama, Mama ... umuntu se fikile"* ["Mother, Mother, a person has arrived."] Her first and instant reaction would be to pointedly enquire ... *"umhlobo bane"* ["what ethnicity"]. If told that the person was "Ibunu" ["Afrikaner", or a member of any of the ethnic groups that she did not accept as equal, access would be often denied, and the person kept waiting at the gate, for such time as, in her view, should accrue in accordance with the lowliness of the person in question. If accepted; the person was immediately afforded access and in the case of English and German folk, in particular, prevailed upon to linger awhile and enjoy a feast which she would immediately cook up.

The above must not be interpreted to mean that Black people practice the forms of racism that White colonizers entrenched in the region; far from it.

It means no more than that racial, ethnic, tribal antipathy and prejudices are not a White prerogative and it is simply wrong and disingenuous to pontificate and pretend otherwise. Over my lifetime I have also seen and experienced pernicious race based treatment at the hands of all the race groups in our region.

For the children visitors were most welcome. In every visit reposed great promise. Not only did it relieve boredom, it provided new opportunities for their natural curiosity. The cherry on the cake was that, every once in a while, a visitor arrived with a parcel from England. If this included confectionary and/or toys their little hearts would all but burst with joy and happiness for a really long while. Thankfully therefore my grandmother's routine of denying entry to some visitors was often subverted by my mother and her sisters, who would clandestinely run off and report to my grandfather in the main house. His then "fortuitous" arrival would save the day for the visitor in these instances.

It was a very happy time for the girls. They had their mother who tended to all their needs and gave them the love and affection that only a mother can. From her they learnt to appreciate the secrets of nature and its endless variety of little creatures. And there were big creatures too, ever lurking in the surrounding bush, with ferocious teeth and terrible claws such as lion which they sometimes imagined they saw or heard.

They did however see hyena, wild dogs, rabbits and various antelope. Their favourite was the prancing tsessebe, especially the new born calves that would run and leap about with the sheer exuberance of life. They learnt stories and fables, handed down over centuries, about the incredible world they lived in, how it had started, how it evolved, where man came from and his long and incredible interaction with the animals in particular. This took place mostly around a fire outside one of their mother's huts. The light emanating from the flickering flames set the scene for little minds to be more than enthralled, captivated and their imaginations teased and titivated.

In daylight she taught them how to identify wild fruit and distinguish what was poisonous and what was edible in the plant world. They also learnt how to trap hares, guinea fowl and birds, prepare and cook them over open fires. However, a little bird, fallen from the nest, would be tenderly nursed for hours and sometimes days on end. Little hearts broke and tears flowed copiously whenever the poor thing died.

Visits by families of African Whooping and Crested cranes were enchanting experiences. Their mother would lead the girls and their friends in a loud singsong chant *"gida dwai sibongile ... gida dwai sibongile ... "* ["dance bird ... dance bird ... dance ... and we thank you'] accompanied by rhythmical handclaps. Lo and behold, the bigger birds in the family would respond by starting to dance, stamping their feet and flapping their wings. This would go on for as long as the singsong chant and handclaps were maintained. It was just marvelous. Like all children, they played games, a favourite of which was "mancala" the African stone game.

They had their father in the big house who often had something new and exciting to tell them or bring to their attention. These things would revolve around England which to them was a mystical far off land full of wondrous things and people. The presents from England that they sometimes received of pretty dresses, dolls, books with pictures, colouring books, musical toys, sweets and confectionary fired up their imaginations and helped to make the world seem a wonderful and magical place. They had aunts in England represented in beautiful black-white and sepia toned photos; grand ladies seated at gilt edged tables on shiny cushions. Their favourite was a picture of an English aunt, regal and beautiful, with an exquisitely groomed poodle on the table in front of her.

They also learnt English history in great detail. The beheading of Mary, Queen of Scots, sent a shiver down their little spines. It was ever so difficult for them to accept their father's stance that what happened to Mary was richly deserved. However, they easily accepted that English and all things English were superior to all else. The exploits of English heroes such as Lord Horatio Nelson at Trafalgar were indelibly embedded in their imaginations.

There was no small problem when they reported to their father that their mother had, whilst enthusiastically confirming English superiority, explained to them how her people, the Zulus, had trounced the mighty English at Isandlwana[1] South Africa. She was at great pains to explain that this had only been achieved on account of the advantage the Zulu impis [Zulu regiments] had in having the madlozis on their side. This, coupled with an

---

[1] **Isandlwana** [IPA: /isanˈdɮwana/][also sometimes seen as Isandhlwana or Isandula] is an isolated hill in the KwaZulu-Natal province of South Africa, 10 miles [16 km] southeast of Rorke's Drift [a ford of the Tugela River, the Buffalo River] and 105 miles [169 km] north by northwest of Durban. On January 22, 1879, Isandlwana was the site of the Battle of Isandlwana, where approximately 22,000 Zulu warriors defeated a contingent of approximately 1350 British and Native troops in the first engagement of the Anglo-Zulu War. The force was largely wiped out by the Zulus under Cetshwayo. The battle remains the single greatest defeat for the British Army at the hands of a native army".
http://en.wikipedia.org/wiki/Isandlwana

attack, configured in the shape of the horns of the favourite bullock Dingaan, had guaranteed victory for her people. Leith was not happy to learn that the girls now knew of this and ranted on about bad luck and "bloody stupid" generalship on the British side.

High points were when the whole family traveled to visit Machisela or a family friend by the name of Mr. Stert at their respective homes. Travel was by wagon drawn by a team of oxen. It was terribly exciting as the wagon was stocked with provisions in readiness for the trip and the oxen in spanned. Each beast had a name and a developed personality intimately known by the girls. There was Dingaan, their mother's favourite, Blixsom, Witboy, Black-Jack, Two-tone and others. Each child had her favourite. My mother's favourite was Jakalaas.

Arguments occurred as to which animal was the strongest or most intelligent. Intelligence was a vital attribute for an ox as only an intelligent animal could be inspanned at the front so as to perform as a leader. Such an animal would react instantly on verbal command, a variety of whistle patterns and the crack of the whip used in driving the team. This was especially important when crossing rivers or spruits. Only quality leadership of the team of oxen would ensure success. Whilst not the favourite with the girls, the bullock Dingaan was regarded with reverence as it was an attack in the shape of its horns that the mighty British were done in at Isandlwana.

These trips always involved having to camp out in the bush. At such times little imaginations were feverish with pictures of those with teeth and claws, especially as the night sounds included the chilling howl of hyenas, the barking of wild dogs, the eerie screeching of owls, and a whole range of other sounds made by animals such as baboon, that made little hearts race, their skins crawl and their hair stand on end. At such times they clung to their mother. She understood animals. She knew all about them. And she knew how to talk to the madlozis and seek their protection. They had also learnt to pray from their father.

Prayers were murmured to a kind and protective God, who apparently lived, at the King's invitation, in an incredibly built Anglican church called St Pauls, in England. At such times their father was the guarantee that they would be protected from harm. This was because he had guns. One was nearly always slung over his shoulder on such trips and close by his side at the evening camp fire. They knew all too well the power of a gun, having often witnessed their father bringing down an antelope with a single shot.

Yes my mother and her sisters had a happy early childhood. Such happiness accrued mostly on account of their mother and her people. They, and Black folk in general, accepted them without question at all times and even treated them with favouritism on account of their status as half English and half Ndebele of the upper class. So they had many Black friends.

Not so as regards White folk. With only one or two exceptions they experienced no meaningful relationship with White folk and certainly had no close White friends except for Mr. Black and Mr. Stert, both of whom were in relationships with Ndebele woman. Machisela had children Regrettably Mr. Stert did not. When contact was made with other Coloured children this was instinctively appreciated and friendship maintained. Whilst eulogizing and extolling the superiority of the English and everything English my grandfather did very little to secure meaningful benefits for his children in terms thereof, starting with the fact that they had no relationship with his people.

He was from English aristocracy. His treatment of the children in not ensuring that they received a full and formal education was hardly excusable. This was so especially as many of his counterparts made sure that their children were sent to schools, designated for Coloureds, such as Embakwe Coloured School, near Plumtree, which was founded in 1902, and which I eventually attended. Even though their mother desired this, Henry Hugefson Leith could not bring himself to at least ensure that the girls attended a Black school such as Hope Fountain Mission School, which some Coloured children did attend.

Still their early childhood was a happy time. They may not have been at school, but they were very much in the school of life in wonderful natural surroundings with warm and loving people.

4. The heart of a mother

This was all to change ... suddenly with little warning. Mafulela decided to leave her English husband ... and for a time she left the children with him. Why? What if I were able to ask her?

So I pose the question in my mind's eye and play the scene out from what I now know about her, gleaned from conversations with my mother and aunts, in particular, and from my own interaction with her as a child *"Gogo* [granny], *why did you leave your children?"*

She freezes for just an instance and then looks at me intently, her jet black eyes misting almost imperceptibly in a face now visibly saddened.

"Sit down my child" she commands as she beckons me to the floor. I oblige. Soon we are seated on the floor of her hut, face to face, and I feel a tinge of apprehension as to what is to follow.

"You are but a child" she says *"who will never understand".* The words fall like tiny hailstones. I start to wonder if I have overstepped the mark, started something that should have not been started. The feeling is accentuated when she straightens herself, and turning her head looks at me directly, but ever so slightly askance. Right there I am acutely aware of her breeding, of her status as a member of the abeZansi.

"But I will tell you ... my child" she goes on reassuringly. *"This thing has pained me deeply; it has been with me ... it has never left me ... all these years. My heart has been so sore, so very sore.*

I was a very good wife to Leith. I loved him as a wife. I attended to all he wanted. Not once did he ever have reason to complain. And yet he disappointed me so. He disappointed me terribly.

How could a man of his status refuse to have our children educated...? How ...? Tell me my child. You are educated. Your poor mother made sure that you were educated. She had nothing ... but you are educated. Was he not educated? Was Machisela not educated? Other Englishmen made sure their children were educated ... and Scotsmen too ... even the Greek storekeeper sent his children away to school. I pleaded with him ... many times ... I cried tears ... I asked Machisela to intercede ... he tried his best ... to talk to Leith ... all to no avail" ... she ends shaking her head whilst bringing her hands together then parting them slowly, opened wide facing me, in a gesture of resignation.

"And" she adds in a noticeably lower tone ... *"he brought Ester to my home... "* The tinge of indignation in her voice is underscored by a pregnant pause.

"But Granny ... Ester was but a child" I say in soft enquiring tones, not wishing to sound argumentative. *"Yes ... you are right my child ... she was a child ... like my children, Naomi, Nellie and Moira ... "*

She looks me straight in the eye and adds with quiet but chilling indignation *" ... but her mother was not a child ... that woman was not even my class ... and Leith brought her child to my home!*

He brought her for everyone to see ... as if there was something wrong with the womb of Mafulela Thebe!"

She fights back the tears welling up in her eyes, her facial expression just betraying the inner turmoil she is experiencing at having to maintain composure as all people of breeding do whatever the situation.

Her tone is now matter of fact *"I settled it with Stert and Machisela. It was settled. As their father intended to disgrace our children I could not kill them. They are my children. I loved them ... so I had no option but to leave them*

... and the English could see what they had to do ..." she ends lowering her eyes to face the ground and shaking her head from side to side.

"These people do not respect us, they will never respect us ... because Lobengula[1] lost ... our assegais, spears and shields could do little against their isgwagwagwa[2] ... which mowed us down like flies ... out of respect for him I have never mentioned Shangani and Wilson ... where we defeated them ... but still treated their dead with honour." And there she ends, pulling herself up, she resumes the posture and bearing of a member of the proud people she belongs to.

Rhodesia, at the time of the arrival of the White settlers, was known as the Kingdom Of Matabeleland and its king was Lobengula. They wrested the land off him and his people in terms of a strategy involving, guile, duplicity and fire power; especially the fire power of the Maxim machine gun.

In mentioning Shangani and Wilson, my grandmother is referring to a notorious historical incident now dramatized in a film "Shangani Patrol."

> "Under the command of Major Wilson, the patrol tracks the fleeing Ndebele King Lobengula across the Shangani River. Cut off from the main force they are ambushed by the Ndebele impi and, except for the few men sent for reinforcements, all are killed. Such was the bravery of the Shangani Patrol that the victories Ndebele said "They were men of men and their fathers were men before them." Depending on your viewpoint, this part of history is one of the great mistakes and military blunders, or last heroic stand of a gallant few. The incident had lasting significance in England, South Africa, and Rhodesia as the equivalent of 'Custer's Last Stand' is for America. "Shangani Patrol" is their story, told in a 1970 movie shot on location in Matabeleland, Rhodesia (now Zimbabwe).[3]

A monument stands on the Matopos Hills, next to the grave of Cecil John Rhodes, credited with founding Southern and Northern Rhodesia. On the monument is an inscription of the salute the Ndebele impi gave Wilson and

---

[1] **Lobengula Khumalo** [1845–1894] was the second and last king of the Ndebele people, usually pronounced Matabele in English. Both names, in the isiNdebele language, mean "The men of the long shields", a reference to the Matabele warriors' use of the Zulu shield and spear. http://en.wikipedia.org/wiki/Lobengula

[2] **Isgwagwagwa** [pronounced phonetically – "is – gwaa – gwaa – gwaa"] is the name given by the Zulus to the Maxim machine gun which name roughly intones the sound of it being fired [in anger]

[3] **Shangani Patrol** - http://en.wikipedia.org/wiki/Shangani_Patrol_(film)

his men that "They were men of men and their fathers were men before them."

It is clear that my grandmother was very disappointed and disillusioned with my grandfather especially as regards the fact that he refused to send her children to be educated. There were children of much lesser status than hers that were receiving an education. She had pleaded and remonstrated with him ad nauseam about this to no avail. She enlisted Mr. Black's support. His children were at school. Leith's response was to shower her with more pretty dresses, jewelry and trinkets from England. Even Mr. Stert's entreaties were to no avail.

Leith also brought a pretty little Coloured girl home and introduced her to the family. Her name was Ester. The girls loved her and were happy at the event. Mafulela was incensed. Ester was the product of an illicit liaison between her husband and another Black woman, a woman considered by Mafulela as being of lesser class.

At the time their mother left the girls were in their early teens. One can only imagine how heartbreaking the parting was. The fact that all three, my Aunt Naomi, my mother and Aunt Moira have steadfastly declined to talk about this period of their lives is testament to the fact that it must have been extremely traumatic.

What is known is that Mafulela left and re-married a Black man with whom she had four children, three girls, Elizabeth, Fatty, Skatele and a son named Willie. There was early interaction between the girls and these children and a lifelong sibling relationship established. It is also known that both Mr. Stert and Mr. Black [Machisela] were involved with providing some support.

Thursday, October 24, 1929 was an auspicious day for a huge chunk of mankind. It became known as "Black Thursday[1]". It was the day that the

---

[1] **Three phrases**—Black Thursday, Black Monday, and Black Tuesday—are commonly used to describe this collapse of stock values. All three are appropriate, for the crash was not a one-day affair. The initial crash occurred on Thursday, October 24, 1929, but the catastrophic downturn of Monday, October 28 and Tuesday, October 29 precipitated widespread alarm and the onset of an unprecedented and long-lasting economic depression for the United States and the world. http://en.wikipedia.org/wiki/Wall_Street_Crash_of_1929. When the Wall Street stock market crashed in October 1929, the world economy was plunged into the Great Depression.

stock market crashed in New York, America and ensured the onset of the depression. Its effects reached Africa. It triggered the untimely death of Henry Hugefson Leith still in his mid-fifties. He had stood guarantor for a relative in South Africa. When the man went under, on account of the Wall Street Crash, the bank foreclosed on Leith and he lost Walmer. He died soon afterwards of a broken heart it is said. Only his eldest daughter, my Aunt Naomi, was in attendance. He is buried somewhere in the Gwanda area of Zimbabwe. I have never felt any compelling need to find out exactly where or to visit his grave. His estate was worth little as the Bank had foreclosed on Walmer Estate. The Leith girls later inherited the princely sum of £300 each.

They never heard from any of their English relatives even though Mr. Stert immediately communicated their plight to them. This abandonment of the girls by their father's family was complete in that much later my cousin Viola, who grew up to be a stunningly beautiful woman and, despite her ethnicity, visually indistinguishable from other beautiful European woman, visited Walmer Estates in England, only to be shown the door with very short shrift. This was articulated in cutting English upper-class intonation, in which she was referred to as "*one of Hugefson's issue*" and told that there was little point in her exploring her pedigree.

The situation was bad for the Leith girls and undoubtedly deteriorated with the death of Henry Hugefson Leith. But just before he died, on one hot summer's day, a Model A Ford made its way slowly through the mopani bush scrub in the district of Kezi. The road was little more than a winding track formed by cattle being driven. Soon it petered out.

The occupants alighted. One was a middle-aged woman, who got out and immediately started walking purposefully along the track scarcely waiting to see if the man, her husband, and a young Black male, acting as a guide, were keeping up with her.

This little party was soon met by children, and the woman asked them in simple matter of fact tones to confirm that they were approaching the village of Mafulela Thebe. The children enthusiastically confirmed this, nodding their heads, and assured the visitors that their arrival would be immediately relayed to the village. Some of the children scampered off. Bush telegraph was in action.

Some twenty minutes later the group of three, led by the woman, arrived at a fairly large collection of huts. Mafulela, accompanied by several male

http://www.bbc.co.uk/schools/gcsebitesize/history/mwh/usa/walldepressionrev1.shtml

village elders, resplendent in traditional garb, was there to meet them. Some younger children stood a short distance away watching everything in childish curiosity; picking up on the theme that "amalungu[1] sebe fikile" [white people have arrived]. The female visitor was a very fair skinned Coloured woman. The older male was her brown skinned husband.

After exchanging warm greetings the visitors are invited to take seats on stools that have been set out under a large shady tree. The elders do not sit on stools. They squat down seemingly also balanced by the spears they have in their hands. Each is in traditional garb with a head-ring and ibetshu[2] covering the genital area. The conversation first centers on whether the trip to the village has been a safe and happy one.

Then one of the male elders says *"we know why you have come ... we were expecting you ... we were hoping it would be soon ... "* Mafulela seated to one side on the ground a respectful distance away, nods in silent agreement. The air is now charged with expectancy.

The woman responds, also in isiNdebele ... *"we are happy that you are happy ... this thing is now so heavy ... "*

"Indeed ... " is the solemn reply ... *" ... it must now all be fixed ... ".* A discussion ensues, conducted in quiet, deadly serious tones, on the "heaviness" of the problem and that it is "so good" that now it will be "fixed", presenting as central themes.

It ends when the most senior elder turns slightly and waves his hand in what is an almost undetectable signal. Immediately an adult female emerges from one of the huts accompanied by my mother, Nellie Helen Leith. The female visitor gets up, rushes up to her, and grabbing her in a vigorous embrace says in English without pausing ... *"hello ... hello ... hello ... how are you ... you are so beautiful ... I am your Aunt Elsie ... Elsie Zerf ... and I have come to fetch you"* finishing quite breathlessly.

Elsie notices that Nellie, my mother, is cradling a baby in her arms. He is tiny ... and wrinkly as babies often are ... and quite black. With hardly a pause, she takes the child whilst announcing ... *"We are going to baptize and register your baby as Frank Joseph Leith".*

---

[1] **ilungu** [singular] amalungu [plural] is a noun exclusively referencing white ethnicity. Traditionally black folk <u>never</u> referred to coloured folk as black. The classifying of Coloureds as black in present day South Africa is an aberration in which a convenient untruth is embedded for political purpose.

[2] **Ibetshu** - a kind of "loin cloth" made of leather, which covered the genital area

Conceived out of wedlock to a sixteen-year-old girl, Frank is thus unhesitatingly welcomed into the Coloured community even though he is physically indistinguishable from Black babies and later from many Black men. In adulthood, he will bear a most striking facial resemblance to Thabo Mbeki, President of South Africa from 1998 to 2008. I imagine though that their personalities were radically different. What a wonderful big brother to me he turned out to be.

The meeting under the tree ends with the most senior elder saying simply and quietly, but in a voice and tone pregnant with authority ... *"Kulungile"*. [It is right]. This is both an observation and a final judgment in approval of what is to be implemented. Mafulela smiles behind eyes brimming with tears. After arranging to collect the younger sister, my Aunt Moira, who is at another village, in the near future, Elsie leaves with my mother who bids tearful goodbyes to everyone especially her Black siblings Elizabeth and Willie.

In these times Aunt Elsie would be certainly classified as a "mover and shaker". As fair skinned as most White folk, with twinkling greenish eyes, she radiated an unmistakable presence conventionally referred to as being "larger than life". She was "up close and personal" without being offensive. Looking you straight in the eye she would connect with you and, in no time at all, you knew where you stood with her, what was required and that she would brook no nonsense. When I met her I inwardly opined "here indeed is a woman of substance". Pressed she admitted that she had heard of the plight of the three girls and made it her business to travel into the countryside, locate them and bring them into the city of Bulawayo to live with her. Their inheritances went some way to paying for their keep.

Not long thereafter Aunt Elsie collected the younger girl, my Aunt Moira, and the eldest sister, my Aunt Naomi, on Leith's death. She was appalled at the plight of the girls and the crass indifference of their English relatives. She was especially dismayed that these young women had received no formal education. It was the reason why she went to fetch them. She also made it her business to conduct formal lessons in reading and writing. Since she would brook no nonsense the girls thus received a very good basic education. They were literate for the first time.

It is notable that of all the children born to my grandmother, brown and Black, only Skatele, her youngest Black child, received a full education and qualified as a teacher.

5. A new life

Bulawayo was Rhodesia's second largest city and was based on colonial style architecture. It was notable for its very wide streets, which were said to have come about as Cecil John Rhodes[1] insisted that a pioneer covered wagon with team of oxen in-spanned should be able to execute a turn in the streets. It was a beautiful city with a burgeoning central business area and surrounding suburbs, well treed and brick under tile residences. Many of these were also in extremely sumptuous colonial style with the White residents waited on hand and foot by uniformed Black servants commonly referred to as "boys" and "nannies". Black folk were confined to "locations" on the fringes of the city. Coloureds lived in designated Coloured suburbs such as Barham Green, Trenance, Rangemore and Thorngrove.

The three main ethnic groups lived and interacted in the symbiotic formula that racism ensures. The dominant group, being the colonialist Whites, acknowledged the other groups but only accorded them such rights as ensured that they remained subservient. In this formula, socio-economic benefits were elusive to the two subservient groups with Blacks being most disadvantaged. Their role was to supply cheap labour with little acknowledgment or reward for their contributions. Coloured folk were a little better off on both counts. So they had access to better jobs and were better paid than Blacks were. In this way the White group grudgingly rewarded Coloureds for having White blood in their veins. Cinemas, parks, waiting rooms ... everything was segregated and "Right of Admission" signs an ordinary feature on many a doorway. Each group had its own schools and hospitals.

The Zerfs had a beautifully appointed but modestly sized home in a suburb called Thorngrove. Most of the houses in Thorngrove were small two to three bed roomed units of brick under tile. The whole suburb covered an area of no more than a couple of hectares. The inhabitants were a small very close-knit community. By also utilizing the outbuildings, usually occupied by servants, Aunt Elsie was able to accommodate her new charges, albeit at a squeeze.

The Coloured community in 1933 Bulawayo was, and still is, throughout the southern African region, an admixture of Euro-Africans, Cape Coloureds, Afro-Asians and others having the blood of two or more of these groups in

---

[1] **Cecil John Rhodes** is credited with having "founded Rhodesia". In colonial times the country was named after him. It became Zimbabwe on 15 April 1985 after a successful liberation struggled waged by the black majority.

their veins[1]. In terms of colouring, skin tones ranged from almost "ebony black" to "lily white". Just as many were indistinguishable from White folk, many were also indistinguishable from Black folk.

This was, and remains, problematical for everyone, my people in particular, and governments; White or Black.[2]

undoubtedly the case that

Like any community there were internal tensions. These were founded mainly on account of the fact that Cape Coloureds were fluent in Afrikaans, spoke no Black language, had no Black relatives, had no Black culture and tended to have straight hair. Euro-Africans and Afro-Asians, on the other hand, spoke no Afrikaans, were fluent in a Black language, had Black relatives, respected and practiced Black culture and tended to have "kroos" or even "corn-curl" hair[3]. Tensions founded on these factors were often very serious and it was

[Picture is of my cousin Viola flanked by Janap Karim on her right and Dorothy Abrahams nee Rhoades on her left]

---

[1] **Euro-African** [of European/African extraction]. Afro-Asian [of African/Indian extraction. Cape Coloured [originating from the coloured community in the Cape Province of South Africa]

[2] For employment purposes and to participate in BEE (Black Economic Empowerment) deals.

[3] **Kroos** = is a colloquialism describing the particularly curly hair of black and coloured folk

corn-curl = is the American version of the same term.

the fairer skinned a person was, with straighter hair to match, the more easily that person attracted social and economic advantages. What united the community however was that, individually and collectively; they were rejected by the White community; regarded, treated and classified as unequal.

To Whites other Whites were regarded as "us", Black folk were regarded as "them" and Coloured folk as "the others".

It was a huge management problem for the colonial government, and its dominant White society, given the incredible racial diversity and colouring of my people. It remains so to-day, in this region, despite revolutionary changes

Since Coloured people are neither truly white, brown nor black, a government obsessed with colour as a basic criterion in the treatment of human beings, is tripped up and confused about what to do. So it resorts to makeshift and unprincipled solutions like artificially defining all "non-white" people as Black. The consequences for us Coloured people are organically induced challenges, ever present, hardly acknowledged; in a minefield of obfuscation.

To get back to the story however. The Leith girls settled down well. With Aunt Elsie they really had no option but to jolly well settle down and get on with life. In the ensuing years they proved to be a hit with the Bulawayo Coloured community. All three were beautiful, incredibly well spoken and could dance, having been taught by their father and Mr. Stert. My mother, Nellie, was so beautiful that she soon received the nickname of "Madame Lazonga" after an apparently seductive night club entertainer who was fabled to have lived in Havana, Cuba.

By 1937 my mother was married to Ganief Mohammed Greenland a South African by birth. The marriage ran into trouble, like so many, on account of couples being parted when husbands went off to fight in the Second World War. They eventually parted ways, and divorce ensued, leaving my mother with four children to support; Frank Joseph Leith, [the eldest] followed by Haroon Zain Greenland [Zain] followed by the writer Christopher Navavie Greenland and lastly Anthony Charles Greenland [Tony]. Another child, David, born before Tony, died at age two.

In terms of colouring, Anthony and I were brown with brown eyes. Zain was fair skinned with greenish-grey eyes. Frank was dark with black eyes. Apart from Frank, who had African type hair, the other children had straight hair in their early years which slowly turned kroos as we got older. We were indeed a Coloured family, not only visually, but also as regards being thoroughly disadvantaged. For reasons known only to Ganief Greenland and my mother, her erstwhile husband never provided any material support.

Nellie Helen Leith, of aristocratic pedigree both paternally and maternally, was in deep trouble once again.

6. A gift of life

I was born on 29 July 1943 in Bulawayo. Like most babies in our community, I was born at home and delivered by a lady named Mrs. Gilgower, who was a skilled and very much practiced midwife. Nearly all our generation, born in Bulawayo, owe our safe arrival to this lady. The birth was unremarkable except that I presented with an unusually loud voice. This was categorized as "good" by Mrs. Gilgower.

Soon thereafter I was conveyed to Kezi for the important business of a "lungisa[1]" ritual. In terms of Ndebele custom it is considered wise, if not necessary, that a new born is taken to a sangoma[2] and subjected to a lungisa ceremony in terms of which the ancestral spirits are invoked to provide support, guidance and protection for the child. The sangoma who performed the ritual on me was known as Fuyane. Apart from being a headman he was both a herbalist and a spiritualist. He was extremely well respected and people of all races traveled from far and wide to consult him.

There was an unusual aspect to my consultation. After the ceremony he presented my mother with 6 goats as a present for me. In later life, 10 - 20 years later, whenever I visited my relatives in their village, one of the first mini rituals that would occur was that goats would be pointed out as being my goats from Fuyane even though the original six were long, long gone. There would be more in later life about my association with Fuyane

My earliest recollection was of lying under red blankets with white coated human beings under bright lights fussing over me and sticking things into me. My mother was utterly astounded when I later related this to her, as it is undoubtedly a recollection of an event in which doctors and nurses rescued me from death's door, after I suffered severe food poisoning. This had

---

[1] **Lungisa** – literally means "to fix up" and is ceremony done by sangoma or spiritualist.

[2] **A sangoma** is a practitioner of herbal medicine, divination and counseling in traditional Nguni [Zulu, Xhosa, Ndebele and Swazi] societies of Southern Africa [effectively an African shaman]. http://en.wikipedia.org/wiki/Sangoma

occurred when I was at age two! She was even more astounded when I intimated to her truthfully that the sticking of things into me had made me feel very embarrassed indeed. It was most difficult for her to accept or understand that a two year old could feel embarrassed. The sin of pride, it seems, was with me from birth.

I remember thereafter living in an unpainted brick house situated on the fringe of Thorngrove in an informal locality known as Brickfields. It derived its name from the fact that the area was used to manufacture the bricks used to build most of the houses in Bulawayo. My grandmother Mafulela would visit. She would throw me high into the air and catch me. Aunt Elizabeth, my mother's half-sister also lived with us at times and we would be visited by Uncle Willie, my mother's half-brother. He too would throw me high into the air and catch me. In all of my later life I would often dream that I could just stiffen my body and fly around like a bird. Maybe this is a "throw-back" to these early games of my granny and uncle. Frank and Zain were hardly around since they were already at boarding school; Embakwe Coloured School.

As I approached age five, things took a very dramatic turn for me. I was playing with other children on a sand heap. We were happy rolling around as children do. I rolled down the sand heap into the path of a passing cyclist. There was contact. I screamed more out of fright than anything else as I was not injured. The cyclist, a well proportioned adult Coloured male, unfortunately fell off his cycle and then got up in a very agitated state. He started shouting at me punctuating his words with Afrikaans sounding swear words. I started to cry out even louder.

Then I heard the sound of a woman's voice. I turned to look. It was my mother alighting from her cycle. Looking at the man straight in the eye she asked him - *"What have you done to my child?"*

Instead of answering the question the man snarled at her *"and who the fucking hell are you to ask me ... who do you think you are ... ?"* My mother repeated the question; this time in wonderfully intoned English but with a just detectable ominous tinge. Advancing towards my mother the man raised his voice further and let out a stream of expletives to the effect that if she could not look after her bastard kids it was not his problem.

"I have asked what have you done to my child ... ?" My mother started to repeat the question but was cut short as the man advanced on, her yelling hysterically.

The whole scene than went into slow motion, with every little detail bright, clear and indelibly imprinted into my memory. One moment I could see his face contorted in anger, veins standing out on his forehead and neck, eyes blazing, mouth streaming invectives. Fearing for my mother I started to scream.

The next moment I saw this pure white streak appear on his face ... a split that materialized instantly from the middle of his forehead down to the bridge of his nose ... open, wide and white ... with the white then turning red in a swamp of tiny little red dots ... which then turned into a stream of solid red ... and down he fell ... lifeless ... blood streaming from his face into the sand.

What my mother had done, as she posed her questions, was to carefully position her body so as to conceal the presence of a shovel that was stuck in the sand heap. The poor man neither anticipated, nor saw her pull the shovel from behind her, and deliver the terrible blow that split his face open.

A crowd gathered. The police arrived. The injured man was hastily removed by ambulance. In impeccable English, my mother explained to the police that after this man, who appeared demented with all his swearing, had beaten her child he had been about to attack her too. As a woman what was she to do faced with a *"mad man"*. Witnesses had heard the swearing. They had also heard my screams, as I upped the decibels, as the man was approaching my mother. The police expressed satisfaction that an otherwise defenseless woman had acted so courageously.

The incident was a valuable lesson in terms of what I was destined for. What is reality depends upon from whose point of view it is being considered.

Truth is often a tantalizingly elusive thing. My mother was never charged.

___

7. Who will love my children?

However I was to suffer the consequences. That weekend my mother and I were driven some 50 kilometers into the countryside by a lady named Dorothy Shimkins, my Aunt Dorothy. This was at my mother's request. It was proving unsafe for me to be at home. Aunt Elizabeth was often away, as she had her own children to attend to. My unsupervised association with a female playmate from next door was also discussed. The two women agreed that if action was not taken I would soon learn to do *"naughty things"*.

I gathered that I was being taken to "Bushtick". This was a railway and power station combined. I was impressed with the steam flowing upwards from the cooling towers. But the car continued its journey, leaving this pretty site behind, and shortly thereafter we pulled up on the road after passing a sign which read "Sacred Heart Home. The reason we pulled up was that there was a figure in the road, a figure in very strange garb. At least that is the way the nun looked to me at that time; seeing a nun for the first time, very strange indeed. We alighted. Greetings were exchanged.

And then I heard Aunt Dorothy say words that are forever burnt into my memory - *"Sister, I have one more for you"*. I will never forget the feeling of utter desolation I felt right then. I looked down and my mind became hypnotically concerned with a stone, embedded in the roadside, its shape its colouring, minute patterns on its surface ... Twenty years later I visited the scene and was able to quite easily locate the very same spot and the very same stone.

The nun put her hand under my chin, and gently but firmly tilted my head up. *"Vaat is your name?"* she asked in a strange accent which I now know to be German. She had to ask the question again, as I was preoccupied with her strange head dress and a meaty protrusion she had on one cheek. *"Vavie"* I finally said *"my name is Vavie ... "*

"Vot ....! " she exclaimed. *"Kookers-nich-nog*[1] *... your name is not Vavie ... it is Christopher ... bearer of Christ!"*

After shooing off my mother and Aunt Dorothy, with assurances that they need not worry as I was a "big boy", she took my hand firmly and, after commanding me to pick up my little case, led me towards a white-washed building.

As I looked back, and took in the sight of the car making off, I felt an indescribable heart-wrench. Part of me died inside. I was to next experience that feeling again, thirty-seven years later, when in 1984, I picked up our two-month-old baby, Nicholas John, to discover that we had lost him overnight to SIDS[2].

That is how I got the name Christopher, contracted to "Chris". That is how I met Sister Dagoberta. That is how I arrived in Sacred Heart Home, sanctuary for orphans and Coloured children in need of care. To use the language of nuns; it was in the year of Our Lord nineteen hundred and forty eight. That night I wet my bed for the first time.

Sacred Heart Home was started by Sisters of the Order Of The Precious Blood, in 1947, as a sanctuary and school for Coloured children. On my arrival there were few buildings with only the church and the residence, housing the priest, constructed of plastered brick. All other structures such

---

[1] ***Kookers-nich-nog*** - *was* what this nun nearly always exclaimed when excited. It apparently has no meaning.

[2] **SIDS** is - Sudden Infant Death Syndrome commonly referred to as "cot death"

as the kitchen and our dormitory had walls made of plastered hessian and tin roofs. Ironically the pigs also enjoyed a sty constructed of brick. Pigs and pork are indeed very important to German people it would seem.

On the evening after my arrival we attended Benediction, which is an evening service conducted in the Roman Catholic Church. I had spent the night before crying my heart out, wet my bed and had been feeling utterly desolate all day. After Benediction I was kept back by a truly wonderful nun, Sister Rocha, and only relieved attendance once I had learnt to say a prayer called "the Hail Mary" preceded by making the Sign of the Cross.

My first religious lesson took place in front of a statue of the Blessed Virgin Mary, Mother of Jesus. The statue impressed me immensely. After the day's tribulations, the beautiful and serene face of Mary, holding a beautiful baby in one arm; the other arm outstretched, soothed and comforted me. So too as regards the Hail Mary prayer itself, especially the second verse *"Holy Mary, Mother of God, pray for us sinners, now and at the hour of our death"*.

That night I substituted some of the crying for a lot of praying to this new, beautiful and truly wondrous mother I had found. I have had a relationship with Her ever since and, even when I go fishing, a quick Hail Mary is often incanted in order to get the fish to bite. Many more solemnly said Hail Marys are said by my brother in law, Mark Lourenço, and I, to stop contact between our boat and hippopotami whenever we fish the mighty and dangerous Zambezi River.

The next morning I went to school for the first time. Classes were conducted in the church building with the section containing the alter partitioned off. There I met John and Mary, not as human beings, but in pictures all over the walls. I also met Spot, pictured as a bright eyed lively looking pup. The walls were full of colourful pictures giving the classroom a wonderland atmosphere. There were no desks however. We sat on a bare cement floor.

Sister Rocha produced a box from which she distributed something truly wonderful - coloured chalk. My first lesson was art. I learnt to draw two pictures, which skill I have retained to this day, and represents the limit of my artistic ability. One was of a house comprising a square upon which sits a triangle as the roof. Doors and windows are represented by appropriately sized rectangles. The other is a cat made up of drawing a large circle for the body, a smaller one for the head and even smaller ones for the eyes. Elliptical shapes adorn the head as ears and the tail and whiskers are added (with a flourish) as appropriately shaped lines.

Soon I was lost in the world of John, Mary, Spot and pictures created on the floor. Then came "1+1 is 2", "1+2 is 3". "1+3 is 4 - ." as our first lesson in arithmetic, which took the form of a loud chant that went on and on until we knew "our numbers" without thinking. The alphabet was learnt as a happy song of "a, b, c, d, e, f g ... " which we sang with great gusto.

These first steps in the process of my education were most riveting in their impact on me and will never been forgotten. Sister Rocha was a kind and patient teacher, who made the business of learning a happy and exciting adventure for fertile little minds behind faces ranging from pure white to dark black in pigmentation.

Because I had arrived mid-term, I was soon back home for holidays. It did not work too well. My Aunt Moira paid us a surprise visit. I can only surmise at what impression she got. Two days later she sent her husband, my Uncle Dick, to "kidnap" me. He arrived by motor cycle and spirited me off to their home in Filabusi. They were not rich. They too were struggling. Obviously, the situation at our home in Brickfields was such that Aunt Moira felt compelled to kidnap me. Upon retrieval I was taken back to Sacred Heart Home, but only after a long a testy discussion in which my mother declined Aunt Moira's request, then insistence, that she adopt me. However the good that came out of this, it seems, is that I developed a taste for motor bikes as in later life I owned different versions of these seductive machines for many years.

On my next holiday I was baptized and admitted into the Roman Catholic faith at St Marys Cathedral, Bulawayo. My godfather was Aaron Milner. He later went on to become Minister of State in the first Cabinet set up upon Zambia attaining independence on 24 October 1964, with Dr Kenneth Kaunda as President.

8. Tending the flock -

As Sacred Heart Home had only just started, there were only a handful of children. At just on five years of age I was one of the "big boys" and remained so for the rest of my time at the Home. There were four of us big boys. The other three were John Peters, George Kenneth and Albert Sammy. Later we were joined by Xaviour Usher, Jimmy Roberts and Winston Potgieter. The other children comprised smaller boys such as Roy Sussman, Gerald Woodend, Stanley Ruddle, Anthony Babbage, Joseph Hickey, Errol Feldman, Peter Bruff, Human Jarvis, Mango Ramjee, Terrence Cook, Atlee Potgieter, toddlers and babies.

One baby was Noel Feldman. He arrived with both his legs broken. There were also two baby brothers whose faces had been so burnt with cigarette stubs that the resultant permanent keloid scars/swellings gave them the appearance of having leprosy. Visually Noel was indistinguishable from any White baby in colouring. The scarred babies were undoubtedly Afro-Asian. One can only imagine the real life scenes that led to Noel's legs being broken and the other two boys having their faces burnt. Even in this small grouping, of no more than 30 children, the rich ethnic diversity of the Coloured community, and its problems, was deeply entrenched.

It is something of an understatement to say that the nuns gave us love, comfort and support. They were firm. They were disciplinarians. They would brook no nonsense. Corporal punishment was administered to the buttocks using a school ruler. However it was never unfair. It was nearly always accompanied by extensive explanation and counseling. We felt safe and secure. However there were a few unacceptable instances involving two nuns only. And therein lies the problem with permitting corporal punishment. There will always be those who will use this to abuse, even brutalize, others. I will never forget the one occasion much later, when I was beaten by Sister Obama, with a piece of hose all over the body with such force that I was unable to cry because I could not ... the air had been forced out of my lungs by the sheer force of the beating.

Fortunately such conduct was a very rare exception. I mention it only as it is in the public interest that physical punishment is maintained as impermissible. I believe that the other nuns who are now all in heaven will forgive me. They were such good people, coming all the way from Germany, to tend to the needs of the homeless, the poor, the unwanted, the other ... ...

If further proof is needed as regards the undesirability of corporal punishment, it was dramatically provided by two of the children. From babyhood Noel was notable for his extremely innovative, funny, infectious and odd personality. He later acquired the nick-name of "Number Plate" by which he has been known ever since. The sheer oddity of his nick name is empathetic testimony to what an incredibly unusual and interesting personality he was. At age four he and another lad, Ronny Miller [nick-named "Mooda"] thought up a plan. It was absolutely brilliant and extremely funny.

Priests are men of routine. So Father Peter, a big man with a huge very gruff voice, would walk past the school at a set time daily. To Number Plate and Mooda this required full exploitation. So one morning, as Father Peter appeared outside the window of their classroom, they set up a duet, comprised of screaming loudly whilst holding their buttocks and stamping their feet. Hearing the screams of little children, the good priest burst through the door and rushed in, cassock billowing behind him. On surveying the scene he assumed, as they intended him to, that these poor little devils were being beaten. He went wild, grabbing the class nun by the shoulders, and shaking her vigorously bellowed -"*S-e-e-e-s-t-a-a ... s-e-e-e-s-t-a-a*, [sister ... sister] *you must not beat the children ... you must not beat the children ...*" repeatedly until the poor nun, now crimson faced, nearly fainted in apprehension.

Father Peter then conducted a thorough search of the whole classroom and broke every ruler he could find. This little game was played out on more than one occasion by these four-year olds. In each instance they had not been beaten. Neither were they under immediate threat of being beaten. A brilliant subterfuge was being employed to remove the threat altogether. It worked. Beatings became rare, substituted by task centered punishment. So the human spirit, however small the repository, will find a way to resist, repel and struggle against that which is wrong.

Such incredible resistance to that which is wrong was instanced, on another occasion, involving Mooda receiving a parcel from home. Sister Obana had on a previous occasion taken his parcel, given him a couple of sweets, in lieu of sweets which we were all given, in any event, by the school every Sunday. Then, having repeated this, she told him that his parcel was finished. She thus nullified any advantage that otherwise accrued in terms of the child having received a parcel from home. This was, of course, grossly unfair.

What does a little boy of four, faced with such unfairness, do? In later life I have often put Mooda's case to adults when conducting a workshop. Not once have our present day crop of MBAs ever been able to come up with a credible solution.

But little Ronny Miller did. He grabbed the parcel and threw all its contents onto the roof of the nearest building. Like monkeys we were all up the roof in no time, collecting the spoils, which were later returned in large measure to Ronny, fully aware that he would respond by sharing the lot with us.

That put paid to that nun's machinations on this score. Mooda - 1. Sister Obana - 0. Mooda was younger than me, but has remained one of my heroes all my life.

He had to be as my life was to be concerned with justice.

9. Fear will make you do anything

Being a hero is good. It's an accolade that humans will bask in. Opportunity presented one afternoon when we were taken for a walk by the female lay staff made up of mainly Shona speaking girls. Going for a walk was a huge adventure for us as it involved venturing into the surrounding bush. For little children bush is an alien world, full of all kind of things, including perhaps the witch from the fable of "Hansel and Gretel" whose favourite meal was little children. The walk went off swimmingly well. A picnic spot was found and the girls kept us happy playing games and telling us stories whilst attending to the little ones. There was no nun with us. We chanced upon some shrubs which were laden with fruit shaped like extremely large elongated grapes. There was much happiness when the girls confirmed that the fruit were toondolooka[1] and edible. Young children in institutions are always hungry. So the find was more than a blessing.

We had our demons, witches, gnomes, goblins, giants ... etc ... gleaned from fairy tales such as those of the brothers Grimm[2]. The girls had their own. One appeared. Well at least one of the girls thought she saw one. She screamed *"Skebenga"*. A skebenga, in Zulu and Ndebele folklore, is semi-human of extremely unsavoury form, manner and habit. Mass hysteria set in. All the staff girls started to scream ... panic overtook them ... and once one of them ran the rest followed. In a moment they were gone. The babies started a crescendo of crying and screaming. In such a situation all your instincts point only one way ... run ... run ... run now ... run fast. So we started to run ... run after the girls ... who being adults were long gone.

But as I started I saw the face of Gerald Woodend, still little, just a toddler. It was a soft round face ... with big brown eyes ... now wide with fear ... streaming with tears ... and a mouth emitting a horse scream of terror ... in an auditorium of other screams ... screams of little ones ... very little ones ... in prams and crawling in circles on dusty ground ... little arms and legs pumping hard to escape that which was now there ... in their little minds ... in their little hearts ... unseen but evil and terrifying ...

I stopped. I was mesmerized with fear ... but I stopped. I just could not leave ... they were just too small, too helpless ... to be left. I myself was crying. I cried more loudly, but seeing nothing, I started to believe ... vaguely believe in what I should do. Taking my makeshift catapult (slingshot) from around my neck I armed it with a stone and looked for my adversary. There was nothing ... but there was something ... I thought I saw something. A mumbled jumbled Hail Mary was accompanied by the catapult being fired at something ... somewhere there in the bush ... where I could see nothing.

---

[1] **Toondolooka -** the Ndebele name - the English equivalent is not known.

[2] **Wilhelm and Jakob Grimm**, German brothers who published folk and fairy tales in the mid 1800s

Gerald stopped crying and his face took on an expression of confidence. He was not too small to know the power of the catapult. He had seen it bring down a dove in the hands of one of the male workers. In his mind it would kill anything. He made me feel better ... fear subsided just a notch. The younger ones were now handing me pebbles which they were picking up from off the ground, where the girls had been playing mancala. The more I fired the better I felt. Then - *"Christof¹ "* they said *"It's gone ... it is gone ... it is gone."* Other children picked the chorus -*"it is gone ... it is gone ..."* and slowly the crying subsided till only a few babies needed comforting by the older ones and then they also stopped.

It was about then that I saw the shape of Sister Rocha approaching in a rush through the bush. It was soon over. We were rescued. On return to the Home all the nuns were gathered. Everyone was breathless. The staff girls swore that they had seen a Skebenga. The nuns displayed little interest. They all turned to me. Sister Dagoberta said - *"Christopher, bearer of Christ ... today you were strong ..."* Some children confirmed that I had "shot it". The other nuns swamped me as I was showered with praise and rewarded with a medal of Saint Christopher carrying the baby Jesus across a river as Roman Catholic legend says he did. I wore that medal proudly around my neck for many years. Every car I have owned has had a St Christopher medal fixed onto the dash board.

I was lauded as a brave boy ... a very brave boy. I had not been brave. Throughout the incident I had felt paralyzed with fear. And yet I had done it. I had seen the thing through. So for me bravery is when fear is so bad that it forces reaction. This was to be confirmed in later life when I was conscripted into the Rhodesian army. The next day I was asked to stand up in front of the class and explain how I had done it ... how I had been so brave. I said - *"When you are afraid ... when you are very afraid ... always say a Hail Mary".* Everyone clapped. My class teacher, Sister Leonora, brimmed in smug satisfaction.

Soon thereafter the power of prayer was put to a severe test. A storm brewed itself up late one night. It was my first experience of such a storm. As the thunder roared the ground shook. The lightening cracked with ear splitting sharpness. We all dived under our blankets not daring to peep out, little hearts thumping in breathless chests. Then the storm delivered its *coup de grace*. In an instant the whole roof was gone, blown off like a flimsy piece of paper.

We all started to cry. This was it. A nun calmly started to lead us in prayer - *"Hail Mary full of grace, the Lord is with thee, Blessed art thou amongst*

---

¹ **Christof -** was a contraction of Christopher, my name

woman ... " Within seconds the rain stopped, the thunder and lightning ceased, except for distant sheet lightening. It was all over ... just like that. Tears were replaced by relieved giggles. Cocoa was brewed and dispensed all round. We carried our mattresses to the nearby dairy, where we bedded down, huddled close together, for the rest of the night.

To me this new mother, Mother Mary, in my life was a smash hit. I would have done anything for her. I would have done anything for Her if a nun had asked me to. So it is all too easy to see how children can be used as suicide bombers[1]. Since I was told, and believed implicitly, that children were pure and went straight to heaven on death, I would have embraced such death if packaged in Her name. In fact I often prayed that I could die in my sleep so that I could go home sooner.

10. Life skills

The nuns were very good teachers both in and out of the classroom. So we did not only learn to read, write, history, geography, English ... etc. We also learnt all about successful vegetable gardening. Virgin ground was selected. It was cleared using picks, shovels and other tools. Beds were marked out, tilled and the soil enriched with cow manure. Manure was transported from the cow kraal using "The Trailer".

Our exploits with this vehicle acquired legendary status and a talking point for the rest of our lives. The trailer was primarily made up of the open boxed section of a motor van, comprising the open rectangular box, axle and two wheels. To the front was attached a 3 meter long wooden boom with a short T-piece.

Once Sister Didima, in charge of gardening, commissioned the collection of anything such as cow manure, compost, bricks, soil ... etc a trailer team would be assembled. This was no problem. Competition for places on the team was fierce. Two boys were "inspanned" to the T-piece at the front to provide control and direction whilst the rest pushed on the back of the boxed

---

[1] In the Israeli-Palestinian conflict, Palestinian militant groups have recruited minors to attack Israeli targets, both military and civilian, especially during the Second Intifada. In some cases these attacks have been suicidal in nature. This deliberate involvement of children in armed conflict has been condemned by international organizations and certain Palestinian groups.
http://en.wikipedia.org/wiki/Child_suicide_bombers_in_the_Israeli%E2%80%93Pal estinian_conflict

section ... and then we were off to make the pick-up. On site the trailer would be loaded with cow manure by the use of shovels. Once loaded the exciting return or delivery trip occurred. The trailer would be always pushed at the maximum speed attainable. The load would have been set so that there was slightly less than "neutral" downward force at the front T-piece. In the result, once mobile, the two manning the front would spend most of their time in the air returning to their feet making contact with terra firma at very, very long intervals. We were always keen to impress and perform more deliveries than specified as there was always a bonus comprising sweets, fruit or biscuits to be earned for extra performance. So the speeds attained by the trailer team were impressive and undoubtedly also dangerous.

The loaded unit would hurtle along eating up the ground with the two front "jockeys" bouncing along "boink ... boink ... boink" like kangaroos. Bringing it to a halt required the highest level of hand/eye coordination, physical prowess, agility and perfect timing. This was accomplished entirely by the two front jockeys, who would have to ensure that their next contact with mother earth coincided with the point of destination and, upon their feet hitting the ground, in perfect coordination, pull the T-piece to one side at such an extreme angle to the line of travel that the following box would perform what is now termed a "wheelie", usually in a cloud of dust, and come to a sudden and most dramatic halt. Everyone always cheered. The higher the preceding speeds, the scarier the stop, the louder the cheers. It was wonderful, it was fun, it was exhilarating, and it was an adrenaline rush. It was what is now meant by "life on the edge" and, dare I claim, the first extreme sport ... routinely performed by largely unsupervised 5 to 8 year olds ... for reward.

A more perfect representation, by this "rainbow coloured" team, of current concepts of "morale", "going the extra mile', "team-work", "efficiency", "effectiveness", "performance" and "reward" you simply cannot find.

Heavy reliance was placed on cow and chicken manure, in our vegetable garden, which was so successful that it graduated to market garden status. So every Friday produce was transported by the Home's brown coloured Ford van to the city of Bulawayo where it was sold at the market. We learnt all aspects of vegetable production, tilling, planting, sowing, cultivation, compost use, manure use, mulching, weeding and watering. What is more, it was all eco- friendly. Pesticides were not featured. Since our produce was always of high quality it fetched good prices on the market, in which profits we participated by increased allocation of sweets, fruit and biscuits. We loved it.

What we did not love was cotton picking. There is something soul destroying about cotton picking. It is hardly surprising that the slave trade occurred. It is doubtful that ordinary folk will voluntarily perform such labour on any meaningful scale. Cotton ripens when it is hot. We had to hand-pick it. Bolls of cotton are picked out of their open shells and deposited into the pocket of an apron worn around the waist. This is how we did it. As cotton is highly compressible an extremely large quantity has to be picked to fill the apron pocket. By this time one would be a very long distance away from the collection/deposit point. After trekking the distance to make a deposit you start again. It was hot, back breaking work especially as there was much cotton to be picked on account of the agrarian skills of the nuns.

11. Politics of the heart

One hot afternoon we were picking cotton. Despite the promise of a bonus allocation of reward I was not happy. I started to miss my mother, really miss her. Then I heard the sound of calling, calling that is peculiar to bush telegraph, voices conveying a message, indistinct at first and gradually assuming clarity. My heart skipped a beat - *"it's Christof's mummy, Christof's mummy ... "* rang the message. I stopped and straightened out, daring to hope.

Through the heat haze I gradually made out the figure of a woman. Indeed it was my mother. My heart broke. I immediately started to cry. All the nun's admonishing that *"big boys don't cry"* were in vain. I cried tears ... not tears that come from the eyes ... but tears that come from the heart itself; and are carried to the eyes by one's veins.

However, this was not out of the joy of seeing my mother. Yes, right there I realized how much I missed her, how much I loved her, how much I needed her. If that was all I felt I would not have cried. I would have run in sheer joy and happiness and jumped all over her.

[Picture is of my mum Nellie Helen Leith]

No; the pain was a realization, thrust like a dagger through my heart, the moment I saw her; that she was going to have to leave me again. This phenomenon of a child crying upon its parent arriving at the Home was common. I am sure the reason was the same realization that I felt. At that moment you are reminded of everything, who you are, what you have lost, the pain of the original parting, what you are missing and that this cycle will now start once more.

Children need their biological parents. A child needs a mother and a father. We were happy and secure with the nuns. However no institution can provide the food that the heart and soul of child needs, only its mother and father. Good institutions can sustain the human spirit, and teach it to endure, but they can never provide comfort to the heart.

The nuns were very good "mothers" to us. But they were not fathers. Deprived of anything a child will resolve it by contriving the situation. We had no fathers. So, without exception, we all "adopted' male adults who worked on the farm. There was fierce competition over this issue, often settled in a fight in order to decide if a particular worker was to be recognized as "my man".

These were Black workers. We were Coloured children in a racist society. It mattered not one jot. The most prized "man" was a worker named Christopher referred to by us as "Big Christof" to distinguish him from me. He became the top prize when he was allocated the responsibility of driving the tractor once the Home acquired one. As the driver of such an incredible machine he easily outranked all others. I claimed him as "my man". This was disputed. The issue was settled in a fist fight. Big Christof was my man. The fight was well worth it.

Conversely the female staff were not adopted even though they were much closer to us and tended to our every need. They were headed by a woman named Merensia who ruled the roost in every respect. She was loved, feared and respected by everyone; but not adopted.

Applying hindsight to all this, it would appear that most of the children did have some mother figure in their lives. This probably comprised a biological mother, grandmother or an aunt who had cared for them before arriving in the Home. Certainly, visits to children were almost exclusively by woman. If a child did not have such a relative it may be that the nuns or a nun played that role in its psyche. What is absolutely clear however is that all of us male children had a father need. Hence the practice of adopting adult males presenting in our space. There is, of course, a certain irony and pathos about boys of White paternal pedigree having to adopt Black men as their fathers.

Of the female staff, other than the nuns, the one we loved the most was a lady named Helena, whom we addressed as *"Miss Helena"*. She was a teacher, a very good teacher in terms of our perceptions. Her strength was that she was exciting in her approach, whereas the nuns tended to be more dour. She also spoke English with a better accent than most of the nuns. She supplemented the coloured crayons with mud with which she used to teach us clay modeling. Modeling clay is an absolutely enthralling business for little children. Such children have a natural affinity for mud. Given half a chance they will wallow in it.

Then the regional educational officer arrived. He was more than incensed. The nuns received a severe dressing down. Miss Helena was tearful. So were we as she was summarily "removed' from the school by government vehicle. The reason - she was Black. The White colonial government was not about to permit a Black to teach anyone other than other Blacks. Helena was Black, but quite indistinguishable in colouring from some of the children in the Home. The problem was that she was a black African and we were coloured African.

On such idiotic premise human lives are wrecked.

---

12. Through the eyes of a child

I am at home for school holidays. One morning I am playing outside when I become aware of a buzz like sound I have never heard before. At first it sounds like bees, or rather a swarm of bees. As the sound is so enveloping it is quite difficult to locate the direction it is coming from. It is both a sound and a vibration coursing through the fresh morning air, augmenting its chill. Eventually I pick up the direction this peculiar buzz is coming from. It is a chilling sight. Rounding the corner of a small hillock, in the distance, is a stream of movement snaking its way forward in my direction. At first it has the appearance of some monstrous centipede with overactive legs. It is a terrifying sight.

Then my eyes start to make out what I am seeing. I start to see people ... more and more people ... Black people ... with spears, sticks and knobkerries ... waving in the air. It is blood chilling. The stream is endless, ever stretching from its source at the hillock and snaking its way towards me. As faces become discernible it is clear that these are angry Black people, shouting, chanting, gesticulating, and waving weapons of death. I am paralyzed with fear and cannot move. Aunt Elizabeth rushes out of the house, picks me up and carries me inside, slamming the door and locking it behind us. Moments later there is a very loud knock on the front door. By this time my mother is with us listening to Aunt Elizabeth babbling an explanation. The knocking continues, louder and louder, against a crescendo of human voices, chanting and singing.

My mother opens the door. It seems to be an act madness to me. I imagine being butchered by angry violent men using their spears, assegais and knobkerries. She stands tall on the stoep looking down on the sea of angry faces. She waits. The shouting, chanting and singing slowly subsides. *"Salibonani obantu bami"* [Greetings, my people] and continuing in the vernacular - *"I am Nellie ... second born of Mafulela Thebe of Mzilikazi 's clan ... "* You can now hear a pin drop. A spokesman returns the greeting adding *"we too are of Mzilikazi ... today is a very important day for all our people ... who must unite in this cause … "*

A conversation, conducted in purest isiNdebele, then ensues in this chilly morning air of this day of the 1948 general strike by Black workers[1]. They want Elizabeth, now seated on the floor next to my mother. As a Black domestic worker she is obliged to join. There is a pregnant silence when my mother tells them that Elizabeth is her sister, born of the same mother, and therefore not a domestic worker but looking after her own child who has not been well. That child is me. In most African cultures such an aunt is regarded as also being a mother to her nephew.

This news is greeted with a hum of seeming appreciation. My mother adds that their cause is good, it is necessary and if there is unity it will not fail. The hum intensifies. Spears, assegais and kerries are lowered. She goes on *"As men ... as men and women ... of a noble people ... we are appealing to you ... that you open your hearts and have sympathy for the plight of two women with our sick child ... we will appeal to the ancestral spirits ... to help you ... to help us!"*

It is soon over. Bidding us *"hlala kahle"* [stay well] they leave, snaking their way up the hill in a crescendo of chanting, sloganeering and singing. My heart continues to thump loudly in my chest for the rest of the day.

Because of the situation at home holidays became infrequent and I, like many other children would spend the whole year at Sacred Heart Home. The home expanded significantly with the addition of a complex comprising dormitories, living quarters for the nuns, laundry and other support structures. Moving into a dormitory of plastered brick under tile with ceilings and electric lighting was an exciting experience especially when the nun flicked the switch and the fluorescent lights magically flickered on. We had never experienced electric lighting and the lights flickering on were met with long *"oohs"* and *"aaghs"*.

---

[1] **Joshua Nkomo**, the railway union leader, was also a representative of the same phenomenon. He was a young graduate who had made his name in the 1948 general strike, sponsored by the railways in the hope that he could help offset the growth of radicalism." Crisis in Zimbabwe by Leo Zeilig.
http://pubs.socialistreviewindex.org.uk/isj94/zeilig.htm

There was also a dam constructed a good walking distance away. This was to provide new adventure in swimming and fishing. A worker named Stanislaus became a favourite "my man" when he taught us to make fishing rods. Wire was friction-sharpened on concrete paving and bent to make hooks. Floats were lovingly shaped from cork material. The nuns provided twine. Rods were cut from tree branches. In this way we had fishing rods to augment our cattys. Stanislaus also taught us the art of fishing using mealie pap as bait. Fishing was a truly satisfying activity and the fish we caught presented as a tasty supplement to the bland food served up by the Home. This was cooked for us by the girls on payment of one fish for each tin of fish cooked. We also sun dried the fish after butterflying them open. Fish was clandestinely feasted upon in the dormitory after lights out.

The regional medical officer was not impressed when some of the boys were found to have intestinal [tape] worms, some of which were of quite frightening proportions, up to a meter in length.

13. A Xmas carol

It is the 25th December 1949, Xmas day. We are excited, very excited, as the nuns have announced that we were going to have a "Xmas party". It is our first, and "Xmas party" are new words in our lives. At midday a stream of cars arrive. We set up our customary chant *"moti cars ... moti cars ... moti cars"* ... ["moti cars" ... Meaning ... motor cars ...] The occupants are all White strangers. One of the cars has "Toc H Society Bulawayo Branch" emblazoned on its side. They engage us. Balls, nets, racquets and other sporting things are produced. We spend an incredibly exciting afternoon learning and playing new games such as the sack race, three legged race, as well as "old games" like foot sprints. Winners are rewarded with prizes of balls, puzzle sets and other occupational toys.

As evening falls there is a fireworks display. It is our first time to see fireworks. We go mad with excitement and *"ooh ... aah"*, shout, giggle and laugh at every stage. And then ... then the Xmas party - that we have all been waiting for. When the door of the hall is opened we are greeted by an unbelievable sight. The walls and ceilings are festooned with brightly coloured paper trimmings, sparkling baubles and twinkling fairy lights. It is like a dream. Many are dumbstruck and have to be jeed up *" ... common child ... isn't it nice ... are you not happy ...?"* as we stand there, bug eyed and enthralled at what we are seeing. Of course we are happy, more than happy, thrilled to the bone, little hearts are bursting, minds are numb.

We are given Xmas hats to wear. We look at each other sheepishly, giggle and then start to laugh ... and laugh ... and heckle each other ... tease and heckle ... and laugh some more ... the happy laughter of children whose hearts are singing a song not sung before. Invited to sit down, we are served our Xmas dinner. A lady approaches me with a tray of rice, meat, fish and vegetables presenting in ways I have never seen. We are invited, entreated, cajoled into making choices. It is hard work for our benefactors. We have never seen such fare before. It is overwhelming to little minds. Spoilt for choice; little brains battle to cope. In the end we get there and eventually we are all tucking in, prodding each other and pointing to this and that on the plate of the other, with Xmas hats requiring constant adjustment.

After the main course one of the sisters excitedly calls out *"children ... children ... quiet ... quiet please ... Father Xmas is coming ... Father Xmas is coming ... "* Little voices peter out in obedience. A hush descends and soon everything is as quiet as a cathedral at midnight. We look around us, and each other ... looking everywhere ... for Father Xmas. The lights go out and the room is now lit only by the twinkling fairy lights on the Xmas tree in the corner. The atmosphere is almost unbearably charged as expectancy and disbelief contend in little minds and hearts. And then we hear a sound ... a sound on the roof ... from a roof that has never made sounds before. It is a rasping sound of something, someone there. *"Oh children"* Sister Leonora calls out *"did you hear Father Xmas arrive on the roof, on his sleigh with his reindeers ... all the way from the North Pole ... I heard it ... yes I can hear it ... "* She is answered in so many voices. Some are bright retorts ... *"yes Sister ... yes"*. Others are forced whispers from mouths hampered by overwhelmed minds. Others simply look wide eyed at the nun and slowly nod ... ever so slowly ... as they struggle to believe ... that a dream is coming true.

Moments later the room is filled with a voice booming out - *"Ho, ho, ho ... ho, ho, ho ... hello children ... "* As the lights go on we are struck with the sight of Father Xmas swaggering into the hall, ruddy faced, bearded, in red/white garb, and a big red bag, over his shoulder just as we had seen him in so many pictures. *"Come ... come children ... "* he booms out - *"Sister tells me that you have been good children ... very good children ... come and get your Xmas presents ... "* The base of the Xmas tree is now covered in boxes of different size and shape, all brightly wrapped and alluring. One or two of us rush forward. Others have to be encouraged, even led by the hand. In the end we all get our presents, brightly coloured boxes held tightly, turned and examined from every angle with disbelieving eyes.

Opening of the presents has to be quite vigorously encouraged. Soon the room is awash with the sounds of squeals, giggles and happy little voices as we make acquaintance with our presents. Mine comprises a dinky toy car, a jig-saw puzzle and a book titled "Under Drake's Flag" by George Arthur Henty (1832 -1902). In the months that followed the adventures of Sir Francis Drake (1540-96); the first Englishman, admiral and buccaneer, to sail around the world, captivated and enthralled me, and my school mates, who would gather around every evening in order to hear me recount what I had read. To this day I have never received a more welcome gift.

Pudding is then served. A lady puts a plate in front of me. She invites me to help myself to ice cream. I have never seen ice cream before, except in pictures. I hesitate. She spoons a huge dollop of ice cream into my plate. *"Have some jelly"* she says pointing to a tray of jelly in all shapes and all colours. *"Help yourself... "* she says entreatingly. *"You can have as much as you like ... yes you can have as much as you ... "* she repeats. I look at all the jelly in front of me ... bright ... quivering ... of so many shapes ... of so many colours ... quivering ... .

I burst into tears. So did one or two others.

What an incredibly wonderful first Xmas that was. A special mass was later held to ask Almighty God to bless the good men and women of the Toc H Society, a blessing that they richly deserved, having given up Xmas with their families to drive out and bring unbelievable magic and joy to others, little hearts beating on the fringe of society.

The next evening we spend firing off fire crackers that we had been given the night before. This is an awesome experience as "bang", "crackle', "whoosh" merge with *"oohs", "aahs"* other sounds of enthralled children. Sister Radigoon does not share in our excitement. She sits on a chair to one side, silently fingering the beads of her rosary. Then she calls us to sit in front of her, as she has a story to tell. Her hazel blue eyes glisten under the night sky, brimful with tears as she recounts a story of nights, many nights of terror ... of the drone of aero planes drawing ever closer ... the sound of their engines heralding the terrible carnage to follow ... the chatter of anti-aircraft gunfire vainly trying to fend off the menacing approach of the birds of death. Then the world would explode, as the first bomb hit ... and then another ... and another ... building to a crescendo of sound ripping out roofs, flattening walls ... exposing the occupants ... men, women, children ... crying, screaming and scurrying around like so many ants whose ant heap has been blown open. And then the fires ... fires everywhere ... coming in a blood chilling "whoosh" ... waves of blinding light and searing heat ... fire storms swamping the world of the scurrying people ... enveloping all and sundry ... singing, burning and cremating ... amidst the screams, gasping, choking and moans of utter despair.

We listen uncomprehendingly to this incredible story of the bombing of the German city of Dresden on the nights of the 13 and 14, February1945, just four years before. The story comes in fits and starts, as this good woman struggles to tell it in a voice that often breaks as she gropes to find the words to describe that which was just indescribable ... how night was turned into day in a process of burning alive, cooking alive, incinerating alive, tens of thousands of ordinary human beings.

There is no anger, only pain, anguish and terrible sadness. After being led in a prayer to ask for forgiveness for those who did the bombing and to welcome the souls of the victims into His kingdom we go to bed, minds and hearts bursting with the experience of what had been a wondrous Xmas and numbed in sadness for the German people of Dresden.

We are too young to see the irony and pathos of a situation, where a German nun was now tending to the unwanted progeny of the very people who bombed her people to death.

14. The grim reaper knocks and is answered

I was a very talkative child. It often got me into trouble. For reasons that escape me it would appear that religious folk such as nuns, prize silence which I was told "was golden". It made little sense to me. As a growing child, new experiences are a continual occurrence. The world presents with so many ever new and wondrous things. These are found everywhere; in the environs, in interaction with others, in the classroom, in books ... the list is endless. What is the point of learning all these things if one is then precluded from talking about them, with the same intensity and commitment that goes into the learning? As said, I often got into trouble for talking too much.

One day I lost my voice. It was gone. I had no voice. My teacher, Sister Leonora, was confident that the reason was that I talked too much, and that I *"had strained my voice"*. To ensure that my vocal chords got a proper rest she promptly taped my mouth over to the not inconsiderable amusement and smug satisfaction of most of my peers. There were many sniggers and giggles at my plight. At a stroke I had lost my status as a brave hero, and was now a dumb something instead.

Surely the reader will agree, that there is something very bad about any silencing of a human being?

A day later the regional medical officer arrived on a routine inspection. On enquiring as to why my mouth was taped he was told, gleefully it must be said, about the events leading up to my mouth being taped. He turned to the nun in attendance - *"you say he lost his voice ... ?"* he said enquiringly. The nun was happy to confirm this, and proffer that the reason was that I talked too much. The doctor's manner underwent a very perceptible change. He stripped the tape off my mouth, and proceeded to take swabs off the inside. In minutes he had packed his bag, got into his car and haired off at some speed. He returned at daybreak accompanied by an army of people in white coats who proceeded to vaccinate everyone within sight and send for those who were not. The populace in the whole area were vaccinated. I was put into an ambulance and rushed at breakneck speed to the hospital in Bulawayo.

I had diphtheria[1], one of the deadliest disorders known to man. The whole school assembled at church to pray for my safe recovery. Prayers were indeed needed. The doctor had informed the nuns that once diphtheria reached the voice loss stage a patient would certainly die unless treated immediately. I had been without a voice for at least two days. That I survived was unprecedented according to the doctors at the hospital, and I was the subject of much attention by many doctors. It was not to be the first time that a medically unprecedented condition would decide to have a go at me.

During my recovery I was visited by two nuns as well as my mother and Aunt Elizabeth. *"It's really a miracle - "* said Sister Leonora. Her companion, Sister Radigoon, in agreeing added *"You see the power of prayer..."*

To which my Aunt Elizabeth further added, in isiNdebele – *"Yes it is true ... God is great. He listens to the ancestral spirits. So you see when Fuyane performed lungisa on our child he really made sure that your prayers would always be answered".*

"Can I have more ice cream and jelly..." I pleaded. I had not eaten for days and it was only my second time to taste ice cream and jelly. Life was so good in hospital. An added bonus was that I was tended to by a beautiful nurse from Thorngrove, Poppy Mckop. She made sure that I had extra helpings of ice cream and jelly.

---

[1] **Diphtheria** is a life-threatening disorder caused by a highly contagious bacterial infection caused by the bacterium Corynebacterium diphtheriae. ··· is especially dangerous when it affects the throat ···
http://www.healthscout.com/ency/68/466/main.html#DefinitionofDiphtheria
Laryngeal diphtheria, which involves the voice box or larynx, is the form most likely to produce serious complications ··· http://medical-dictionary.thefreedictionary.com/diphtheria

I am not so sure that Fuyane had much to do with what happened on one of my school holidays. I was at home with Elizabeth when she decided to do something about an itchy rash that I had developed all over my body, reddish and blistery in appearance. She concocted a mixture of potash and water in a tin bath outside. I was immersed into this crimson mix. The spots on my body were than scrubbed off using a bath stone. On my mother's return she was very concerned. The doctor was called. He was more than shocked and bemused at this perfunctory and novel way to treat chicken pox. However diagnosis revealed that I was in recovery phase. Little more was needed other than that I remain in bed and out of sunlight. I recovered well without a trace of a scar on any part of my body.

It was very difficult for my mother. So I would also spend some time with my grandmother at her village in Kezi. On one of these trips I developed ear ache before we left. My mother took me to the doctor. He treated me and assured us that it would soon be over. On the way things got worse. A stage was reached when I was in unbearable pain. What to do? The fully laden bus could not return to Bulawayo. Somebody suggested we try an *"African store"* a short way ahead. We did. The owner produced a small tin which contained a foul smelling greasy mixture which he said only *"the natives"* ever used. We had no option. The smelly grease was heated in a teaspoon so as to reduce its viscosity and poured into my ear. Within a minute the pain was gone. I have never had another ear ache in some 60 years.

Mostly I traveled with my Aunt Elizabeth. We would go to the bus rank in Makokoba Township and catch an "African bus". It was all very exciting with the hustle and bustle of humanity at the bus rank. Goods were laden on top of the buses. The range included suitcases, blanket rolls, wire mesh rolls, live chickens and even the occasional goat. On the trip nourishment comprised roasted mealie corn and/or bully beef sandwiches, washed down with cold tea, poured out from a bottle. Late afternoon the bus conductor would signal the driver to stop, at a place quite indistinguishable from the surrounding bush, except for a tiny mark on a tree. Upon alighting Elizabeth would hoist all our possessions, tied up as a huge bundle, onto her head and then offer to carry me on her back as well. I always declined and would strut off at a pace intended to impress her. At some stage my mother had bought me a pith helmet which I donned.

It was a long walk, and I felt for her having to carry the load on her head. However it never seemed to bother her much, as she followed me, ambling almost regally along the bush path to my granny's village. We must have made quite an interesting cameo; a five-year-old brown skinned lad, with a pith helmet, followed by a Black woman, with the whole world bundled on her head, meandering through the mopani scrub.

Noticing that I was flagging, she would repeat her offer to carry me on her back. I always declined, feeling quite ashamed that I was tired while she had such a burden to carry. Upon reaching the village my granny would run out to meet us, clapping her hand, exclaiming loudly in words and song of welcome. *"Ah, ah, aah ... who is this ... aah ... it is my child ... oh ... it is my child ... no ... oh no ... it is my children ... but my child Lizzy has brought my child u-Vavie ... today I am so happy ... we are so happy."* She would pick me up and after showering me with kisses, throw me high into the air, laughing and cooing in expression of pure joy.

Then I would be offered my favourite treat of sour milk, sweetened with sugar and regaled to eat as much as I wanted. *"My child, Gogo knows that this is what you love most from your Gogo",* she would say.

15. A question of identity - and mentorship

I loved being at my granny's village, comprising a cluster of pole and dagga huts with thatched roofs. However I was extremely resentful of the fact that all those around me were black and I was brown. Also my hair was almost completely straight. This induced a serious identity crisis. When my mother arrived to fetch me she called me by name Vavie. I protested bitterly and tearfully in isiNdebele - *"I am not Vavie ... I am Ndiweni ... me I am Ndiweni..."* My grandmother was not impressed. From then on she would always stress to me that I was not *"umuntu um'nyama"* [a black person]- that I was *"umlungu"* [of white status] - that I should never forget this and be proud of what I was, otherwise she would have to use a switch to get me to understand.

This counseling was routinely reinforced by my Black aunts and Uncle Willie, then and throughout my development years. In present day South Africa, Coloured folk are significantly prejudiced in their life prospects and struggles, unless they accept government sponsored classification that they are Black. In order to benefit under "affirmative action" and "Black empowerment' schemes they must prove they are "Black", whatever their physical colouring. This is vomitus stuff.

Internationally there is a most curious phenomenon, in which political correctness insists that we be classified as Black. Barrack Obama who, like me, is ethnically Euro-Africa, is referred to as America's first Black president. That he is 50% White is thus seen as an *inconvenient truth* to be submerged by the *convenient untruth* that he is Black. What is it that children, in particular, think of such blatant lies? What effect does it have on them?

My grandmother taught me many of the things that shape my value set and personal code. Included was that, in relating to people, I should be most wary of three types of people - *ugly people,* [sour faced], *unhappy people* [mean spirited], and *stupid people.* Of these three groupings, *stupid people* were by far the most dangerous, she always stressed. Life has taught me that she was 100% right. People who have a complex about their mental ability will always feel threatened, and especially threatened by those possessed of talent and ability. The latter than stand to be suppressed and victimized. Ignorance is very dangerous to humanity. Ignorant leaders are the most dangerous.

On occasion my elder brothers Frank and Zain would also be on holiday at home with me. It was just marvelous to have elder brothers as they taught me things. What impressed me most, in my first recollection of them, is that they had catapults around their necks. When they decided that it was time for me to also have a real catapult I realized that they were indeed my brothers, wonderful, special ... my big brothers ... to be looked up to ... to be revered ... admired ... and that they loved me and would protect me against all. I felt safer in this world.

The making of the catapult was a very serious business. The surrounding bush was scoured for just the right Y-shaped twig. This was cut and honed to size and shape that was the best fit for my hand. In a two-man operation car tubing was cut with extreme care into two strips which, in terms of length and width, would provide optimal tension in the draw-back phase of firing the weapon. As I watched my brothers making up my catty[1] my heart was pounding with excitement. Even more exciting was my training in its use. A tin was set up as a target and I was then trained. Hearing the sound of the tin being struck, and seeing it jump into the air, as the pebble I had fired made contact for the first time was a very special moment. I had vindicated their decision that I could be entrusted with possession and use of such an important weapon. This was my first graduation in a lifetime on many graduations.

Just then Zain shouts - *"hawk ... "* We look up and sure enough there is a hawk circling high in the sky. On Frank's command we all take cover. This confuses me, as we have a hen with her brood of chickens scratching around in the yard. On such occasions Aunt Elizabeth would always run out, and do everything to shoo off the hawk, by shouting invectives and waving her arms. Not so on this occasion. Frank insists that we be out of sight. He crouches down on one knee, adjusting the angle of his hat as he does so. I crouch down beside him. It is bright morning. The hen is oblivious to the threat circling

---

[1] **"Catty"** - colloquialism for catapult].

above her. On other occasions I had seen her gather all her chicks and conceal them under her wings. Not so this time; she has not spotted the hawk. She is unaware that, in a moment, a winged projectile will come hurtling down from the sky in a dive of awesome power and accuracy ... terrible claws will be extended ... and one of her precious chicks will be plucked from the ground and carried off, never to be seen again.

The hen is clucking contently as she scratches the ground. *"Peep, peep, peep ... "* her chicks chorus as they too scratch and run around exploring the earth. My heart is pounding. High above the hawk seems to pause imperceptibly and then turns into a dive. Everything goes into slow motion. The black meteor of death descends, at incredible speed, on a flight path leading to the brood of chicks. They all start to scatter as the attack is betrayed by a whoosh sound, when the hawk extends its wings, in order to air-brake the dive, level off and execute the take. Its claws are extended. Capture is assured.

My heart stops ... but just then the whoosh sound is interrupted by another sound ... the sharp sound of contact ... contact of a projectile ... a bouquet of feathers fly off the hawk at the point of contact ... the hawk loses its flight path ... it tries to regain height ... but it has been fatally wounded ... and spirals off into an uncontrolled dive soon, hitting the ground some distance away. Frank Joseph Leith has just taken care of things. He carefully checks his catty and then hangs it around his neck. I was to witness him perform this incredible feat of marksmanship on one other occasion.

Such marksmanship was needed. Our sustenance as a family depended on it. Hunting trips were organized. The quarry were wild doves and guinea fowl. The three of us made up the hunting party. My brothers, darkly dressed, provided fire power. I would wear a huge ex army great coat despite the midday heat. The great coat had pockets, huge pockets, in which dead doves could be transported. The hunts were always successful. My brothers were incredibly efficient in the art of stalking and bringing down a dove with a catty. Suppers, which we found delicious and filling, comprised sadza[1], vegetable relish and roasted or braised doves or brisket. This was prepared by Aunt Elizabeth on our "Welcome Dover" stove that we were all so proud of. When it arrived we built a kitchen from bricks scavenged in the local brick field. The roof comprised corrugated iron sheeting, weighted done with bricks, concrete slabs and other building rubble.

Eating was communal. After washing our hands, we would all sit in a circle and, taking a dollop of sadza from a dish in which it was set in a round mound, one would form it in the hand before dipping into the bowls of relish

---

[1] **Sadza** - also known as "pap' - A thick porridge made from maize meal

and meat, before transfer to one's mouth. The relish often comprised the leaves of a weed that grew freely in the surrounding hedges. Sometimes we got a guinea fowl or a rabbit. That was more than a blessing. We also netted fingerling fish in nearby stream using our vests as nets. On Sunday we had chicken. Those meals, that we shared in a smoke filled room, were truly delicious and felt like a feast for kings. It never did feel that it was all about survival for a woman earning £5 a month as a nanny in the White suburbs, to feed and clothe a family of five.

It was home and we were family.

Frank was a hero with younger ones in the Thorngrove community. Undoubtedly his prowess with a catty had much to do with this. He was also an incredibly talented boxer. On weekends we would go to the African location of Makokoba to attend what was then referred to as bioscope. African locations were sprawling human settlements, comprising match-box houses with water being drawn from communal stand-pipes. But they were alive, noisy, vibrant and colourful, with the smell and taste of humanity. The films were always westerns, with their customary punch-ups. These were loved by the Black audience who would scream and shout - *"Jagee – Jagee ..."* whistle and ululate in approval. *"Jagee"* was a reference to Jake Tuli, a legendary South African boxer.

Afterwards everyone gathered outside and an impromptu boxing ring set up. The previous champion would enter, dance and prance around, ducking, weaving, and feigning as he threw punches at imaginary opponents. Anybody wishing to challenge would then enter, be gloved up and the fight would be on. Frank was a heroic favourite with the crowd as he would roundly beat all contenders in his weight class and many heavyweights as well. When he entered the ring there would be a rapturous roar of *"Makiti ... Makiti ... "* which is a colloquialism meaning *"cat ... cat"*. This was in keeping with his boxing style, which was the employment of speed, guile, agility, and generally effective technique. I am sure the lion, king of the jungle, and greatest of all cats, would have gladly acknowledged Frank as a worthy human version of their renowned kind.

Frank, unlike other dark skinned folk, had little difficulty in finding his first job, when my mother announced that he had to leave school to help our struggling family. It took only a few days before Petie McKop, brother to nurse Poppy McKop, arrived to announce - *"Frank, you have got a job ... come to-morrow ... "* The Mckops were a Cape Coloured family, who lived in a house closest to us. They were all brown skinned, with straight hair, and would resort to speaking Afrikaans with little provocation. Culturally they were very Afrikaans; a people who were renowned for racism in the region.

In the Thorngrove community however, although the brain undoubtedly knew that Frank was black, this information was never confirmed by the retina. Being colour blind, it seems, was a local pandemic.

Another legendary hero, for all Thorngrove at the time, was an African by the name of Ginger. We all loved him. He was the one who imparted the life skill of catapult use. He also took us on forays into the bush and introduced us to what was edible such as "sadende", a root fruit shaped like a potato which was absolutely delicious. He also taught us how to set traps for hares, guinea fowl and birds. Mostly though we would gather at the sweet factory, where he worked and, at a pre-arranged time, he would give us bricks and chips of brown sugar; a truly delicious commodity to be traded in amongst growing children.

On many a day, the Thorngrove scene included this Black adult male, followed and surrounded by a troupe of Coloured children, like some modern day pied piper. At the Home each of us had our own "my man".

In Thorngrove we all shared Ginger.

16. And deliver us from evil

My mother, like millions of other women all over the world, was also vulnerable in other ways given that she was a beautiful woman living alone without husband.

It is early evening when the man arrives. He is a big man, well proportioned and muscular. I have seen him before. He has always been very nice. He sometimes comes over and helps fix things. I like him. I greet him as *"uncle"*. To-day there is something different about him. He is loud and exhibitive. He grabs me and, picking me up, all but shouts - *"Helloooo sonny boy ... what's up ... you are soooo big and strong my boy ... just like me hey ...."* On meeting my mother he insists that he needs to talk to her in private. They go into a section portioned off by a curtain to serve as her bedroom. Once inside my mother asks if he has been drinking. This is discussed shortly and he protests -*"what does it matter if I have had a drink or two ... you know I have been thinking about you ... missing you ...?"* He attempts to put his arm around her. When she resists he persists. There is a mini physical tussle, as woman tries to ward off the attentions of lustful man. *"You had better leave ... "* she says and goes on to insist that he go now.

He is adamant that he needs her, he loves her, and she needs him ... they would be *"good together"*.

As this insistence fails he becomes aggressive, and things deteriorate rapidly. The man presses home his attentions as my mother tries to calmly resist ... *"Look ... you must be drunk ... don't behave like this ... I don't like it ... now please leave ... "* This is to no avail and bad becomes worse when he says - *"Common ... common ... what's up with you ... you know you want me ... what's the problem ... why you playing hard to get ... after all who is fucking you these days?".*

At that point he grabs her, she pushes him away. As he lunges forward again, he sees her about to hit him with a kerrie that she has suddenly pulled from under her bed. He raises his arms to ward off the blow, but then feels a sharp pain in his knee. Striking an opponent on the knee, as the first blow in mortal combat, is a classic Ndebele/Zulu combat tactic. The enemy expects a blow to the face or upper torso. When delivered, he is able to ward it off, as it has been anticipated. A blow to the knee, is not anticipated, so it finds its mark. The knee is a critical component, for efficient and effective movement of the human body. Once disabled, all movement is badly sabotaged. The man is now crippled. He can hardly move, let alone press home the attack on my mother.

She calmly straightens herself, and pulling a hippo's tail sjambok[1] from under her mattress, whips the man across the torso. *"Look ... "* she says *" ... you said you were going to fuck me ... so you can fuck me now ... "* Another blow is delivered. The man tries not to cry out but, on feeling the searing pain, on being struck again, go through his body like an electric shock, he screams. She takes off her dress and throws it in his face. *"Common ... I want to be fucked ... you said so ... since I have no husband ... you promised to do the job ... now do it ... !"* she commands him. When he looks up at her, in helpless pleading, she sjamboks him again ... and again ... all the while reminding him of the promise he is now failing to fulfill.

I hear the sounds of the man crying. I have never again heard such sounds emanate from a human being. It is an admixture of a muffled scream, a reverberating moan, a mournful groan and the bleating of a sheep in death; rising in pitch as each blow is delivered.

I run to the first house in Thorngrove and report. The man is rescued soon afterwards. He is almost comatose. An ambulance conveys him from the scene. The police are here. My mother appears distraught. She is dressed only in a petticoat and bra, one side of which is undone. Her hair is disheveled. A neighbour puts arms around her comfortingly. There is a discussion with the police. I hear the words *"rape"* and *"attempted rape"* for the first time in a

---

[1] **Sjambok** – is whip made from animal hide

life in which I am to be greatly familiarized with these words. The police are satisfied that the *"drunken bastard"* got his just deserts. Women all over this planet will agree. The man never did ever return.

The police return a few days later. They enlist the help of the whole community. An extensive search is conducted, in the surrounding bush, in the river, down wells. The search goes on all afternoon and well into the night. It is fruitless.

A child is missing. My mother is heartbroken. That child is me. I have run away after my mother threatens to give me *"a hiding"*, i.e., beating. I assumed she would use her sjambok. I have seen how it can reduce a grown muscular man to a mass of blue-black pulp. So I ran away from home. Making my way to the African location, I boarded a bus bound for a tribal trust land in Lupane, some 180 kms away. The bus owner knew me very well. He was a man named Nicholas Scott. At the time he was my favourite uncle. I assured him that my mother had given permission. I paid nothing for the trip and my Uncle Scott gave me enough pocket money to see my way.

As the bus meanders into the African bush, night falls, and the passengers start singing. It is magical. Three, four, five voices join in, join off and rejoin, in a heartwarming meeting of harmonious sound, song and refrain. First one, and another, then another picks up the melody with other voices rich in background chorus, rising and falling, wave upon wave, wave into wave, on and on, drowning the senses in rich, vibrant sustenance of the soul itself. It is magical, soothing and comforting to the unhappy little heart of a lost child, and I soon fall into deep and peaceful sleep.

I spend two weeks in the rural area of Lupane, living with different families in their huts in different villages. I am welcomed everywhere, treated with kindness and afforded lodgings and food as if I were a family member. Being a child of Ndebele extraction guarantees that. There is much competition to "claim" me by different families. This is because I was considered "a catch"; not on account of my brown skin and staightish hair, but because I can do something they have never seen before.

I can walk on my hands and perform hand and fly springs. This I learnt in the Home where we did this almost daily. We could even walk up and down stairs on our hands. Everywhere I go I am heralded as *"the one who walks on hands"* even though I have told them my name is Ndiweni. Crowds gather to watch, in awe and appreciation, as I demonstrate these weird skills. Every performance attracts rapturous applause. Many try to emulate me, and there are some comical instances of young urchins almost breaking their little necks, as they near dive onto their heads and roll in a cloud of dust.

Once again I am a hero. Life is good. It is 1952. The community is well knit, seemingly content and happy. No one is to know that, some 31 years later, in 1983 North Korean trained troops will arrive to, amongst other things, bayonet open the stomachs of pregnant women, on behalf of Robert Mugabe in a search for "dissidents'.[1]

Fortunately, by the time I return home, my movements have been traced by Ginger and it is known that I am safe. On arrival at home I find my mother sick in bed. She never threatens to beat me again.

17. Heroes

Back at Sacred Heart Home, three White adult males arrive one day. They are welcomed by the nuns and provided lodgings. A huge *"my man"* squabble ensues, as each of the three is claimed and adopted. We are in awe and reverence of these men. This is because each has a gun, with long shiny barrel, riflescope and polished butt. To a male child a gun is a thing of almost mystical status with fearsome power. We notice that even Father Peter nods approvingly, as he examines the guns, stroking each one reverently. These are the real thing ... not the little 4/10 shot-gun that he uses to kill snakes on the farm. He who has a gun is lord. The reason for their presence is that a leopard has made its presence known by taking livestock.

Leopard! This is shocking and exciting news. We know little about leopards. But what we know is more than enough to ensure that we hold them in terror. We are convinced that this leopard is here to eat little children as well as livestock. It is the most exciting period of the seven years I am to spend at the home. The atmosphere is charged with expectation. No one walks alone. No one goes out in the evening, let alone at night. Some children have bad dreams and cry in their sleep. Others insist on sharing a bed. Every morning we watch in awe as the White hunters leave, armed with their guns. Bets are taken as to which one will bag the leopard. Bets sound in marbles; perhaps the most prized of many a young boy's possessions at that time.

But to digress for a moment. An oldish Black man arrives, accompanied by a dog. Immediately we set up a chant, which is the routine regarding most events, *"a beggar ... a beggar ... a beggar ... "* On occasion beggars did arrive

---

[1] **The Gukurahundi** (Shona: "the early rain which washes away the chaff before the spring rains"[1]) refers to the suppression by Zimbabwe's 5th Brigade in the predominantly Ndebele regions of Zimbabwe.
http://en.wikipedia.org/wiki/Gukurahundi

at the Home. The nuns taught us to always treat them with respect and kindness. This is what Our Lord Jesus did for the poor and the homeless, when He was alive. We are happy to do the same. So the old man, whom we referred as *"the madala[1]"*, once we had made his acquaintances, is treated respectfully by us. He and his dog are given food and water, but no more. No one adopts him. There are no squabbles over ownership of him. He presents as no more than a curiosity that serves to further break the monotony. He sets up camp under a tree.

Then everything changes. Our world is turned upside down. In the bright morning sun comes the madala, approaching our school, dog at his side ... a leopard slung over his shoulders. Everyone rushes out of school. We are chattering like monkeys. The nuns are rushing about also chattering excitedly in German. German is the language of choice whenever there is a happening. The madala almost reverently deposits the leopard in the shade of a large tree. We gather around and are joined by the three hunters, who proceed to barter long and hard with the madala. Eventually a deal is struck, payment made and they take the leopard away with them, after a long photographic session.

For the first time we take full note of the fact that the madala has a spear and knobkerrie. These weapons now assume a new character and are scrutinized in minutest detail. He explains, in a slow calm baritone, drawing lines and arrows in the sand as he goes, how he had bagged the leopard. It had been a two-day process involving reconnaissance, studying the behaviour of the resident platoon of baboons in particular, and making the kill with he and the dog employing tactical guile in execution.

It was all too clear that, whereas the three hunters had skills, technology and tools, the madala had the precious commodity of understanding; understanding of both the environment and the quarry. We are mesmerized. The madala is immediately adopted. A near fight breaks out over the adoption of the dog. For the first time we ascertain the madala's name. He is Ndiweni. His dog's name is Captain.

When he and Captain bed down for the night, under the tree in front of the Home, having politely declined an offer of better lodgings, they find sleep only after a long and searching conversation with us little ones. Before leaving the next day Ndiweni is paid a gratuity by the nuns. Our driver Moses is summoned, and instructed to drive our heroes to wherever they need to go.

---

[1] **madala** – isiNdebele meaning "old man"

Their hitherto modest possessions are augmented by presents of much clothing and food.

Applying hindsight to this marvelous event we must conclude that qualifications, skill, technology and tools are undoubtedly important but that *understanding* is key. If this were universally applied surely society would be so much better served by leadership.

Surely understanding outranks all other criteria in the appointment of persons to posts?

18. The angel of death knocks again

It is a hot balmy afternoon. We are busy in a new vegetable garden, being cultivated behind the wall of the dam. Sister Didima calls a break, and invites us to our reward for having worked hard so far. I pull a turnip from its bed. Pulling a turnip from the ground is not unlike dipping one's hand into a lucky packet. There are no guarantees that what is pulled will be entirely to one's liking. I am happy with my turnip. It is big, round and smells so good. Instinctively I turn and brandish my prize to others round me, inviting their envy. That is in the nature of children as is one-upmanship in adults.

A fresh turnip straight out of the ground is truly delicious, and I am about get stuck in when the bush telegraph comes to life. Faintly at first, we hear the call of human voices. As they become louder it is clear that the message being conveyed is one of urgency. We run towards the voices. I am able to make out *"It is Leonard ... it is Leonard..."* Soon we meet the messengers, smaller children, sweating, stuttering, stammering and panic stricken. My heart sinks as the message changes - *"Leonard has drowned ... he drowned in the water ... he has drowned ..."* We rush to the scene. I am inwardly ambivalent as to what we will find. I have never experienced a drowning ... drowning means death ... death is something I am terrified of. But the momentum of my own running, and the running of others, keeps me going.

We arrive at the scene. It is a not so small weir on the river serving the dam's overflow or spillway. Everything goes silent and into slow motion. I see a child standing at the water's edge. He turns to me with big eyes, big and glazed inside a mask like face. The child is pointing ... pointing at the water. My eyes see the water ... all of the water ... the admixture of ground and grass forming its edges ... its blue green colouring ... the light dancing on its rippled surface. All of these minutiae of detail forcefully imprint themselves into my mind. And then I see the shape floating ... the unmistakable form of a human being floating ... floating in the water. We all freeze, cowered by the sight before us. Once again I am terrified. My inner self is now a conflict zone of mass negativity.

But I cannot stop, I cannot do nothing ... I am a *"big boy"* ... that is my status ... a status that I relish ... a status that is now being tested. It is the sin of pride that forces me on. So I go on. I enter the water, half wading, half swimming and with a few swimming strokes I reach Leonard, floating face down. I grab and pull and, not really conscious of what happens next, we are soon on dry land. Suddenly my fear has left me. It leaves me as I see his face. It is not the face of death, certainly not as I have imagined what death must be. It is a peaceful face ... just sleeping ... not dead ... sleeping ... well that is what I think and feel. I pick him up and start running. Leonard is cradled in my arms. He is not a baby. He is a boy just two years younger than me, but I am not conscious of his weight.

The bush telegraph does its business again. Soon we meet Merensia, and she takes over with Leonard piggy-backed. As we run she starts to chant plaintively in isiNdebele, "Maria M'sante ... " [Hail Mary] We are met by Sister Radigoon. She grabs the child and puts him on the ground. Seeing her lips meet his paralyzes my mind. She is a nun. She is the closest being to Mary, the mother of Jesus. My mind is blocking a scene it finds incomprehensible. But the business of administering the kiss of life and CPR goes on. We are now all praying loudly - *"Hail Mary, full of grace, the Lord be with thee .... Pray for us sinners, now and at the hour of our deaths"*. Merensia is pressing on Leonard as Sister Radigoon is kissing him.

Moments later we hear a splutter. Water starts oozing from his mouth ... more and more water ... until he makes a sound ... opens his eyes and tries to move. Sister Radigoon turns and looking upward she says *"Thank you Jesus ... "* and makes the sign of the cross. We all follow suit.

Leonard Usher recovers fully. He has been unconscious for at least 20 minutes[1], a period that assures the accrual of brain damage on account of oxygen depletion. He is not brain damaged. He grows up to be an extremely intelligent, resourceful human being and finally settles in Canada. This story is published in 1956 in a magazine called "Youth News". I am sent a postal order of 10 shillings for what I had done, on account of being too proud to do otherwise.

One afternoon we are all playing "Tarzan" games in a tree grove near the Home. John Peters starts to shout *"stop it ... stop it..."* He is remonstrating

---

[1] Friends and I worked this out some 15 years later by returning to the scene and re-enacting the sequence of events

with another lad, named Judas, who is using a long stick to poke Peters in his nether regions. Judas does not stop. Peters loses his grip and falls. However he does not fall to the ground below. His body is arrested by the pointed end of a broken branch, which impales him in the rear upper thigh. And there he is, hanging like a carcass, head down, completely limp, face ashen in shock and semi-consciousness. Blood starts to stream from the site of injury. It is a shocking site to us young lads. Everyone makes off, and an eerie silence envelopes the scene.

I am mesmerized, especially as to how my senses are heightened. All kinds of detail imprint themselves in my mind. I clearly hear the sound of a lone bird, chirping intermittently. But I also "hear" an incredible silence.

I see a small stream of crimson red blood, jerkily streaming down the stem of the tree, and also dark red drops falling to the ground, where they seem to instantly turn black. John's arms hang limply below his head, but his little finger twitches, stops ... and twitches again. His face is so peaceful but ashen grey, light yellow-green eyes half open.

Robotically I find the way he should be held, and lift him off the tree. As I do so I hear a squelch and see a chunk of flesh hang away from the wound site. Then I carry him home, some two or three hundred meters, where I am met by a nun who is hurrying towards me. John is slightly older and bigger build than I am. However, not for one moment, am I conscious of his weight or any effort on my part. It is to be many years before I learn about adrenaline. The nun is surrounded by the other boys all chanting - *"It was Judas ... it was Judas..."*

It is an immense relief that I am not being blamed. John has suffered a very bad injury, involving the gauging out of a huge chunk of tissue from the rear of his upper thigh, exposing blue/green veins and arteries which fortunately remain intact. The nun pushes the chunk back into place and bandages his thigh. He is rushed to hospital and recovers. To this day he has an ugly scar on his thigh. Judas Peterson was expelled, the only boy to have ever been expelled from the Home.

Sacred Heart Home was my home from home, until the end of 1954. The Sisters of the Precious Blood Order did their best with us. Sometimes it was problematical, as when you were required to hand-hold your bed sheet up to the rising sun, to dry if you wet your bed. One nun was undoubtedly cruel in the way she beat children on occasion. Most of the children were very poor and clothed in "home clothes", supplied by the colonial government. These were of very poor quality and, in winter, children were so cold that often their wrists, the back of their hands and the heels of their feet would crack and bleed with cold. Shoes were only ever worn on a Sunday.

However, we received a really good education, both in the classroom and out. We learnt nothing of Hitler and the holocaust. We were taught Roman, Greek and English history; learnt all about the great British Empire and taught to sing "God save the Queen". In 1953 we were ferried to Bulawayo, to partake in the British Centenary celebrations. The nuns were exceptionally good teachers and especially strong in imparting a sound value set and moral code. They had a serene, radiant aura about them.

This served to offset the tinge of vacant glaze, to become known as the "Bushtick look", in the eyes of their charges. These faces reflected what has been called "the dark brown taste of being poor[1]". We, "Bushtick children", are forever indebted to them.

More importantly though, is that society must be indebted to them, this group of good people who came all the way from their home country, Germany, which had just completed the most horrific ethnic cleansing of a whole people[2]. They came from a far off land, diabolically purging itself, in the cause of racial purity. They came to love, care for and teach the homeless, the poor, the unrecognized progeny of their British conquerors, the unwanted ethnic other of a foreign land. They did this to the very end.

They are all buried under a tree, in the front of the dormitory complex at Sacred Heart Home, far from their native land.

---

19. Ancient wisdom

At about age ten or eleven I travel back to Lupane, with Nicholas Scott, who I come to regard as my father. I have been sent for by Fuyane. He says he is *"so glad"* to see me, and wants to be taken to Bulawayo where White people will allow him to die. He is dying of cancer. He already has the appearance of a corpse, extremely shriveled, with flies in attendance, even at night, on account of a pungent smell he is giving off. He has been like this for weeks.

We travel back to Bulawayo. Mostly I sit next to him, because he wants to talk to me. The nuns have taught me respect for older people. So, as uncomfortable as it is, I sit with him and listen. It is about respect and love,

---

[1] **Attributed to Ruth Gordon Jones** (October 30, 1896 – August 28, 1985), better known as **Ruth Gordon**, an American actress and writer.

[2] It is estimated that 11 million people were killed during the Holocaust. Six million of these were Jews. The Nazis killed approximately two-thirds of all Jews living in Europe. An estimated 1.1 million children were murdered in the Holocaust.
http://history1900s.about.com/od/holocaust/a/holocaustfacts.htm

for elders, others, self, animals and all that God has bestowed. He tells me a story in truly marvelous isiNdebele idiom *"goku kona, kudala, amadwala angaqini, umumtu owele situnzi okumangalisayo ... ."* [There was, a long time ago, before the mountains had even hardened, a man of incredible integrity ... .]

It is a simple story about a man who at every stage declines to do *"dirty things"* in order to secure wealth, influence and power. The man counsels others –

```
"a man is not a crocodile ... so he cannot behave like a
crocodile ... concealing himself and springing to grab others
from beneath

he is not a lion ... so he should not try to roar like a lion
–

he does not have eyes like an owl ... so he should not be doing
things in darkness –

he is not a hyena ... so he should not scavenge –

he is not a snake ... so he should always stand up straight
and not slither around furtively –

to look down is to see only the ground and your own image in
the water ... to look ahead is to see where you are going ...
."
```

This man's reward is to be blessed by the ancestral spirits, with a heart brimming with contentment, knowing of the great welcome beyond, guaranteed by *Mulimo* [Almighty God]. He wants me to accept that I must never do *"dirty things'*. By *"dirty things"* he includes all unprincipled behaviour, central to which is the doing of intentional harm, to others, to the environment and to creatures of the planet.

He adds that his spirit is ready to go now, but that he will be with me. He dies within two hours of being admitted to Impilo Hospital in Bulawayo. If only I had known the importance of all this at the time, I would have been far more attentive to what Fuyane was telling me. However I do know that the essence of his counsel has been always with me. As a person I have always been concerned that behaviour should not be unprincipled.

This has led to much trouble in my life.

---

20. Go teach my dogs

It is January 1955. I am 11 years of age and on a train to Plumtree; on my way to Embakwe Coloured School, P O Box 54, Plumtree. I am about to start my secondary education. The train clikkaty-clacks its way slowly along the track. It is called the "Bombela", the slow train, that stops at every station. Three carriages are packed with Coloured children being transported to be educated in a mission school far off in the African bush.. Nearly all are older than me. For the first time I am no longer a *"big boy"*. It's the first of a litany of further discomforts.

My next discomfort follows quickly when I see some boys running off, and boarding the moving train, without paying track-side vendors for goods taken. I find such conduct greatly offensive to what I have been taught in Sacred Heart Home. I say to my elder brother Zain, who is with me for the first time in my life, ... *"it is stealing ... stealing is a sin!"* His curt reply is *"You had better wake up my boy ... this is not Bushtick ... this is Embakwe..."* greeted by a coo-eep ... coo-eep ... coo-eep ... whistle-blast from the steam locomotive, drawing our train. Zain hands me an apple, part of the ill-gotten gains. *"Yaaa ... ou Vavie"* others chorus *"you must wake up"* they say in an accent that I would soon learn as being unique to Embakwe.

Thus, in my first association with Embakwe, my name reverts to Vavie, and I am hardly referred to as Christopher, let alone Christof. The reason for this, I am to learn, is that just about every child was given a nick-name, by which they were referred to almost exclusively. My name reverted to Vavie because of a misconception that it was a nick-name.

When the train finally pulls up at Plumtree, a south-western border town of Rhodesia, our carriages are disconnected and parked on a shunt rail. There we await our transfer. This arrives in the form of an open three ton Bedford truck, onto which we are loaded with baggage going first. In consecutive trips the truck conveys all to our destination, some 38 kilometers away in the bush near the Bechuanaland[1] border.

Embakwe Coloured School was a mission school for Coloured children. It was started in 1902 when, so legend has it, King Lobengula said to Roman Catholic missionaries ... "Go teach my dogs ..."

This is what Michelle Faul, writing for Associated Press, has to say —

"Embakwe Mission was founded in 1902 by the spirit medium Njemhlophe, who gave up throwing the bones after he converted to Christianity. He came at the behest of Catholic missionaries who soon followed, a Jesuit priest on horseback and three

---

[1] **Bechuanaland,** a British Protectorate at the time is now the Republic of Botswana after becoming independent within the Commonwealth on September 30, 1966. It is bordered by South Africa to the south and southeast, Namibia to the west, Zambia to the north, and Zimbabwe to the northeast.

intrepid nuns fresh from England in an ox wagon loaded with provisions, including a hen, a cock and a cat.
First they turned back because of a thunderstorm with forked lightning. On the second attempt, the wagon got bogged down in mud. So the nuns, from the Belgian-based Sisters of Notre Dame de Namur, trudged through the sludge to their new home, a loaf of bread under one arm and a bottle of altar wine tucked under the other."

By the time of my arrival in 1955 it was well developed, with the main buildings constructed of unplastered red brick, contoured and ornate. It

Some Embakwe Boys – 1956

Back - Edward Evans, Sheeree Khan, Michael Louis, Waldo Payne, Claude Kinnear, Billy Wright, Dennis Howes, Achmet Cader, Patrick Wallet, Robin Kinnear, Albert Muir, Gus Evans. **Middle** - Charles Peters, Mark Williams, Chris Greenland(Author), Herbert De Souza, Stephen Sudan (pulling face) **Kneeling** - Louis Le Grange, John Peters, Popye Rice, Zain Greenland

would be wrong to imagine that because it was reserved for Coloureds, we were highly privileged. The privilege, undoubtedly fundamental and vitally important, was that payment of basic fees by government was guaranteed. African black children were denied this.

However, as an educational institution, Embakwe was the poorest and most under-resourced of all Coloured schools in the colony. It was without both a science block and a library. It is pertinent to point out that two great African schools in the Plumtree area, Empandeni and Tekwane, were both better resourced and each had a science block and a library.

All three schools however were "slums", when compared with nearby Plumtree High School, reputably one of the best schools in the history of the country, and therefore reserved for Whites. Most of the children in Embakwe were from poorer families. The school also served as a "reform school", to which problematical children were committed, on Court order.

Not to put too fine a point on it, we were a rough tough lot of proverbial ragamuffins.

There was a girls' hostel at one end of the complex and a boys' hostel at the other end. In between were the administrative blocks and living quarters for the main staff, being the nuns and priests. Also present was the refectory and laundry. The school, in rectangular configuration, was nearer the boys' hostel.

At one far end was a primary day school reserved for local Black children exclusively, many of whom were fairer skinned than many of the Coloured children, for whom the main school was reserved.

On such madness is racism predicated.

---

21. A baptism

On arrival, we disembark in front of the boys' hostel. A crowd gathers. New comers, like me, receive special attention. There is little friendliness in the manner and tone of those who point and bay out - *"a new kaaamaa ... a new kaaamaa ..."* [new comer]. The head boy, Achmet Cader, introduces himself in a *"you better*

understand who is boss" tone. He allocates me a bed in the middle boys' dormitory, as in terms of physical size, I am neither a big boy nor a small boy. The bed is made of plain steel with a thin coir[1] mattress and pillow. On this I unroll my blankets which, like everyone else, I have conveyed from home in a roll strapped with leather belting. My steel trunk of belongings is deposited under the bed. There is not a sign of any adult authority. Father Anscar, nicknamed *"Tickey"*, occupies a room in the middle of the hostel but presents as nothing more than nominal head of things.

The boys' hostel runs itself, divided into a "big boys dormitory", "middle boys dormitory" and a "small boys dormitory", with each having a prefect in charge. The triumvirate of prefects have a head boy as boss.

---

[1] **Coir** fibers are found between the husk and the outer shell of a coconut

At supper time we are lined up, and walked in procession to the dining hall referred to as a refectory. We are seated at long wooden tables, 16 per table, with a bigger boy seated at one end, as head of the table. The fare is maize-meal porridge, served into a tin bowl without milk. This is augmented by one brown bun and a cup of cocoa. The head of table shares out butter and syrup. The syrup is doled out onto the table surface, next to my plate, from whence I struggle to retrieve it by scraping with a spoon. It is not much, not enough to sweeten my porridge and cocoa.

Things get worse. My share of the butter is allocated by a knife being stabbed into the rectangle of butter, pulled out and then wiped against the table edge next to me. The resultant oily smear is all I am to get. I try to protest. Everyone glares at me. Old Sister Bridgett, the only nun in attendance, slowly patrols the aisle of tables, surveying all through thick lensed spectacles, totally unaware of these shenanigans occurring right under her nose. That night I sleep fitfully after crying myself to sleep ... and wet my bed.

Things deteriorate to become a baptism of fire. The next day I am summoned to the front of the hostel. A boy of my size and weight is also summoned. A pile of sand is formed on the ground. *"That ees your maathaa..."* [that is your mother] they scream at me referring to the pile of sand. On a signal the other boy kicks the pile of sand over. *"He has kicked your maathaa ... . He has kicked your maathaa..."* is the chant ... *" ... you must fight ... you must fight ... fight fore your maathaa "* .

I have very little interest or inclination to fight, but a fight is now inevitable. The group are baying for blood. Although the other boy is of similar build to me, he is an "old boy" [not a new comer], has been especially selected, on account of his pugilistic prowess, and has the mob on his side. It is a set up, but I have no option. We engage, fists flying. My face stings as I start to lose the fight. Instinctively I go into my comfort zone. Pound for pound no one can match me in wrestling. The hard manual labour, I endured in Sacred Heart Home, has ensured that I am muscular, fit and strong for my age. I grab him and soon he is on the ground, helpless, as I cover his face in sand and punch him up. The mob rescues him. I am shouted at and derided for *"fighting unfair"*.

We had arrived on a Friday. Nearly the whole of Saturday, and the Sunday, are spent with new comers made to fight unequal battles. By Sunday evening I have had two fights, each intended to subdue me and teach me a lesson for fighting unfair. Even my brother Zain tries to encourage me to fight *"fair,"* and gives me a few lessons. It is no use, I am not a boxer, I am a wrestler and in the heat of battle I inevitably fall into my comfort zone. My opponents are wrestled to the ground and deprived of oxygen. It is a very unpopular resolution of things, but it works.

By Sunday evening I have sustained what doctors refer to as *periorbital hematoma*[1] of both eyes. Like many others, my face is bruised and swollen.

As I arrive at my classroom on Monday morning, I feel assured that these injuries will attract attention and ensure intervention by authority in the anarchical situation that is the boys' hostel.

My heart sinks when my teacher, Mr. Abe Davies, scarcely raises an eyebrow as he allocates me a desk in his Standard 5 classroom. Facial swellings, referred to as *"knobs"* and black eyes are the norm in Embakwe. As the Americans would say - *"no one gives a shit"*. I am 11 years of age. The next eldest boy is my own brother Zain, at age 15. The oldest boy in the class is Willie Robinson, at age 19.

That is how I started my secondary school education at Embakwe Coloured School. It is how I regained the name of Vavie. It is when I met new nuns, Sisters of the Order of The Notre Dame, wonderful human beings all the way from the emerald green island of Ireland.

The reason why the school has children of 19 or more years of age is that people, like Aunt Elsie, have made it their business to scour the native tribal trust lands, seek out and retrieve Coloured children, the unwelcome progeny of colonialism. Exploiting the law that entitles such children to education at government expense, Coloured Schools like Sacred Heart Home, Martindale and St Johns receive their share of *"raw"* Coloureds.

The term *"raw"* is used to denote a poor command of English in particular.

---

22. Where are my bones

Soon thereafter a hostel master appeared on the scene. His name was Richard Brown. He was an ex-Embakwean and had just returned from South Africa, where he had qualified as a teacher. Richard arrived full of revolutionary zeal. He was determined to *"change things"*, starting with stamping out smoking. Since this was 1955, Richard Brown has the distinction of having pioneered the anti-smoking lobby, which is now ever so understandably fashionable and politically correct, it must be said.

Barrack Obama is to be admired for seeking to *"change things"*, knowing how risky this always is. Brown's purge on smoking was to expose him to

---

[1] **periorbital hematoma** – medical term for "black eyes"

great risk and little admiration. From the start he was on a collision course with the boys, many of whom smoked. Once something is criminalized, it becomes more attractive to a certain sector of any social group. Brown's anti-smoking crusade had as much chance of succeeding as did the American attempt at "prohibition[1]". Both succeeded only in making the targeted product more attractive, and in inducing users to organize themselves into deviant ridden gangs. Embakwe was to prove all this in microcosm.

An anti-Brown campaign was immediately started. First he was given a nick-name or rather a number of nick-names. Adverse labeling is a tried and tested stratagem in conflictual situations. All Brown's nick-names where bad - *"Bolganin"*, after Nikolai Bulganin the Russian leader then seen as an enemy of the west. *"Zhizhizhi"*, a made up name said with intonation that conveyed illusions of evil. *"Bruin"*, a play on the name Brown. War had been declared.

Your enemies will soon find out your weakness. So too as regards the showdown with Brown. A gang, led by a boy named Joseph Waldman, nick-named *"Baldy"*, finds out that Brown believes in and is terrified of ghosts. From that moment Brown's fate is all but sealed. At Embakwe, electric power is provided by one DC[2] motor that goes off at 9 pm. Brown often works past this time.

He is sitting at his desk in the classroom he teaches in, working studiously by the light of a hurricane[3] lamp. Since the lamp is not bright, there are areas in the classroom which are darker and even dark. Shadows are also cast and these move, even dance, as the flame flickers. As a person who believes in ghosts Brown is not comfortable, and is already feeling just a little bit uneasy. The sound of the breeze outside and entering the room seems to include an eerie moan. In fact the whole scene is a little bit eerie, especially as night sounds made by insects, such as crickets, get louder. When an owl screeches in the distance Brown's feels his skin start to crawl.

---

[1] In the history of the United States, **Prohibition**, also known as **The Noble Experiment**, is the period from 1919 to 1933, during which the sale, manufacture, and transportation of alcohol for consumption were banned nationally as mandated in the Eighteenth Amendment to the United States Constitution.
http://en.wikipedia.org/wiki/Prohibition_in_the_United_States

[2] **DC** – direct current as opposed to AC [alternating current] with the latter being the modern standard

[3] **Hurricane lamp** – simple paraffin lamp with a small tank, wick and protective glass orb surround.

It is then that Baldy makes his move. Donning a football boot on one foot, and a tennis shoe on the other, he steps out onto the paving forming the floor of the verandah outside the classroom. Because the classrooms are configured in a rectangle around a central courtyard the whole complex resonates any sound made, magnifies it and echoes it. As the boot lands, and studs make contact with the paving, a sharp "crack" of sound is produced, followed shortly by a *"shhhhhhhhhooooo"*, sound as Baldy drags the bottom of his tennis shoe on his trailing foot along the paving. Then he stops.

Brown has heard the sound. Well he thinks he has heard the sound; he is not sure. Silence! Deathly silence! Just as he settles down again ... *"kraaaak"* ... pause .... *"Shhhhhhhhhooooo"* ... long pause ... and then again ... *"kraaaak"* ... pause ... *"shhhhhhhhhooooo"* –

Brown now knows he is not imaging things. The sound, clear and reverberating, being carried to his ears sits on his skin, which starts to crawl, and then permeates through to his heart. His breath shortens; he is rapidly being overtaken by the paralyzing effects of fear. His mind is racing. His imagination is playing havoc as to what it is that is approaching. It is certainly something unnatural; it must be. He has experienced evil spirits before. He is trapped as the sound leads to the door of his classroom.

It is right then that Baldy delivers the *coup de grace*. In an as unearthly voice as he can muster he half cries ... half groans ... moans - *"Where-r-r-r-r - e-e-e--s me bo-o-o-nesssss ..."* ["where is me bones"] and then louder - *"Where-r-r-r-r - e-e-e--s me bo-o-o-nesssss ..."* ... repeated, reverberating and echoing in the enclaved courtyard through to the ears, heart and mind of Brown.

It is too much. The poor man, stricken in terror, dives through the window and runs. This has been anticipated and planned for by his enemies. As he makes the first turn there is a full-sized figure, greyish white and ghostly approaching and shrilling - *"Where-r-r-r-r - e-e-e--s me bo-o-o-nesssss ..."* Brown bolts, covering the ground with all the speed he can muster. Upon reaching his room at the boys' hostel he dives in, slams the door and locks it. The ghost team assembles behind the toilet block to gloat over their victory. The boy in the "ghost sheet" re-enacts how he put the fear of God into their victim after he had dived out of the window. They allow themselves an extra celebratory fag.

Baldy's ghost team is to score this victory a few more times in the coming months, tweaking their model for maximum fear effect. Brown never did manage to stamp out smoking. The gang's reputation went up. An ordinary gang became legendary. This gave much impetus to the formation of more gangs. Nicotine addiction was soon supplemented by benzene inhalation. This would reduce clusters of boys to loll about laughing uncontrollably for hours on end. Eyes wide and glazed, they would point at each other, at the sky and at imaginary things and shout, moan and whimper, drooling at the mouth. *"Look at ou Blackie"* [a nickname for one of the boys], one would shout - *"the guy is black ... ou Blackie is black ... blue black ... no man ... one minute to midnight..."* and the others would all laugh uncontrollably as they joined in pointing unsteadily at the boy.

And then there would be tears as a chorus would start - *"where is your maathaa...-* [where is your mother] *... you got no maathaa ... I got no maathaa ... we got no maathaa ..."* tears streaming down faces of boys now mindless. Then they would start -*"Look at ou Dutchie..."* [nick-name for a very fair skinned boy named Norman Ras] *... "look at ou Dutchie ... a white rat ... white like a rat ... a white rat..."* These benzene parties reduce boys to mindless buffoons. It was the apex drug at our hostel. Dagga[1], a later favourite in the Coloured community of the country, was unknown in Embakwe.

Richard Brown eventually reconciled to reality. As Prohibition failed in America his efforts to stamp out smoking failed. He became a different highly respected leader, with friendship foremost in his style.

So much later, in the very early morning of 20 June 1960, we all assembled in Brown's room to listen to a broadcast of immense importance to all of us. Floyd Patterson, a Black American boxer was to fight a rematch with Jens Ingemar Johansson, a Swedish boxer, who had defeated Patterson by TKO in the third round, after flooring Patterson seven times in that round, to win the World Heavyweight Championship on 26 June 1959. Old debates about Aryan supremacy, first mooted when Max Schmeling beat the legendary *"Brown Bomber"*, Joe Louis, in 1939 were revived. Patterson needed revenge. We needed revenge. We were mad with excitement, having been fully briefed on all the nuances of the issue by pipe smoking Enoch Stool, another local hero with us, who was the school's jack-of-all-trades.

Richard's small round radio is hooked up. An antenna is led out of the window and as far up a tree as one could climb. Another cable is stuck into a pot of earth and secured to a point marked "earth" on the radio. It hums and crackles into life. Everyone in the room sides with Patterson. He carries a whole gamut of undefined hopes and dreams, of all of us, into the ring with him. Unbelievable elation overtakes us when "Patterson knocks Johansson out in the fifth round with a leaping left hook to become the first man to recover the world's undisputed heavyweight title. The punch caught

---

[1] **Dagga** – local name for *cannabis sativa* also referred to as marijuana.

Johansson's chin and he hit the canvas with a thud, out cold before he landed flat on his back".[1]

We rush out, whooping in delight, just as the first rays of the sun break the horizon. Father Adalbert, our dashing young resident German priest, comes to investigate. We all love him for his intellect and fascinating personality.

Fr Adalbert: So what is it that you are so happy about? [We breathlessly explain what has just happened].

Fr Adalbert: But that is on the other side of the world? [he says quizzically with a mischievous glint in his eye]

We: Yes Father - in America –

Fr Adalbert: And what do you know about the two boxers ... ? [setting the trap ... we are forced to accept that we know very little about either]

Fr Adalbert: For all we know Patterson could be a sinner and Johansson a saint ... not so?" [We are forced to agree]

Fr Adalbert: But you have supported Patterson ... why ... ? [we are unable to proffer the reason as the realization sets in as to what this brilliant man is leading to]

Fr Adalbert: You must agree that you are really no better than the German people, you are always so happy to criticize ... is that not so?[we can only look back and each other sheepishly as the trap is sprung]

Fr Adalbert: Just as Hitler's supporters took a stance against the Jews, you have taken a stance against Johansson ... a stance based purely on race!!

Brown: Ah, but Father you are omitting the symbolism of the oppressed needing champions in the front of their struggle ["that's got him" we thought, nodding vigorously in agreement]

Fr Adalbert: Not at all, your point on symbolism has great validity. However, it must never submerge truth. As I often hear you [referring to my then best friend Edmund Ambrose and I] proudly say - *"cogito, ergo sum[2]"*.

---

[1] http://en.wikipedia.org/wiki/Ingemar_Johansson

[2] **Cogito, ergo sum** - (Usually translated in English as: "I think, therefore I am", but can be less ambiguously translated as "I am thinking, therefore I exist" or "I am thinking, on the account of being"), ⋯ is a philosophical statement ⋯ by René Descartes, which became a foundational element of Western philosophy. The simple meaning of the phrase is that if someone is wondering whether or not he exists, that is in and of itself proof that he does exist (because, at the very least,

The great gift that God gave us is the power of reason. It distinguishes us from other creatures. It is natural to have prejudices. It is part of human nature – *"man's imperfection"*, part of original sin in terms of Catholic teaching. However, it is when prejudice, and its responses, are intellectualized in dishonest reasoning that natural prejudice is translated into evil and real evil is perpetrated by man on man as Hitler has done. The biggest sin is dishonest reasoning, and is always the start of systemic sinfulness, abuse of other people, other creatures and the world God has given us. You must not intellectualize justification, for taking a stance against Johansson, just because he is White and for Patterson, just because he is Black. To do so is also to adopt the very dishonest reasoning that produces the oppression you are trying to overcome.

Me: Father, my grandmother always said stupid people are the most dangerous.

Fr Adalbert: She was right. Those who are unable, but mostly unwilling, to use the great gift of intellect that God gave us cannot rectify that which is wrong or evil. As they are unable to distinguish good from evil, so they perpetuate evil. In that sense most of my people who supported Hitler were, as your grandmother would say, stupid ... incredibly stupid.

You must not just babble *"cogito, ergo sum"*. It is your duty, not being a dumb animal, to always be sapiential or you too will become a vehicle for evil! [he finishes with a flourish and leaves us quite dumbstruck .I turn to look at the horizon and watch in fascination as the huge bright yellow orb, that is the sun, rises up seemingly out of the far off bowels of the earth. It is an uplifting experience as I feel the full effects of what is a defining moment. I have a new understanding of what sin is and how it can influence peoples' lives. All evil starts with intellectual dishonesty.

Sapiential! What a wonderful thing! I quietly resolve that I will always be sapiential. As for Brown, he is grinning from ear to ear as he gathers us around him and says *"Father is right"*.

Brown has long since become a very different hostel master and we have built up an incredible rapport with him over time. He becomes much loved and respected by all thereafter and never takes offence when we tease him about his ghostly experiences.

He too became a smoker.

---

there is an "I" who is doing the thinking).
http://en.wikipedia.org/wiki/Cogito_ergo_sum

23. And the meek shall surely endure

But we must return to those first days at Embakwe. Not being in a gang or having gang protection left you exposed to bullying and victimization. A surreal scene was when the *"Bulman gang"* decided to attack one boy. His name was Timon Brown. He must have been at least 18 years of age, but of very frail built and somewhat sickly. He was also a very quiet unassuming boy, tending to stick very much to himself. Undoubtedly his non aggressive nature, and attitude of common decency, made him attractive as a victim to the bully-boy Bulman gang. The gang was named after their leader Freddy Bulman, a 15-year-old with an inflated imagination, ego and ambitions. It must be said that his elder brother Tom, and his sister Dolly, were wonderfully kind and gentle of disposition.

The whole thing plays out in front of the boys' hostel. A member of the gang peels off from the rest, standing in a group under a Syringa tree, having just had a plotting session, and approaches Timon. He is Edmund Ambrose, nick-named "Pra-Pra-". The nick-name was probably chosen on account of Edmunds's wonderful turn of phrase in both English and isiNdebele. Getting real close, up and personal, he gives Timon *"a warning"*. A warning is a standard ploy, and involves employing language calculated to intimidate and humiliate from start to finish. *"Look here myee boyee[1] ... you like to act cheeky ... you are trying to be funny ... if you are not sorree we are going to hlaba[2] you ... say you are sorry ... !"*

Timon Brown says nothing, and just looks the cheeky strappling in the face. The demand is repeated, with emphasis and finger waving added. Timon does not respond and we all fear for his safety, knowing all too well what is to follow.

Freddy gathers his gang of six around him and, after a final consultation, shouts out an exhortation - *"Charge my men ... !"* They all charge, with Freddy in the rear. They are all of similar or only slightly smaller stature than Timon. He seems doomed. Fists fly. I am conscious of a particular smell. It is the smell of violence, which is sickly sweet, strong and slightly overpowering. It seems to enhance the senses as everything looks brighter, sounds louder and burns itself into the psyche. The sound of blows on flesh is sickening. Blood appears, not as red, but as bright crimson. One can instantly smell it, strong and warm around and in the nostrils. I feel so bad

---

[1] **Myee boyee** = Embakwe pronunciation for "my boy"

[2] **hlaba** - is isiNdebele for "prick, puncture, gore or pierce" and used in Embakwe to mean "beat"

for the victim, very bad and helpless ... utterly helpless. This is cruel, it is inhumane ... and nobody is doing a thing about it!

Surely Timon must be overwhelmed ... but he is not. After a few minutes, first one, than two, than all six retreat nursing various wounds ... ballooned ear, black eye, bloodied nose, facial swellings and other wounds we colloquially refer to as *"knobs"*. We are somewhat bemused at the failure of the attack. I have an immense sense of relieve. God is good I think.

The gang regroups under the syringa tree and, after a short conference, Pra-Pra is sent to repeat the demands that Timon exhibit contrition for whatever nebulous crime he has committed. He maintains a stony silence. They charge again. He inflicts more pain, injury and suffering on all of them. After what is now a fiasco, is repeated for the third time, the gang decides they have had enough. Having been completely humiliated in public, they then have the astonishing temerity to all approach him and loudly issue further warnings that, if he does not mend his ways, he will be knocked good and proper. We have great difficulty in concealing our sniggers at this obscene attempt at face saving. We have to conceal our glee. If spotted, we will be turned on like hyenas on a kill.

About a month later various member of the Bulman gang are noticed to be all sporting a variety of facial knobs. If you dare look at any of them you are immediately set upon and threatened with physical violence. Nobody knows, or is allowed to enquire, as to how this gang of rascals have suffered their injuries. Our curiosity and speculation, conducted in great secrecy, was unbearable. However truth will out.

It emerges that, after the Bulman gang suffered their public humiliation, they issued a demand to this quiet, decently behaved boy, Timon Brown, that he meet them in secret at the river, some 3 kilometers away. There they set upon their intended victim in a cowardly attack, employing all kinds of "dirty tricks" that they had thought up. All alone, in a secluded river bed, the intended victim had not only survived; he had also given the gang a thoroughly good thrashing. It was typical of Timon that he did not think that his victory over these thugs was worth mentioning to anybody.

When he later leaves school Freddy Bulman is rumoured to have emigrated to Johannesburg, South Africa, where he joined a gang.

24. Together we stand - and business is business

Adventure Boys was conceived out of necessity. It was a coalition of boys who did not quite fit in. We were all big for our ages, of above average intelligence and not disposed towards violence. It received impetus on account of what happened at the term ending 1956. The gang culture had taken such hold that a stage was reached when a catapult war broke out of such proportions that the boys' hostel was in a state of siege for two whole days and nights. Rival gangs shot it out in various skirmishes. I spent most of my time hunkered down behind a mattress. My brother Zain had a front tooth knocked out in a skirmish.

The school authorities dealt with the situation by allowing it to play itself out, knowing that hunger would eventually win, as no boys were able to access any food. Since it was near end of the term we were allowed to go off on school holidays, during which period the parents or guardians of 56 boys were written letters stipulating that their charges were expelled. In this way a sanitation process was affected. Boys perceived as hard core or bad elements were excised from the school. Regrettably this included one or two innocent boys, such as Patrick Muir from Botswana. Patrick was nick-named *"Jerry Lewis"* after the American funny man on account of his innocuous and funny disposition. Patrick had been an altar boy with me for nearly the entire period covering 1955 -1956. Why he was expelled is a mystery and undoubtedly unfair. That, of course, is the problem of decisions being made about people in their absence without due process and representation.

Our gang of four was led by Mark Williams, a fair skinned good looking lad with a "Tom Sawyer" look and an attitude. He was an orphan, having lost his remaining parent, his mother, at the age of 5 years. He never recovered from this, and became visibly upset whenever the issue of having a mother arose. He was angry and rebellious and would seize whatever opportunity presented to act out his inner pain and bitterness. So during a maths class he would stand up and start a protest engagement with the teacher by executing a waist level sweep of the upper arm, with an open hand faced downwards, whilst uttering the word "nevaaa ... ".[never] This was a standard Embakwe devised start to dispute. The arm gesture foretold strong disagreement. The teacher would then be challenged to explain why he, Mark Williams, should believe any of it ... formulas, theorems and the other components of mathematics that have been established over centuries.

All efforts by the teacher to explain why, what has been established, proved and now universally accepted was right, would be met with stubborn refusal. During such confrontations Mark would become very emotional, body quivering, face contorted, eyes welling up and tears streaming down his cheeks. He did nothing for his cause when he disputed the fact that Mary, the Mother of Jesus, could have been a virgin, as stipulated by dogma of the Catholic Church.

Mark was in trouble as a human being, serious trouble, on account of the terrible loss he had suffered at the most impressionable stage of his life. To Mark the whole world was predicated on the one big question. Why had he been singled out to be father and motherless? He had been permanently traumatized. However, at that time, there was little understanding of such issues, let alone sympathy. During school holidays I visited his home. He was being fostered by his elder brother Patrick Williams, a very nice man indeed. He explained to me forlornly that he and his wife had tried everything with Mark to no avail. *"We just don't understand why Mark is like that..."* they lamented at length. They didn't. PTSD ... and counseling was still far off, over a very distant horizon.

Our other senior member was Michael Brown, nick-named *"Troll"*. He was dark skinned with somewhat bulbous features and big-boned in the limbs. If cast in a movie he would have been the "plantation nigger". He had been "committed" to the school on account of behavioral transgressions. Quiet, at most times, it was all too easy to underestimate him as a person and subject him to teasing, ridicule and even bullying. This occurred very early after his arrival and he was picked on. The stage was reached when the 20 year or so old head boy, Achmed Cader, joined in. Troll repeatedly protested - *"Leave me alone you guys ... just leave me alone..."* They did not leave him alone and intensified the ridicule ... *"Troll, Troll, Troll ... ugly ... big and thick ... and black..."*

Eventually he pushed one of his tormentors out of sheer frustration. Cader immediately intervened, punching Troll in the face. It was a big mistake. This 13-year-old gangling, seemingly inoffensive boy, retaliated with breathtaking speed, efficiency and effectiveness. With one punch Cader was sent flying through a low classroom window just like in western movies. It took Cader some 10 minutes to get up and return. His mates assured him that they had taken care of Troll. They had not. He was left alone then and forever thereafter. Having seen that punch, I sure was glad that Troll was my friend.

Over the years he developed into one of the most likeable characters in the school. What Troll was short of in looks he more than made up for in personality. Typically he would stand up in front of the class, when the teacher was absent for some reason, and mimic the antics of the teacher to the amusement of all, especially the girls. His gift was art and we would be entertained with hilarious cartoons drawn at lightning speed on the blackboard. I suppose Troll was to us what Whoopee Goldberg is to the world to-day ... not that pretty, not a "pussy cat", but extremely talented, larger than life and loved by all.

As he would have undoubtedly made a fantastic teacher our Headmistress later sent me on a trip to talk his mother out of taking him out of school in 1959. At their home I met his sister Elizabeth, as fair skinned as many White girls and beautiful to boot. Troll's mother, despite strenuous pleas on my part and a letter from our Head Mistress stating that Troll would make an excellent teacher and that she would ensure he was accepted for teacher training, refused saying he needed to work and help support their struggling family. This decision proved to be a real tragedy in the making.

He was to die penniless many years later, having failed in a lifetime struggle, checkmated by his colour and ethnicity.

Mark however was good looking, intelligent and imaginative. He was our leader. Our ethos was to use our wits to survive. There was more space for such an operational culture now that most of the violent brigade had been expelled. One of our first projects was "Operation Love Letter". As said, many of the bigger boys had poor command of English, let alone possessed of writing skills. However, like most older boys, they were interested in girls and in securing girlfriends. In stepped Adventure Boys. We wrote the love letters for them. They paid for the service in kind, comprising oranges, bananas and buns. I was good at writing English. Mark had the imagination to provide the "spice" needed to impress the intended recipient of the letter.

Typically an opening line of a letter would read - *"Dear Molly, as God is my witness you should know that you are like a big bright star in heaven, lighting up my ever miserable life. When I see you, I see Cleopatra. When I think of you, I hear a nightingale singing in my ears and feel so much joy beating in my throbbing heart. My love for you is ever divine* – SWANK[1] . Troll would festoon the letter with a drawing of cupid and a heart with an arrow through it. Perfume was added. No girl could resist such proposal of love. Business flourished.

The last member of the gang was Raymond Naidoo, referred to as *"Ou Ray".* His father was an Indian who remarried. His mother was a Coloured and had run off to England, leaving her two children stranded. He and his only sister, Queenie, had been committed to Embakwe as children in need of care.

Adventure Boys did a roaring trade in the love letter business and a huge spin-off was that we became "untouchable". As the anointed scribes of the big boys we were protected by this cabal and immune from all bullying. We also scored when standard tasks were being allocated. Instead of being assigned to being lavatory boys or laundry boys we secured the least onerous assignment of being "wood boys". So instead of cleaning lavatories or doing

---

[1] **SWANK** - acronym for "Sealed With A Nice Kiss"

laundry we would wonder off into the bush collecting wood to burn in the hot water boilers.

In order to maintain our turnover we also devised a rather unpalatable, but effective ploy, to break up boy-girl relationships that we had been involved in actually securing. So typically a human turd would be discovered somewhere near the girls' hostel. Next to it a boy's belt would be found ... a belt bearing the name of the big boy whose love affair we intended to break up. Girls are "sugar and spice, and all things nice". They do not like boys who are going to crap near their hostel. The boy whose name appeared on the belt would inevitably be dumped by his girlfriend. He would not know why. He would then re-engage us and business would go on. We had a captive market and were in control of it. Profit was guaranteed. The acquisitive and mercenary nature of man knows no bounds.

The other area in which we happened to chance upon an effective panacea was bullying. Bullying has always been somewhat endemic in boarding schools. Embakwe was no exception. Somehow we discovered that bullies were cowards at heart. We engaged a cluster of victims and, for a fee comprising bananas, oranges and/or buns, guaranteed resolution of the problem. Each victim was supplied with a live chameleon and trained in its use. In an orchestrated exercise each would then approach his tormentor and feign transfer of the creature onto his person. The reaction of the bullies was incredible. Without exception, each cringed, recoiled and then fled in abject terror, being chased all around the hostel by his erstwhile victim. There was little doubt that the whole experience proved extremely traumatic, in the medical sense of the term. Their spirits broken in such public humiliation, the bullies would cry out, even scream, for respite. This was only afforded once it was clear that understanding had been reached that there would be no more bullying.

By and large it worked.

25. And necessity is the mother of invention

It is 1958 and there is a terrible drought in the area. Cattle are dying. Carcasses are retrieved and dragged to the mission by tractor. The meat is served up in our meals. It smells rotten. We cannot eat it. Hunger is now the order of the day. Adventure Boys needs to deal with this privation. On Sunday afternoon the hostel master, Richard Brown, assembles the boys as is the routine. An audit is conducted as to what we will be doing that afternoon so that he knows where boys are and what they are up to.

Adventure Boys is going fishing to the dam. We have constructed fishing rods which we hold up in a show of true intent. He waves us off.

We run off, but do not go to the dam. We hive off to a farm owned by a Mr. Skinner some 5 kilometer away. On arrival we survey our target. It is the fowl run, situated some 100 meters away in an open grassland clearing. Baiting our hooks with mealie rice, we leopard-crawl up to the fowl run. We cast our hooks into the run and soon bag two fowls.

It is just then that an ambush is sprung. Skinner's gang of workers have been waiting for us. They now start to emerge from behind a building a fair distance away. Mark starts to laugh uncontrollably. I shout out *"belt it ... !"* and we start to run. Given the head start we have, I have every confidence that the workers will never catch us. But then we hear the sound of barking dogs behind us. Dogs are quite another matter ... bad news ... very bad news. There is something terrible about knowing that you are being pursued by dogs. Dogs are fast. They will catch you, and when they do they will bite you, with big sharp teeth, and tear your flesh apart.

We run for all we are worth through the bush towards the river. The barking of the dogs grows louder as they gain on us. I think of dropping the fowl I am carrying in the hope that the dogs will stop to investigate it. Instinctively I change my mind, concluding that it is a vain hope. Ill gotten gains are never easily parted with. The river is in front of us. We run down the bank, across the dry river bed and up the other side.

Immediately we all stop, turn and crouch down, untangling our cattys from around our necks as we do so. Everything now goes into slow motion. As the first dog courses down the other bank, and reaches the river bed, the cattys twang in unison. There is a loud yelp from the dog and it half keels over. The second and third dogs meet the same fate. They yelp and howl out loudly as they are hit again and again. One runs back, the other two run around in circles howling and whimpering in pain. The workers have arrived. They stop and take cover on the other side of the river. There is a deathly silence, broken only by the now occasional whimper of the dogs, who have all rejoined their masters.

It is a classic stand-off. After a while we crawl away and make good our escape. Later the fowls are roasted on an open fire and eaten with some meat packed and reserved for consumption in the days to follow. Mark starts to laugh again and mimics the running around of the dogs after being hit by slingshot. *"Did you see that...?"* he says, face brimming with joy - *"did you see how the garu[1] was yowling and yowling? "* and shamelessly we all join in with peals of laughter.

The next day an identification parade is conducted. Skinner's workers pick out the other three members of our gang, but not me. Fuyane's magic is at work. The punishment is six cuts and one week in the cellar. The cuts are administered in public, at the boys' hostel, on towel-covered buttocks, using a sjambok. Heads are then shaved and the culprits confined to a dark cellar receiving a little light via a very small ground level iron-grated window. Food consists of unsweetened mealie porridge served in the morning and the evening. After a week my friends emerge with eyes as big as an owls and a strong greyish white tinge to their skins on account of sunlight deprivation.

Sjamboking was reserved for serious transgressions, which included attempting to run away from school. Attempts by boys to trek across the bush and make it to Bulawayo, some 140 kms away, was the stuff of school folklore, spoken about with admiration and reverence. Some had made it and regarded as heroes. They were always caught, brought back, sjamboked and put in the cellar. All took this in their stride except one boy, Norman, who went into a state of absolute panic and fear at the prospect of being sjamboked. He ran around screaming, in abject terror, and when the strokes were administered, after he was forcibly held down, he hyper-ventilated and nearly passed out. There can be little doubt that he was traumatized for life. This experience was to help inform a historic and important decision I was to make in later life.

I was also not picked out in an identification parade after our gang was seen gathering wild fruit off a tree. Unfortunately the tree happened to be in the field of a subsistence farmer. In African culture entering the field of another without permission is regarded as a grave breach of behavioral laws. It is taboo. The man approached shouting *"Went off my field ... went of my field..."* My mates were in the three. I was under it standing guard. Certainly I was the one he had the best view off and yet he accurately picked out my colleagues the next day and failed with me. It is all too tempting to believe that surely I was under the protection of Fuyane.

On another occasion intelligence indicated that the big boys were up to something. We followed them. They stole a piglet from Skinner's farm and roasted it up in the bush. From our hiding place we spoke out loudly, in isiNdebele, saying to each other *"can you smell something ..?"* It did the trick. On hearing our voices, and thinking capture was at hand, the big boys ran off deserting the scene. We had a feast on the roasted pig-let. I was so satiated

[1] **Garu** – is an Embakwe term for "dog'

that I felt giddy and nauseous. That evening the big boys were walking around the refectory scanning around to see who was not eating. It was a real close call but somehow we escaped their attentions by feigning chewing.

26. The truth about sex

Having a girlfriend was an exciting business. You belonged to an exclusive band who met late at night after having gone *"snugging"*. Snugging was the label we accorded the happy business of meeting with a girl and indulging in petting and kissing. Snugging took place at a secret secluded spot near the girls' hostel. Arrangement of such dates was nearly always by love letter, with our gang having exclusive rights as paid-for courier services. As said, after snugging you met to smugly discuss your prowess and exploits at this happy business.

Some Embakwe girls – 1959

Back - Maureen Taylor, Agnes Wilson, Gladys Smith, Pamela Pullen, Mable Williams, Martha Kavanagh, [?], Dorothy Khan, Ester Gleek
Front - Effie Weir, Queenie Naidoo, Jayne Cohen, Sarah Van Beek

Techniques were discussed, sometimes even sold at a price of a banana, orange or two. If someone was your friend you might even whisper to him a sure fire snugging technique that would make any girl giddy and mad with passion.

And then the 64,000-dollar question - sex? Did we have sex? Well this was as mundane an issue as you like. We were all having sex, lots of it!

At least that was what everyone claimed without the slightest hint of dispute. Since the older boys were undoubtedly of sexual maturity, sex was a natural preoccupation in their psyche. As they were a dominant cabal, whose will, whim and every word ruled; then what they claimed was accepted as the norm for all of us.

And what sex were we having? Unless the girl had fainted, simultaneously emitting a huge sigh, at the moment of penetration, you were a failure; and a pretty hopeless one at that. These claims were made, bandied about and accepted without question. It was thus fully confirmed that the convenient untruths disseminated, by a dominant majority in any social grouping, is nearly always accepted as a societal norm. Oh yes, I was to meet more of this in later life ... convenient untruths.

Apart from six Coloured teachers, the other teachers were all Irish Sisters of the Order of Notre Dame. Our Head Mistress was Sister Mary, stunningly beautiful, incredibly inspirational and loved by all. Aware that so many of our girls soon fell pregnant after leaving school she came up with a strategy to counter this regrettable trend.

It is a bright morning in 1957, a Saturday morning. Sister Mary has called a special class of all seniors and prefects. *"I want us to talk about sex"* she says. We are all astounded. Sister Mary is a nun - who has taken a vow of chastity!? None of us has ever heard a nun mention the word *"sex"* before and none ever expected that we would. *"From next week Sister Superior is going to hold classes on sex education. Now don't be shocked ... "* she says with a glint in her eye *"I know you think we nuns know nothing about sex ... on that you are mistaken ... sex, like everything else is part of God's plan ... and should not be regarded as dirty, bad or something to be spoken about only behind the lavatory ... or in secret"*.

You can cut the atmosphere with a blade. You can hear a pin drop. She goes on to explain that, in her view, we are all ignorant about sex, which was absolutely true, and that this is the main precipitant to early and unwanted pregnancies after our girls leave school. Ignorance is dangerous ... just as my grandmother had insisted! It is the main reason for most failures. The philosophical underpinning of her stance takes shape as we listen in wondrous fascination. Unless boys and girls learn earlier, rather than later, to mix, communicate and interact in a meaningful way, disaster is assured she expounds. So we are to have "social activities" in which such closeness of contact occurs. We are going to all learn to behave responsibly with each other. Do we understand? Hardly, but that matters little. My mind is spinning, but spinning happily. This is all too good to be true.

In the result in the week following Sister Superior commences sex education sessions with the first question being - *"All those of you who have had sex ... hands up please?"* There is a long and deathly hush. The game was up. At a stroke the lie is given to the hitherto convenient untruth that we have all been having sex, with our girlfriends routinely fainting during the experience. The lessons are explicit and down to earth without the "birds and the bees" nonsense. She has spent most of her life in Sophia Town and Alexandra, both Black townships in Johannesburg, South Africa. She knows all about illicit sex and its dastardly consequences. Her lessons are punctuated with case studies of living beings. We also have social sessions where we mix with the girls in the absence of teachers, have cold drinks and tea and discuss things in a lounge setting.

It gets better, much better, oh so much better. One Sunday morning Sister Mary sends for me and Raymond Naidoo. *"So Christopher Greenland; who is your girlfriend?"* she asks mockingly. We are quickly forced to somewhat happily confess who our girlfriends are and spill the beans on others. Having extracted the information she needs we are invited to spend the day totally unsupervised at the river with our girlfriends. To make our day more enjoyable we are given a portable record player and a selection of records which she produces. To our utter amazement these comprise all the latest hits in long playing format. Once all assembled, including our girlfriends, who have been sent for, refreshments secured, she sends us on our way. *"There is only one condition ... only one condition -"* she stresses in a slow and authoritative tone *"You can do anything you like ... anything ... but you solemnly promise me that you will never leave each other's sight ... never ... that is the only condition"*. Needless to say we uphold the condition and have a wonderful day.

The icing on the cake is when Sister Mary commissions Vernon Bowers, a newly arrived South African born teacher, to conduct ballroom dancing lessons. These had some not so funny moments. A 15-year-old boy is a repository of certain very powerful biological urges. As his hormones do their business he has little control.

So it is not good form to leave such a boy, holding a girl for minutes on end, whilst you check whether other couples are in the right pose to execute a dancing step. Given the general poor quality, even absence of underpants amongst boys at the school, the situation that arises thereafter will often end up with the girl administering a slap to the boy you have left, and the girl walking out red faced and embarrassed. Vernon Bowers! What planet you on?? Mind you, Vernon B was a great teacher.

We all become accomplished ball room dancers. We master the waltz, the quick-step, the tango and the fox trot. Social activities, including a weekly dance function, were now part of our normal routine. We chose the music. So we had all the records of the legendary stars of the rock and roll era such as Elvis Presley, Chuck Berry, Bill Haley and the Comets, The Platters, Bill Black's Combo ... the lot. And we also had our crooners like Brook Benton, Pat Boon, Johnny Mathis, Dean Martin and the silky voiced Nat King Cole. This privilege was extended to films shown once a month.

All Elvis Presley's films were shown. It was truly wonderful. We were also allowed to follow clothing trends. Being with it, cool, casual, and hip included wearing moccasins, "screaming" neon bright socks, blue jeans and shirts with upturned collars. So despite being out in the remote bush we were culturally connected to the real world in this very important and special way thanks to a truly incredible Irish nun.

As said Sister Mary was light years ahead of her time as regards the concepts of life skills and sex education.

27. A start to the roaring 60s

A high point was when she gave permission for us to put on our very own concert in 1959. During the school holidays Rhodesia had been treated to a tour by an ensemble then styled "The Coon Carnival". The carnival or "Coons", the name by which they were called at that time before the age of political correctness, were exclusively Cape Coloured. The show they put on was incredible. You had Madjiet Omar, whose singing was indistinguishable from Bing Crosby, whom he emulated. You had Danny Williams[1] whose take offs of Elvis Presley sounded indistinguishable from the great man himself. In fact they reproduced all current hits with incredible "authenticity".

Their selling point and brand however was their presentation. Dressed in the most colourful costumes, faces painted black and white vaudeville style, they would enter the stage performing their "coon dance" and re-perform it at the slightest provocation throughout the show. This dance was unprecedented

---

[1] **Danny Williams** later seized the opportunity to desert racist apartheid South Africa on one of the tours and settled in the United Kingdom where he became a singing star recording "Moon River", "White on White" and other great hits

and unique to them. It involved highly rhythmic bouncing and shaking of bodies, which seemed to be made of rubber, on legs seemingly spring loaded.

 The stage would be awash with colour and alive with movement. Their exuberance was electrifying.

Our concert was a first. It was the first time that students put on a show for their school. There was great excitement. Sister Mary and her team of nuns was supportive throughout preparation, and excited too as they had no idea what to expect.

[Picture is of Sister Mare Nugent SND]

Preparations involved making up the costumes including paper millinery as regards our colourful coon hats. The show was a complete hit with everybody. The girls left their seats and, crouching at the foot of the stage, put on a good show themselves of screaming and swooning madly. This they had picked up from watching Elvis's films no doubt.

The high point was our coon dance which certainly brought the house down. More sober contributions included my rendition of Russ Hamilton's 1957 "Rainbow", delivered in full costume and cane in hand. It was a magical and beautiful night. Stirling performances were put in by Bunny De Souza, Michael Hoffman, Scotty Brown and Victor Pinto

It is a gross understatement to say that Sister Mary SND was ahead of her time. She was light years ahead. It is astounding that an Irish nun, in the middle of the African bush, was so enlightened. Sex education, social learning and life skills, only hit the rest of the world nearly two decades later. The pregnancy rate amongst our female school leavers all but vanished.

We were able to venture into the urban world confident, well resourced and with enhanced social literacy. There was a tendency for children from "snootier" schools to refer to us as *"those Embakwe kaffirs"*. This was on account of the dearth of resources at our school and our propensity for speaking in an Africanized "Embakwe" accent

This was exacerbated by the fact that nearly everyone was given and referred to by an isiNdebele slang nick-name such as "Pra-Pra", "Wabayi",

"Zantondo", "Zizi", "Machipisa" and "Umkuliki"[1]. Well the smiles were soon wiped off their faces once the band struck up. Young ladies like to dance and we were champions at ballroom.

A regrettable biological change that occurred in my mid-teens was that my hair started to go kroos. This was most inconvenient, considering the hairstyle of my idol Elvis Presley and the "kiss-me-curl", that I included in my own hair style. I had long since lost all enthusiasm to be Black, and to be called Ndiweni, and remonstrated with my God for this unwelcome change to an important social asset. Whereas for me the change in my hair was an unwelcome change, for a lad named Robert, nicknamed *"Uborden"*, his corn-curls were a major issue which was not to be left unresolved. A tin was obtained. A nail was then used to make holes in the bottom. As the nail was driven from the inside the resultant holes would have serrated edges on the outside. These presented as "the teeth" of his comb. The tin was then filled with hot embers and Uborden would spend hours combing his hair in the vain hope that the heated contraption would force the hair strands to permanent straightness. The limited success he achieved made him try harder, and the lad was at it for most of the rest of his school days.

Straight hair was considered an advantage in our community and "ironing" hair till it was straight was very much a norm. This was accomplished by combing the hair with a brass comb heated on a spirit stove. For me, however, although my hair went kroos, it never changed to corn-curl condition. I felt relieved about this and cannot be condemned. Today the cosmetic industry for Black folk is one of the biggest in the world. Most products are concerned to ensure that hair is either straight or fashionably curly.

So too as regards skin lightening. A product called Ambi started gaining acceptance in the 60s and went on to take the Black world by storm soon thereafter. Its purpose was to transform black skin to a nice shade of brown. The rest is history. Today most Black celebrities *et al*, including all the female presenters of South African national television, (2010) are a nice dark to golden brown complexion with curly hair ... the natural look of my people, whatever the multi zillion dollar "black like me" brand is saying.

We often ruefully observe that, one of the reasons why it was felt necessary to classify Coloured folk as "Black", was so as to "hi-jack" our skin colour and hair condition.

---

[1] **"Pra-Pra"** = talkative. "Wabayi" = owlish. "Zandondo" = receding forehead. "Zizi" = an owl. "Machipisa" = prone to bargaining. "Umkuliki" – little Indian

28. Testosterone - and the truth shall set you free

It is a Saturday afternoon in 1959. I am with two classmates who have also become my close friends, Bruce Abrahams and Edmund "Pra-Pra" Ambrose. We are walking on a path through the bush making our way to Skinner's store on his farm. We overtake two young Black girls. Soon thereafter we hear the sound of a bell ringing. Turning I see a young man on a cycle, on which he has one of the girls, followed by another pair also on a cycle. My friends jump out of the way. I stroll to one side. This seeming lack of enthusiasm on my part, to afford him right of way, annoys the young man. He and the girl alight from the cycle, whilst he announces loudly in isiNdebele that he intends to *"smack this puppy ... this insolent puppy"*.

My heart sinks. As he approaches me I am all too well aware that he is now brimming with testosterone. I know its effects. I have recently surprisingly won the pole vault event at our annual athletics championships, and broken a 10-year-old record, only on account of my girlfriend standing close, clasping her hands and sighing *"I know you can do it ... I just know you can ... "* When he adds - *"mina ngiya vela e Goli ..."* [me, I come from Johannesburg], and goes on to say that in Johannesburg puppies are taught respect, my heart sinks to the bottom of my feet. All locals have a reverence for anyone who has lived and worked in Johannesburg, the "golden city", with all its mines, gangs and legendary deviance. Such men are to be feared ... very much indeed.

Desperate, I try to talk to him saying that he does not know me and I don't know him; implying that in this truth there may be unforeseen risk for him. He smirks from ear to ear, in bemusement, and assures me that he is not interested in my whining like a puppy. I am cornered, sick in the stomach, mind racing. A cornered rat is dangerous. Admonitions from my grandmother's people that *"a man cannot die like a fowl"* swirl vaguely in my mind. I have to do something or I am dead.

I tell him that he has a beautiful watch, and that if intends to finish his business he should take it off. In an exaggerated gesture, and one motion, he strips the watch off his wrist and, turning, throws it to the doe eyed lass. As he turns back towards me I punch him, and with a sickening thud, catch him square on the mouth and nose, with blood and mucous splattering out into the bright afternoon sun. He reels twice and keels over onto his back. I jump onto him and, straddling his chest, apply a strangle hold to his throat, intending to deprive him of oxygen. But he is quite lifeless, his eyes open, eyeballs fixed and in tilt. I turn triumphantly to my companions and hope they get the message ... what a tactic I have employed! what a punch! Surely I deserve their admiration?

Looking for admiration is a big mistake. As I stand up in triumph and rejoin them, all hell breaks loose. With an ear piercing shriek of *"vrastaag[1]"*, he springs up from the ground, like a jack-in-the- box, to an incredible height, eyes wide and blazing like beams from hell, and in a flash he is onto me in a murderous charge. Instinctively I throw a straight left punch, only just taught to us from a book on boxing by Richard Brown, who made us practice it *ad nauseam*. Thank God he did! My attacker runs into it and, is once again, caught flush where mouth meets nose. Down he goes onto his back and lies lifeless. My slip-on shoe has come off. The ground is hot. I have just enough time to slip the shoe back on when the "vrastaag" routine is repeated, fortunately with the same result. God and the ancestral spirits are on my side so far.

Bruce and Pra-Pra think that this might not last, that my luck so far might run out. I am but a boy, up against a man, who will soon change tactic, and I will be found wanting. In high isiNdebele Pra-Pra entreats the other man, telling him that the thing should end with a handshake and acknowledgment of honour on both sides. It is a long shot, since my opponent is a bloody mess and I am unscathed, but it works. The friend grabs the man and talks sense into him. I am very reluctant to shake his hand for reasons I cannot formulate. My friends insist. It is the honourable way to settle the matter. That is the packaging. The truth is that we all believe that the tide will turn to my detriment. I allow my adversary to take my hand. He does so and, after an exclamation in classic Zulu idiom - *"Hau! Indoda[2]"*, punches me full in the eye causing me to see stars for the first time in my life.

I am not violent by nature. My mother would often even refer to me as *"chicken-hearted"* on account of my non-aggressive disposition. I am relieved that the fight is over, very relieved, but cannot stop myself on insisting that it must now go on. It is the sin of pride dictating. The man's companion agrees, saying ruefully that the punch in the eye was cowardly in the extreme. Indeed it was. The fight goes on. Fortunately my opponent never changes tactic and runs into my counterpunch with sweet regularity. It ends with him propped up against a tree, barely able to stand, with an awful bloody mess for a face.

The next day the police collect me and I am taken to Plumtree hospital outpatients where my opponent is. I am shocked at the state of his face.

---

[1] **Vrastaag** – pronounced with flattened "a's" and a silent "g" is Afrikaans and apparently has no meaning

[2] **Hau! Indoda** – is classic Zulu/Ndebele meaning "a man" said in a tone intended as recognition and honour

Overnight swelling has made his face into a blue-black contorted balloon in the middle of which is a very badly split upper lip. He looks like he has been hit by a train. *"You are charged with Assault GBH[1]"*, the police officers tell me repeatedly and *"tomorrow the magistrate is coming and you will get 6 cuts[2]"* they taunt. I am examined by a doctor. The result is bad. I have no injuries only a fracture to the middle knuckle of my left hand. This all confirms a belief by the police that there was never a fight, in which I was defending myself, only a savage beating administered to a victim. Applying hindsight, it is somewhat understandable that they were disinclined to accept a story that the injuries were self inflicted by the man charging his face into my fist.

I am in desperate trouble and the Hail Marys, I now silently reel off, must sound pretty desperate to Mother Mary because She eventually comes through. Whereas they decline my insistence that they interview Bruce and Pra-Pra, as they are my friends, the police agree to interview *"the complainant's"* friend, who they are forced to agree was a witness.

When he arrives, in the back of a police Land Rover, he takes my hand and greets me warmly. With the clarity and simplicity, that characterizes truth, he tells the police that the complainant is a jumped-up pest from Joburg[3], lacking in respect for elders and others, prone to harassment of people's wives, and that the beating he got was richly deserved, as he had been a most cowardly aggressor from start to finish. I am freed.

Truth is ever simple and by simple truth, unbeknown at the time, history was shaped for me and my country.

When we next played Empandeni, our arch rivals at soccer, the local Black supporters would enthusiastically roar *"Dabula umlomo"* [meaning "the one who tears the mouth"] every time I played the ball.

It made me play that much better I dare say.

---

29. The devil you know

On a certain day, at an earlier date, I am called by a priest who I think was of Austrian ethnicity. He is of quiet disposition, rarely engaging in

---

[1] **Assault GBH** – assault with intent to do grievous bodily harm

[2] **6 cuts** – a whipping of six strokes with a cane

[3] "Joburg" – short for Johannesburg

conversation. He invites me to *"go for a walk"* with him. I feel honoured that he has singled me out for such privilege.

As we walk on a path in the surrounding bush the conversation is slow and stilted.

Priest: How old are you?

Me: 12

Priest: How long have you been an altar boy?

Me: Since I was eight years old in Sacred Heart Home

Priest: You are a good boy

Me: Thank you Father [I respond feeling flattered. We are now truly alone deep in the bush]

Priest: You need to unbutton those buttons - [he says pointing to my trouser fly buttons. I hesitate. This is confusing. It is difficult for me to reconcile a priest with any concerns about the area of my loins.

The world stands still. I can hear the shrill of the cicadas in blanket of awful silence]

Priest: Yes - [he mutters insistently] ... you must unbutton your trousers ... [unbuttoning his own trousers ... my mind is swirling]

Me: Yes Father [I stammer ... but still hesitate ... looking at his face ... I see eyes ... kindly eyes ... stained with terrible sadness but kind and gentle behind a mask of authority ... ultimate authority ... the authority of a man of God. So I unbutton my fly buttons -]

Priest: Good boy ... you see fresh air is very important [he adds looking at me with an intensity that I will never forget] ... fresh air is very important ... it is very important!

I comply.

The rest of the walk is without remarkable incident; and is to be repeated on several occasions thereafter. On each occasion the routine is the same. However, at no stage, am I ever touched, fondled or molested.

At some stage Father Adalbert informs me that this priest had been a prisoner of war in the custody of the Japanese. He had been subjected to unspeakable privations. It was then that he had developed an obsession with the male pubic area needing fresh air. In later years I was to become aware of what prisoners of war in Japanese camps went through ... and then I started to understand.

From the age of just 8 eight years, in Sacred Heart Home, I had always been an altar boy. This usually involved donning red and white vestments and helping a priest in the conduct of mass, which is the basic religious ceremony of the Roman Catholic Church. The ritual included Latin being the language of choice, and the burning of pungent sweet smelling incense. To me it was always a spiritually uplifting business, in which I felt greatly privileged to partake.

One morning, in 1958, Father Elmar Schmidt[1], administrative head of the school, sends for me. It is an emergency. Someone important is dying. That is the news that has been conveyed by two locals, now waiting anxiously for those who do God's work to come and administer to their loved one, in his final moments on this earth. Priest and altar boy don their robes of office, purple for this ritual, with all due speed, climb into the Land Rover and hair off to the village in question.

On arrival we are directed to the hut in which the dying man lies. We prepare the implements of our sacred office. Father has his books, holy oil and water. I have my incense burner, which I now stoke up felling pleased with my proficiency, as the sweet smelling smoke rises, signifying instant success. I am ready to do my bit.

As we enter the hut I see a partly covered man lying on a low bed. He looks grey and lifeless. Suddenly all hell breaks loose. Upon becoming aware of our entry the man jerks up to a sitting position, and starts to shriek a string of invectives in the vernacular starting with –

"U funani lapa ... " [What do you want here] ... *"Suga lapa ... "* [get away from here] ... . *"Sata nyogo* [Fuck your mother]

He is angry. No; he is wild with anger ... in a rage ... as he continues berating us. I am shocked at the level of aggressive energy confronting us, and instinctively step back. Father Elma immediately grabs me by the shoulder and pulls me forward. This priest is an imposing giant of a man, at some 6 foot seven, with a booming voice to match. *"Come on boy - come on boy..."* I hear him say *" - you must pray with me..."* I can feel the enormous physical and spiritual strength of this great man of God, and bravely step forward. He starts administering the last rites. The man goes mad, waving his arms and screaming invectives. *"Jesus is nothing - he is not my Lord - he is nothing - Satan is king - I embrace Satan - I love Satan - Mary was not a virgin - she*

---

[1] **Father Elmar Schmidt** – a great German missionary now buried at Marian Hill in Kwazulu, South Africa.

was a prostitute - and Jesus was her spawn - with no father - get out - leave me - leave me now - !"

The priest is undeterred. He raises his voice, in supplicating prayer, calling on our God to intervene. The man raises his voice in response. The inside of the hut is now a crescendo of sound as the situation takes on the characteristics of a shouting match. Then I hear something different - chillingly different. It freezes my heart. I am certain that I can detect more than one voice, emanating from our adversary, and adversary he certainly now is.

[Picture is of Father Elmar Schimdt and Sister Mare Julie SND]

My knees start to buckle. My voice goes faint and I go woozy. *"Come on boy - come on..."* Father Elmar booms at me *" - you must pray with me - pray with me..."* It takes time for me to summon up courage, and try to add volume to the strangled hoarse whisper that my voice has degenerated to. To help I swing the incense burner more strongly. Perhaps the increased production of this holy smoke will help overcome what is clearly now a terrible enemy, unseen but there all the same.

The confrontation, and that is what it clearly is, goes on for what seems an interminably long time; priest and altar boy on one side; sick man and unseen entity on the other side. Our prayers and supplications to Almighty God are drowned by the screaming of the man on the bed. He radiates strength and energy that is disempowering. The priest radiates a strength and energy that is empowering. It is overwhelming. It is frightening. I am able to stand my ground only because of the presence of this huge man of God so close to me.

In the end it is all to no avail. The man will not relent. He will not give up. Father Elmar finally says *"so be it"* and closes his book. We retreat leaving him sitting up, eyes blazing in ferocious anger, mouth churning out rejection, curses and invectives. *"Impisi"* [hyena] *"inja"* [dog] *"indwangu"* [baboon] and other classic Ndebele swear words, all continue streaming out of a frothing mouth. There is, and has been, no indication that he is sick, let alone dying.

Upon reaching the Land Rover we are called back. Reluctantly we return. The man is dead. It has been hardly two or three minutes since we left him. In that short time all the incredible strength we had witnessed, and his life, left him forever.

Father Elmar summonses the elders of the village. He tells them coldly and matter-of-factly that they are not to bring his body for burial at the mission cemetery, which is holy ground. On the way back he explains to me that this man had once been a devout member of the Church and had been an exemplary catechist. However a stage had been reached where, inexplicably, he had lapsed and reverted to the practice of witchcraft. He also tells me to remember that, as a soldier of Christ, I must never succumb to fear when faced with evil. *"The devil"* he says ... *"has many hands that work for him - you must always stand up to such people - that is your duty".*

I hardly tell a soul that I had heard more than one voice emanating from this man until many years later when the world is treated to a film titled "The Exorcist[1]"

---

30. Inspiration

Children need heroes. In Thorngrove our hero was Ginger. In Embakwe it was Danny Pillay, a Coloured teacher of South African extraction. He was nicknamed *"Torro"*, a word that one associates with the style of matadors. He certainly came across as stylish, more in personality rather than dress sense. When he spoke, you listened, because he would intone his speech so as to make any subject so much more interesting. Although Danny was our soccer coach we also received a lesson from another teacher, Abe Davies, on how to kick a soccer ball. Davies prepared and delivered the lesson extremely well using all the right materials, graphs and demonstrations. Our kicking skills hardly improved. When Torro took us for the same lesson he produced no course material and/or diagrams - etc. Instead he told us, in reverential tone, about two legendary teams being Manchester United of England and Dinamo Moskva of Russia. In the context of the then cold war, his build up of these two teams took on special significance and really got our interest

---

[1] *The Exorcist* is a 1973 U.S. horror film directed by William Friedkin, adapted from the 1971 novel of the same name by William Peter Blatty, dealing with the demonic possession of a young girl, and her mother's desperate attempts to win back her daughter through an exorcism conducted by two priests.
http://en.wikipedia.org/wiki/The_Exorcist_(film)

and attention. There was no television those days. What we learnt about these great teams and their players was in terms of brilliant mind-mapping induced by words from the mouth of a great teacher.

Spellbound we listened, as he set the scene of a historic encounter, settled when a great player Manchester half-back Duncan Edwards[1] was assigned the taking of a free kick. His description of the kick had us awestruck. He introduced us to Stanley Matthews and his legendary "Matthews swerve". We also learnt of the Nat Lofthouse volley. The icing on the cake was to hear about a brown-skinned football genius, Pelé[2]. When he thereafter put the ball down and asked each of us to kick it, the ball was hit with full force power and accuracy.

Under him we scored a famous victory against our arch rivals, Empandeni, annihilated Founders High School, who were reputed to be kings of Coloured school soccer, and secured a 4 all draw with Tekwane in a thrilling match talked about for many years. A memorable feature of this game was that I was involved in an incident with a fantastic player nick-named Zoo, who donned pure white boots, and who went on to become a legendary player and coach for Zambia. We were both going for a high ball. He jumped first and had the advantage of having done so. However it was a false advantage, as he had jumped too early, and gravity would bring him down as I jumped with correct timing.

But he did not come down. He hung in the air until after I came down. Incredibly he remained in the air and then, bringing the ball down the front of his body, trapped it with both feet. I imagined that he had defied gravity. But I had not. All the spectators and other players shared my impression and their calls of *"Zoo – Zoo..."* built up to a deafening crescendo. It was

---

[1] Matt Busby described **Duncan Edwards** as the most 'complete footballer in Britain - possibly the world'. The greatest tragedy is that his death aged just 21 from injuries sustained in the Munich air crash meant his full potential was never realized. He died on 21 February 1958.

http://www.manutd.com/default.sps?pagegid=%7B847FFC5F-947A-470D-A13B-E757FD63C2A8%7D&bioid=92124

[2] **Edison Arantes do Nascimento**, KBE [born 23 October 1940], best known by his nickname Pelé - a veteran of four World Cups, scorer of 1,283 first-class goals - 12 of them in World Cup final tournaments - a member of those magical Brazilian squads that won soccer's greatest prize in 1958, 1962 and 1970.

sensational. The incident is recalled to this day. If one is to be beaten then it is palatable if it is by sheer genius.

I have always been in the highest degree bemused by the reticence with which to-day's soccer players at world cup level approach the taking of penalties. Some of these fabulously paid stars even appear to tremble. In many instances their obvious fears are realized when they then bungle the kick. Had they been taught by Torro they would relish the prospect, demand to be one of the kickers and smash the ball onto the net every time giving the goalie not the slightest chance.

We now also have the "bend it like Beckam" hype. Well, when Bruce Abrahams took a corner kick the ball would sling out at least a meter or more in mid-air and then curl right back in to brush so close to the inside of the crossbar as to give the goalie immense problems. Our right winger Joseph Shirto, nick-named "Banana Joe", would take a defender at full speed right to the corner and then sling the ball inward only to curl back to the inside of the crossbar again making the goalie's life miserable. It should be noted that such prowess was accomplished with boots, soccer pitches and footballs that were vastly inferior to to-day's fare.

In the Empandeni game the goalie was a show-off and a comic. Dressed all in black with a cap to match, the game started with him performing antics such as cart-wheels and handsprings much to the approval of his adoring fans, especially the girls. He also had a chair in his goal area on which he would sit like some great professor in nonchalant pose so as to show disdain for us the opposition. Five minutes into the game we were awarded a 30 yard free kick. I took it. I was doing it for Torro. I was doing it for Manchester United's Duncan Edwards, who had just been killed in the infamous Munich air crash. I played half-back just as Edward's did. The result was an Exocet missile that turned the goalie's fingers inside out and found its way into the top left hand corner of the goals. Well that is the way I saw it. My team-mates insist that the ball floated serenely into the top left hand corner. Either way that cured the man of all his monkey business and he abandoned his chair.

Teaching is not a science. It is an art and all art is founded on inspiration. Danny "Torro" Pillay was truly inspirational in everything he did with us. This included forming a band with us in which he played the saxophone and Stan Abrahams played guitar.

Early one morning I accompany Torro on a drive to the dam. I feel happy and privileged that he asked me to. Near the dam, standing a short distance from our track, we come across a magnificently conditioned kudu bull. We stop, slowly reverse and drive back to the mission in order to get a rifle. After explaining how it's done he lets me drive as he needs to take the shot. I am a bit clumsy but do a good job of driving. Which boy wouldn't with such a teacher?

The bull is still standing there on our return, tall with antlers seemingly reaching to the clouds, and a long flowing grey-white beard. A kudu bull in its prime is a truly magnificent sight.

Resting the rifle carefully on the sill of the open passenger's side window, Torro carefully takes aim. I hold my breath as my heart pounds away. It is a clear shot, some 60 meters to a large, still and easy target. The seconds tick - and tick - and there is no shot. He makes a small adjustment and aims again. The bull is standing quite still looking at us. The shot that I expect with unbearable anticipation never comes. Instead Torro pulls the gun in and signals me to drive. He is dead quiet, and to my repeated questions as to why he did not shoot the kudu, he just shakes his head from side to side.

At the time the hunting of game, and antelope in particular, was a much prized activity. Whatever disagreements the different races in the region had with each other, there was no disagreement about the hunting and killing of animals. Conservation was a yet to be invented concept. The bagging of such a magnificent kudu bull would have earned Torro, and me, unmatchable bragging rights across the community. He never spoke about the incident, let alone explained it.

The next weekend he put a gun to his head and pulled the trigger. Why would this wonderful man, an exuberant epitome of life itself, who spared the life of a dumb animal, choose to ends his own? Nobody knows why. We are still shocked and numbed at his loss. He remains forever imprinted in our psyche.

He was a great inspiration to children needing so much.

---

31. A sojourn to the north

My mother's situation was such that she was unable to have me home for the mid-year holidays in 1959. One of my friends, Scotty Brown, wrote to his parents asking if he could have me home for the holidays. After an anxious wait we received their assent by letter. We traveled by train all the way to Ndola, Northern Rhodesia. It was my first trip out of Southern Rhodesia.

The train left Bulawayo in the evening. Being Coloured we were booked into a "second class" compartment. It was a Bombela, [slow train] stopping at every railway siding. We received a print-out of its arrival and departure times with our tickets. As the journey progressed we amused ourselves by checking to what extent the train adhered to it's scheduled times. Over the two-day trip it rarely was more than a minute or two off scheduled time. With all our modern technology it is now extremely rare to find modern transportation that can match this. For this credit must accrue to the plate layers of the time, almost exclusively Coloured, who were responsible for ensuring that the track was in good order.

Seeing the great Victoria Falls, in the early morning light, as the train crept across the engineering masterpiece that the Victoria Falls Bridge is, was an awesome experience. On arrival at Livingstone we got off and made a mini-tour of the town returning with a good supply of mangoes, which were there for the taking, off trees that grew wild by the roadside. It was a wonderful holiday during which Scotty and I were able to display our soccer skills playing for local teams.

I was mad with excitement when the local soccer committee submitted my name to play for Northern Rhodesia against a great English club, Bolton Wanderers, who were visiting the country. Regrettably the fact that I was born in Southern Rhodesia put paid to my candidature. However watching the game and seeing some of the great English players that Torro had enthused about was a dream-come-true experience for Scotty and I.

The other notable experience was attending the cinema house. To my surprise, unlike the situation in Rhodesia, there was no racial segregation in the seating. We sat next to White folk and nobody minded one bit. Ironically though, I did meet up with a person who did mind, and was extremely unhappy at our meeting. Her name was Judy, as light skinned as any White person, who I had known well as the sister of a girl named Denise.

We had all been together in Sacred Heart Home. At the Home Denise would suddenly jump up, run around emitting blood curdling sounds whilst frothing at the mouth. These were terrifying experiences for young children not yet 10 years old. She was an epileptic. I was assigned the onerous duty of attending to such attacks by, catching and restraining her, until the attacks subsided. Every time I did this I was terrified through and through.

This duty, I dare say, I must have discharged with distinction as not once did she do herself an injury. To that extent her family was, in effect, indebted to me. Not so when I met Judy and her other family members at the cinema. They embarrassed me deeply when they rebuffed my greeting, pretended that I was a pest and marched off in a huff.

It was ironic in that all the other "real" White folk around didn't seem to care less about my presence. Given the situation, it was understandable that this fair skinned Coloured family believed that it was to their advantage to "play White". It was! This was the White dominated colonial society of 1959. "Playing White" was quite a common occurrence and some Coloured families had a "white sheep" of the family, whose existence was kept a closely guarded secret.

More ironic, however, was that on the very distant horizon of South Africa, would emerge a world acclaimed Black government, with a world acclaimed Constitution, that would insist that we Coloureds prove that we are Black, in order to secure rights and privileges as human beings, under Affirmative Action and Black Empowerment stratagems and laws.

32. My brother - and the Queen

I spent my next holidays with my eldest brother, Frank Joseph Leith in Salisbury[1]. He was an incredible mentor and tutor. One night, on a weekend, he decided it was time for me to learn about life. To that end he took me on a tour of nightspots and shebeens. A shebeen is an informal pub where people gather to hear music, eat, drink and socialize. Their allure is their informality. Shebeens are common in the southern African region.

Frank was a great fan of Audie Murphy[2], a star in western movies. So he emulates his hero as he speaks to me. I listen captivated and enthralled at my brother, my legendary big brother. Physically I am already taller than him but he is a giant in my eyes. As these words hit my computer screen, my heart breaks and I fight back tears as I remember my brother, Frank Joseph Leith.

Everywhere we go he is treated with infectious respect with people glad-handing him and back-slapping him with unrestrained enthusiasm. It is obvious that he also a giant in their perception, despite his small frame and dark skin. I am introduced to alcohol and given my first beer. I feel like I have just become a "made man[3]".

---

[1] **Salisbury** is now named Harare – in Zimbabwe.

[2] **Audie Leon Murphy** [June 20, 1926 [?] – May 28, 1971] was a much-decorated American soldier who served in the European Theater during World War II. He later became an actor, appearing in 44 American films, and also found some success as a country music composer. http://en.wikipedia.org/wiki/Audie_Murphy

[3] **A made man**, also known as a wise guy, made member, made guy, man of honor, soldier or friend of ours to the family as opposed to "friend of mine" [not made], is someone who has been officially inducted into the Mafia [La Cosa Nostra]. http://en.wikipedia.org/wiki/Made_man

I am counseled throughout by my brother; counseled at great length about life, people and behaviour in particular. I learn to distinguish been those people that can be trusted and *"shady characters"* who must be avoided. So too as regards treating a lady and avoiding *"dirty women"*. Dirty women will steal your money and give you *"notch"* [venereal disease]. To mix with shady characters is to be *"a mug"*. A mug lacks motivation, is an under achiever and will inevitably end up in *"boop"* [prison] or at the bottom of the societal pile. Everything is said in a particular voice and tone.

[Picture is of my brother Frank Joseph Leith]

At 3 in the morning we start walking home as Frank explains that traveling on his 650cc Norton Motorcsycle would be in breach of the law, in lieu of the amount of alcohol he has drunk. It is a clear night. There is little traffic and the streets are devoid of people. I feel a bit tired but on top of the world as I listen to my brother and hang on his every word.

My world is rudely interrupted when I hear a voice shout - *"Hey you - hey you - you better stop right now ... "* We turn to see a White uniformed policeman emerging from the shadows. Frank puts one hand on my arm and whispers that I must say nothing, whatever happens. The officer stops real close to us and glares down at us. He wants to know what we are doing, what we *"up to"* at 3 in the morning. *"Don't think I don't know you Coloureds - "* he goes on and implies that our presence in the street, at that time of night, is only consistent with an intention to steal, a propensity amongst Coloureds with which he is all too familiar.

Audie Murphy tries to explain - *"no officer - I am out on the town with my youngster - I am teaching him about life - not to be a shady character..."* The policeman makes it clear that he does not want to hear *"fucking bullshit"*. He is in no mood for it; and what does Frank mean when he says this is *"his youngster"*. Crass rudeness changes to rage when Frank explains that I am his younger brother. *"So you think you are a clever pikkie[1] hey - trying to be smart with me ... talking shit ..."* is the response. Discourse becomes confrontation; and confrontation becomes heated, as my brother and the police officer talk at cross-purposes. Frank is attempting to make things go away. The police officer is escalating the situation. He is incensed that this *"kaffir"*, a label he now accords Frank, has the temerity to pretend that he has

---

[1] **Pikkie** – racial slang meaning a young African

not been caught in the act of training a Coloured kid in the business of stealing. Not for a nanosecond does he believe that Frank is my elder brother.

Things take a turn for the worse when the officer says that what Frank really needs is a good *"fucking up"* as prison only makes pikkies like him worse. I can only think that, also on account of his small stature, Frank was always sensitive about anyone threatening him. He reacts in a way that I was to witness in later life in similar situations. Hitherto a cool and respectful Audie Murphy, his tone changes markedly as he rubs his wrists together and mutters darkly - *"if you ever think you can fuck me up - me - dabula nyosi*[1] *- you had better prove it mister..!"* The officer is visibly amused by this counter challenge. *"So a stupid fucking pikkie like you wants to fight hey... "* he guffaws enquiringly. *"Anytime officer – anytime... "* is the response, in a quiet but pregnant Audie Murphy drawl.

An obscene cameo is then played out. The two protagonists agree to find a place to fight. I am asked to help in the search. We walk through the streets of the city looking for a secluded spot, where they can have their fight. We even walk right past the main police station. The absurdity of it, the sheer wrongness of it is not lost on me. But with every fiber in my body I am aware that it is unavoidable. This thing has to be played out. It has a momentum of its own that cannot be stopped. Racist contempt and arrogance will endure until it is checked by the spirit, strength and belief of the oppressed underdog.

We find a small courtyard in a sanitary lane near the railway station. Frank says to the officer - *"I respect the Queen - I will not fight unless you remove your cap and belt - as they have the Queen's badges".* Mentally I note that "The Queen" is also our national anthem which we sing at school. The officer is only too happy to oblige, and I am handed both cap and belt to safe-keep.

The two are a physical miss-match. Frank is no more than 5 foot 8 inches and of lightweight build. His opponent is around 6 foot 2 and burly. I am concerned but not afraid for my brother. He has built up my faith and trust in him over many years. I know that he would never take on something that is to fail. That would be a betrayal of all he stands for and believes in.

Their physical miss-match is soon conversely mirrored in the fight. It is a no-contest as Frank proceeds to give his opponent a boxing lesson. Punches, thrown by the officer, turn into wild swings as they fail to find their mark. Frank is "Makiti" [the cat] once again, back in Makokoba Township, feigning, ducking, weaving and counter punching with deadly accuracy. Soon the man's face is a bloody mess - a huffing, puffing, snotty bloody mess.

---

[1] **Dabula nyosi** – isiNdebele literally meaning "to tear that which is sweet"

We leave him on his knees in the courtyard and walk home. On the way we review the fight, and I am schooled into the key elements for success in this department.

A whole year later we are at Frank's home preparing for Xmas which is the next day. A black car pulls up outside and soon there is a knock on the door. I open to find a White man at the door, impeccably attired in a black pin striped suit and tie. *"Good evening"* he says very politely and then in a slightly firmer and more formal tone - *"Please hand them over - we don't want any trouble - just hand them over…"* and as I look at him quizzically he adds - *" … the cap and the belt".*

Frank's eyes convey an instruction of assent. I go to the bedroom, and from the top of a wardrobe, I retrieve the police officer's cap and belt. The man takes these from me saying - *"Have a very happy Xmas - goodbye"* and leaves.

In this way the CID[1] section of the BSAP end one of many mini struggles played out so often in Rhodesia.

---

33. Dangerous games

Travel to and from school was by train. This involved an overnight leg between Salisbury and Bulawayo. We always traveled on the Bombela which stopped everywhere, sometimes for up to an hour. This gave Adventure Boys plenty of time to run into a town and have fun.

This would include asking a shopkeeper if he had a *"left handed screwdriver"* in stock, or a red shirt with yellow, blue, white and green polka dots. Requests were made with extreme politeness and a tone of feigned naiveté. We would ask a baker if he could sell us a leg of lamb. A Jewish hardware store owner became so exasperated, as we peppered him with these "loony' requests, that he threw a primus stove at me, which we had requested and then rejected for not being pink and able to run on water as paraffin was too expensive. I ducked and the stove smashed through the large glass pane fronting the whole of his shop undoubtedly causing damage costing an enormous amount of money.

Mark would also leave a turd on the doorstep of a butchery or bakery, in the dead of night, and laugh long and hard as he projected the prospect of the owner arriving early in the morning to find that *"he too had so much crap in*

---

[1] **CID** - Criminal Investigation Department of the British South Africa Police

his life." I did little to discourage him. Mark needed to act out the demons that were deep inside him.

We soon formulated a grievance, one of many, about the fact that our train was overtaken by the passenger mail train. Something needed to be done about this train with its posh occupants, all snooty and ever so superior. The overtaking procedure was that, at a station called Hunters Road, our train would stop for ever so long and the mail train would catch up, draw alongside it for just a minute, and then move off ahead.

In the minute or so, that the mail train was parked, we got to work uncoupling the carriages and undoing as many brake hoses as we could. This was easy as it was about 11 o'clock at night. Pandemonium broke loose and Hunters Road became a hive of activity as railway staff proceeded to investigate, shouting in excited consternation. A hunt for the perpetrators started. I had visions of the Gestapo looking for French resistance fighters. We took refuge under a tarpaulin of one of the goods carriages of our train. We believed that we would not be found. We were found; found quite quickly by railway police dogs, whose employment we had not anticipated. It was decided that we would be conveyed by train to the next city, being Gatooma, [now Gadoma] and handed over to the regular police.

As our train moved off again we found ourselves kneeling in one of the carriage passages being guarded by a railway police officer. Things were looking very bleak as the train trundled along. I knew with absolute certainty that we would be handed over to the police, prosecuted and subjected to a whipping. However, the slow pace at which the train traveled conferred an advantage. It gave young, fertile, overactive, mischievous minds time to think. In whispered tones a plan was hatched.

As our guard turned away for some reason I reached up, undid a latch, opened a flap to expose a rotary switch which, on my turning, killed all the carriage lights. In the darkness we made our escape to a compartment of trusted school mates. When the guard and policeman arrived, searching the train, and opened the compartment with their master key, we simply monkey-climbed out of the window of the moving train to the next compartment and back again when they were gone. Anticipating that the train would be more thoroughly searched at Gatooma we alighted at the next stop and made our way to the main road. There we managed to prevail upon a truck driver into giving us a lift, after first getting him to stop by standing in the road, waving and blocking his path.. The truck traveled much faster than our train and so we were able to rejoin it in the early hours of the morning, after waiting at a siding near Salisbury.

Thus ended an escapade involving rebellious fun for us, Adventure Boys. Had this occurred later, under the Ian Smith government; it would have been classified as sabotage of an essential service, under their infamous Law and Order Maintenance Act, and we would have been liable for the death penalty.

By 1959 I had been appointed as head boy. A situation arose in which a younger lad named Clive [not real name] was going berserk trying to gratuitously stab other boys with a dagger he was wielding in his hand. When I arrived on the scene it was clear that the only thing preventing serious injury or death was the agility and athleticism of his intended victims in taking avoiding action. The lad had a glazed facial expression with eyes beaming in the "vrastaag" mould. It was clear that he was deadly serious in his attempts to stab someone, anyone within range, as he chased after one boy and then another - and another.

No one is trained to deal with a deranged person, wielding a dagger, and bent on doing serious mischief to others. I felt my inadequacy very keenly. I also felt the paralyzing effects of fear as the murderous blaze in his eyes was matched by the glint of the dagger blade. However, as the head boy, I had no option but to bring the matter to safe resolution. Instinctively I feigned a punch to his head and, as he warded this off, I kicked the hand in which he had the dagger. It spun off, landing a short distance away. Other boys then waded in and soon the deranged lad was completely subdued.

About an hour later whilst sitting in a classroom I felt a "squishy" sensation in my shoe. On taking it off, my foot immediately "blew up", becoming very swollen. The shoe was full of blood. Investigation revealed that, when I kicked the dagger out of Clive's hand, it had penetrated through and through the shoe, and my foot, severing the tendon of the right "ring" toe *en route*. To this day that toe has limited function.

It was to be many years before light was cast on the reason for Clive's demented behaviour.

34. Auld Lang Syne

I was at Embakwe from 1955 to the end of 1961. Although it was badly under resourced the teaching standards were superb. Certainly the teaching staff, comprising Irish nuns and Coloured lay staff had an interesting challenge given the pupil material they had to work with. This aspect can be illustrated by recounting an essay competition that was run. Entries were published. A legendary entry, that had been entered by a lad named Etwell, was titled "The Storm". It read –

> "The lightning roared, and the thunder flashed, and
> swiped the tree from its earthly portable position - ..."

Etwell did not win but, like many others, did go on to full literacy and a successful life thereafter. Apart from being a veritable hotchpotch of ethnicity most of the children were from severely disadvantaged and underprivileged backgrounds. They were also from a range of countries in the region being Southern Rhodesia, Northern Rhodesia, Nyasaland[1] and Bechuanaland.

We had a dashing German priest named Fr. Adalbert. Apparently his family were wealthy media moguls. In 1963 Adalbert had an article published in Europe titled "God's Step Children". It was a graphic portrayal of Embakwe with dramatic emphasis on the realty of Coloured children being shoved off some 140 kms into the bush despite, and on account of, their pedigree. The newly elected Rhodesian Front government had him summarily deported.

The curriculum was British and students left on attainment of either Cambridge School Certificate of the General Certificate of Education [GCE]. It achieved a pass rate in excess of 95%. The current pass rate for South Africa [2008] as regards its Matric results is 62, 5%.

Just before leaving school Sister Mary called me in and with eyes brimming with tears she explained that, despite all efforts, they had been unable to secure a single scholarship for any of us. Overseas agencies had black-listed us on account of the fact that we were classified as White in terms of Rhodesian statutes.

The result of this state of affairs was that the only way any of us had a chance of attending University[2] was the attainment of at least three distinctions at Higher GCE level and private funding. Embakwe did not teach Higher Level GCE. White students had full access to South Africa Universities which would accept three credits at GCE level for entrance. Our Black counterparts in Empandeni and Tekwane were eligible for a range of overseas funding for tertiary education at international universities. I left school having scored

---

[1] **Nyasaland** - The Republic of Malawi is a landlocked country in southeast Africa that was formerly known as Nyasaland. It gained independence on July 6, 1964 after the Federation of Southern Rhodesia, Northern Rhodesia and Nyasaland was dissolved. . It is bordered by to the northwest, to the northeast and, which surrounds it on the east, south and west. The country is separated from Tanzania and Mozambique by Lake Malawi

[2] University College of Rhodesia only

credits in 5 subjects, including French and Latin, an upper distinction in English and a lower distinction in English Literature.

By most criteria Embakwe was under resourced and the children disadvantaged. However, I know in my heart and mind that I was greatly advantaged in terms of the fundamentals imparted. This gave me the tools and skills, even advantage, to do the best I could in later life. It was a great school staffed by wonderful human beings who selflessly gave their all for us.

My last evening at Embakwe is spent, as is the custom, with the whole boys' hostel gathered around a huge bonfire. Stories are told with the Bechuanaland boys excelling themselves in this department. John "Goldie" Stoneham and his elder brother Harry are legendary in the practice of this ancient skill. It is not surprising. Bechuanaland folk are in closest contact with the San people who many believe have been with mankind from the beginning. Their stories therefore ring with the authenticity of the story of mankind with all its mystery, mystique and magic. These stories are interspersed with songs sung in great harmony, the favourite being an Embakwe composure whose lyrics are-

```
Are you ready mafana¹ [then the refrain] ready - ready - oh'
ready
Tra ' la ' la ' la - [" refrain] ready - for the moto car
Are you heppi mafana [then the refrain] heppi - heppi - oh' heppi
Tra ' la ' la ' la - [" refrain] heppi - for the moto car
```

The song is led by a senior named Trillet "Toti" Weir, who sings the first line before the refrain, with the rest of us joining in the refrain. Tenor, soprano, contralto, falsetto, deep rumbling bass; all these voices rise and fall in resonant harmony responding to the question- *"are you ready - are you heppi - "* The song approximates that great Negro spiritual "Swing Low, Sweet Chariot", which we also sang, by Wallis Willis, in all its enrapturing splendour.

It is more than just a song; it is plaintiff call from the heart - from so many hearts - a call for hope, for deliverance ... full of emotion and pathos. The question being put to those who know homelessness is- *"are you ready - to go home - are you ready to go home on the motor car"*, in reference to the Bedford truck that will ferry us to catch the train at Plumtree tomorrow; and *"are you happy - to go home"*.

---

¹ **Mafana** – isiNdebele meaning "boys". **Heppi** – "happy" with African intonation. Ditto **"Moto"** – Motor.

The African intonation is an instinctive acknowledgment, that we brown people have Black blood in our veins.

The night air reverberates and leaves in the trees rustle with the sound of so many voices, joined in so much yearning, from so many hearts, in hope of finding home after tomorrow's truck ride - train ride - to so many cities, towns, villages, kraals in Northern Rhodesia, Nyasaland, Bechuanaland and Rhodesia itself.

35. Adventure into citizenship

Before commencing employment I spent some months at Morgan Secondary School in Salisbury with a view to securing A Levels and going on to University. During this period I was chosen to embark on a course titled "An Adventure into Citizenship", run by the Salisbury Chapter of Rotary. Senior boys, identified as having leadership potential, were selected from all schools and assembled on the "adventure".

Rotary was taking its cue from the then United Federal Party Government, the "UFP". The UFP had come to the conclusion that the Black majority could not be excluded from participation in society anymore. Society therefore needed to be reformed so as become nationally unified. A policy of "Partnership" was devised and implementation started in 1961, under which White and Black were to be schooled to live in harmony.

This was a far-sighted policy in the prevailing circumstances. Moreover it was a prudent agenda in that Black majority rule was on the horizon and it was an imperative that progression to that event involved harmonious race relations. Most importantly though, the partnership policy would ensure that, by the time Black majority rule occurred, Black people would be fully equipped to govern.

Adventure into Citizenship, run in early 1962, was my first contact with members of all other races inter-acting very much as equals. It was an all-male affair comprising about 16 boys of Black, Coloured, White and Asian ethnicity. We got on very easily during formal sessions, but tended to revert to out racial groupings during breaks. At first there was a natural reticence, and boys tended to be conservative about venturing opinions or expressing viewpoints. This soon changed as the ice broke.

By the end of the course, which lasted two weeks, a very natural mood prevailed, with boys behaving like boys, talkative, mischievous and just a little bit uncontrollable. There was a total absence of racial antipathy, let alone racial friction. What was evident though, was the fact that I was able to more easily mix with both White and Black, as compared to a Black boy getting close to a White. It was also the case that White boys asked technical questions. Black boys were concerned about opportunity, removal of barriers and racial discrimination. Throughout, a resonant assurance was given that only merit would be the criteria in future.

The adventure involved visiting centers of power and influence, such as Parliament, the Courts, Mayors office and Police headquarters, where we received detailed briefings on the workings of these entities. The idea was that we should become fully acquainted with how the State functioned, and the relationship between the public and private sector. By the time the course ended we had even attended a full blown public company general meeting, in which sparks flew, as shareholders took directors to task. It was a most instructive exercise and an undoubted success. However, once over, I am not aware that any further contact between the boys occurred.

Interaction was easy; inter-racial bonding less so.

36. Silence in Court! - and the wind of change

As my mother could not afford to keep me in school, I left, and started applying for jobs. Whilst waiting for something better I secured a job as a groundsman at a school. The workmen were somewhat bemused when I would join them in wielding a pick and shovel and push a wheelbarrow. Given my background in Sacred Heart Home and Embakwe, this was a natural operational mode. After about two months my mother took me to see a Mrs. Jessie Templeton, to have my fortune read. She used tarot cards. At the end of the session she told me, as matter of factly as one would tell the time, that within days I would find myself in a big building and then start work, after traveling to another town.

Sure enough I received a letter inviting me to Public Service HQ, where I was asked to choose which ministry, of a small range offered, that I would like to work for. There was little difficulty in making the choice. I chose Ministry of Justice, as justice was the only thing I could meaningfully relate to, in the world I had hitherto experienced, where injustice was such an ever pressing issue. That choice however meant that I would have to relocate to Bulawayo, some 400 kms away.

I reported for work at the Magistrates Courts, Tredgold Buildings, Bulawayo, on the morning of 02 July 1962, having traveled to work on a bicycle, bought for me by my mother. My job title was Clerk of Court. I was the only Coloured in the whole ministry. Also employed was Cyril Ndebele, the only Black. In Harare there was Moosa Ismail, the only Asian. All three were recruited under the UFP Government's newly implemented policy of partnership.

Soon thereafter we all attended an "induction course" in Harare. For me the objectives had been foreshadowed by the "Adventure into Citizenship", run by Rotary. However the induction course had public administration as its central theme. Already there was a subliminal message that Black folk were going to have to be accepted, as full equals and eventually as rulers, under the black/white partnership theme. Again the message that, merit was to be the criteria in future, was drummed into us at every turn.

For perhaps the first time in my life I felt that there was hope. Despite my disadvantaged background, here I was on equal terms with all others. Moreover I seemed to have an edge over my counterparts, despite the poorly resourced schools I had attended. My command of English, and ability to express myself, appeared stronger than most. So too as regards my general knowledge and comprehension. I could not have been imagined this as, during both the Adventure into Citizenship and the induction course, I was often honoured with appointment as a session leader, perhaps only on account of a perception of ethnic neutrality it must be said. However I relished the prospect of merit determining the future for me. Life felt good despite the extremely lousy remuneration.

With one exception, the White staff at Tredgold Buildings appeared to be comfortable with my arrival. I was treated with civility and good grace, particularly by the female staff. The exception was a man named Rodney, burly and ruddy faced, who had an unfortunate addiction of digging his fingers, deep and long, between the cheeks of his buttocks as he sullenly attended to the public at the counter. At first I thought I might be imagining the antipathy. I became more certain when he posted me to work in the cellar, tidying up Court records stored there. The cellar was an underground dungeon. I spent over a month tidying up the records. As it turned out, it proved extremely interesting, as I perused old records of famous trials, many of which had photos of the most gruesome murders. A picture, that I have not forgotten, was one showing a beautiful young Black lady who had been murdered by her jealous paramour. He had cut her stomach open. Her intestines formed an incredibly large gruesome heap on her stomach, in stark contrast to the serenity of her face. Another unforgettable picture was of a very good looking sixteen-year-old White lad. In his left temple was a small neat hole to which an arrow pointed with a note "Entry Point of Point 22 Caliber Bullet". Both these pictures filled me with a deep sense of sadness that has never left me.

Rodney also spends a good part of the day phoning around. Typically he phones Johannesburg airport, and speaks to anyone available, enquiring on the arrival of say the British Lions rugby team. Then he phones a porter at the hotel the team is booked into and pursues more small talk. In this way he runs up a very considerable phone bill for the office. At month end a senior magistrate, nick-named *"Tapping Tommy"*, as he is in the habit of typing the evidence as he hears it in Court, comes round to reconcile the phone bill with the staff. Private calls above a certain limit are meant to be paid for. Rodney admits to having made just one international call and unashamedly denies the rest. I was gob-smacked.

He cures me of all doubts, regarding his antipathy towards me, when he picks on me because I will not exchange my Saturday off day with his. The Courts maintain only a skeleton staff presence on Saturdays, so we take turns being at work. *"Look Greenland - I have had it with you - you don't seem to understand that when I say we are swapping - we are swapping"* he bellows at me. When I reply that I am not prepared to swap, he bellows on and concludes *" - perhaps you will understand if you are fucked up - ?"* I walk right up to him, stand in his face and tell him what I had heard my brother Frank say to the police officer - *"If you think you can do that Mister - you are going to have to prove it...!"*

All bullies are cowards at heart. They cannot take being taken on fair and square. To ratchet things up for him I go to the door, close it, lock it and then march back. This is more of an act on my part rather than a commitment to violence. I am messing with his mind. Just then there is a loud knock on the door. Rodney rushes off, to open it, and leaves without greeting Mrs. McMullin, a vivacious happily married Court stenographer, who has come to deliver cakes as it is someone's birthday. *"What's up with him?"* she asks quizzically. *"I think someone was just about to stamp on his foot"* I reply in half-truth. Mrs. McMullin senses that there is a problem, sits me down and I have my first counseling session. *"Don't worry"* she says with a twinkle in bright green eyes *"we all know how he is"*. She is to remain a good friend for the rest of the years I spend in the Bulawayo Courts. Rodney never again gives me trouble and later becomes quite pleasant.

My time is divided up with paper pushing, such as processing summonses, and attending Court as clerk to the presiding magistrate. I knock loudly on the door of the Court, shout *"Silence in Court"*, let the magistrate in, and then take my place in front of him, facing the battery of lawyers and the general public behind them. Thereafter, it is my job to swear in witnesses and deal with any exhibits produced.

What strikes me is how fiercely lawyers fight, during a session, only to be best of buddies, sharing a smoke at intervals. This culture of *"agree, disagree, agree to disagree, in a climate of mutual respect..."* indelibly infuses itself into my psyche. It is at this time that I make the acquaintance of two soon to be famous lawyers, Aubrey Hewitt and Leo Baron, who were then partners in the same law firm.

Baron went on to become the equivalent of what George Bizos was to become to South Africa, in his routine courageous defense of Black people charged under the infamous security legislation.

He also joined Joshua Nkomo's ZAPU[1] during the struggle for liberation. Pathos is to intervene. Using a SAM-7 Soviet made missile ZAPU shoots down a second Viscount civilian passenger plane on 12 February 1979. Aubrey Hewitt is on board. There are no survivors.

Life seemed good for a short while, only to be spoilt by the rumblings of the racist right. The Rhodesian Front Party, "the RF", is now regaling the White electorate with the language of fear. The theme is that the communist inspired UFP government is selling White folk down the drain and that, if they are not stopped, the Blacks will be taking over their land, their houses, their jobs. The subliminal message is that the takeover will include wives and daughters.

The leverage the RF has is that the UFP government has been incrementally dismantling racial discrimination. So cinemas, public parks, hospitals and schools have been de-segregated. To the RF this is the beginning of the end. The RF and its followers have paid scant attention to the speech by the British Prime Minister, Sir Harold Macmillan, to the parliament of South Africa on 3 February 1960, in which he voiced the view of the free world that –

> "the wind of change is blowing through this continent. Whether we like it or not, this growth of national consciousness is a political fact."

General elections are held in November 1962. Despite the entreaties and wise counsel of leaders of great stature, such as Sir Garfield Todd[2], and the best efforts of the UFP to convince the White electorate that partnership is the

---

[1] **The Zimbabwe African People's Union** is a once militant organization and political party that fought for the national liberation of Zimbabwe from its founding in 1961 until it merged with the Zimbabwe African National Union in December 1987

[2] **See "Sir Garfield Todd and the Making of Zimbabwe" by Ruth Weiss**

only sane route, the UFP suffers a crushing defeat and the RF government comes to power.

I am an electoral officer. It is so disheartening counting the votes. It is so difficult to reconcile my recent life experience with what I am now seeing. White people have seemed sensible, fair minded and appreciative of the need to have an all-equal society. It is White people who gave up their Xmas day to come to our orphanage and give us a Xmas, never to be forgotten. How could they vote for a party espousing politics of hate and division? A bitter sense of deep betrayal infuses me, especially as I stand on the balcony on which the results of the constituency we have managed is announced and I see White folk crying tears of joy at the result.

I am sickened for its madness, for its stupidity, for its racist content. I am once again back on the roadside at Sacred Heart Home, on day of my arrival looking down broken-heartedly; only this time it is not a stone in the road, but a sea of White faces, mad White faces that I see. It is impossible to reconcile these people with the members of the Toc H Society that gave us our first Xmas all those years ago. In my mind the "adventure into citizenship", and all the counseling on a new spirit of "partnership", fade into a vomitus abyss.

So starts an incredibly naïve, irresponsible and foolish attempt by the White folk of Rhodesia to thwart the "wind of change". Under the RF government there will be no other non-white recruit into the civil service (Courts) for the next 15 years, until the appointment of Ernest Tsomondo, as a magistrate in 1979.

In the result I am to be guaranteed a place in history.

---

37. Man is but born to serve

In June 1963 I am conscripted into the Rhodesian army, to perform four and half months of initial compulsory military training at Llewellyn Barracks, for later part time service in the Territorial Army.

The army was not racially integrated and Coloureds were confined to a supply and transport unit. Blacks were not conscripted but could volunteer for service in the regular army in which they could never be officers. Coloureds could not. So the regular army was made up of White and Black units; but no Coloureds and Asians. The territorial forces were made up of White part time forces and a Coloured/Asian part time supply and transport unit; but no Blacks. Woman were simply not considered for uniformed service. The composition of the army therefore showed in microcosm the *"civilization"* and *"western standards"* that the RF government was seeking to preserve. It was on such premise that Blacks, Coloureds and Asians were being denied equality. It was this brand of *"civilization"* that Ian Smith espouses as having been betrayed in his book "The Great Betrayal: Memoirs of Ian Douglas Smith[1]".

As drafting into the territorial army occurred every four and half months, there was a cycle in terms of which, at any given period, forces in training comprised a platoon that was about to complete its period of training, referred to as *"seniors";* those who were in mid-training phase, referred to as *"juniors";* and new recruits referred to as *"rebels".* After reporting to the Drill Hall in Bulawayo, where I met other conscripts, we were conveyed to Llewellyn Barracks. I quite looked forward to being a soldier. Most young boys relish the thought of becoming proficient in gun usage. At age 19, I was no different, and imagined that I would become some kind of heroic soldier.

All positive thoughts are rudely dashed as we disembark at Llewellyn. The truck is surrounded by a screaming mob of Coloured soldiers. *"Tuff shit - tuff shit rebel..."* is the chant I hear all around us, loud and vindictive. It is difficult to comprehend the behaviour of these people. Why the anger? Why the language, which soon gets much worse -" - *tuff shit rebel - smelling of puss - smelling of puss".* *"Puss"* - also spelt as *"poes",* in this context, is a vulgar synonym of *"vagina".* We are soon subjected to a process that supposedly rids us of the offensive smell. Stripped naked, we are made to take a cold shower and then high-step naked around the barracks to dry off, all the while shouting -*"I am a puss - I am a cunt..."* and accompanied by the screaming mob. This incredible welcome ends abruptly, and all is quiet, after the third cold shower. So ends our first day initiation. Apparently we no longer smell of puss, but we are still rebels, and fair game for seniors and, to a lesser extent, the juniors.

Our instructors were exclusively British and were very good at turning us into soldiers. For me the military aspects of my stay at Llewellyn represented an exciting and rewarding learning curve. Driving trucks, route marches, firing weapons, drill sequences and throwing grenades were all on the menu of a range of exciting competences acquired.

The army also followed through on what I had already learnt from my Roman Catholic tutors. Discipline is an essential attribute. It is also the cornerstone of a good army. It is an attribute that should be at the heart of all human endeavour. Even in the World Cup, being played out as I type these words, the most disciplined teams are doing the best. I did well in all departments,

---

[1] http://www.rhodesia.nl/betrayal.htm

eventually made Lance Corporal Greenland N C 37226T, and was one of only two Coloureds then known to have been recommended for officer training at end of training period assessment. The other was Churchill Martin.

An amusing aspect was that I had two cousins in my platoon, identical twin brothers, Esau and Jacob Williams, half brothers to my Aunt Moira's husband. Misdemeanors and failures in the army results in a soldier being charged and sentenced to "jankers". A misdemeanor often involved being "manky". You were screamed at and charged for being "manky" if so much as a hair was found on your bedroll. If on "jankers" you were required to report, on the hour, from 5 pm until 10pm to the guardhouse, where you would be put through various punishment routines by the regimental police. Whenever one of the twins was on "jankers" the brothers would alternate reporting to the guardhouse and the regimental police would be none the wiser not being able to differentiate between identical twins.

38. And the meek must endure

Whilst the official military training was excellent, under British trained instructors, there was much that was really bad.

Firstly there was the racial segregation. We were condemned to being no more than drivers, with some generic weapons and other military training thrown in. Symptomatic of the absurdity of the situation was that, in order to have a swim, we had to drive all the way to Bulawayo, some 40 kilometers away to access a pool in the Coloured suburb of Barham Green.

Secondly there was almost daily victimization of soldier on soldier. Rebels were subjected to a variety of practices, ranging in character from humiliating, to downright depraved. For instance, a rebel would be required to present at the bedside of a senior at 6am, and crow like a rooster to wake him up. There were even instances of a rebel having to then carry the penis of a senior, as he walked to have his morning pee. So some mornings were greeted by a truly obscene procession, as rebels performed this ritual. Other humiliations involved *"jacking up"* uniform items, such as boots and belts, of seniors and washing their meal trays.

There would be concerts, on Sunday afternoons, with adjoining tables set up as a stage. A rebel would be presented with a broom and told to chat up *"the chick"*, convince her until she complied with hot *"smooching"* on his part. So the broom was chatted up, hugged and kissed to the cheers of the audience. Some were made to push matchsticks with their noses across the floor. It was mostly gratuitous, humiliating and degrading.

To all this I stubbornly refused to cooperate, apart from the odd polishing of the brass buckle on the belt of a senior in an attempt to compromise. At first there were three of us in my platoon that stood our ground. Of course those in power will always pressurize the rest to be pliant and cowed. So, within a couple of weeks there were just two, as pressure was brought to bear. Peter Shadreck, known as *"Shuren"* from Embakwe days, was the other. The senior corporal would exact revenge for our stubbornness, on the whole of our platoon on the parade ground, where rank was king. We would be drilled to exhaustion. We would be sent running to collect leaves from a far off tree and, on our return, told that we had stolen government property and sent back to replace the leaves.

Then I was all alone. There was one senior I really disliked. To me he fitted my grandmother's description of a bad person. In particular he was ugly [of disposition] and very stupid. He actually was not stupid but, as a person whose sin is pride, it was my perception given the bad situation. So I descended to the perceived level of my enemy and indulged in shameful conduct.

I took his meal tray off him, offering to clean it for him. He was delighted that I had apparently capitulated at last. In the toilet I retrieved what we referred to as *"a floater"*, which I subdued with a stick into his tray. Human faeces shrinks when dry. After drying in the sun, my handiwork was represented by black spots not readily detectable, especially as I returned his tray to him just as he was about to have it filled in the mess. The bad news was conveyed to him once he was tucking in.

In the subsequent fall-out even my own platoon members deserted me, by pulling their beds away from mine, leaving me physically and psychologically isolated. All the seniors created an awful intimidatory din by running sticks along the outside of our corrugated iron barrack room walls and screaming *"tuff shit rebel"*. The *"r-r-r-r-r-r-r-r"* sound, that the running of their sticks produced, could be likened to the sound that a Zulu impi would make by tapping theirs shields before battle. It was terrifying, especially when my last platoon ally remarked - *"that they will kill you - and you know the army - they will cover it up"*. I was cornered and isolated with a mad mob waiting to pounce.

A cornered rat is dangerous we are told. Grabbing my Sten gun, in wild desperation, I fixed the bayonet and charge to the seniors barrack room. I do not have a fixed plan in mind, just an idea in my panic-stricken mind. They are momentarily stunned, at this intrusion, as a rebel never enters the senior barrack room. Before they can recover I grab their corporal, a weasley, diminutive creature, and announce in colourful language, that this little rat had been to town and falsely boasted to people, my girlfriend included, that I had been washing his underpants. Holding him up against the wall, I threaten that it is now going to me or him.

It is an exhibitive, instinctive show of force, often involved in situations of self-preservation in the animal world. Thankfully it works. Embarrassed by this sensational but true revelation, my victim hesitates for long enough in response, to lose the momentum of the situation. First one, than more of his platoon turn on him; expressing disgust as to how he could have done such a thing especially as he has really let them down by not having *"tamed"* this cheeky rebel as they had been demanding. In military terms I have succeeded in creating a diversion, and the attentions of my enemies are now elsewhere. Having scored the point I leave amidst somewhat subdued howls that- *" - you are going to see rebel - tuff shit for you"*.

My platoon goes through hell, on the parade ground the next, day as the Corporal starts to exact revenge, in compliance with the wishes of his men. Just as I am about to crack two things happen. Lieutenant Leigh, our Deputy Commanding Officer, is so impressed with my map reading skills that he assigns me to lecture a platoon of White soldiers. This is unprecedented, and such a remarkable thing, given the racial situation, that it must have made my enemies see themselves at risk. In addition a guitarist is needed for a band being assembled for an army concert. Being a confirmed Rock n' Roller, from Embakwe days, I have an electric guitar. Suddenly I am being swamped by White soldiers and senior officers who want to hear me play. I get into the band, and am then excused duties for band practice.

The army is favouring me. A soldier does not mess with the army; or a friend of the army. I have immunity. I now have a new organically induced rank of "privileged private". The Corporal and gang perceive that the game is up and embark on a strategy involving more bark than bite, about the issue of taming me, until they pass out of training soon thereafter.

The pressure of military environment brings out both the worst and the best in people. Part of our entertainment was to engage in "pillow fights". Despite the name, this was not a game for the faint hearted as the "pillows" were canvass kit bags filled with weighty objects, even half-bricks, and one could easily be knocked quite senseless. In these fights Thomas Zerf, carrying the nickname of "Peezway", from Embakwe, quite easily emerged as the soldier I would have most relied on in actual combat. Despite his small stature he was a lion in battle. It is not surprising that, in later life, he joined the liberation war and served with the ZIPRA forces.

I received promotion to Lance Corporal, in which capacity I then served as joint leader of our platoon. The other was Peter Shadreck. We put a stop to the abuse of rebels, except for harmless initiation, such as giving them a rough truck ride on arrival and mundane skivvying. One day, on my return from a day pass, I discovered a huge bunch of flowers in my room. It was from all the Indian members of the unit, as a token of appreciation for my ending victimization, which they were traditionally subjected to as an ethnic minority. Receiving flowers was completely out of keeping with the norms I was accustomed to. In my macho mind I associated flowers with everything feminine, *"sissy stuff"*, not soldiering. However I was immensely surprised to find that it touched me deeply. It still does.

Thank you, Imtias Ranchod and Dudubhai Gandabhai. My appreciation received even greater impetus, when I found that they had deposited a crate of beer under my bed.

As said, the situation also brought out the worst. Notable was the fact that those who were most spineless, pliant and crybabies during our rebel phase, turned out to be the biggest bullyboys once they graduated to become seniors. As said, bullies are cowards at heart. After I passed out one such member, named Farry [name altered], took despotism to such a level as to involve recruits being made to spit and polish their testicles. There was an enquiry and he was sentenced to serve time in military prison. I was invited to military HQ and interviewed by a Lieutenant about the situation.

When he asked why I had apparently been one of very few to resist, and where had I got the courage from, I replied to the following effect, after some thought, not mentioning that at school I was diagnosed as suffering from pride or that my mother thought I was *"chicken-hearted"*-

```
"I was not brave - not at all ... I was never so terrified in
my life - but the thing is that I just cannot - I just cannot
suck someone's dick - I just cannot - and when you see a person
doing this in films because there is a gun to his head - well,
they would have to shoot me - not because I am brave - but
because I cannot - some people can - but I just cannot - bravery
is not involved - it must have something to do with those
German and Irish nuns - programming by them when I was with
them as a child."
```

I was not to know then how this inability to be pliant and cooperative in the face of nonsense would affect my fortunes in later life.

---

39. A double whammy - and the innocent 60s

After a rousing passing out parade I am back in "Civvy Street" but, this time, I am armed also with a heavy vehicle driver's license. Upon attending the local cinema house I see the most wonderful advertisement inviting immigration to Queensland, Australia. Oz desperately needs immigrants, with heavy vehicle driver's licenses in particular. Queensland is presented as an incredibly beautiful, unspoilt, rugged land of opportunity.

Given the appalling turn Rhodesia has taken, with an avowedly racist government in power, I am passionately interested. With a heart, brimming with faith and confidence, I report to the office at the Australian embassy whose address appeared in the advert. As I enter a White man looks up from behind his counter, leaves the two White persons he is attending to and facing me, bawls out - *"We don't want no kaffirs in Australia"*. He then shoos me out. In this conversation, my brown skin has done the talking for me, and racist xenophobia has replied loud and clear.

When I get back to the office a letter is waiting for me. It is from Rhodesia Railways offering me a job as a fireman. I have a real dilemma. The starting salary for a fireman is around £100 per month, easily topping £150 with overtime. As a clerk of Court I make a measly £35 per month. It is massive difference. All the Coloured lads, working as firemen, are driving brand new cars and are flush with cash. I ride a bicycle and I am always skint. My schooldays sweetheart has lost interest in me, remarking on the fact that I ride a bicycle. In my mind I see myself arriving at her house, in a brand new car, and the joy in her face as she falls back into my arms.

Just then the phone rings. It is her. *"Vavie - "* she says, and after a long pause - *"I am pregnant – from..."* and names her lover. It is shattering news. Leaving the office, I walk two blocks to St Mary's Cathedral, where I was baptized so many years ago, and kneel in confused prayer in front of the statue of Our Lady, an exact replica of the one I first saw in Sacred Heart Home as a child. That night I decide to stay in the Courts. The next day I enroll with Rapid Results Correspondence College for certification in Rhodesian Civil Service Law.

From 1963 until 1965 I work as a clerk of Court in the magistrates Courts of Bulawayo and Salisbury. The country is regressing politically under the RF government and its insistence on racial inequality. This however does not stop a wonderful cameo played out on a Saturday afternoon in Bulawayo. In 1963 I bought myself a motor cycle, British made Matchless 500cc, souped up with a G80CS over square engine. Other Coloured lads had faster bikes, with the fastest being the Triumph Bonneville T120 otherwise known as the "Bonnie". Our bikes put us on equal terms with White youngsters and their bikes. Number plates are stripped off or disguised. So we all meet outside the Princess cinema, making a real din, roaring up and down the street on our bikes to the cheers and amusement of the young Rock n' Rollers gathered to watch films like "Bill Haley and the Comets" and "Jailhouse Rock". It is all macho and testosterone driven as we *"burn each other off"* in order to impress. Attire includes leather lumber jackets with "Slow Down to 90" typically emblazoned on the back.

The police dutifully arrive on their polished BSA Golden Flash machines. These are very good looking bikes, but the slowest of the lot. A ritual then ensues in which, to cheers from the crowd, the police chase us. They never catch anyone and, I dare say, never expect to. The police are obliged to put on a show of force by appearing to be attempting to arrest us. This bike party ends with a race to Esigodini, some 50 kms away, after the film show. Apart from one instance, we Coloureds always win. On one occasion a White girl leaves the hippie sub-group of the crowd, jumps onto my bike, and rides pillion for the race. Right there a line was crossed. There was a just perceptible drop and change in the tone and volume of human discourse on the fringes of the event; nothing more. On our return she jumps over and rejoins her kind. We have not spoken once.

We feel good. We are faster, more macho, better bike riders than the Whites. In this way the status quo was challenged and the lie given to its claims. It's what we felt.

One evening I go to the Waverley Bar for Coloureds in Bulawayo, having heard that there is to be a fight between two sets of brothers. My intelligence proves correct, and a stage is reached where the brothers square off, two against two. It is an awful business as fists fly and blood flows freely. That sweet-sour smell of violence hangs thick in the air and permeates everything. I am so glad not to be involved.

It is just then that the police arrive. Without warning White police officers burst through the doors and start laying into all and sundry with wooden batons. Being young, fit and quick witted, I manage to find an opening and escape through a window, only to find another officer standing guard outside. As he attempts to grab me I feign a punch at his face. When he raises his arm to block the punch, I aim a kick at his knee, which lands. Then I run for all I am worth. At first I am conscious that the officer is chasing, but it is soon apparent that he is not going to catch me, and I lose sight of him. Upon reaching the Town Hall, I reduce my run to a slow trot and decide to make my way through the lawn covered grounds. In my mind I am thankful to have escaped the clutches of the police whose actions were to gratuitously contribute to violence instead of redressing it. The feeling of relief is accompanied by smug satisfaction at how I had dealt with the situation.

Pride comes before a fall. This feeling of invincibility is comprehensively ended when I am hit from behind, with such force, as to be flattened, onto my face, in but an instant. My first reaction is to think that I have been hit by a train; such is force with which I have been flattened. Just as I start to realize that this could not be so I hear, feel, sense and smell the presence of a dog. It is a police Alsatian, with my upper arm firmly in its jaw. In such situations everything goes into slow motion. My mind is racing. I feel terribly afraid. But I also feel anger, terribly angry, resentful at what has happened; and what is happening to me. It is all very hurtful and demeaning - relentless victimization.

In an instant I know what to do - and I do it. Turning I grab the one leg of the dog and then, turning some more, I quickly maneuver myself so as to be somewhat astride the animal which, in accordance with its training, concentrates on maintaining its grip on my upper arm. Fortunately the leather jacket I am wearing prevents serious injury. Hanging on to my arm is a mistake on its part; as I am able to get my other arm around its body and then grab its other leg.

From that moment the pendulum is now swinging in my favour. In accordance with stories I had heard from my Adventure boy friends, Mark and Troll, I proceed to pull the animal's legs apart. Apparently this is real bad for a dog. It is not as easy as my friends had predicted, because the animal wriggles and squirms. However it's undoing is that it will not relinquish its grip on my arm. As I pull I feel a need to do something more, something extraordinary. It strikes me that Mark would have been thrilled in endorsement of such an act on the part of an Adventure boy. I sink my teeth into the ear of the dog and bite as hard as I can. In an instant it is over, as the effects of having its legs parted, and being bitten, take effect. It lets go and starts half crawling in circles yowling terribly in pain and agony. The policeman arrives as I start to amble away. He goes to his dog and I hear him talking to it in tones of extreme concern.

Soon I am at another pub. As I enter I am met by Nicholas Scott, now regarded as my father. It takes him but an instant to notice that something is wrong and, putting his arm around me, he expresses his concern and sits me down enquiring about the traces of blood in the region of my mouth. I feel good to be with this man. He makes me feel safe again.

Much later we are joined by another man, whose company I really appreciate, as he insists on buying every round of drinks. Moving his stool closer to me we start developing a spirit of camaraderie, with him slapping me on the thigh. It is then that Scott insists that I accompany him to the toilet block. Once there he turns to me and quite angrily says - *"what is wrong with you - what is wrong with you my son"?* He has to repeat the question several times, when I look at him in bemusement, not at all knowing what he is getting at. He is referring to the man with whom I am bonding at the bar. His deft slapping of my thigh has caught the attention of Scott, and alarm bells have gone off. It is then that he tells me, with bar room explicity, using the "F" and "A" words, that I need to understand that I am in grave danger of experiencing anal penetration by a penis.

I am shocked to the core. It is the first time in my life that I become aware of homosexuality. I am 20 years of age. Such a thing has never crossed my mind. In all the years at Sacred Heart Home, Embakwe School, with my granny, my brothers - not once has the issue of man-to-man sex even been mooted.

I am astounded and disbelieving. Certainly at school there were one or two boys who were teased as being "girlish" and were referred to as *"moffies¹"*. We have a couple of these types in our community in Bulawayo. There is a delightful character by the name of Bassy Levendale. There is also a young lad called Honey West and another nick-named Bishy-Wishy. However to my mind no one even imagined homosexuality. However Scott is serious, and since I instinctively love and trust this man, who never uses crude language, I believe him. It is only much later that this refinement of my sex education is extended to the issue of lesbianism - and that also comes as a huge shock.

It is also then that it is revealed that the dagger wielding lad, Clive,² who, was responsible for severing the tendon of my right "ring toe" at school, is now living with a White man *"as his wife"*. The reason why he had gone berserk on that afternoon at school had everything to do with him being unable to come to terms with his sexuality, in an environment that was ignorant and undoubtedly completely intolerant of such orientation.

The lad had been acting out inner psychological pain and suffering on realizing what terrible misfit he was in this world at that time.

40. An Afrikaner lady - and a sangoma

In Salisbury I was one of only two males in the office. Our boss was a wonderful lady named Mrs. Helen, who spoilt me rotten, but was somewhat less generous to the female staff. There was an over 80 year old lady, Mrs. Gray, who was a fantastic typist, and came in on a casual work basis. She loved me; not for my good looks and charm, but because I had a motor bike. So I would often take her for a ride into the countryside on a weekend. This

---

¹ **Moffie** – is a South African term for a gay man
² See towards end of Chapter 33

must have bemused many road users at the time; a young man with a deliriously happy, mature pillion passenger. As helmets were not compulsory at the time, they were hardly worn, and we would have been recognizable for what we were. We made quite a sight for the times we lived in - a young Coloured man riding a bike with a venerable White lady as pillion.

Also in the office was an attractive young lady named Louise Odendaal. She was of pure Afrikaner stock having just arrived from Vereeniging, a real Afrikaner stronghold in South Africa. It soon became clear that Louise was a naturally warm and loving person, and by no means racist. She must have been suffering some inner tensions on account of her background. This made her so much more curious about me, as the first Coloured she had ever associated with, and on equal terms at that. We became very close, but not romantic, with consummation of our relationship occurring at our Xmas function, when we danced together. She loved ballroom or *"langarm*[1]*"* as she called it and, of course, Embakwe had schooled me well on this score. When she returned to work, after her Xmas break, she told us that she had announced at her family's Xmas dinner - *"Papa - I danced with a Coloured "*. The response was such a deathly hush that she knew never to mention the matter again.

She belonged to the Dutch Reform Church, which I would refer to as *"the Much Deformed Church"*, in religious arguments we engaged in. Regrettably we lost Mrs. Gray who passed away. Soon afterwards I met a lawyer who wanted to know what I had done to Mrs. Gray. Expressing surprise I assured him that the good lady loved me as a biking soul mate. *"Well - "* he said revealingly *"your bike soul mate came in and disinherited you of a legacy she had bequeathed"*. I was confused and shocked, especially as I had not been aware of the legacy. Later Mrs. Helen confirmed that Mrs. Gray, a staunch Catholic, had been very upset with me after overhearing me concede to Louise, in argument, that indeed there had been some bad Popes in Roman Catholic Church history, who may even have fathered illegitimate children. What rotten luck! I never forgave Louise for having cost me a small fortune. It would have been better if she had been racist and not spoken to me. As *"the other"* you just cannot win, it would seem!

One morning a Black lady came to see me. She had a 11 year old Coloured girl in tow. She explained, through an interpreter, that the girl was her daughter, conceived before wedlock, but whom her dear husband had accepted without rancor. Their problem was simply practical. As a Coloured, whom she referred to as *mulungu* (White), their daughter was entitled to

---

[1] **Langarm** – pronounced with flattened a's is Afrikaans for "ballroom".

better things, not the life they led in the tribal trust land. They could not afford these *"better things"*. Could the girl's father be contacted and made to assume responsibility for his child.

With simplicity that usually underpins truth, she explained that conception had occurred when she had visited a shop owned by a certain Greek man. While she was bending over, browsing through objects that had caught her interest, he had grabbed her from behind, lifted her dress, with sexual intercourse then occurring with no resistance on her part. She had never returned to the shop or confronted him with the fruitful product of this brief and apparently intensely passionate encounter. When the issue of possibly laying a charge of rape was mooted she became very perturbed and tried to leave. To her what had happened was no more than a privilege that had accrued to the man on account of his ethnicity.

In somewhat bemusement I opened a paternity suit against the Greek man. He later arrived, accompanied by a lawyer, in a state of extreme agitation at the allegations, waving his arms around in wild indignation. I fully sympathized with him. The story advanced by the mother of the child sounded - well - shall we say - fanciful. The case was set down for hearing.

He arrived an hour earlier without his lawyer. He saw the child for the first time. As he approached, the child snuggled up closer to her mother sitting beside her. He stopped just a pace away from mother and child, his eyes riveted on the bright eyed little girl, now slightly cowering in posture, averting her eyes. No words were spoken. After what seemed like an eternity, he turned and left in a great hurry.

A few minutes before the hearing he returned. There was great commotion. As his lawyer tried to talk to him he was brushed aside. Approaching mother and child again he held out his arms. "*My child - my child - you are such a beautiful girl - you have touched my heart...*" he said in tones tinged with the heartfelt tenderness that only people of Mediterranean ethnicity can muster.

The child hesitated but her mother gently pushed her forward. A tearful father and daughter embraced as the first step in a long overdue journey. Two workers came forward carrying a brand new Singer sewing machine. "*Thees is forr you*", he said to the mother, "*thank you forr looking after my child - you have done well*". Dismissing his lawyer, he turned to his daughter and said, with passionate intonation - "*I am going to poot you in Convent School* (one of the best private schools), *you maast not be like me - and no speek eengleesh - but first we go shopping*". They left, with father and daughter leading, hand in hand. A more moving scene I have never witnessed in my life.

It was at about this time that Salisbury was visited by a renowned sangoma apparently all the way from Malawi. He set up a tented surgery on the grounds of Rufaro Stadium. Aunt Moira pleaded with me to take her for a consultation as no one else would. When we arrived there was a very long queue of persons of all races, though mostly Black. Aunt Moira eventually has her consultation and, on emerging, insists that I have one too.

I try to decline, protesting that it is a lot of money at £5 a consultation. I take home about £40 per month. She insists saying that she will pay for me. I do not have to queue, as she convinces the receptionist that she had intended all along that I have a consultation. The receptionist gives me instructions, telling me to take off my shoes, enter the inner room, via a reed curtain, turn to my left and then sit down to face the sangoma.

I follow her instructions and enter the inner sanctum which is festooned with the bric-a-brac associated with persons plying their trade in the spirit, occult and herbalist world. There are gourds, masks, clumps of plant material, pots of herbs and other artifacts everywhere. I am not in a doctor's surgery. I am in a den of wizardry. As I turn to face the sangoma I notice that he has a white enamel dish, containing clear water, on his right hand side. On his left hand side he has a live tortoise.

The tortoise suddenly spins onto its back.

The sangoma jerks his head up to look at me and, with his left hand, pushes me firmly in the mid-drift, so as to indicate that I remain standing. With his other hand he takes the tortoise and places it next to the enamel dish facing me. It turns to face the dish and stops. He bends over and the dish and the tortoise are now concealed from my view by his back. There he remains perfectly still for what seems a long time with his left hand still in my mid-drift.

Suddenly he jumps up, face alight with expression, and exclaims - *"Do not sit - no, no - do not sit..."* and then switches to a dialect, which I do not understand, seemingly addressing someone in a tone of incantation. I have seen and heard this before when my Aunt Mamquebu, Uncle Willie's wife, invoked the ancestral spirits except with her I was able to understand some of it. Then he fixes his eyes on me and says excitedly - *"Today is a great day for me - a very great day - I am so happy - I am so honoured to be in the presence of so great a spirit - the spirit of a man who was the greatest sangoma at that time - the time of your birth - when he came to know you - his spirit is with you - he will be with you..."* I have little doubt that something extraordinary is taking place as I feel the hairs on my skin pricking up. The man has surely picked up my link to Fuyane, the renowned sangoma who "fixed" me up at birth in the "lungisa" ritual. But how????

- 127 -

He goes on to counsel me. It is not all that good news. All my life I will be in the public eye - but will have to face evil - but I will be protected - if I do not meet evil with evil. The good news is that I will have a long life. There is so much power in the voice he speaks in. The last time I have felt something similar was in 1958, at my Confirmation[1] in the Catholic Church, when the great Bishop Adolph Schmidt[2] said *"Pax Tecum"* and smacked me on the cheek symbolically. He embraces me tightly and, after reverting to the unknown dialect for a short while, he bids me farewell again repeating that it is the happiest day of his life. The receptionist is instructed to refund the fee of £5.

When I re-join Aunt Moira she wants to know how it went and why the refund? I am unable to say anything for a long time as I am in a state of deep astonishment. Then I say to her - *"Do you know that Fuyane is with me?"* She looks at me intently and quizzically. Then she asks -*"Who is Fuyane?"* She knows nothing about Fuyane. The sangoma was from out of the country and could never have known Fuyane either.

I am astonished to the core as to what has occurred. How right was this man to be proved - about me being in the public eye and ... ...

---

41. Summary justice

One morning I give my girl friend a lift to work on my motor bike. She works at the telephone exchange, which is right next to the High Court, separated only by a sanitary lane. Riding a bike feels good, especially when I open the throttle, in timed sequence, so as to produce a throaty roar of power.

To others, however, this is noise, very unwelcome noise. Before I can pull off I feel a hand on my shoulder. There is a burly police officer, standing straight, stern faced and glaring at me. *"You are required to come with me at once"* he says in a commanding voice. He points to a spot and says -*"You can park you machine right there"*. When I park the machine he barks at me - *"Not there - but there!"* pointing to a spot a foot or so from where I have parked my bike. My heart is sinking fast. I am in trouble, what trouble, how

---

[1] **Confirmation** – a formal step in the religious life of a Roman Catholic where " soldier of Christ" status is conferred.

[2] **Rhodesian Selous Scouts** claimed a member of Nkomo's group, Albert Sumne Ncube, killed Bishop Adolph Schmitt, Father Possenti Weggarten and Sister Maria Francis, on a road near Lupane on December 5, 1976. ZAPU claimed that the Selous Scouts were responsible

much trouble - ? Very big trouble it would appear when he says – *"I am the Sergeant at Arms and the Chief Justice has ordered that you be brought to Court this minute - so move it!"*

As a clerk of Court I am well aware of the existence of the Chief Justice. Whenever a letter arrived from a judge querying the verdict or sentence of a magistrate everything stops as it is attended to. Magistrates live in constant trepidation of judges. Judges are like some up-stairs gods who can strike at any time. Now I am being hauled before the Chief Justice, the chief of the cabal of the most feared. He is the one always referred to in the most reverential tones.

I am led, like so many prisoners that I have seen in the Courts before, into "A" Court of the High Court. It is my first time to be in a High Court. It is large, many times as large as any magistrate's Court that I have ever been in, and it is completely empanelled in formed wood, embellished with carvings and patterns. It is imposing and in my circumstances, intimidating to the core.

Apprehension turns to fear, as I see men dressed all in black flowing robes. They glare at me, their eyes conveying condemnation to the man. The sergeant instructs me to stand at a spot and, putting his hand on my shoulder, says gruffly -*"Face the judge"*, indicating with his hand where I should face. Confused and frightened, I take in the scene in front of me. High above me sits a man, so imposing in a tingy white wig and flowing red and black robes. I realize that he is the Chief Justice; the man most respected and feared by all of those involved with law. The voice of Sir Hugh Beadle cuts through the air and hits me like a whiplash –

Chief Justice: Young man you have disturbed the proceedings of this Court and frustrated the administration of justice with your hooligan behaviour. What have you got to say for yourself?

Me: My worship –

Chief Justice: You do not worship me ... [he snaps] - do you understand?

Sergeant: Address the judge as "My Lord" ["Worship" refers to magistrates]

Me: Yes My Lord [my voice is hoarse] I am sorry

Chief Justice: What are you sorry for?

Me: For - for - having disturbed the proceedings

Chief Justice: You are going to even more sorry - [my heart sinks] - a lot more sorry - [it sinks lower, I am doomed] - if ever I see you again in this Court - [it skips a beat] - do you understand?

Me: Yes - yes - yes –

Chief Justice: Yes what - yes what?

Me: I understand - yes My Lord - I understand - I am sorry - and will never do it again - My Lord [I whimper pitifully]

Chief Justice: Sergeant - take him away - and I hope to never again see him in my Court!

Phew! It is over. I am free. I am not going to the gallows. I have been spared. It seems miraculous. I push my bike a hundred and fifty meters out of the sanitary lane, start it and tootle away, slowly and sedately.

My introduction to the inside of a High Court has been a baptism of fire. Even my first day at Embakwe was not so bad. The trepidation I feel lingers on and is never to leave me for the rest of my life.

---

42. Madness entrenched - fighting the wind of change

The political situation in Rhodesia was deteriorating as it became increasingly clear that the RF government intended to be racist in its approach. It's Minister Mark Partridge introduced a Bill called the Property Owners Protection Bill, the "POP Bill". The Bill was primarily aimed at reversing and preventing the ownership of property by Asians and Coloureds in White areas. It was an RF version of the infamous Group Areas Act of South Africa, a cornerstone of apartheid.

We formed a committee that met in secret. Here we heard about the "cell" system in South Africa as a basic component of struggle strategy. I was studying law and an avid reader of books sourced from the Parliamentary Library of which I was a member. This now paid off handsomely. *"Under the Constitution - "* I declared *"Rhodesia is a self governing colony - however any law that affects other races has to be specifically assented to by the British Government - so the POP Bill will be illegal and unenforceable unless the British sign it - and they won't."*

The mood is exuberant as we set out a plan. That weekend a dance function is held to raise money to fund future legal challenges. It is attended by Asian, Coloured, Chinese and some Jewish folk, raising the most money of any fundraiser in the history of the Coloured community. It was the first and last time we see Jews and Chinese at our Community Hall. A delegation led by

Gerry Raftopolous[1] is tasked to give Minister Partridge notice that any racist laws would be challenged on the basis of lack of British assent.

The RF government is checkmated and hamstrung. The significance of this cannot be overemphasized. It is a truth that has been routinely ignored in history books, and particularly by Ian Smith himself and his apologists. To that extent, his book "The Great Betrayal" is a fatuous lie, in justifying the course he eventually took on the basis that the British had betrayed the country.

The Smith government had come to power in order to implement racist policies. None of it was now legally achievable, and that fact was rammed home when their POP Bill was stopped in its tracks in early 1965. As it so happened it was never to be introduced again. We need to be clear. Ian Smith was hamstrung on account of the British constitutional right of veto over racist laws. Moreover, it was our committee that put that to him as an issue beyond a shadow of doubt.

The fact and the law of the matter was quite simple; on account of its racist agenda, the RF government had to rid itself of British government veto.

On 11 November 1965, Ian Douglas Smith, the doyen of an incredibly naïve White electorate, announced a Unilateral Declaration of Independence "UDI", for Rhodesia. Under constitutional law, in place since 1928, the RF could have continued governing the country with full recognition and respect as the legitimate authority of an independent state.

The British Government had never interfered in the internal affairs of Rhodesia, and was constitutionally barred from doing so. One needs only to point to the fact that British Government had never so much as made any kind of fuss about blacks being continued to be denied the vote in Rhodesia as proof that it was serious about its complicity in the continued subjugation of the populace.

Ian Smith chose to declare UDI because of the constitutional veto that the British government had over racist laws - not because of any threat of interference or some kind of *"betrayal"*. Over the years thereafter Ian Smith, in particular, attempted to conceal and obfuscate this inconvenient truth with blinding spin and tautology. This inconvenient truth has also been badly under-reported on in the media.

When Smith's infamous UDI was broadcast over the radio only two members of staff in our office did not go into rapturous celebration at this act of folly;

---

[1] First and only coloured member of Parliament for the United Federal Party that lost the general election in November 1962

Richard "Dick" Mallinson and I. Mallinson was thereafter marginalized by his peers.

Britain announces the imposition of economic sanctions on the Smith regime. I write a letter to the then Governor, Sir Humphrey Gibbs, who is now holed up at his residence in Salisbury and hand-deliver it to a post box especially set up at his residence for public submissions. There is a long stream of concerned people, many of them who are there in order to ascertain what Britain proposes to do, and what are the implications of what they see as treasonous conduct by the Smith government.

In my letter I opine that sanctions will not work and that its effects will be simply passed onto to the very people Smith is oppressing. In my respectful, but forceful view, the answer is incredibly simple.

The rail and road links to South Africa should be bombed at uninhabited spots by plane sorties flown from a Royal Navy carrier positioned in the Mozambique Channel. As the Rhodesian Hawker Hunter planes were outdated in relation to the British fighter planes there was simply no risk of armed conflict as the Rhodesian air force would know that taking on the British planes and/or the carrier would be suicidal. It was my belief that the security forces themselves would see the operation as a cue to withdraw support for Smith.

The whole nonsensical Smith agenda would be brought to an immediate and effective end. I receive no reply, but the British government issues a statement ruling out the use of force. Clearly I was not alone in my view. An inconvenient truth was being suppressed for nefarious reasons. A strong perception developed that the British government, whatever its posturing, secretly wanted Smith to eventually succeed, and the problem to go away, in terms of whatever nonsensical solution Smith could sell internally to the Black majority.

Some would argue that this perception was subsequently vindicated in the Pearce Commission saga of 1971/2 in which the British government attempted to sell such a solution to the Black majority.

43. And we are all so different

Sometimes I would be called up to serve in the Territorial Army, on weekends, and for a week's stint in the bush. These "call-ups" were a very welcome break from the hum-drum of the office and city life. Playing soldiers is great fun. As said, our unit was Supply and Transport, and confined to Coloureds.

It is a Saturday at Cranborne Barracks, where a group of us are deep in discussion. The word is out that the unit needs to effect promotions. My school-mate Eddie "Pra-Pra" Ambrose is here. So is Farry, famed for the ill treatment of rebels in Llewellyn. We discuss the issue at length and resolve that none of us in the group will accept promotion. We will not support a racist regime. We are to make a stand on principled grounds. It is the sapiential thing to do. We are a band of brothers and will stand together, that is a precious commodity inculcated in our training at Llewellyn Barracks. Soldiers always stand up for each other.

Soon thereafter I am called and marched into the office where there is a panel of senior officers waiting.

Me : Private Greenland CN 37226T [I call out after coming to a smart halt]

Officer: At ease soldier - we will come straight to the point - you have been earmarked for promotion - the army - sorry - the unit needs non-commissioned officers and we think you can make Warrant Officer Class II, which is a very big promotion

Me : Thank you Sir. Permission to ask a question Sir?

Officer: Permission granted

Me: Am I not eligible for officer training Sir? [A tension overtakes the room and the two other officers sit back in their chairs and glare at me]

Officer: What do you mean soldier. Make yourself clear?

Me: I believe that my Llewellyn assessment includes a recommendation that I am suitable for officer training Sir! [There is now a momentary and deathly hush. The sound of papers being fiddled with can be clearly heard. This is not information that soldiers normally have access to]

Officer: That is exactly why we determined that you can make Warrant Officer Class II. We cannot reverse government policy. It is not government policy to appoint Coloureds as officers. Will you reconsider?

Me: No - but Sir –

Officer: Will you or will you not reconsider soldier? [he barks at me]

Me: No - but Sir –

Officer: Very well - thank you - dismissed. [I am marched out]

I feel good inside that I have stood on principle and that the regime would be frustrated. Eddie, when interviewed, also declines promotion and as he comes out we all look at each other in smug satisfaction.

Farry is marched in. He emerges in no time at all sporting a Warrant Officer Class I band on his wrist. It is greeted with a sigh of disgust by all around us.

He is not the only one who then betrays the "band of brothers" and the unit soon has a full complement of Coloured non-commissioned officers none of whom can ever make officer on account of their skin colour; nor can they join the regular army. Collaboration with those in power is as natural as breathing with many in any society.

The situation becomes immensely bemusing and quite sickening to Warrant Officer Farry and his cohorts when Eddie and I are thereafter routinely invited to the officer's mess, by a Lieutenant Langton in particular, to drink long and hard at their expense. Normally the officers' mess is holy ground that non commissioned officers can never tread on. Langton is curious, fascinated and intrigued by the eloquence with which Eddie is able to serve up pseudo-intellectualism and plain bull packaged in marvelous turn of phrase.

So typically the good Lieutenant gets a lecture on the X-Plane program in America *"and its significance in the geo-political context of the cold war"*, all boned up by us from the American embassy library, of which we are members. To a military man like Langton this is worth every beer bought - and more. It is unlikely that he is taken in by our nonsense. But for him it is a change; it is intriguing, it is fun. He is also genuinely disgusted that he cannot have us as officers, pointing out that some of the best soldiers he has ever known are Black soldiers in the famous Rhodesian African Rifles Regiment, "the RAR[1]" None of these legendary soldiers are officers. Farry and his sycophantic mates can do nothing. Eddie and I are "privileged privates".

44. Straightening out history

There was one particular lad who had also been conscripted, and done his stint at Llewellyn Barracks. He was good looking and personable. However,

---

[1] **The Rhodesian African Rifles,** or RAR, was the oldest regiment in the Rhodesian Army, dating from the formation of the 1st Rhodesian Native Regiment in 1916 during the First World War. This was followed by the creation of the Matabeleland Native Regiment, and the 2nd Rhodesian Native Regiment, formed in 1917. In 1918, the Rhodesia Native Regiment was formed by combining the 1st and 2nd Regiments. The regiment was raised again in 1940 during the Second World War and staffed with black non-commissioned officers [NCOs] from the British South Africa Police Askari Unit.
http://en.wikipedia.org/wiki/Rhodesian_African_Rifles

like the rest of us, his existence was unremarkable in the context of Rhodesia. Had he not died he would have remained just one more member of the insignificant *other*. It was a longstanding tradition in our community for everyone to pack goodies, and make off to the Matopos National Park, to spend Easter Sunday. It was on one such trip that the lad unfortunately met his death. Diving off a ledge at the Matopos Dam his head struck a submerged rock, resulting in fatal injury.

His untimely demise ensured that his hitherto anonymity ceased up to a point. The Bulawayo Chronicle carried a banner leader which read - "The last of the Selous". In stirring language the supporting article made out the case that the nation had just experienced the passing of the last in the line of a great dynasty. It graphically described the tragic circumstances of his death at Matopos. It gave his name.

He was Courteney Fisher, -

```
"direct descendant of the great Frederick Courteney Selous[1]
DSO (31 December 1851 - 4 January 1917) who was a British
explorer, officer, hunter and conservationist,, famous for
his exploits in south and east of Africa. His real-life
adventures inspired Sir Rider Haggard to create the fictional
Allan Quatermain character. Selous was also a good friend of
Theodore Roosevelt, Cecil Rhodes and Frederick Russell
Burnham. He was the older brother of ornithologist and writer
Edmund Selous."
```

The young lad was given a State funeral with full military honours - but there was no lying in State with public viewing. That would have revealed an inconvenient truth. His coffin was conveyed on a gun carriage through the streets of Bulawayo. At his graveside a 21 gun salute was fired.

However no one, except our community, knew who he was, his ethnicity and who his family was. In asking the nation to share in the passing of one of the British Empire's sons the media ensured that these facts were deftly omitted.

Courteney Fisher was honored, but not recognized, in death. His ethnicity guaranteed this - and still does. So if one Googles the name "Selous" and/or "the last Selous" the information highway, that is the Internet, will regurgitate a plethora of information without one mention of Courteney Fisher, the Coloured lad killed in a diving accident at Matopos in Rhodesia.

---

[1] http://en.wikipedia.org/wiki/Frederick_Selous. **FREDERICK COURTNEY SELOUS** (1851-), British explorer and hunter, was born in London on the 31st of December 1851, and was educated at Rugby and in Germany.
http://www.1911encyclopedia.org/Frederick_Courtney_Selous

As a Coloured he is the "other" Selous who cannot be acknowledged for simply who and what he actually was - despite his noble pedigree.

45. Finding your own freedom

By the mid to late 60's the Black majority had started the war of liberation and were intensifying it incrementally. Under the RF government the country was maintained in divided format with each ethic group kept in its place. So Coloured folk were almost exclusively confined to suburbs designated for Coloureds, such as Thorngrove, Trenance and Barham Green in Bulawayo and Arcadia, Ardbennie and Southerton in Salisbury.

A somewhat positive outcome of the racist policies was that there were no Coloured policemen in the country, only White and Black officers. This conferred a degree of freedom that was exploited. As a White English visitor expressed it - *"this pub is by far the very best in the bloody country"*. He was referring to the Arcadia Club in Salisbury. It was indeed a free and happy place which we patronized enthusiastically. For me the attraction was to meet with friends, have drinks and play darts in particular. The dart games were marathon sessions in which teams of two would play for money against other teams. I had often heard expert medical evidence given in Court that inebriation first affects the extremities of the body such as hand/eye coordination as the *"faculties become impaired."* Well the medical experts are wrong in my book. The more inebriated I was the more deadly accurate I would become with darts. It is no exaggeration to claim that often my day-to-day expenses were, for more than a month at a time, financed entirely from winnings claimed in darts matches played *"whilst under the influence"*.

I think what impressed our English friend the most was that he was free to join the "users" group" at the Club. Dagga[1] smoking was a free option to members of our community, there being no policemen around, and many indulged in it almost openly. It was no big deal and certainly did not appear to induce the social problems that alcohol abuse did, not by a long, long way.

What always intrigued me was a group that may be referred to as "the debating committee". Its members were an ad hoc assemblage of free spirited and loquacious social commentators unrelenting in according issues a unique perspective. Most had nick-names and typically their conversation would take on the following attributes.

---

[1] **Dagga** – local name for *cannabis sativa* also referred to as marijuana.

Zozo: Look man - what do you know about the law - let us call Vavie Greenland and we can settle this issue once and for all. [I am then summoned to join the group]

Mabeans: Hey Vavie - have a dop ek se - you are a man of law - these okies reckon that a man can rape his own wife - and be put in jail - they talk such cuck – [1]

[I then proceed to clearly and simply explain to them what the law says on the issue and preen myself on my competence in law. Almost immediately this is met by unanimous agreement that I too talk "cuck", as always]

Nags: Ou Vavie always tunes us cuck man - you remember how he was praising ou Chidzero [Bernard Chidzero is our new Minister of Finance, United Nations trained and incredibly articulate]

Crossley: Ja man - just because the haute can speel English better than the honkies he reckons the manna is great –

Mabeans: He don't see that the haute has swallowed a dictionary and is just eating us in the ear - you will see - he will be as useless - just wait and see

Crossley: Kools kile we deem rome reebs nam. Ou Mabeans - tis rouy nurt nam - yub nam - muc no nam - yub dop - rof eth sammes - goffals[2] kaams rof reebs nam –

Crosley has reverted to a now well entrenched communication medium where words are reversed. We all speak it almost exclusively in social discourse. Translated what he has said is –

```
Looks like we need more beers man. Ou Mabeans - it is your
turn man - buy man - come on man - buy dop - for the masses
- . Goffals smaak for beers man - "
```

Their irreverent assessment of our Minister of Finance, Bernard Chidzero, somewhat surprisingly and regrettably is to prove correct. His stirring speeches, littered with 21st century buzzwords, delivered in better than

---

[1] "Dop" – local slang meaning "a drink". "Ek se" – is a South African expression used to get one's attention on a point. "Cuck" – local synonym for "crap". "Haute" – pronounced '"hoe tee" is local slang referring to an African black. "Speel" – pronounced "spee el" is local slang meaning to articulate. "Honkies" – is slang referring to white folk. "Manna" – pronounced "maa naa" is local slang referring to a male person. "Okie" – has same meaning. "Smaak" – pronounce with flattened a' s is South African slang meaning "to like"

[2] **Goffals** – colloquialism for "Coloureds"

Queen's English were matched by a decline in our country's finances of equally impressive proportions. It is somewhat worrisome that their opinions about my advice is also routinely disparaging. "Goffal" is a reference to a Coloured person; and "honkie" and "haute" to a White and Black person respectively. It is rare to hear the different race groups referred to in any other way. Whatever their origins such references are not considered or meant to be disparaging. It is just the way it is in the discourse culture of our community.

Whatever one may have thought about this "debating committee" what emanated from within it was often chillingly disconcerting. It is said that *"facts are awkward things"*. The committee would serve up a plethora of awkward things with brutal irreverence.

Why were White folk busy tanning their bodies to achieve a nice shade of brown, and curling their hair, whilst despising Coloured folk? Conversely why were Black folk lightening their skins, and straightening their hair, whilst mouthing slogans about *"black power"* and *"black is beautiful"* and *"I am black and I am proud"*? One day the whole world would be some shade of brown however much racial prejudice there was. The need for inter-racial sex was just too strong.

Support for their stance can be found, for instance, in this passage at page 227 of "Scribbling the Cat', a book by Alexandra Fuller: -

```
K glanced at the women.

"The Porks weren't afraid of dipping into the oil drum, hey."

"Plenty of goffles around here,"

Mapenga agreed. "Beautiful as well. There are some that are
almost white, I promise you."

Mapenga lit a cigarette. "Its tempting, sometimes.

There's a Bar in Maputo that I go to where all the prozzies
hang out. You Know, the classy ones.

The ones with Pork blood in them.

You've Never seen such women. More beautiful than wazugu women.
I'm telling you."

Mapenga cleared his throat.[1]
```

To the members of this committee the world seethed with convenient untruths and suppression of inconvenient truths. *"You cannot talk about justice, O'Vavie"* they would say, *" - when most people in this country simply cannot afford a good lawyer to defend them - justice is only for the rich".*

---

[1] **"Porks"** = Portuguese . **"wazungu women"** = white women

Nags: last week you guys prosecuted a whole lot of Black girls - for loitering …

Mabeans: … saying they were prozzies - and the paper made a big thing about it - about cleaning up the city ...

Me: well loitering for the purposes of prostitution is a criminal offence - the law is the law

Nags: yah - but what about their clients? - cruising around in their smart cabs hunting for the pros - what about them - it takes two to tango - not so?

Me: well - hmmnnn - .

Crossley: yah O'Vavie - what type of justice you talking about - the Black girls are nailed as prozzies but their rich honkie clients - nothing - its as if they don't even exist - these girls are prostituting with who hey? Who is bonking who - ?

This would be followed by the group bursting into a favourite song –

> "Whose fooling ah who? … whose fooling ah who?
> Ah man is a rolling stone … but a w-o-o-o-man is a
> gri-i-i-nding sto-o-ne …"[1]

ending with a cheer in acknowledgement of the incredible power of the fairer sex.

And so it goes on about a range of issues. If the White man had not come to Africa, the mosquitoes, lions, hyenas and crocodiles would have still had the locals in check. The consistent failure of Black governments was sure proof of innate incompetency. Botswana and Namibia, as exceptions, were still on the horizon in the 70s and early 80s. After all Africa had still not even invented the wheel on arrival of the White man. Zimbabwe was doomed despite the fact that the Mugabe cabinet had *"... more degrees than a thermometer..."* The Jews were forever cursed for having killed Jesus. Starting a religion was *"the best business"* and most were about making money. White people had decimated all wild life in their own countries and now wanted to *"preach conservation"* to blacks. The United Nations was nothing more than an incredibly expensive club for political leaders to peddle power, assets and influence for themselves with little corresponding love of humanity. It should be called the *"Disunited Nations"* or *"The United Corrupt Leaders"*. I was not spared and routinely castigated for being part of a system that was inherently unjust.

---

[1] I believe these lines are from a composition by Ray Phiri and group named Stimela of South Africa

The list was endless. It was irreverent - it was not politically correct - it was brutally impolite - but mostly it raised terribly awkward questions that were very difficult to answer. Facts are indeed awkward things. The committee was a heaving hive of cynicism and skepticism. The disturbing thing however is that its predictions are being proved right with monotonous regularity.

Zimbabwe has joined other countries in Africa as a failed state. The United Nations is a spectacular failure in terms of a cost/benefit test. One needs only to point to the continuing instances of genocide that occur, despite pontifical statements mouthed off at the UN. A brown tan and curly hair is - well - more desirable then ever - and - by the time Michael Jackson died he had all but rid himself of all his blackness - the list is endless.

There is little doubt that they would have been very enthusiastic about the following poem selected as the best from Africa -[1]

```
When I born, I Black,
When I grow up, I Black,
When I go in Sun, I Black,
When I scared, I Black,
When I sick, I Black,
And when I die, I still black..
And you White fella,
When you born, you Pink,
When you grow up, you White,
When you go in Sun, you Red,
When you cold, you Blue,
When you scared, you Yellow,
When you sick, you Green,
And when you die, you Gray..
And you calling me Colored ??
```

As to their sense of humour there is the following exchange –

Me: You know there was this inquest to-day at the Court

Crossley: Ya, our Vavie, tell us who frekked [died]

Me: This guy had crabs - you know - pubic lice

Nags: Naa, crabs don't kill man - they just tickle - and itch like mad

Me: He tried to get rid of the crabs - with paraffin and stuff - when that failed he finally rubbed Rogor CE [garden pesticide] onto his testicles - he was dead in 2 hours

---

[1] http://forums.bollyent.com/african-kids-poem-t-14586.html

Crossley: Wow .. doed [dead] in 2 hours - because of Rogor - that's heavy man

Me: You see Rogor is an organophosphorus poison, [I add sapientially] it is absorbed through the skin into the blood stream. So when it got to his kidneys and liver - that was it - in just 2 hours …

Mabeans: The haute was dwaarse [slow witted] - if he was a goffal he would have soaked his balls in brandy so the crabs could have had a lekker party.

Then, when they were high on dop, he would have added river sand and the crabs would then have all stoned each other to death - problem gone - [he finishes amidst peals of laughter]

The police would, on occasion, attempt to raid Arcadia. These were always futile and unproductive since they had neither a foothold in the community nor the hearts and minds of its members. Things came to a head one evening when the police conducted a raid at our community hall where a weekend dance function was in progress.

Their behaviour was, gratuitous, provocative and intimidatory in the extreme. An otherwise peaceful and happy event was completely marred by White police officers parading around in our hall with police dogs in some obscene and provocative show of force. Supplications to leave us alone fell on deaf ears and irritation became resentment, resentment became anger and anger became mob fury. In the ensuing physical altercations the police got the worse of it and were put to flight. Regrettably a police dog met its death by being drowned in one of the toilets. It was terrible.

Ian Smith made arrangements with some naïve older members of the community and one or two sympathizers of the RF cause such as a man named Jack Jones. As result a tea party was organized and conducted one Sunday afternoon in which he gave a well publicized speech promising that *" - we will take you Coloured people with us. "* Being Coloureds we were not considered part of the society; we were *"the other"* - and needed therefore to be especially *"taken"* along with the rest of his community. What a privilege!

Another favourite drinking hole was the Castle Hotel where we would meet after work on a Friday and keep it up till late on the open patio under the stars. Proceedings often involved rousing renditions of our own revolutionary songs such as -

```
"Siti Banda, Kaunda, Joshua Nkomo - . Sikalela iliswe letu - - .
[repeat]
Siti tina abafana be liswe - si kalela liswe letu - ."
```

[We call on Kamuzu Banda, Kenneth Kaunda and Joshua Nkomo - we are yearning for our land

We, the boys of this land - are yearning for our land -]

These sessions, of drinking and singing about freedom, just about represented our political activism.

This, whilst others left home, kith and kin, to go for training and then return to be killed by the thousand in battle for our freedom.

---

46. A dung beetle mind

As with all disadvantaged communities, America ["Native Americans"] and Australia [Aborigines] included, there was over representation of drinking as a past time in a colony where, in any event, alcohol use was something of a national hobby. So a drinking culture was well established. Drinking and driving was also something of a norm. Its deadly effects were only starting to emerge. This does not by any means mean that the community was riddled with drunkards; far from it. It means that culturally drinking with friends was very much part of the social scene.

George Anderson [my then father-in-law], and I are on a car trip to Bulawayo. He is dozing. It is a long drive and I am bored. *"George"* I say- *"Do you see that little mouse under the tree over there - ?"* Without a moment's hesitation he quips - *"Which one - the black or the grey one?"*

Phew! The man has a razor sharp mind. I decide to test him again. *"What year did Luther King make his "I Have a Dream" speech"* I ask.

"August, 1963 - " he replies and goes on *" - I have a dream that one day this nation will rise up and live out the true meaning of its creed: "We hold these truths to be self-evident: that all men are created equal ... "*

I interrupt him - *"George, do you know what a isigiqathuvi is - ?"* I ask. When he says he does not I explain that - *"a isigiqathuvi is a dung beetle and the name means to roll a ball of dung. I see your brain as the ball - rolling along - getting ever bigger as it picks up material - for a person of only standard 7 education you sure is sharp".*

This man, with only a mid-high school education, but a voracious reader, is easily the most brilliant human being I have ever known; and this includes university professors that I have met.

We decide to stop at a pub in Gwelo [now Gweru]. It is packed with White folk. The barman serves us, only for a waiter to approach a minute later to say that we should leave pointing to a "Right of Admission Reserved" sign on the door. A burly White man, obviously intoxicated, stands up and says-

"Why should they leave - they are also people just like us - they are Rhodesians - this is nonsense..."

The manager arrives and says that if we don't leave he will call the police. The man remonstrates with the manager, pointing out that Coloured folk also serve in the army. George asks the man for his name. He replies *"Erasmus"*. We are on high stools. There is a large group of whites sitting in chairs below us. From the twinkle in George's eye I anticipate what is to happen. He starts - *"You know that, as an Erasmus, you should understand and be proud of your pedigree. The name Erasmus is of Latin and Greek origin and means "to love". Originally there were two Erasmus brothers who arrived in this part of Africa ... ..."* and he goes to trace the fortunes of the Erasmus regional clan from the time of their arrival in Rhodesia.

There is stunned silence as our audience becomes absorbed in the dissertation; enraptured by what he has to say. A truly great mind is in its element. Then he switches to telling one joke after another. They are risqué and racial. He asks a lady what is her name. When she replies *"Dawn"* -

"Dawn" he responds with scarcely a pause – *"... and from the smile on your face we are all sure that your husband is always up at the crack of dawn".*

The risqué innuendo is not lost on the audience and they double over in laughter. They demand more and the waiter is commanded to serve us more drinks which they pay for.

" ... as they lie in the servants quarters in a Gwelo suburb the house-maid Mary - whispers tenderly to Jonathan the house-boy - [he goes on in decidedly African accent] *"... Oh Jonathan my dearest one - you are the very most sweetest - much more sweeter than the baas"* [White boss]

Jonathan replies – "yes Mary my loveliest one - even the missus[1] she says so".

This otherwise highly offensive joke to White folk is met with peals of laughter. Only George could get away with that. However these happy proceeding are soon brought to a rude halt when two White police officers arrive and announce that if we do not leave immediately we will be arrested. Amidst howls of protest from the patrons we leave. I work in the Courts. I cannot risk arrest.

It is 11 o'clock at night as I bring my car to a halt at a police road block, at Insiza, some 80 kms from Bulawayo. The three of us met after work, had a few drinks and then decided to hit the Bulawayo scene.

---

[1] **Missus** – colloquialism use to refer to a white madam of the house

Woman Patrol Officer Ford, the first female police officer appointed to the force, approaches my window and asks me to wind it down. As I do so she mutters as the smell of alcohol emanating from the inside of the car assails her nostrils. Directing the beam of her torch into the back passenger floor area, she notices fifteen empty beers bottles lying there. I have little doubt that she is doing her sums in her head and 15 divided by three equals 5 beers each on the trip.

Patrol Officer Ford: Please step out of the car. [I comply and stand facing her]

Patrol Officer Ford: Are you drunk?

Me: No officer ... I am definitely not drunk

Patrol Officer Ford: I want you to use your right hand, bring it up and touch the end of your nose

This is not good news - she is going to conduct a standard test for faculty impairment. I know this as I work in the Courts. People who have been drinking fail these tests]

Me: Yes Officer - [and I succeed in complying with her request]

Patrol Officer Ford: Now the other hand - [and again I manage]

Now - I want you to walk along the centre white line of the road until I tell you to stop. [I comply successfully]

Patrol Officer Ford: Patrol Officer Ford: This time I want you to do it with your arms outstretched

[I manage with no hint of unsteadiness. I am happy I have passed - and then disaster strikes -]

Patrol Officer Ford: I am taking you in for a blood test. [Oh no! This must not happen - a blood test will surely sink me]

Me: Look Officer - I am not drunk - [as I proceed to perform a perfectly still headstand on the road]

Patrol Officer Ford: Hmnnn - - no - I am taking you in

Me: Look Officer - I will even walk on my hands to prove to you that I am not drunk -[and I proceed to walk on my hands along the white line]

Me: Please tell me when you want me to stop ...

We are soon your way again. My friends spend the rest of the trip describing in minute detail how gob-smacked the police officers were at my head stand/hand stand performance.

I say a silent Hail Mary that I was not blood tested. It was a close thing indeed. I am offered an open beer to celebrate. For the first time in my life, I decline.

WPO Ford has induced a fundamental change in me. Till to this day I do not drink and drive. I can also stand on my head and walk on my hands under any conditions.

What you learn as child in the care of German nuns is with you for life.

47. A prosecutor

In 1966 I was appointed as a public prosecutor having successfully passed Civil Service Lower Law, Parts I and II.

It was news. It was history being made. I was the first Coloured public prosecutor appointed in the country. There was one Asian State counsel, Ahmed Ebrahim [later to become a Judge] but not one African Black in the Courts. The RF government was making sure of that. The sangoma was right. I was to be in the public eye and would be very much confronting evil it seemed.

My boss, mentor and tutor, was Mrs. Wilson. She was a wonderful lady, who had passed both the lower and higher Civil Service law exams, and therefore fully qualified for appointment as a magistrate. This was denied. The madness of inequality did not only accrue on account of skin colour. Her appointment as a magistrate was denied purely on account of her gender, despite the Rhodesia Herald publishing an article, with her picture, titled "Qualified as a magistrate". UDI was also trumpeted by Ian Smith and gang as preserving good order, values and governance. Allowing a White woman to prosecute in a Court, but not preside over the same Court, was the type of mind blowing logic supporting their thinking it seems.

In the prevailing climate the concept of "merit" becomes somewhat problematical. By this time the establishment has managed to rid itself of Cyril Ndebele, the only African Black in the Ministry of Justice. He was found to have been helping convicts under the Law and Order Maintenance Act with their appeal procedures. The fact that, as a public servant, he was obliged to assist was irrelevant. There were mutters that " - *this munt*[1] - *Cyril - is dangerous* - " So a stratagem was put in place to hound him out of office.

---

[1] **Munt** – pronounced "moont" was another derogatory reference to a black person.

Only Moosa Ismail and I remain in the Magistrates Courts, and Ahmed Ebrahim in the office of the Attorney General. There is always the nagging question as to whether or not we will also be perceived as *"dangerous munts"*. I realize that my position is inherently tenuous in the prevailing climate, so I am diligent and conscientious in my duties, after being given a good start by Mrs. Wilson. It pays off. Life for a magistrate is hard, if not sheer hell, if the prosecutor in his Court is incompetent or ineffective. The magistrate is also out of Court earlier if he has "a good prosecutor". So, despite my ethnicity, I am popular with the magistrates, always in demand by the more senior ones, and enjoy my work.

As a prosecutor my attitude is, as with all human beings, influenced by experience. I am confident and somewhat self opinionated, a fault that Sister Mary had publicly dressed me down for on any number of occasions, accusing me of having *"intellectual pride"*. It is hardly surprising that I suffer from such pride considering that I recollect being embarrassed at doctors sticking instruments into me, when they rescued me from death's door on account of food poisoning, at age two. Amongst other things I believe that I can beat any White given fair opportunity and that I am to become the best lawyer in the business.

Gert Schaap, a magistrate, and I decide to attend the Appeal Court hearing of the famous Rhodesian case of Daniel Madzimbamuto v. Lardner-Burke, in which the legality of the Rhodesian Front government and their UDI is put in issue by the wife of a detainee and lawyer Leo Baron, now also detained. The appeal is argued by an advocate from South Africa, Sydney Kentridge. We listen in wondrous amazement as Kentridge takes on a largely hostile Court and, in a mind boggling display of memory, oratory and advocatory skills, puts the merits of his client's case and seemingly demolishes the illegal government's case.[1]

Schaap and I agree that it is simply unbelievable that a human being can have such a mind. It is just awesome. During one tea break I see Kentridge standing under a tree pondering his thoughts and summon up the nerve to greet him. He is warm in response especially when I tell him that I have been reading the biographies of great English Advocates like Marshall Hall and Norman Birkett. He talks to me as if I am someone important, ending with

---

[1] **Beadle CJ** led the judges into upholding the legitimacy of the Smith government even though they had been sworn, on appointment, to uphold the previous constitution that Smith and gang tore up. The Privy Counsel reversed this decision to no avail.

encouragement in my pursuance of law, which he says is an honourable profession.

Like Louise Odendaal he is a South African but no racist; just a great human being in whose presence I feel honour. It is an inspirational moment in my life that will never leave me. As a person I am chastened into the realization that I will never be able to match the level of advocacy that Kentridge displays. Certainly I will not match many that I will meet. My "intellectual pride" is gone forever.

But my commitment to be always sapiential, in accordance with the admonition by Fr Adalbert in the early morning of 20 June 1960, is strongly reaffirmed.

---

48. A river of substance

By the late 60's I am promoted to Regional Public Prosecutor, and stationed once again in Bulawayo, reporting to a truly wonderful boss named Joe Kristafor. Joe is slightly built, has an infectious smile in a kindly face behind a pair of rather thick lensed glasses. He is a graduate from Rhodes University, down in Grahamstown, a fact that he is enormously proud of. My work also involves scheduling trials in Wankie[1] just 40 kms away from the mighty Zambezi. I schedule these for a Thursday and Friday, leaving the weekend free for fishing excursions on the Zambezi. Joe has a boat and schools me in the art of Tiger fishing.

It is my first sight and experience of the Zambezi, and the start of a life-long long love affair with this mighty river. The river is an admixture of timeless incredible beauty, grace and power. Its captivating splendour is replaced by a realization that it is also very dangerous, with death ever lurking. The deep flowing water, with its swirls, eddies and dancing patterns of light, also has black jagged rocks waiting to tear the bottom out of our boat. The awesome tranquility of its wideness, smooth and lazy currents is soon replaced by the blood chilling threat of howling, treacherous rapids emitting a crescendo of sound that assails the ears, freezing the heart. Large crocodiles, mouths

---

[1] **Wankie** – now Hwange in Zimbabwe is a centre for the coal mining industry with being the largest coal mine in Zimbabwe [with reserves for over 1000 years]. The Wankie Coal Field, one of the largest in the world, was discovered here in 1897 by the America Scout. He is reputed to have sold the coal field for £100 and a bottle of whisky.

frozen in an evil smile laze on sandbanks. Clumps of hippopotami grunt and display nearby.

You are chastened to the core, alive to your mortality. Man is but just one more creature on this planet, just one more puny creature. The incisive call of a fish eagle softens the heart and dispels that which is worrisome to the mind.

Words are inadequate to describe the feelings of joy and exuberance that are at play when you are on the mighty Zambezi and have just hooked a tiger fish. It fights with electrifying power, speed and agility, displaying all the colours of the rainbow as it leaps, twists and tail-walks in the African sun.

En route I had hit two guinea fowl with the car. Joe hangs these in the shady foliage of a large tree after, we have taken out the intestines.

That night we make a mud bath into which the still feathered birds are placed. Our camp fire is then made over the mud tomb of the birds. Next morning they are retrieved, feathers and skin easily pulled away with the now dry mud, leaving the most perfectly cooked meat. This is delicious fare, after seasoning, for the day's sandwiches and the next evening's meal.

[Picture is of Joe with a tigerfish, *Hydrocynus vittatus*, at Deka Fishing Camp. 1970]

Sadly, at just about the time I ran over the guinea fowls, another deadlier drama was played out on the same stretch of road. Poppy Mckop, now Mrs. Manickum, who had tended to me when I had diphtheria, spoiling me with ice cream and jelly, was killed in a road crash. It broke all hearts in Thorngrove and so many others in our community.

Interesting also is a make-shift "medical clinic" set up by the wife of a Coloured road builder at Deka Fishing camp where we, and hundreds of mainly South African fishermen, stay when on tiger fishing trips. The area is infested with scorpions of such size that when they scurry around they give the impression of being miniature squirrels. A sting from one of these can

- 148 -

induce anaphylactic shock, sometimes with fatal results. Incredibly the "sure-fire" prescription, our good lady has devised, is that the patient is given a tot of diesel fuel to drink and the wound site covered with a compress soaked in diesel. It works every time. Whatever reticence our friends from South Africa might have about this brown lady and her treatment; when death came knocking on the door, ethnic antipathy vanished.

On another trip, I ask to be left on an island after receiving a tip-off about catching fish known as Nkupe [Distichodus mossambicus] which, pound for pound, are perhaps the most exciting fish to do battle with on ultra light tackle, which was my passion. No sooner am I left on the island then deep regret starts to overtake me. This regret is induced by a feeling of extreme vulnerability. Regret quickly changes to serious apprehension when a herd of some 30 or so elephant assembles on the main shoreline with a huge pod of perhaps 50 hippopotami appearing in the main stream nearby, on the other side of the island. I feel alone and extremely vulnerable. As beautiful as the Zambezi is, it is not my environment. I am an intruder - and a pretty puny one at that.

Apprehension turns to panic when I realize that the herd of elephant are staging to swim to "my" island. Stupefied I watch as the whole herd organizes and enters the water to make the swim across. Babies are put on the "up-current" side of the adults so that the current cannot sweep them away but pushes them against the bodies of the adults. The adults link themselves in a line, trunk to tail, with a large bull taking the lead. They quite easily make it to the island, with scarcely a downward drift despite the strong current. By the time the lead bull steps onto the island I have slunk to the down-current end of the island, trying to make myself as inconspicuous as possible. He is not taken in and immediately ambles in my directions ears spread wide. In abject terror I start to actually enter the water, my mind a confused jungle of thoughts involving being trampled and gored by an elephant and/or being grabbed by a crocodile. I reel off some "Hail Marys", struggling to breath. I am more than petrified with fear.

Fortunately this magnificent animal stops after only a few steps. It has not even been a mock charge. He was just having a look at me; puny inconsequential me. Having done so he turns disdainfully away. I then watch in utter fascination as the herd re-assembles, enters the water and swims some 3-400 meters or so across the main current, arriving safely on the Zambian side after skirting around the pod of hippos.

This terrifyingly engrossing experience is topped off by the Nkupe arriving to do battle. It is quite impossible to describe the gamut of emotions that I have been put through in just one afternoon, except to say that I feel emphatically unimportant, insignificant and somewhat irrelevant in the grand scheme of things.

That night, at our camp fire, I tell Joe about the terror I had been in. He smiles whimsically and assures me that I had never been in danger. *"You see - "* he concludes *" - it is only man that will harm or kill another creature gratuitously"*.

The reason why we are able to put in more fishing time is that trials in Wankie do not last long. In the regional Court the diet of matters is almost exclusively attempted murder and rape. These are more serious crimes and the Regional Court is configured to deal with them. Nearly all the accused are from the BaTonga people who inhabit the Zambezi valley. They are an incredibly forthright people who consider mendacity unthinkable. They just never tell a lie.

It is their custom that a man, who way-lays a girl and has sex with her, has first claim to her hand in marriage. Unfortunately this is considered as rape under laws imported with colonization. So when charged with rape the accused readily admits his conduct, knowing that he now also has official proof of the act founding his later claim, before the chief, to the girl's hand in marriage. The time spent in prison for rape presents as a price to be paid in the process.

So too as regards attempted murder which invariably involve spear attacks motivated on the basis of honour. They are fearless and honourable. Legend has it that they are the only tribe to have given raiding Ndebele impis such a pasting, in the past that, Lobengula stopped his raids on them. The criminalization of a people largely on account of their age-old customs is completely lost on the colonial government.

Another fascinating fact about this tribe is that some of their members, known as the Vadoma, have feet comprising only two toes.

> "Just when you think the world has revealed all of it's curiosities - you get the Vadoma people of Zambezi River valley, all of whom share the condition known as ectrodactyly, in which the middle three toes are absent[1]".

What an incredibly rich and wondrous environment our Zambezi valley is.

---

[1] http://blog.synthesis.net/2007/04/02/the-two-toed-tribe-of-zimbabwe/

49. Justice must be done[1]

It is at this time, 1970, that I travel to Gwelo to prosecute a case involving a White lady socialite and community activist, on a charge of fraud. On arrival at the Meikles hotel I am refused admission until the manager is sent for and relents, recognizing me as he has previously worked in the Courts. I receive royal service from all the Coloured and Black staff, who are overjoyed about the admission of a non-white patron for the first time in the hotel's history.

The accused in the case I prosecute was incredibly imaginative and innovative in the commission of her crime. She replicates these traits in Court and is brazen, tough and artful in her defense. By more luck than skill I induce her to make a fatal error under cross-examination. Against her advocate's advice she immediately changes her plea to guilty and elects to give evidence in mitigation. The performance she then puts on about how tragic it would be for her, a mother with two daughters at their most impressionable age, to be sent to prison would have won many Oscars in Hollywood.

Everyone including her legal team, comprising a seasoned advocate and two hardened lawyers, as well as Court staff, is reduced to tears. The magistrate fights back his tears, adjourns Court, returns a few minutes later and imposes a patently inadequate sentence. Our good lady immediately turns off the tears and, grinning all over, hugs her lawyers, family ... and gives me a special hug. Throughout my career I have seen plenty to prove that the female species is very much more artful, resourceful and deadly than the male as an adversary.

The intriguing nature of this case was more than matched by the numbing revulsion induced by another Gwelo case. The accused, a White man, also of high social standing, raped his 14 month old baby. The physical damage included the fact that this child would have to wear a colostomy for the rest of her life.

The child's mother was hysterical in Court, screaming and throwing herself on the floor - not at the plight of her child - but at the prospect of her husband being sent to prison. She pleaded tearfully, long and hard, for mercy. I was numbed at the crime committed and numbed by her attitude. The Magistrate (very senior) must have been taken in by this oscar winning performance by the wife as he imposed a totally inadequate sentence.

---

[1] **Justice must be done and seen to be done** - is the judicial motto of the free world

Years later the creature that was her husband raped another child. This time the Court sent him away for a very long time indeed.

In another rape case the child's father is under cross-examination by the accused. He is a very dignified mature Black man and has given his evidence well, explaining what a wonderful daughter the complainant has been, always respectful of herself and her elders. He maintains his dignity and speaks in a calm and clear voice despite what has hitherto been a most provocative and offensive line of questions by the accused.

Accused: Your daughter has no morals and is a temptress of men. [Note[1]]

Witness: That is untrue

Accused: In fact she asked me for sex and cried when I had to get off her. I could not even satisfy her lust. [There are murmurs from the public gallery]

Witness: We brought her up well - she would not do such a thing

Accused: I will end by telling you that the whole world knows that she over-uses her vagina. [The murmurs grow louder]

Witness: You have no respect - for anyone - you are insulting my child and the Court - have you no shame - a young man like you?

Accused: I am finished with this father of a whore [he says with a huge smirk on his face]

Amidst a welling up of angry mutters in the public gallery, the old man turns respectfully towards the magistrate and says thank you. He walks across the front of the well of the Court to where the dock is.

The accused is turned, looking smugly at the public gallery, to whom he has been playing. The prosecutor becomes aware of the sounds of a scuffle. As his eyes pick up the scene the scuffle is already over as the old man turns and offers him a large knife and, addressing the public gallery, he says in classic isiNdebele idiom - *"Nga hlinza indwangu*[2] - ["I have skinned a baboon"]

In the background the prosecutor sees a crimson jet piecing the air - and then another - as the precious fluid leaves the jugular vein of the accused. He has had his throat slit. The old man calmly proffers his apologies.

---

[1] All dialogues are reconstructions unless stated otherwise

[2] *"Nga hlinza indwangu"* - literal "I have skinned a baboon" "Hlinza" usually refers to dressing a carcass.

Very fortunately for him, the accused is saved by the skills of a White doctor called from a nearby surgery. He is later convicted of rape and sentenced to 7 years imprisonment.

The old man is later charged with attempted murder. At his trial he is the picture of dignity as he pleads guilty to attempted murder, asking the magistrate if, as a father, he would not have done the same for his daughter.

An understanding and merciful Court imposes a sentence of imprisonment wholly suspended on grounds of good behaviour. The man is the epitome of dignity as he thanks the Court and leaves.

Somehow I feel that justice was done.

---

50. ... and seen to be done

One day I am walking from one Court to another when I see Alan Noah, as we know him, but recorded as Alan Douglas Noach in Court records. The Noach family is very well known in the community. They are resourceful and street wise to the man. Alan, in particular, is personable, good looking, charming when not crossed, and extremely plausible. He has the gift of the gab and could quite easily sell coal to Newcastle. He is happy to see me and wants a "second opinion" as he is about to go into Court. From what he tells me I decide it is well worth attendance.

In Court the drama of contest is played out. A car dealer, notorious for shady deals at the expense of Coloured people in particular, sold Alan a flashy car. A stage was reached when the dealer agreed to have the car traded in provided Alan bought an even more flashy and expensive version. This Alan did. The dealer is now suing Alan for the value of damage that Alan had allegedly concealed when he traded in the original car. Alan is cross-examining the dealer –

Alan: Do you see this receipt I have? [producing and showing the receipt to the witness]

Dealer: Yes

Alan: What is it for?

Dealer: The cost of tending to problems with the reverse gear of the car you bought first –

Alan: You mean the one you are now suing me for.. that I traded in?

Dealer: Yes

Alan: So it had a problem with the reverse gear and you charged me a lot of money to fix it ?

Dealer: You paid for repairs – yes

Alan: At least you are being honest for a change [he says sarcastically]

Magistrate: I will decide who is honest - proceed with your questions

Alan: You see these other receipts? [and producing four other receipts] - you agree that they are all payments I made for you to fix the gear problem?

Dealer: Well ... er ...er ... yes –

Alan: So I paid you a lot of money for this gear?

Dealer: You paid for repairs that we did

Alan: So I don't understand - your Worship - as you can see - a poor man like me has paid these people a lot of money .. - [he says pleadingly with as wide and as innocent a look on his face as to make a baby look like a psychopath in comparison]

Magistrate: er - yes - I see that - er –

Alan: These people are now suing because they say when they got the car back it had no reverse gear - your worship - so what where they charging me for - this is robbery of poor people - who can't afford lawyers

Magistrate: Now wait a moment - [to the witness] - it is clear that you charged this man for fixing this gear - this reverse gear - you charged him several times in a period of just 2 weeks ... and now you say there was no reverse gear - what were you charging him for - what for ? [he concludes irritably]

Alan: That is exactly what I mean your Worship - it happens when you are a poor man ...

The magistrate shuts him up and takes over. The lawyer for the dealer does his best but he is checkmated on the evidence. His client has apparently made Alan pay money on five occasions over a 2 week period for a non-existent gear.

Does the lawyer not know that this is fraud? It gets heated, but in the end the Magistrate says - *"You are wasting the Court's time - that is contempt of Court - you know that don't you? - now do you have any more witnesses?"* When the lawyer says no the Magistrate dismisses the case saying he has heard enough nonsense for one day. He reverses all the transactions and Alan is to get all his money back.

Alan and I meet in my office and we laugh till the tears are running down both our faces as he explains how he set the whole thing up. In the preceding

2 weeks he had taken the car to the dealer on five occasions on a completely spurious complaint about the gear. There was nothing wrong with it. Being dishonest they had charged him anyway, five times; and he had paid as part of his sting operation. Being an accomplished mechanic, he had then removed the actual reverse gear cog in the gearbox, before he finally traded in the vehicle for the flashier model. Game, set and match!

At the office the magistrate, who was new, received a real roasting from the other experienced magistrates who were all too familiar with the guile and cunning of the Noach brothers.

Like little Ronny Millar, who threw his parcel onto the roof all those years ago in Sacred Heart Home, in my eyes Alan was a hero. He had struck a blow for justice!

Years later this incorrigible but lovable member of our community drove his car to a lonely spot on a road, connected a hose pipe to the exhaust and died of carbon monoxide poisoning. As with Danny "Torro" Pillay, how such a "larger than life" personality could decide to take his own life defied comprehension and deeply pained all of us.

The other instance when a new magistrate would be especially assigned a case was in respect of Solomon Guter. Guter was a Polish Jew who had arrived in the colony penniless after apparently escaping the holocaust. By 1962 he was a multi millionaire, owning considerable chunks of real estate in downtown Bulawayo. However this fact was not reflected in his lifestyle; not by a long way.

He lived as a recluse with his mangy ill-fed dog, sleeping on straw under one of the dustbin shelters in the back of one of his rented-out properties. Typically he would then set up a vendor's stall selling matches, razors, cheap rings and other knick-knacks on the pavement outside, in breach of some petty bye-law or other. For this the authorities would dutifully issue him with a notice to pay a fine in a menial amount. This he would always decline to pay, despite his enormous wealth.

On being summoned to Court he would arrive, scruffy, unwashed and unkempt; pulling a trolley on which were stacked outdated, repealed and disused law books that he had retrieved from the dump. After pleading not guilty to the petty charge, he would proceed to conduct his own defense, putting every aspect of the State case in dispute, starting with the constitutionality of the Court. On average Solomon Guter's cases lasted a full week, by the end of which the entire Court staff would be at their wit's end and in a state of complete exasperation. Trying Guter was one of the ways that new magistrates were blooded, especially as regards the requirement to have patience as a judicial officer.

It was at this time that I also made contact with two school colleagues who I do not propose to name. One was charged with having way-laid and raped a Black woman. He had simply failed to maintain Coloured status and had reverted to living in the African tribal trust land from whence he had been originally retrieved in order to attend Embakwe. Changed completely as a person, he was now sullen and rebellious in the extreme. In Court he declined to cooperate and at one stage turned to the presiding magistrate and shouted *"Sata nyogo"* [Fuck your mother].

The other was on a charge of stock theft. He was so happy to see me and told me, with a broad grin on his face that *"I am a cattle rustler"*, as if to say this was an honourable profession. These contacts filled me with great sadness, especially as the cattle rustler had been a soccer star at school. The rapist had been such a wonderful and personable character.

The sentence imposed for the rape was seven years imprisonment. Nine years imprisonment was imposed for the stock theft. The RF government's main constituency was the White farming community. So a law had been passed that the minimum sentence, under stock theft statute, was nine years even if it was for being found in possession of just one piece of meat from a carcass of stolen stock animal, obtained to stave off hunger.

So stock theft was decreed as far more serious than rape. This was Ian Smith's "civilization". The interests of its constituency are always paramount even with supposedly democratic governments. It would seem that this is why the Kyoto[1] remains unsigned by America and some other countries.

It is a warm November evening. The shapely form of a woman stands on the kerbside. Car after car stops next to her. In each case she waves the driver off.

Loveness Chipisa [name altered] is in a good mood. She is expecting someone special. She is quite sure that in their last encounter she had given him more than he had expected. That he would return for more she had very little doubt. As she walks slowly down Charter road she surveys each approaching vehicle with heightened anticipation. *"My rich Jew boy client is bound to come back for me"* she had boasted to her friends - *"It was his first*

---

[1] **The Kyoto Protocol** is a protocol to the United Nations Framework Convention on Climate Change [UNFCCC or FCCC], an international environmental treaty produced at the United Nations Conference on treaty is intended to achieve "stabilization of greenhouse gas concentrations in the atmosphere at a level that would prevent dangerous anthropogenic interference with the climate system."[1]
http://en.wikipedia.org/wiki/Kyoto_Protocol

time to taste chikapa". Chikapa is sex involving serious hip gyrations in which only Black girls are reputedly skilled.

She was right. It is not too long before a brand new dark blue Jaguar XJ6 motor vehicle pulls up. The driver gets out and he and Loveness meet in sweet embrace in a darkened corner, away from the flood of the street lights.

"I knew you would come - but I was worried - not that you would not come ... because I know you love me - " she cooes huskily into his ear *"but that perhaps something had happened to you - my heart was getting sore sometimes - I have been waiting so long for you - my man - my bull".* Turning she pulls him by the hand, leading him with an urgency that he is sure signifies desire - a mad desire that must surely match his own.

Soon they reach a door which she opens and, once he has entered, she impales her loins on his, steering their entwined bodies against the door, so as to ensure that it is closed, with a firmness that is pregnant with delicious promise. Swooning with unmitigated passion the man is soon undressed, lying on a bed, pleading with Loveness to start her magic.

It is just then that everything changes. There is a loud bang on the door. A booming male voice demands entry. A cameo is then played out. Loveness has apparently been caught in *flagrante delicto* by her very big and irate boy friend. Her White lover is roughed up and relieved of the sum of £200, but only too grateful to be allowed to get back to his car, clad only in his underpants.

Things take a further dramatic twist when members of the Crime Prevention Unit (CPU) arrive, having been tipped off by one of Loveness's own friends. She and the boyfriend are arrested. However an exhaustive search fails to locate the £200.

It has vanished. Loveness is insistent that she is innocent of any wrong doing. The White man is her lover, she pleads, trying to snuggle up to him coquettishly. No money was ever involved. She is not a prostitute, she protests, wild with indignation. Her White boyfriend, whom she loves deeply, is probably being vengeful because her jealous ex-boyfriend had caught them in the act.

The police are dumbfounded. They have little doubt that Loveness is lying - and that she is a seasoned pro. However it is a fact that, despite all their efforts, no money can be found. Facts are awkward things. The absence of any money changes everything. Some White men did have long standing clandestine love affairs with Black women. This was nothing new. Perhaps Loveness had, at last, found her own "sugar daddy".

She is just about to be released when one of the officers has a whim. Loveness is taken to the casualty department of the central hospital. Soon thereafter she and her accomplice, the so called ex-boyfriend, are charged with robbery.

At their trial it is very difficult to maintain Courtroom decorum and order when, as the prosecutor, I stand up and say –

```
"Your Worship, I now produce Exhibit "A", £200, made up of 20
x £10 notes, retrieved by the casualty doctor from the 1st
accused, Loveness Chipisa".
```

Everyone's eyes are riveted on the money coiled in a neat, but not so small bundle, that I have had wrapped in transparent plastic and that is now dangling high from a hook at the end of a rod that I am holding.

```
"The doctor will give evidence that the money was retrieved
from inside the vagina of Accused 1, Loveness Chipisa"
```

I add, letting every word drop, bright and clear, into the fascinated minds of a people in hushed and intrigued attendance.

Loveness and her accomplice were convicted and sentenced to long terms of imprisonment for their robbery scam.

Later at our club, the debating committee took bets as to whether or not the victim, *"being a Jew boy"* and *"a chikapa addict"*, had returned to Court to claim his money.

He had.

51. Collegiality

Throughout the years I spent as a public prosecutor I worked exclusively with White colleagues, except for the Court interpreters who were Black. The climate of racism being fostered by the RF government was hardly noticeable in my work environment. All my colleagues and the presiding magistrates behaved with professional collegiality. However, with two exceptions, not once was I invited to any of their homes and the contact was confined to the office. The exceptions were Tim Cherry, who was to become a lifelong friend, and Joe Kristopher who later moved to South Africa.

The interpreting staff included Ismail Pedze, who was very experienced, mature and worldly wise. We became good friends and would go fishing together. This gave him the opportunity to bemoan, at some length, the situation with his two wives.

Pedze: You know I was so happy when my first wife came to me and asked me to marry her sister

Me: Hmnnn - - why so?

Pedze: Her sister is very beautiful - too beautiful - young and beautiful - you know what I mean - . I thought I am so lucky as a man - a very lucky man indeed - .

Me: So, of course, you married her - ?

Pedze: Yes - I did - and it was a big mistake - woman are very clever - so clever –

Me: What do you mean - ?

Pedze: It was all a plan by my first wife - a cunning plan - since I married her sister she does nothing in the home - all the cleaning, cooking - looking after the children - even looking after her own children - is done by the junior wife - her sister - my first wife is so lazy –

Me: Hmnnn - why do you allow it - ?

Pedze: Well you see - when I ask her - she just tells me that it is the custom - it is our custom - and I can do nothing

Me: Is it the custom - ?

Pedze: Yes - yes it is - and if you were a Black person you would understand - [he ends ruefully shaking his head]

This rueful shaking of his head would also often occur when he was swearing in a witness being called. The reason was that he was able to predict with near complete accuracy that the witness would prove to be a liar and often a scoundrel as well.

This prediction was founded entirely on the basis of tribal ethnicity and place of origin. Obviously Pedze was displaying ethnic prejudice in stereotyping human beings in this way. The problem was that he was unerringly accurate in his assessments. Many, of course not all, Court cases in the Fort Victoria [now Masvingo] Court tended to be acrimoniously drawn out affairs with some witnesses obviously lying through their teeth. Just 250 kms, in Chiredzi, very little would be disputed in Court as the truth, once unearthed, was hardly ever challenged. Chiredzi folk are a different sub-group of the Shona tribe to which their Fort Victoria counterparts also belong. Pedze's linking of ethnicity to personal integrity seemed to be confirmed.

Interesting also was what happened in many cases involving the issue of identity. A Black witness is asked to describe who he/she says committed the particular offence in issue. The witness is pressed on the issue of identity –

Prosecutor: How can you be absolutely certain that it was the accused in the dock?

Witness: Because he is ugly

Prosecutor: What do you mean when you say that he is ugly?

Witness: Because he is black

As said, colour based prejudice is simply not the sole preserve of any particular ethnic group.

Woman however, it seemed to me, were not always as clever as Pedze might have thought. I did not think I was popular enough with the girls and spent much time pondering ways as to how to remedy this. It was Alan Noach who gave me a sure fire remedy. So at our dance functions I would contract with one of the "ruff-neck" girls, offering to pay for her refreshments. In exchange she would be tasked to approach whichever girl was "my pick" for the night, but who had hitherto displayed little interest in me. My envoy would approach the target, engage her in conversation which included - *"You see that Vavie Greenland - he is a real dog".*

Classifying me "as a real dog" guaranteed success for me thereafter. When I then approached the target, and asked her for a dance, there would be no separating us thereafter. An ordinary male mortal is instantly transformed to being "tall, dark and handsome" once his reputation with the ladies is questionable.

The workings of the female mind will remain forever unfathomable, fascinating and mysterious.

I also had occasion to work with a Scotsman. Mac was big, very big, and also very big hearted … to me. He treated me like his own son. This was entirely gratuitous … unsolicited by me.

However this big heartedness was not extended to everybody. He was decidedly testy and contemptuous of the Irish and, to a lesser extent, of the English. Germans, Japanese and Italians, in particular, induced a glower of dark antipathy.

It was a matter of some cognitive dissonance that this White man treated me better than he treated most White folk. Still I was very appreciative indeed, being the only non-White in the office.

One day he appeared unusually perky. I was invited to his desk. Spread out were a good selection of his war photos. He had served in the Horn of Africa in an intelligence corp.

There was a young uniformed Mac having breakfast with other platoon members. They were all brimming with youthful smiles, radiating the aura of a band of brothers in arm.

In the background was a wooden structure resembling goal posts. Hanging from the cross beam were 5 or 6 Somali men. They were dead; hanging by their necks.

"We used to interrogate them at night, and hang them in the morning" Mac chortled, in happy reminiscence.

It was just about then that I first appreciated the qualities of a treble shot of brandy.

---

52. A giant leap for me - a small step for man

By the end of 1972 I have obtained certification in the Civil Service Higher Law Examinations Parts I and II.

As with Mrs. Wilson the fun starts. The qualification makes me fully eligible to be appointed as a magistrate. There has never been a non-white appointment to the magisterial bench. My boss Joe Kristopher is glowing in his assessment of my competencies. As is the routine with eligible candidates, the matter is referred to the Minister of Justice, Lardner-Burke, one of the chief architects of UDI.

The man has a dilemma that is fundamental. Appointing a non-white to such a position would be a paradigm shift for him, for his party, for his government and for the White constituency he represents. It would be a betrayal of his commitment to reverse *"communist inspired"* liberalism. It would be the thin edge of the wedge, a dangerous precedent giving the Black majority more justification to complain, resist and fight for equality. He flatly refuses to appoint me.

A Coloured delegation, headed by Gerry Raftopolous, goes to see Ian Smith, the Prime Minister and now internationally infamous UDI declarant. Smith has now had 8 years of international condemnation, sanctions and a country with borders increasingly porous to infiltration by Black guerrillas prosecuting the liberation war with increasing boldness and effectiveness. After a discussion Smith leans back in his chair, executes a thumbs up sign and with a grin on his face says loudly - *"Make him a magistrate!"*.

This is news, quite big news for the country, carried by all media; "Christopher Navavie Greenland, is to be appointed as the first Coloured magistrate for the country."[1] History is being made. Why Smith did it must remain within the realms of conjecture considering he was bent on the

---

[1] And for the southern Africa region

suppression of all non-white people and the concept of advancement on merit was alien to his political philosophy. Such conjecture includes the realization that at the time he had his back to the wall on account of the application of international sanctions on the country and the intensification of the liberation war by the Black majority.

A friend, James Devitte, later put it thus –

> "Your appointment had nothing to do with good faith - it had nothing to do with application of merit, fairness or promotion of the interests of justice - it was hypocrisy - intended to augment his case to the world that his government was not racist - a ploy to deceive and obfuscate - in war truth is always a casualty - "

I had much reason to agree, starting with the fact that I was immediately transferred from Bulawayo all the way to Mbare Magistrates Courts in Salisbury, which dealt almost exclusively with Black folk.

Soon after the announcement of my appointment I am visited by a White lawyer generally recognized as a man and professional of great stature. He says he wants to proffer perhaps the best advice that I will ever receive as a judicial officer. As a lawyer who had represented the majority of White juvenile delinquents in the Courts I should know that only the imposition of whipping on first time offenders guaranteed that they would not offend again. He exhorted me to employ this form of punishment if I imagined that punishment could ever be in the interests of both the offender and the general public. His view was based on lifetime of experience.

He must be turning in his grave as a more "enlightened" world now classifies his ideas as barbaric, cruel, degrading and inhuman.

I commenced duties as a judicial officer on the first working day of January 1973. Soon thereafter as I am entering a social club a voice rings out that grabs everyone's attention. *"Christopher Greenland - "* It is Bassy Levendale, addressing me in the delightful intonation that gay men are renowned for. Everyone turns to look. *"I sentence you - "* he goes on *"… to three months … to three months in bed with moi!"* and embraces me possessively. Everyone collapses in gleeful amusement at this wonderful bit of theatre.

The office of magistrate is a long standing and honourable in society. Wikipedia states –

> "A magistrate is a judicial officer; in ancient Rome, the word magistratus denoted one of the highest government officers with judicial and executive powers." According to William Einwechter from the National Reform Association [natreformassn.org] the Biblical standards for appointment as a magistrate are 'men who are able; men who fear God; men committed to truth, men who are opposed to covetousness; men

who are wise; men who have understanding; men who are known to be wise and understanding; men with natural ability, integrity and spiritual maturity".

In the southern African region the magistracy had always presented as the *"face of justice"* in that for the vast majority of persons it is the magistracy that administers to their needs when issues of justice arise. In Rhodesia, magistrates presided over criminal and civil trials, dealt with most licensing issues and conducted civil marriages. The black gown of office helped to instill a generally held sense of prestige and honour.

An American female judge came to give us a talk at the university. In the end it was somewhat embarrassing for her to find that we all had much higher jurisdiction than she had. As a class, magistrates presented in the upper middle social-economic sector of society. A magistrate lived well and could afford a new car and bi-annual holidays.

My imminent appointment to this honourable office was therefore of significance in the greater scheme of things. For me and my family it was to be an honour and something of a "giant leap" in the journey of life. For the oppressed majority it was to be a "small step[1]" but a not insignificant one. In a nuanced way it gave the lie to central themes of the RF regime's philosophy of racism.

All this would have never happened had a simple villager not displayed diamond hard integrity in witnessing to truth that embarrassed his bully-boy "vrastaag" friend all those years ago after a fist fight on a bush path near Embakwe Coloured School.

53. In the heat of the night

Despite the announcement the ugly face of racist oppression still lurks and soon strikes.

It is late evening in December 1972. My brother and I are walking from the Monomatapa Hotel, where we have been celebrating the announcement of my soon to be made appointment as the country's first Coloured magistrate. We decide to walk the distance of some 3 kms to a favourite haunt of Coloured folk, the Queens hotel. We are smartly dressed. An unmarked car

---

[1] At 02:56 UTC on July 21 [10:56pm EDT, July 20], 1969, Armstrong made his descent to the Moon's surface and spoke his famous line "That's one small step for [a] man, one giant leap for mankind" exactly six and a half hours after landing. http://en.wikipedia.org/wiki/Apollo_11

comes to a screeching halt next to us. Two White men in plain clothes approach, identify themselves as members of the Crime Prevention Unit, "CPU", and announce that they are taking us in for questioning. We try to protest. It is of no use. We are conveyed to the Salisbury Central Police Station and marched into the main charge office where they start to record our details. At this point some senior Black officers of the uniformed branch, who are in attendance dealing with the public, quietly alert these bright sparks that - *"Today you have arrested the wrong man"*.

These officers have recognized me. They are keenly aware that I have just been designated as the country's first non-white magistrate. The CPU members now have a problem and disappear to another office, undoubtedly to find somewhere private to discuss the problem. The two Black sergeants are smirking in smug satisfaction at the plight of their White counterparts and give us a knowing look.

Moments later, in struts another White man in plain clothes. He has a gun belt with two holstered guns, cowboy style. He goes to the first occupant of a bench in the office, a Black man, and barks at him - *"So what are you here for?"* The man tries to explain but is rudely interrupted. This bullying of human beings is repeated as he moves down the line being gratuitously rude and offensive to Black folk on the bench. One or two are slapped across the face. The sergeants watch this ruefully. There is nothing they can do. Sergeant is the highest rank they can hold. They are outranked by their White counterpart.

In my mind I make an association with Sidney Poitier in "The Heat of The Night[1]". The public molester eventually arrives at the spot where my brother and I are standing. He stands right in my face and says- *"So - what are you here for hey?"* I do not respond.

He barks variations of the same question to both of us adding gratuitous observations like - *"We know what you buggers get up to - drug merchants - but better not fuck with the CPU "*, prodding me hard in my stomach. *"Your mates know me - they all know Ossie Cowan - they know they can't fuck with Ossie - so you better not try ..."* he adds.

I now make a connection. Ossie Cowan is renowned in the Coloured community for "stitching-up" our youth in particular. So many youngsters

---

[1] *In the Heat of the Night* is a 1967 film, based on the John Ball novel published in 1965, which tells the story of an African-American police detective from Philadelphia who becomes involved in a murder investigation in a racist small town in Mississippi. http://en.wikipedia.org/wiki/In_the_Heat_of_the_Night_[film]

have told me how he would plant dagga on them once he received information that they were users. He would also set his police dog on them. Many of them were subsequently convicted. *"I know that I am a rooker*[1]*"* they would lament *"but this is unfair ..."*

As Cowan prods me in the stomach I feel that something must happen. In such a situation it is not the mind that takes over, neither is it the heart; but the spirit, the spirit of one man, the spirit of all mankind; confronted with that which is unjust, that which is evil.

Just as I asked my tormentor on a bush path so many years ago, in Embakwe, to take off his watch, on a decision made more in the subconscious rather than a plan consciously formulated, I say to Ossie - *"You are only talking tough because you are wearing a gun belt - like you are some sort of cowboy - "* He replies, an arrogant smirk on his face, *"Aah - so we have got a tongue hey - we can talk - and talk big - "* as he pokes my lips with his finger.

He then unclips the gun belt and, turning away, throws it onto the charge office table. As he turns back towards me, I punch him, and with a sickening thud catch him square on the mouth and nose, with blood and mucous splattering onto the front of my suit and shirt. He reels and flies across the top of the charge office table landing heavily on the other side. It was a good punch - with good results. Before he can make his way back other police officers charge in and the two sergeants take control by putting themselves between Cowan and me.

When senior uniformed officers query the situation Cowan, mouth bleeding, is incoherent in his anger and splutters out that he wants to *"get this bastard"*. All the police officers disappear once again to discuss, I presume, the now very big problem. A senior ranking officer is sent for. As he is apparently in bed, when phoned, his arrival takes some time. When he interviews me in an office, as part of "preliminary enquiry" he has instituted, he starts off by pointing out that I should know that assaulting a police officer on duty is an extremely serious matter.

It is a game of chess. He is seeking an advantage. Instinctively I say to him - *"there were two witnesses - can you please call them and let us hear what they have to say - "* The police sergeants come in and are asked to recount what happened. They give a factual account of the incident from the time when Ossie arrived, and all his bad behaviour of abusing Black people in the office. When they reach the stage of the confrontation with me - *"Officer*

---

[1] **Rooker** – from the Afrikaans word "rook" – to smoke - pronounced "rooeker" meaning smoker of dagga

Cowan - who never identified himself - also started to assault Mr. Greenland - poking him in the face - and started to draw his gun ..."

It is soon over. The police undertake not to press charges and I will reciprocate. Ossie is transferred to Bulawayo. Soon thereafter some Coloured youngsters, when confronted by Ossie, knife his dog to death. He ends his service in the force some years later as a wanted man.

54. Justice is blind

I commence duties as a magistrate in January1973. There are facial expressions and mutterings of satisfaction amongst the gallery of Black folk as my clerk barks "Silence in Court" and I enter the Court in the black robes of office. I feel good. This soon changes.

One of my first trials is that of a young attractive Black female accused of Malicious Injury to Property, "MIP". She pleads guilty, asking for mercy whilst setting out the circumstances to which the prosecutor fully agrees. The complainant is her boyfriend who had *"plucked her like a flower from the garden of education"* where she was about to complete her first year of a degree.

Because she was pregnant from him she had to leave university. On the night of the offence he arrived with a new girlfriend whom he wanted to sleep with. It was cold and rainy. This did not stop him from turfing her and their three-month-old baby out into a cold and rainy night. Piqued at his actions, she had then thrown a brick into the windscreen of his car; hence the charge of malicious injury to property.

To my mind she is more sinned against than sinner. I say so, in delivering what I imagine is a Solomonic judgment, ticking her off for having taken the law into her own hands, but recognizing the appalling circumstances of provocation and gross irresponsibility the complainant displayed towards her and the child. In the circumstances, I postpone the passing of sentence for three years on conditions of good behaviour on her part. She is free to go. I am certain in my mind that justice has been done.

There are audible mutterings and murmurs in the Court. During the tea break these increase outside my Courtroom. On enquiry the Court staff inform me that my sentence has been greeted with unanimous disgust by the general public in attendance and there is a consensus that I am a really bad magistrate who perhaps should not have been appointed.

In Black culture the actions of the accused, involving smashing up her "husband's" property is totally intolerable. A woman simply has no right to do such a thing. The interpreter assures me - *"If you were a Black person - you would understand - "*

I am not Black - my grandmother made that all too clear to me - I hear him loud and clear.

---

55. And in the heat of the day

The 70s saw an intensification of the bush war of liberation and of a "Black Power" culture, which had started in 1968, finally taking root in our community. Our heroes are Malcolm X, Nelson Mandela, the Black Panthers and other Black civil rights champions. We spend evenings playing long-play records of Mandela's Rivonia trial speech and Dr Martin Luther King's "I Have a Dream" speech.

I decline call ups into the Territorial Army, taking full advantage of a law under which members of the judiciary may claim exemption from compulsory military service. With the black power[1] culture came the "afro" hairstyle. Like millions of others around the world I joined in solidarity with our Black brothers in America and adopted the "Afro".

Suddenly it was an advantage to have kroos hair, and I now thanked an all-wise God for having turned my hair kroos in my late teens. Sporting an afro did not go down well with all of my White colleagues though and there were disapproving remarks passed. I was called into his office by my boss, Des Utting, and pointedly asked whether I thought an afro was becoming of a person holding the post of a magistrate. My answer was that surely he accepted that those over whom I presided over in my Court must think so. This check-mate was met with an expression of ill concealed disgust.

On a car trip from Bulawayo in 1975, we stop at the Kadoma Motel for lunch and refreshments. All members of our group of four, Edgar Rogers, Felix Galloway[2] and Anthony Charles Greenland and I, are smartly dressed. As we approach the tables a waiter stops us –

---

[1] **The 1968 Olympics Black Power salute** was a noted black civil rights protest and one of the most overtly political statements in the 110 year history of the modern Olympic Games. African American athletes Tommie Smith and John Carlos performed the Power to the People salute at the 1968 Summer Olympics in Mexico City. http://en.wikipedia.org/wiki/1968_Olympics_Black_Power_salute

[2] **Edgar Rogers** nick-named "Jabbar" after the American basketball star Karim Abdul Jabbar, **Felix Gallaway** nicknamed "Soul"

Waiter: Have you not read the sign? [pointing to a sign which reads "Right of Admission Reserved"]

Felix: What do you mean? - What has that got to do with us?

Waiter: Well, I am sorry, but you will have to leave

Felix: What do you mean - that we must leave?

Waiter: We cannot serve Coloureds - we are not allowed to serve you

Edgar: Please call your boss - [which request Edgar repeats in Shona. Soon thereafter the proprietor, a recently arrived Australian named Tony Barker, arrives]

Barker: You people need to leave and leave now, or I will call the police

Tony: On what charge - what is the problem - all we want is a meal and refreshments - we are not criminals …

Barker: We have right of admission - and there is the sign - so you better leave now - or I will call the police and you will be arrested

Felix: Do you know that this man is a magistrate - he is a magistrate in the Courts -?

[Barker looks at me, with my suit and afro, and the disdainful expression on his face betrays a deep-seated antipathy]

Barker: I don't care who he is - I am within my rights as admission is reserved at this Motel … now leave or I will call the police …

We leave shortly thereafter.

Within days the print media give prominence to a story titled "Coloured magistrate refused drinks at Kadoma Motel". There is a picture of me sporting a really big afro which I had especially combed out when the reporter visited me. We felt that a statement should be made to the world.

On the Monday morning my boss Des Utting asked me, in passing, whether or not I knew where the paper had got its story. I replied that I did not. Utting knew full well that this was "a white lie" telling him, in effect, to mind his own business since the press had published my photo and a statement attributed to me in which I said I intended to go to Court and oppose renewal of Barker's liquor license.

The next day I was summoned to his office and informed that I was being put on "very serious charges" and that there would be a disciplinary hearing conducted by Head Office. In the meantime, he went on, I was required to file a full written statement about the matter.

The charges were conduct unbecoming of an officer of the Courts and being untruthful to my superior. I filed a written explanation that our rights to fair, equal and dignity had been gratuitously violated and that my denial to Utting had been proffered in "unofficial" circumstances, conferring no obligation on me to disclose my personal affairs.

In response Utting wanted to know if I was resolved in my intention to take Barker to Court and oppose the renewal of his liquor license. In a series of further interviews it became all too clear that what government did not want was further publicity which was guaranteed if there was a Court case about Barker's license.

[Picture shoes Magistrates at Mbare Courts in 1973: Left to Right - Author, Des Utting, Dick Mallinson, Bill Lunt]

I refused to relent. Utting wanted to know what I hoped to achieve. I truthfully stated that I was not too sure but that what had happened was intolerable and akin to the Rosa Parks[1] saga.

I was not going to acquiesce. Soon thereafter I received a "private note", from a senior officer in the office of the Attorney General, drawing my attention to the fact that regulations passed under the Liquor Act conferred a right on a licensee to discriminate against persons on any grounds. He was counseling me to be realistic. Racism was legal and I would be embarrassed when the

---

[1] **"On December 1, 1955, Rosa Parks**, a 42-year-old African American woman ⋯ boarded this Montgomery City bus to go home from work ⋯ Soon all of the seats in the bus were filled. When a white man entered the bus, the driver (following the standard practice of segregation) insisted that all four blacks sitting just behind the white section give up their seats so that the man could sit there. Mrs. Parks, who was an active member of the local NAACP, quietly refused to give up her seat.

Her action was spontaneous and not pre-meditated, although her previous civil rights involvement and strong sense of justice were obvious influences. "When I made that decision," she said later, "I knew that I had the strength of my ancestors with me." http://www.hfmgv.org/exhibits/rosaparks/story.asp

Board ruled accordingly. This same officer, John Giles, was to later commit suicide by jumping out of a hotel window in London during one of the several "settlement talks" sessions that Ian Smith had with the British government. I refused to relent.

We traveled to Kadoma Licensing Court. It was jam packed with Black and Coloured folk, all of whom surrounded me expressing solidarity. Barker was pathetic as a witness and even more so when I cross-examined him, a skill that I was, of course, much versed in. His problem was that he did not want to tell the truth and say that his motives had been racist. So he took the stance that we appeared to him as persons bent on making trouble. It was his prerogative to reserve right of admission and deny access to trouble makers. The proceedings then took on a very comical texture at his expense.

Me: So you say we looked like we wanted to cause trouble?

Barker: Yes

Me: Is this what your waiter reported to you - you agree he saw us first and was called - ? [Knowing that the waiter, if called, will not support his claim he now has a difficulty]

Barker: Well - er - that's the way it looked to me ...

Me: Hmnnn - that is the way *it looked* to you Mr. Barker - an experienced hotelier. We were in suits - and the waiter had not reported misbehavior - so how did it seem to you that we were about to cause trouble - explain please?

Barker: Well - er - er - it was the way you were standing ...

Me: I see the way *we were standing* - were we not standing as people normally do - each standing on two legs?

[There are audible giggles in the Court]

Barker: er - there was something about the way you were standing - er - moving your feet ...

Me: Moving our feet - how Sir? - stamping our feet - dancing - jiving - explain - this way that people who want to make trouble stand?- [The Courtroom fills with laughter]

Barker is finished and cannot answer. The Chairman of the Committee suggestively asks him if he is aware of the regulations.

He wants Barker to admit that it is racist and that he was within his rights to be racist. Barker is a racist, but he is simply not going to say so in open Court and have the media splash this all around the world. So he simply nods in the affirmative. The Chairman is frustrated as he undoubtedly would prefer to uphold Barker's right to be racist under the regulations and irritably asks me to move on. It is time to give the man a way out.

Me: If you are prepared to solemnly undertake never to discriminate against another person on grounds of race I am prepared to withdraw my objection to renewal of your liquor license?

[He is visibly relieved]

Barker: Yes - I am prepared to do that - [he says taking the bait]

Me: Raise you right hand

Barker complies and I put him through the indignity of having to swear before God, right hand held high, that he will never again discriminate against a human being on grounds of race. I then withdraw the objection. I have won. However, it is a Pyrrhic victory. Within weeks Barker is back to his old tricks. It is amazing. A man comes all the way from Australia to come and abuse Africans in their own land. But then again - what is new?

The story is carried in the press. Des Utting is incensed. I am summoned before a disciplinary committee, headed by the Permanent Secretary of Justice. The Committee is polite and questions are temperately put. It is an uncomfortable affair. They have the manner and demeanor of persons who have little faith in their "fault finding" cause. This is what sometimes happens when bad leaders force good people to do bad things. They go through the motions and I stick to my guns that –

> our rights as human beings had been violated; that opposing the renewal of the license was my constitutional right; that publicity of this would have inevitably occurred; that Utting had not been acting in his official capacity when he first questioned me and that therefore my denial to him was an innocuous "white lie" which human beings tell every day as when in answering "fine thank you" when asked "how are you" even though not at all well.

After a few days the Committee's written findings arrive. I am cleared of conduct unbecoming of an officer of the Court.

They are not prepared to classify me as a *"dangerous munt"*. Had I been Black??? However they "note" a concern at my lack of complete forthrightness with a superior. It is a token slap on the wrist. I have not been fired. Utting is sick.

When Black majority rule overtakes the country in 1980 he immediately leaves and apparently heads off to Australia.

56. Sapiential and other games

Oppressed people will find all kinds of ways to act out resistance to the oppressor. In the early 70s, we found chess, and imagined that it was a good way of striking just one more blow against the culture of racism. After all racist thinking seems to be premised on the proposition that a Black person is stupid, and therefore deserves to be treated as inferior. Chess is a struggle of minds. It is intellectual; sapiential, the very antithesis of what racists believe Black folk to be.

In 1972 Bobby Fischer[1], a non-conformist American had beaten Boris Spassky of Russia at chess, ending the Soviets' long-standing domination in this field. The sensational style of play that he employed in destroying, even humiliating, the Soviet grandmaster, gave huge impetus to the popularity of the game, Rhodesia being no exception. The symbolism of the east - west cold war was not lost on the world and us.

So we were determined to do battle of our own, in the now thriving weekly chess league, in order to embarrass the white mindset of superiority being avidly promoted by the RF government. Ganief Jenkins, who was also our captain and coach, my brother Tony and I entered, playing under the name of "Continentals". We studied the game long and hard, paying particular attention to the Fischer/Spassky duels, and practiced long into the night. I was extremely fortunate in that I worked with Les Donnelly, brother of the national and then South African champion, Brian Donnelly. Les and I spent many lunch hours at it and he was a great tutor.

However I lost my first league game to a White teenager. It was devastating. All my life I had played sport and had experienced loss on some occasions. From school days my motto had been "modest in victory, gracious in defeat." I took the defeat extremely badly without an ounce of graciousness.

It did, however, strengthen my resolve. For the rest of the year, playing every week, we did not lose one match against White opposition. A most enjoyable encounter was when, playing as white[2], all three of us opened, in synchrony, with Fischer's famous pawn-to-queen-bishop-four move. It was a bold, dangerous and revolutionary move which amateurs steer clear of. Our opponents, log leaders at the time, never recovered from the shock and were demolished in no time. It was sensational and we felt good especially as the results of the games were routinely covered in the weekend print media.

---

[1] Robert James *Fischer*

[2] In chess opponents use white and black pieces respectively

We had won the sapiential battle. The establishment needed to know that, whatever our pigmentation or hair type, we were not stupid and could beat their kind on any level playing field. And our captain, Ganief Jenkins, was especially strong in this attitude.

The other front on which battle was joined was in the basketball league. The game had been adopted by our community and given impetus after a visit by the world famous Harlem Globe Trotters. The show that these Black players put on, a kaleidoscope of skills, colour and antics was incredibly entertaining and inspirational to us. Here were Black people who were simply unmatchable. They did on the basketball Court what the Cape Coon Carnival did on the stage - prove that on a level playing field we could be unmatchable. Every year thereafter a nearly all-Black American team named Venture for Victory would visit and conquer all before them.

I was chairperson of Arcadia Bucs, a Coloured team. Traditional league champions were a Greek dominated team named Hellenics. Throughout the 70s we set out to unseat them from their throne. From the start they were well resourced in all respects, including having their own champion standard Court. We had nothing and had to make do on school grounds. So the war involved having to build ourselves up from scratch. A basketball Court ensured that, in terms of economy of scale, we were all on a relatively level playing field even though only a small and under resourced community.

Tony, my brother, was our coach. It did not take too long for us to overcome the other White teams such as Police, which victory had its own special flavour. Hellenics, however, was quite another matter. Slowly the encounters became more closely contested until the stage was reached where they were heart-stopping, breath-taking duels of epic proportions with the result in doubt to the very last second, and their winning margin by Hellenics just one point. To our minds much of this had to do with the referee, as the same gentleman was employed in every final. He was a well respected advocate of the High Court. Given the stakes, it is all too probable that our own view of him was coloured by sub-conscious bias. In race-orientated wars, this is all too likely.

Anyway the stage was reached where our supporters, who would outnumber theirs, would start singing the Boney M smash hit, as we went on to play, - "There are Brown Boys in the Ring - traa-la-la-la- la - there are brown boys in the ring - traa-la-la-la-la - " and keep it up throughout the game. I do not think we slept the night that we finally beat them in the national final. Once we toppled Hellenics the whole war started all over again in a long drawn out saga in which they tried vainly for years to regain their crown. It is pertinent to point out that we had one White player in our team. Hellenics, on the other hand, was all White.

In 1975 Tony and I decide to take Edgar and Felix on a fishing trip to Lake Kariba[1] On arrival at Charara Fishing Camp, where we intend to stay for a week, a plan is hatched so as to halve our accommodation fees. Edgar and Felix decide that they will book in as our servants. Servants pay only a nominal fee. The camp manager is a Black man named McLeod. Since Edgar and Felix both speak perfect Shona, the main Black dialect, the plan goes off without hitch and only Tony and I pay fees.

In the camp our companions take to doing their evening exercises in close proximity to neighboring campers. Their exercise routine is incredibly impressive, a forerunner to modern aerobics, except that they include basketball touches of each other high in the air, their bodies soaring up and up till fingers meet. Phew! One could lose weight just watching them. The problem with all this is that both are clad only in exercise pants that are so skimpy as to qualify them as being just about naked. Even I, their friend and colleague, am uncomfortable with this display. In Court an argument could be made out that here we have a case of "indecent exposure". It is one thing to show off the male physique. It is quite another thing to do so in a way that puts the whole of Africa's testosterone toolbox on exhibition. It is difficult to see them as anything other than two black "six-packs", doing a provocative dance on a dusty stage, washed over by the rays of the setting sun.

It is not surprising when two White men from the neighboring camp approach us and very respectfully request that this display stop or be taken somewhere else. After all *"there are women around"*. Their request is met with a deluge of new found black rhetoric gleaned from speeches by new heroes such as Malcolm X, Eldridge Cleaver and other hard line American Black activists. Edgar and Felix give them a long lecture on *"the need for the White man to appreciate, recognize and accept the beauty and superiority of the black body - especially since the White man has long since been adept at accessing the wondrous sweetness of the black female body under cover of darkness - "* You don't know whether to laugh or cry. They don't mean any of it. It is pure theater on their

---

[1] **Lake Kariba** is over 220 kilometers [140 mi] long and up to 40 kilometers [20 mi] in width. It covers an area of 5,580 square kilometers [2,150 sq mi] and its storage capacity is an immense 185 cubic kilometers [44.4 cu mi]. The mean depth of the lake is 29 meters [95 ft]; the maximum depth is 97 meters [320 ft]. It is one of the world's largest man-made reservoirs.

http://en.wikipedia.org/wiki/Lake_Kariba#Physical_characteristics

part but with a serious politically nuanced message. The complainants retreat in numbed incredulity. Shamefully we all reflect smugly on this put down of our White brethren - but not for long.

One evening Edgar and Felix go for their run along a track that winds its way through the African bush to Kariba Town. They return earlier than usual, much earlier - with Felix in the lead. They collapse on their camp beds panting as if their chests will burst. Our neighbors arrive soon afterward and drive right into our camp. I realize something is up as they alight from their van smiling broadly. Confirmation that something is up comes swiftly as Felix jumps up and breathlessly tries to order them to leave. The two White men turn towards me, and with big grins on their faces and say, - *"You need to hear this - man you should have seen your friends here ... "* pointing to Felix and Edgar. Against the protestations of our colleagues I invite the visitors to take seats in camp chairs and offer them beers. *"We need to hear this"* I say.

It emerges that as Felix and Edgar were running along the path our neighbors drove up to them and offered them a lift. Once again they were treated to a colourful lecture about the "softness" of White folk who need cars, the "hardness" of Black folk and other gratuitous rhetoric intended to niggle and irritate them as White folk. *"So be it"* our boastful friends were told - *"look over there ..."* as the van proceeded to accelerate away. Just some 70 -100 yards away was a pride of lion ambling roughly in their direction. Soon Tony and I are in stitches as we are told about the terror stricken escape back to camp that our friends set about accomplishing, with each overtaking the other in rapid succession; Olympic times being shattered as fast as you like. As the lions seemed interested our neighbors thankfully kept their van in between the pride and the fleeing pair.

The trouble is not over. McLeod arrives soon afterwards. He demands payment in full of camp fees for Felix and Edgar. They try to protest stating that they are servants.

"Rubbish - " says McLeod - *"I have never seen such lazy servants in my life - every evening I see you people come off your boat - the servants run to camp sit down and start drinking - while these MaBaas[1] unload the boat, carry the fish, clean the fish and make fire for the night. They do the cooking and the washing up while the servants have more beer. In the morning it is the same - the servants sleep while the MaBaas get up, make fire and cook breakfast. Then they wash up and carry the things to the boat ... even in the*

---

[1] **MaBaas** – colloquialism meaning "these bosses"

morning the servants are drinking some beer - no - no - you are not servants and you must pay"

When we try to say that we are very good bosses McLeod says emphatically - *"No - no, never - not in Rhodesia - "*

Our White neighbors are doubled over in laughter. The day is saved when Edgar counsels McLeod that he should charge visitors for the privilege of viewing the penis of one of the workers in camp. Some time before the man had been naked in the waters of Lake Kariba, drawing his nets, when a tiger fish struck. His most precious organ was reduced in an instant by jaws filled with razor sharp teeth. Fortunately the bite was lengthwise and the man was able to still procreate thereafter. His penis, however, was something well worth viewing and many a patron paid for the privilege, starting with our two White gentlemen neighbors in camp.

By this time I was enrolled as an external student at the University College of Rhodesia in a program devised by Professor Richard "Dick Christie" for persons like me who, for reasons of fate or the vagaries of circumstance, had not had previous opportunity to access tertiary education. Those who were admitted under this program are forever indebted to Christie and his fantastic team of lecturers, including Andrew Lang, Dennis Robinson and Jeff Feltoe, for having afforded us this opportunity.[1]

For seven years I study deep into the night in order to secure my BL and LLB degrees[2].

My routine was to come from work, have an hour's sleep, then study till midnight after a "freshening up" shower.

57. The right partner - and a sojourn south

At university I meet a girl named Elizabeth Gutu. She is beautiful and incredibly well groomed. On a whim I decide that I will invite her to be my partner at a dance function to be held in Arcadia, our suburb. It is not at all common for a Coloured male to escort a Black female to such a function. What I propose to do will be a deviation from societal and cultural norms.

---

[1] **Professor Christie** is an international expert on contract in Roman Dutch Law and author of **Christie on Contract.**

Andrew Lang eventually moved on to Rhodes University in the Eastern Cape, South Africa. **Jeff** has soldiered on in Zimbabwe.

[2] **"BL"**- Batchelor of Law. **"LLB"**- Bachelor of Laws.

My mother is bemused and asks me if I am sure. Soon thereafter the issue is formally raised in the presence of my Aunt Elizabeth. My Black aunt sets out the rules clearly and firmly. I will do no such thing. It is out of the question. This is the consensus of my Black relatives that she has been asked to convey, and is not to be questioned.

To them any association by me with a Black female, especially one of Shona extraction, is taboo. However much I try to explain that Elizabeth Gutu is only a friend and that I have no romantic interest in her the opposition is the same; any man/woman relationship between me and her is out of the question. Then comes the crunch. If I defy their wishes Elizabeth will strip naked in public. Such an action on her part is the ultimate representation of disapproval in Ndebele custom and generally regarded as a curse. My intentions have been completely vetoed and unless I propose to incur the grievous disappointment of all my Black relatives, and the wrath of the ancestral spirits, I dare not persist with my plan.

I had married young at age 22. It failed and finally ended in divorce in 1974. It was also subsequently annulled. I have two lovely daughters by this marriage, Shereen Elizabeth and Helen Angela.

On Xmas day 1974, a young newly qualified teacher named Palmira Rozaria Lourenço, visits our home. My brother and I have included one or two condoms in decoration of our Xmas tree. Pam wants to know where we obtained *"these kinds of balloons"*. My mother wants to know where I have found such an innocent girl. I tell her that she received all her schooling under Roman Catholic nuns. *"They seem to have done a very good job - "* she observes. Aunt Elizabeth agrees. We tie the knot three years later on 11 March 1977.

In 1978 we visit the annual agricultural show at the Salisbury showground. Pam and the kids refuse to leave until we have purchased a ten-foot Turner Wren caravan with full awning and extras. It is an "impulse buy" which pays off that December when we decide to go on holiday to South Africa for the first time. At Fort Victoria [now Masvingo] all vehicles are assembled in a convoy and drivers called to a meeting to be given a full briefing by an army officer about the 250km trip to the South African border.

"Make sure ..." he says in a cold mater-of-fact tone *" - that your vehicle is in good order - coz if you break down - especially near Bubye river - you are a gonna - you will be slotted - the escort vehicles cannot stop for stragglers ... their responsibility is the convoy ... and if the convoy is attacked - please keep the outside lane open for me - I want to be able to get at these bastards - "*

He is referring to the possibility of our convoy being attacked by guerrilla fighters. It is the height of the bush war of liberation. My vehicle is assigned to be the lead in a convoy of 104 vehicles. As we pull off an armed vehicle takes station in front of us. On the back is mounted a machine gun manned by a soldier on a swivel chair. The convoy moves off and snakes its way along the winding road. Two light aircraft patrol the sky, flying up and down the length of the convoy. In our car the air is pregnant with apprehension; our throats dry up and we drink a lot of fluids. At irregular intervals the gunner in the vehicle ahead peppers the surrounding bush with bursts of machine gun fire as he swivels around scanning for a faceless foe perhaps lurking, ready to strike at any time. The children keep asking in very worried tones why there is a man with a gun in the vehicle ahead. As young as they are they know we are in danger. You cannot fool children. Platitudes in reply fail, and they keep asking questions as to who wants to shoot at us. We drink more fluids, lots more - and conversation is stilted and strained.

We finally make it to the coast, and see the sea for the first time in our lives, from the top of the pass at George, in the Western Cape. It is an awesome sight, swallowing up the horizon in its blue green endlessness. The next morning we cannot wait to get onto the beach and experience what it is like to swim in the sea. Our arrival is greeted by a sign "This Facility is For Members of The White Group Only". In the near distance the White group is enjoying its facility. However we are not about to be denied after having traveled over 2500 kms. So we find a spot and start our swim.

In no time at all I see what must be an immediate descendant of Neanderthal man. He is big; he is muscular, he is hairy; and he is approaching us with a gait that signals trouble, big trouble. He booms out something in Afrikaans. I put on the bravest face I can muster and, in tourist Afrikaans, greet him and say I am sorry I do not speak the language.

We then get a severe dressing down for swimming at this spot. What is the point, he laments, of him going to all the trouble of setting up a safe swimming area demarcated by red flags, and protected by life guards, if we are going to put our lives at risk by swimming here? Do we not understand, or care, how much pain we will bring to the lives of other people if we drown? And how will he be able to explain our deaths? We are shooed off to join the all White crowd on the beach. No one raises an eyebrow and the children soon make friends with other children, giggling and cavorting happily in the sea and on its shore. We have a wonderful day, brown intermingling with white in strife torn South Africa on an all White beach. In my heart I have little doubt that the situation would not have been tolerated had we been Black.

We are the first Coloured caravanners to secure a berth at Lake Pleasant Caravan Park, at Sedgefield, George. The park owner, an ex-Rhodesian, allocates our little 10-foot Turner Wren caravan a site amongst the luxury 17 foot Jurgens models owned by wealthy Free State farmers. Considering that this is a racist apartheid state a surreal situation develops. These die-in-the-wood supporters of racism treat us to a wonderful holiday with nightly braais [barbecues] and our children are collected for special treats in the day time. They are quite clear in attitude. Races are not equal. Blacks were biblically assigned to be the "hewers of wood and drawers of water". That is their role, not governing anybody. As proof they point to the many failed governments in Black Africa. To be good to strangers and travelers is a Christian duty. When we pull out 10 days later we find that the bill that we have run up at the site shop has been paid. It is confusing; it is unreal; it is unbelievable, but something of a strangely heartwarming island of weird sanity in a sea of madness.

Thereafter we travel down the famous Garden Route, which is a marvelous experience, and finally berth at Sonesta, a holiday resort "for members of the coloured group only" situated at Hawston. Hawston is a small town that supplies cheap Coloured labour to the beautiful tourist town of Hermanus, famous for its whale watching. Again our little caravan is the smallest of the lot and our kids are teased about this. However we have the last laugh when the Cape Doctor[1] comes up one night and rips the awnings off 176 other bigger caravans with ours remaining intact.

I enter the annual hotly contested chip/putt golf competition which I eventually win. One of the opponents I knock out is a certain Alison Coert. When he escorts me to the lounge in order to buy me a drink, as loser, he shows me the newspaper. The front page is covered in pictures of fuel storage tanks that the guerrillas in Rhodesia have managed to set ablaze. It is not pretty. He then asks me to call my wife and says he will call his wife, Virginia.

We all meet soon thereafter. These two then solemnly announce that they have discussed the matter and have agreed that they will keep our three children until the war in Zimbabwe is over. Pam and I are gob-smacked. We have never met the couple and Alison and I hardly spoke during our game as

---

[1] **Cape Doctor -** [usually The Cape Doctor] is the local name for the strong, persistent and dry south-easterly wind that blows on the South African coast in summer [around Christmas in this hemisphere]. It is known as the Cape Doctor because it has long been held to clear Cape Town of pollution and 'pestilance'.
http://en.wikipedia.org/wiki/Cape_Doctor

his English was just a little better than my Afrikaans. But they are serious. When we express reservations about their request they turn it into a demand pointing out that it is in the highest degree irresponsible for parents to expose children to such danger.

It is a long time before they are forced to accept that we cannot leave our children. Hoping that we will change our minds they invite us to spend our last week with them at their home in Cape Town. In the meantime Alison offers to obtain all our provisions from Cape Town, at a newly opened Hypermarket, as it is considerably cheaper that way. Thereafter he steadfastly refuses to accept re-payment saying that we can settle things before we leave. On the eve of our departure they hold a farewell braai for us during which Alison insists that we should not spoil the party by bringing up issues about money. The only way we are able to repay them is by putting the money in an envelope which we leave on the dining room table on our departure at 5 am. On our trip back we stop over in Kimberly where we are treated to the wonderful hospitality of the Coopstad family who had extracted a promise from us at Sonesta that we visit.

In our honour Coopstad puts on an evening braai which is well attended. During conversation I mistakenly hear one of the guests referring to himself as a "bastard".

Me: Well the trouble is that if you regard yourself as a bastard, you will always find that the word has even bigger bastards than you ...

Guest: What's that - what are you saying - are you calling me a bastard - ? [as he advances seized with rage]

Me: Look - I am simply acknowledging what you have said about yourself

Guest: Hey Mister - . [and advances with malice aforethought - .]

Coopstad: No - no - gentlemen - there will be no violence in my house - there is a misunderstanding ...

Guest: there is no misunderstanding - this bugger here is calling me a bastard –

Coopstad: No, no, no - Chris here is from Rhodesia - he does not understand - he has never been to South West[1] [now Namibia] - he does not know about Basters.

The problem is soon settled and peace restored. That is how I came to know about the Basters. "The Basters (also known as Baasters, Rehobothers or Rehoboth Basters) are the descendants of liaisons between the Cape Colony

---

[1] **South West** – referring to South West Africa – now Namibia.

Dutch and indigenous African women. They largely live in Namibia and are similar to Coloured or Griqua people in South Africa[1]".

Physically most are very fair skinned. Hair tends to be straight, sometimes curly. Many have blue, grey, green - Caucasian coloured eyes. What strikes me most about them is their attitude. I am not ever to be confused about who and what they are. These people are Basters - not Coloured - not Black – not White - not anything else - they are Basters, and they are incredibly proud of it!

We return home, re-joining the convoy at Bietbridge, to war ravaged Rhodesia. It has been a truly wonderful adventure. What has been most striking was the hospitality of South Africans. It was all unreal. Human kindness to strangers completely masked the depraved savagery of the apartheid system. Proof of that savagery reposed in the invisibility of Black people. They comprised the vast majority and yet throughout the trip we have seen relatively few of them. Evidence of their existence reposed in the numerous shanty town stretches of poverty on the edges of cities and towns.

A moment of great sadness was looking across Table Bay at Robben Island on which Nelson Mandela remained incarcerated. The high point was re-unification with the coons, now referred to as minstrels, my childhood idols. On the day after New Years day we had attended Green Point Stadium in Cape Town to witness the spectacle of the annual parade of Coloured folk formed into troupes of minstrels, painted, costumed, colourful and so alive - so very much alive with their music, dancing and singing.

We are to repeat these caravan trips to South Africa three more times, including a stay at a Black park, Umgababa, outside Durban. On the way to Durban I stopped to assist a family who were having trouble with their vehicle. My wife was quite irritated as time was of essence. Fortunately I was able to sort out the problem in just 30 minutes. When we arrived at Middelburg we found a scene of complete mayhem and destruction. This included hundreds of caravans reduced to matchsticks. The worst hail storm

---

[1] **The name Baster** is derived from the Dutch word for 'bastard' (or 'crossbreed'). While some people consider this term demeaning, the Basters proudly use the term as an indication of their history in the same way as the Métis or "New People" of Canada. http://en.wikipedia.org/wiki/Baster

"They feel they are different from other coloureds due to their unique history and the fact they have been settled in their own area for more than 100 years." http://www.namibian.org/travel/namibia/population/basters.htm

in history had passed through just 30 minutes earlier. Had I not stopped to help - These holidays made complete sense.

Our dollar was worth R1.40 in 1978. How things are to change. By 1981, a year after independence it is worth R1.10.

By 2005, under Mugabe, it is worth considerably less than one sheet of toilet paper.

58. The mind cannot be contained

As a magistrate I performed prison visits in order to afford prisoners access to independent oversight. Notable was the attitude of condemned prisoners (those awaiting execution) about property. They were nearly always concerned with extracting a solemn promise from me that their property, or specified items of property, was to be handed over to a particular person upon their execution. Sometimes the subject matter of such concern would be something as mundane as a blanket worth just a few dollars. It was obvious to me that property is of huge significance in the African psyche and has strong links to spirituality. It is therefore not uncommon for a sangoma to advise, for instance, that the reason that misfortune has befallen a consultant is that ancestral spirits are angry on account of the fact that lobola has not been paid.

I also picked up a particular phenomenon that does not appear well represented in criminology. A long-term prisoner gave me a story that was incredibly detailed and had what judicial officers term "the ring of truth" about it, on account of its detail and objectively verifiable factors. According to him he was still in prison because of an illicit deal, involving the sale of cattle and gold, which had gone wrong between him and the governor of the prison. He was able to furnish dates and full details of the governor's house where, according to him, clandestine meetings had occurred. The story covered a saga that had occurred over a three-year period and he was able to provide complex details on all its aspects including the nuances that attach to stories that are true.

In all aspects he appeared to be what Courts refer to as a "credible and reliable witness". Testing his story only induced him to clearly and calmly reveal even more supportive details. The point he was making was that he had been due for release many years earlier but was being kept incarcerated by the governor manipulating the system so as to ensure that he, the governor, could get away with having cheated him on their deals. A more convincing story was hard to find.

I called the prison officials, whom I always excluded from such interviews, so that a prisoner was free to divulge information, and asked them for his file. Only then did the truth emerge. His story was an incredibly fanciful invention of the mind which was blocking out the true reasons for his situation. The man had originally been convicted of a particularly horrendous double murder, involving the use of an axe, and sentenced to death. Fortunately for him he was reprieved, at the last moment, by the then British Governor and the sentence commuted to life imprisonment. Of this he had served about 10 years by the time I saw him. His mind had long since blocked out the horrendous events he had experienced in committing the murders, his trial, sentence and reprieve, and substituted it with the story he was now advancing.

I then discovered that this phenomenon was quite common to long term prisoners with similar histories, i.e., the psychological blocking out (hysterical suppression) of the terrible true reason for their incarceration.

For society the problem that arises is that, once the phenomenon takes hold of such a prisoner, he his utterly convinced, in his mind, that he is innocent and being victimized. He is in no different a position to a person who is actually innocent, and being unlawfully kept in prison. Both "know" that they are innocent. It can be strongly argued therefore that their continued long-term incarceration, on both a subjective and objective test, constitutes "cruel, inhuman and degrading punishment" as understood in jurisprudence, and a human rights perspective. Put differently, to keep a human being in prison who neither knows, understands or accepts that he is guilty of anything, is cruel, inhuman and degrading. Facts are awkward things.

This has serious implications for the abolitionist camp that opposes the imposition of capital punishment and sees life imprisonment as acceptable. In terms of the phenomenon I discovered, long term imprisonment is cruel, inhuman and degrading once a prisoner's mind suppresses the reason for his/her incarceration. It therefore cannot be a credible substitute for capital punishment.

Now if you can't kill people as a punishment - and you also cannot keep them in prison for too long - what then? To this day I have not found an answer to these "awkward facts".

As a result of the urbanization of the war the RF government introduces what becomes known as "the 6 0'clock law." The cities are divided into white and black zones and between the hours of 6pm and 6am there is a curfew based on ethnicity. White folk may not enter Black areas and Black folk may not enter White areas.

So we immediately have fun with the thing. Our Kariba foursome is joined by a friend named Eugene Robinson who is physically indistinguishable from a White person. The five of us travel by car and are stopped at a police road block enforcing the curfew. We insist that we are not White and therefore entitled to visit Mushandire Pamwe Hotel which is in Highfields, a Black area. The poor police officers are driven to distraction as to what to do. They finally let us through ruefully bemoaning the idiotic laws they now have to enforce. We play the game conversely by attending parties in White areas.

It is a rare instance in which being "the other" accrues an advantage.

---

59. Self delusion

The bush war is now in full stride and almost nightly there are special televised security briefings regretfully announcing yet more and more casualties. It is obvious that the liberation war now has the momentum of a tsunami and is not going to be stopped. The successes of the liberation forces is matched only by the crass obstinacy of Ian Smith, the RF government and most of the White community who keep up a *"good ol' Smithy"* chant of naïve loyalty to their leader as he makes speech after speech of delusional rhetoric railing against betrayal by the British and postulating Rhodesia as the last bastion of civilization in a world crumbling in the face of Communism.

The Smith government is not too happy with the sentences being handed down by the Courts when *"gooks"*, *"terrs "* and their collaborators are charged. So they devise a plan. A plane load of Judges, Magistrates and prosecutorial staff is flown by Dakota aircraft to the north-eastern *"sharp end"* of the country in order to see for themselves the reality of the situation. The plane flies very low, its wing tips seemingly just inches from mountainsides. This is to give the enemy on the ground less *"lead-in"* time to aim and fire at the plane. The view outside is breathtaking; the atmosphere inside the plane is chilly apprehension. There is only small talk and nervous giggles.

We land on a bush strip in a cloud of dust and are taken on a tour of a Protected Village, *"PV"*. This comprises huge clusters of huts surrounded by high stockades built of wooden poles lashed together by the fibers of inner bark. The complexes are guarded by armed soldiers and entry in and out impossible without their consent. Protein takes the form of guinea pigs that are farmed within the stockades. Guinea pigs have never been part of local diet. Smith has trumpeted the PVs as much appreciated protection of a peaceful and loyal rural populace.

The reality is the imprisonment of an oppressed people so as to ensure that they cannot cooperate with their liberators.

A French built Alouette helicopter circles in an angled dive and lands as we are led away to be addressed by Lieutenant-Colonel Derry MacIntyre. His words are clear and clipped, dropped like icicles on a mountain pass. It is also a matter of fact, but chilling reality check, hitherto unheard in the heavily censored and RF propaganda riddled and controlled public discourse. For some time now, the independent media has produced newspapers festooned with huge blank spaces from whence Smith's censors have excised the truth under newly passed censorship laws.

McIntyre explains that incursions by the guerrilla forces are no longer just incursions. Rhodesia is actually at war. It is a war in which one army seeks to liberate its support base comprising the vast majority of the populace. The other army seeks to maintain the status quo. The key to success for either is to secure the *"hearts and minds"* of the people. The reality is that *"we cannot win this war, as we do not have the hearts and minds of the people on our side. The best that our army can do is to maintain a holding operation"*.

The guerrillas are soldiers, just like he is, and some of them have incurred his respect. In particular, Josiah Tongogara, the Commander in Chief of the ZANLA forces, is a good soldier and masterful tactician whom he holds in respect. The guerrillas were also capable of acts of utmost depravity, with atrocities committed as part of a Communist taught strategy to obviate betrayal. However, one guerrilla in particular has incurred his admiration as a tactical insurgent. His name was Mabonzo. This man had run rings around the security forces and driven them to distraction, even having the temerity to attack a guarded helicopter single handedly and the resourcefulness to escape after capture.

The stage would have to be reached where a political reconciliatory solution was arrived at. In the meantime, the security forces could do no more than hold the enemy at bay.

This news is sensational and sickening to nearly all my White counterparts. McIntyre referring to the enemy as *"guerrillas"* is new to them. They have only heard of *"gooks, terrs and "CTs "*. The unpeeling and exposure of inconvenient truth induces instant disillusionment and a pall of utter dejection grips the whole group on the flight back.

"When McIntyre says that we can only keep the terrs at bay ... what he means is that we have actually lost ... surely ...?" is a now oft repeated lament spluttered by mouths in bewildered dejected faces. Mallinson looks at me and remarks mischievously for the benefit of his erstwhile detractors' *"good ol' Smithy - !"*

One of the most senior State Advocates in the country snaps back - *"well ..*

that's it ... I am fucking off ... out of this shit hole ..." This is met by a burbling stutter of agreement as one, than another, moots similar intentions. The trickle of Whites leaving the country thereafter soon becomes a stream.

Mabonzo was *"contacted"* ["engaged in combat"] not long thereafter. On capture it just so happened that his leg was *injured "necessitating amputation of the lower half"*. A man with half a leg cannot escape. He was tried and hanged.

Eugene Robinson tells me that he is collecting signatures on a petition to have the life of a young Coloured lad, Richard "Sweetpea" Robinson, spared. He is a captured guerrilla member of the Frolizi arm of ZIPRA. I realize that he is actually asking whether it is at all possible that I sign since, as a Magistrate, I am a State employee and member of the judicial system that has condemned his cousin. I sign and add an endorsement in thick font **"Magistrate"** in a shared and vain hope that this might count for something.

It does not. Robinson is hanged. Neither he nor Mabonzo are buried at Heroes acre in liberated Zimbabwe. I have made a point of never visiting Heroes Acre despite having been invited there as a VIP on a number of occasions.

South Africa withdraws its support for the RF government. Smith and gang try a last desperate gambit. They engineer an inclusive government in which a new political player, Bishop Abel Tendekayi Muzorewa takes over as Prime Minister. The gambit predictably fails. The game is up. At a conference held at Lancaster House, England, Muzorewa agrees to a settlement in which the war will cease and free and fair elections will determine our new rulers. Josiah Tongogara is interested in unification between ZANLA and ZAPU. Robert Mugabe is not.

Immediately after the conference Tongogara is dead. Mugabe acolytes put out a story that he has been killed in a vehicle accident. To this day there is speculation and belief that he was murdered. Robert Gabriel Mugabe has made the top spot of the now triumphant ZANLA forces, the armed wing of the majority black party ZANU, with impeccable historical timing. From that moment ZAPU, and its leader Joshua Nkomo, the man who started the Black liberation struggle in Zimbabwe, are doomed. After winning 97% of the vote in elections ZANU PF is our new government.

On 18 April 1980 the reins of power are ceremoniously handed over to Mugabe by Britain's Lord Soames. A legendary brown-skinned reggae star from the West Indies, Bob Marley, is invited as chief entertainer for our independence celebrations. The crowd goes wild at Rufaro stadium when he gives a rendition of a new song "Zimbabwe" especially written for us and the world.

"Every man got to decide his own destiny - .
And in this judgment there is no partiality
Divide and rule could only tear us apart - .
In every man's chest there beats a heart...".
No one is to know that Mugabe is set to decide our destiny, with ruthless
partiality, dividing and tearing a young nation apart and stopping the
beating of hearts in over an estimated 20,000 thousand chests in his
Gukurahundi genocidal saga.
It is an inconvenient truth that lurks, looming on a distant horizon, waiting
for its time.

---

60. Is this my country?

Soon after independence I was transferred to Chiredzi, to take up the post of
Resident Magistrate there. Chiredzi is in what is known as *"the Lowveld"* on
account of its low altitude. Apart from the heat and mosquitoes it is an area
that represents all that is so magical about Africa. The vegetation is lush, and
awash with wild animals, with troupes of impala, at that time, routinely
accessible on an evening walk. The community was very close knit, with
everyone knowing everyone, and a spirit of comradeship prevailing across
the racial spectrum. Court trials took very little time, as there was hardly any
dispute about issues, once uncovered by the police. The local populace was
simply not given to mendacity.

Soon after our arrival it was recommended to us that we visit what were
referred to as *"hippo pools"*. Access was via a narrow grassy bush track. *En
route*, Pam and I saw an elephant suddenly appear ahead of us, and enter the
track, approaching us. This elephant was immediately followed by another,
and then another. I could do nothing, as the track was too narrow and winding
for me to either turn around or reverse. We had no option but to sit tight, as
the huge beasts approached, ambling along majestically.

In our minds majestically" was substituted by "menacingly". I had
experience of such situations before from my fishing trips. So I was better
able to control the fear rising up in me. My dear wife was understandably in
a state, and there was nothing I could do but reassure her that it would be
alright, as long as we remained still and quiet. So we sat saying our *"Hail
Marys"*, awaiting our fate.

Suddenly all three elephants stopped. A short while later one of them knelt
down. Almost immediately the figure of a man, a hunchbacked man,
emerged from the tall grass. In astonishment and awe we watched as he
mounted the kneeling elephant, which then stood up, and all three resumed

their approach. Apart from pausing momentarily to perform a disdainful inspection of our vehicle and its contents, these lords of the forest ambled past - majestically!

We were to renew our acquaintance with the troupe when they later visited Tamboutie Lodge, where we were staying. It turned out they regularly visited to the delight and amazement of Sunday afternoon visitors at the Lodge. The point to be made here is that these were not tame or domesticated animals. They were not in game farm. These were wild animals that had somehow come to form a truly extraordinary relationship with a human being. There was much speculation on the matter but no authoritative explanation.

Most parents lament the fact that they have little or limited influence over their offspring. *"My child will just not listen!"* is a mournful cry we have all heard on many an occasion. In my case, unlike other parents, at least I am aware of where, when and how I lost just about all credibility with our children.

We are seated at Tamboutie Lodge, Chiredzi, whiling away the time on a Sunday afternoon. Suddenly a troupe of mongoose arrives. Curiosity turns to pandemonium as the troupe starts running amongst the many children who are present. They take flight amidst squeals, screams and other sounds that children are wont to make when in a state of extreme excitement. When one child drops a packet of glass marbles the mongooses quickly snatch these up. We watch in amazement as one of these little animals holds a marble in the claws of is forelegs and then, with power and accuracy, throws it backwards through its hind legs, smashing the marble against wall. Finding nothing other than shattered glass for its trouble it deals with the next marble with the same consequences.

Dissatisfied with its hard-won prize the mongoose than runs up to our eldest son and confronts him, bobbing up and down on its hind legs, chirping, clicking and hissing in seeming aggression. Instinctively our son wants to run. I immediately bark an order to him that he should stand still. He is reluctant to obey. I have to bark louder and repeatedly. *"Listen son - I am your father - I know about wild animals - listen to me - don't run - you must never run from a wild animal - it will see you as prey - and then it will attack - so please son - don't run - stand still - stand still!"* I insist. With great reluctance the lad stands still.

After staging repeated mock attacks, the mongoose loses patience with him - and bites him on the knee - drawing blood and tears. All the other children, who have run when challenged by these marvelous creatures, suffer no harm. It is simply a game that these wild, but intelligent and mischievous creatures, play with them. Right there my credibility as a parent and head of the household suffers irreparable damage. Alas, like so many other parents in this world, I am never to regain it.

Taking advantage of the prevailing situation in Chiredzi, I formed a completely multi racial darts club which met on two evenings a week. The club was very successful. Our darts evenings were always well attended and competitions ended with a range of locally donated prizes, comprising glassware, camp chairs, cooler boxes etc, being awarded to the winners. In addition we would meet on Sunday afternoons for picnics and fishing competitions. The community spirit was greatly enhanced by the phenomenon of CB Radio that had just taken the world by storm. So everyone had a CB radio and *"good buddy"*, *"good lady"* contact was made on the slightest excuse. It was wonderful.

Because of our success we formed the Lowveld into a Darts Province and affiliated to the National Darts Association. We were therefore eligible for, and invited, to compete in the National competition held in Gweru. Our darts teams at the competition comprised the first fully racial and gender integrated teams in the competition. It was satisfying to see Betty Bezuidenhout, an Afrikaner woman, joyously hugging her darts partner Noel, an African Black, after they scored a victory. Our province did so well that, much to the surprise and chagrin of other provinces, we took three of the six cups on offer including the singles and team formats; on this our first attempt.

As my wife Pam was with me, but not part of the Lowveld team, I convinced her to, just for fun, enter a knockout competition known as the Alan Dobson Cup, that was open to anyone. She was quite depressed to find, that in the first round, she was drawn against 6 times national champion Bertie Booth. She beat him. It was absolutely sensational and the hottest topic of conversation for the whole competition.

The next day everyone just wanted to see this petite lady from Chiredzi, who had knocked out the legendary Bertie Booth. She made history also in being the first lady to beat any man at darts in open competition. My dear wife was totally unused to such attention and fame and found it very difficult to cope in the next game before a huge admiring audience. She undoubtedly had the skill to beat this opponent but not under the glare of so much publicity. She lost but went down bravely. Most understood her predicament.

It is a hot October afternoon. In the shade of a leafy tree a scene that has been with mankind from time immemorial is played out. A mother contently suckles her child, humming an ancient lullaby to herself and surveying the world around her through half closed eyes. It is a beautiful world. It is a landscape of shrubs, trees, termite mounds, outcrops and clumps of grass of all shapes and sizes, through which runs a river providing the life sustaining gift that is water. The mid-day heat also imposes a tranquility that is serene. All is quiet except for the shrill of cicadas and the intermittent low grunt of hippopotami in nearby pools.

It is a scene that has repeated in Africa for millennia - from the time a Black woman held a child as the mother of all of modern mankind. Mitochondrial DNA indicates that all living humans descend from one maternal source - christened Mitochondrial Eve[1] - who lived in Africa between 100,000 and 200,000 years ago.

Her world is suddenly and violently shattered when she feels a force on her lap and hears a muffled cry from her child. Her eyes open to see a scaly monster with her child in its jaws, still as a rock, evil eyes unblinking. As she starts to move the crocodile makes off in a slithering run. She screams and starts off after the monster. It pauses momentarily, she pauses in reaction, and then it hurtles off at lightning speed, its huge head shaking obscenely in the bright sunlight, her baby in its jaws.

There is a huge splash as it enters the waters of the Mtilikwe River and then silence - a terrible silence that matches the small ripples that mark the spot in the river where crocodile and child disappeared.

She screams - and screams - and screams - and screams - the heart wrenching scream of a mother - for her child. It is all in vain. Her precious child is gone forever, taken by an apex predator that had crawled some 70 meters in order to snatch her child from her lap.

The awful details of this incident came to my knowledge when, as the resident magistrate, I was required to conduct an inquest into the circumstances of the death of the child. After the hearing, the Court interpreter, Mr. Moyo, engaged me.

Moyo: Mr. Greenland, what do you think about this matter - how this child died - eaten by a crocodile - ?

Me: well - it is difficult to think of something more terrible -

Moyo: yes - it is so terrible what people will do -

Me: I don't understand - what do you mean - "what people will do"

Moyo: This happened at mid-day, when the sun was up and at the hottest time of day

---

1

http://web.mit.edu/racescience/in_media/what_dna_says_about_human/index.html.

Me: yes

Moyo: crocodiles do not hunt at that time of day - they hunt mostly late afternoon and early evening or at night '

Me: yes - you are quite right

Moyo: and they hunt at the edge of the water - they do not come out of the water to catch their prey

Me: well yes - that is true

Moyo: and this crocodile traveled over 70 meters in the heat of the day to stalk this woman and her child like a leopard and then grab the child

Me: yes - I have to agree that it was quite extraordinary - we have all commented on that

Moyo: to us it is very clear - there is no doubt that this was the work of an enemy of the family

Me: [realizing what he is leading up to] - you mean witchcraft?

Moyo: without doubt - it was witchcraft - the crocodile was sent to do its business - there can be no doubt about that

Me: - and now I suppose another witchdoctor is going to be consulted and someone is going to be blamed - and then we will have more trouble - probably blood shed

Moyo: the culprit will be uncovered - that is for sure - you should understand that - there can be no justice until he or she is uncovered

Me: Mr. Moyo, I hear you loud and clear - and yes, I do understand that - it is the way of Africa

Moyo: - and it cannot change - you yourself have seen the same thing in the book you have lent me "The Man-Eaters of Tsavo".

He is referring to a book by John Henry Patterson recounting how some 35 persons were killed and eaten by lions in 1898 whilst a railway was being constructed in Kenya. All the locals believed the lions were really "insects" operating in terms of witchcraft and that only the local witchdoctor could stop their rampage. Although Patterson eventually bagged the two lions that were responsible, local people however attributed the end of the scourge of lions eating people to intervention by the witch doctor. Scant credit was accorded to Patterson.

A Coloured friend, Moffat Frank, and I are out one afternoon, on a small rowing boat, fishing in a very large reservoir, known as Section 18. As is starts to drizzle people leave except for one White gentleman who knows us well. Soon thereafter the boat capsizes on account of my clumsiness. As I turn to look for Moffat I notice that he is thrashing about wildly flailing his arms, eyes white and as big as saucers. The realization that he cannot swim strikes through me like a knife. I grab him and with great difficulty convince him to be calm, put his hands on the hull of the overturned boat and trust that it will hold him up. Understandably this takes time as Moffat is in a panic; in the grip of the fear of drowning. What this means is that my plan to right the boat is a non-starter, as this cannot be done given the state that Moffat is in. Another far more chilling realization grips me. The reservoir has resident crocodiles big enough to take a grown man. As the local magistrate I have conducted some inquests into such events.

I shout out loudly, turning towards the shore which is a mere 90 meters away, waving my arms frantically. Through the rain I can clearly see our friend, or should I say, the White gentleman, and even make out his features. He looks at us as I continue the shouting and waving. All he needs to do is to row out to us in one of several other row boats within yards of his spot. The man does nothing but continues to sit there looking at us. Moffat continues to panic and I again spend time calming him down. This is difficult as he becomes more terrified when I tell him I am going to have to swim to the shore. All the while my mind is envisaging the silent presence of a scaly monster approaching, grabbing one of us in those teeth-filled jaws and pulling us under - forever gone. It is one thing to face other human beings shouting *"tuff shit rebel"* or one man saying he is going to *"just smack this puppy"*. A crocodile, perfected as a killing machine from the time of the dinosaurs, and an apex predator, is a very different proposition.

"Hail Mary, full of Grace, the Lord is with thee, blessed are thou amongst women - " I pray - and pray - as I swim towards the shore. Slowly I realize that I am making no headway. It is confusing. As I try harder I start feeling the onset of cramp in my upper thigh muscle. Knowing how dangerous this can be I immediately return to the boat. Moffat is shouting out so loudly as to be heard for a mile round. Our friend on shore does nothing but continue to just look at us. The adrenaline now flowing wildly in me ensures that his face is telescoped within my vision to such an extent that I can make out a facial expression of crass indifference. We were being left to our fate. I try to swim again with the same result. I can make no headway and cramp starts its business when I try to force the issue. I return to Moffat and we watch as the man on shore, packs up, jumps into his vehicle and drives off, disappearing into a blanket of teeming rain. We are trapped in the domain of terrible scaly killers. *"Hail Mary ..."* is all that I have.

As I pray, suddenly through the driving rain the figure of a man on a cycle appears traveling at speed, the speed of rescue. Soon one of the Black workers rows out to us and we are mercifully rescued. The man heard our calls at nearly a kilometer distance. It is then that I discover that the reason why I could make no headway in swimming to shore was that I was being held back by a hook, in the very back of my jersey, attached to a line from my fishing rod which was now at the bottom of the reservoir.

Why we had been left to drown, or to be eaten by crocodiles, by the man who deserted the scene is never explained when he is later confronted by other White members of the community in the local pub. His hitherto friends make life so difficult for him that he soon leaves the Lowveld. It would appear that the veneer of interracial bonhomie may have masked an ugly inconvenient truth in this case, with this one individual at least.

Soon after our arrival there was a bad accident in our home. Our son David, still a toddler, pulled on our gas stove, dislodging the grid, which then fell onto his face. As it was hot he sustained burns to his face which immediately swelled up like balloon. We rushed him to the local hospital where the only doctor was a hitherto guerrilla by the name of Davies. He had been trained in an eastern bloc country. The facial burns were bad, so bad that there was a real risk of our son losing his vision in one eye. Since the hospital did not have a properly resourced burn unit there was also a great risk of infection, as is the case with burns, with further disastrous consequences. We had a choice. Either we entrusted Davies, with his limited resources, with treatment of our son, or we drove some 500 kms to Harare. A trip to Harare would have greatly increased the chances of infection. There were mutterings from others that we *"would have to be mad to trust "a gook" just out of the bush and trained in some "useless commie university"*.

We made our choice and Davies, was entrusted with our son. To my mind he had been tested fully during the bush war. From my military training I had a good idea of the type of incendiary burns that are inflicted in battle. He treated David whose facial burns improved to the point that Davies advised that he could be transferred to Harare be seen by a burn specialist. When we did, the burn specialist was effusive in his admiration and praise for the treatment that our son had already received. Certainly his sight had been miraculously saved. In his view the treatment could not have been better and he expressed bewilderment at how Davies, "the gook", had been able to do it.

When our son was fully recovered there was a truly remarkable incident. Understandably he now knew what to be burnt was and gave the electric heater in the room a wide birth. One day he was crawling around when he came across a knob-kerrie kept hidden under our bed. He grabbed it, turned it so that he was holding it as one holds such a weapon, stood up and, at the fastest toddle he could muster, charged the electric heater whilst emitting a blood curdling scream. Upon reaching the heater he struck it a tremendous blow with the knob-kerrie; as efficiently and effectively as would have done any Zulu warrior proud. The heater was reduced to smithereens.

We were all absolutely stunned. This toddler had no experience of knob-kerries. I had never produced it in his presence and, more importantly, had certainly never used it in his presence. How had he recognized it to be a weapon? How did he know how to use it? How did he know that it was to be used against one's enemy? What about the "war cry" as he charged the heater. Since he had been badly burnt in the face the heater certainly was an enemy in his mind. He was just three years old. We were completely lost for explanations to all these questions.

Our domestic worker, Annie Grace, was not. She was also quite bemused as to why we were confused about the event. She explained that David's second name was Sigidi[1]. I had chosen this name in acknowledgment of my ethnic link to the Zulu people. *"Sigidi"* was a battle cry that a Zulu impi would call out in unison, after rattling their spears and kerries on their shields. They would do this at the instant of charging the enemy, ending with a resounding exclamation *"Zhee!* The combination of the rattle, the battle cry *"Sigidi"* and the exclamation *"Zhee"* had a blood chilling and terrifying effect on the enemy. Our worker explained that it was simply a case of the Zulu ancestral spirits having guided David in the use of the knob-kerrie against his enemy, the electric heater. It was as simple as that, and she could not understand why we were so amazed. Since there was no other indicated explanation we were indeed even more amazed; utterly so … and still are!

At about this time Pam and I treat ourselves to a sojourn in the Gonarezhou National Park, in south-eastern Zimbabwe. It is situated in a relatively remote corner of Masvingo Province, south of Chimanimani along the Mozambique border. The park is a lowveld region of baobabs, scrublands and sandstone cliffs.

We are seated in our camp chairs on a sand bank in the Mtilikwe River, now known as the Mutirikwe River. It is a glorious morning. Before us the river stretches out comprising an admixture of languid pools, main and sub streams of gushing water. The shrill cry of fish eagles is complemented by the low grunt of hippopotami whose heads routinely break the water's surface, ears wriggling. Crocodiles start to slither onto sand banks to take advantage of the warm rays of the rising sun. We are imbued with a sense of solemn exaltation at the wonder of it all.

---

[1] **Sigidi** – pronounced "see –gee – dee" Zhee – pronounced – "jhee" [softened "j"]

Me: Pam, isn't this just magical [as I take yet another fish off my hook]

Pam: Yes, and even though I feel a bit scared as the bush has wild animals like lions and elephants, I also feel that only a God could have made all this and He is looking after us

Me: So, you know what. As much as I have misgivings about the future of this country, with Mugabe in charge, I have decided not to apply for the magistrate's post in Samoa.

I am referring to the fact that a New Zealand friend of mine, Warner Banks, now stationed in Hong Kong, had advised me that Samoa was in desperate need of magistrates.

It is just then that we hear the sound of human voices emanating from somewhere behind us. We skirt around a clump of reeds, otherwise blocking our view, and soon take in a truly extraordinary scene. On the high bank of the river, some distance away, is a rather portly build White man. He is dressed in full safari suit with pith helmet, and as we later found out, boots and puttees to match; just as the great White explorers used to be attired in the last century. He looks like a character straight out of King Solomon's Mines[1].

It gets better; quite incredibly so. He is testing the strength of overhanging vines to see if one of them can take his weight. The man intends to use a vine in order swing out and over a deep stream of water onto a sand bank in the river bed, just as Tarzan would do. Disbelievingly we watch as he goes through the testing ritual, performing mini-swings with vine after vine, until he finds one that he is satisfied with. Then, after a short very energetic run, he swings out and is airborne, body dangling over the stream, swinging towards the sand bank on which is a Black man, undoubtedly his guide, stretching out his arms to help him land safely.

He doesn't make it. The vine snaps whilst he is in mid air. By the time he hits the water arms and legs are in such an energetic "free style" mode that would do an Olympic swimmer proud. His guide dives in and thankfully soon has him out of the water safe on the sand bank. It is all so incredulous. We look

---

[1] *King Solomon's Mines* (1885) is a popular novel by the Victorian adventure writer and fabulist, Sir H. Rider Haggard. It tells of a search of an unexplored region of Africa by a group of adventurers led by Allan Quatermain for the missing brother of one of the party. It is the first English fictional adventure novel set in Africa, and is considered to be the genesis of the Lost World literary genre.
http://en.wikipedia.org/wiki/King_Solomon's_Mines

at each other in disbelief. Have we really witnessed such an extraordinary piece of theater so deep in the African bush? Yes we have, as confirmed by the African guide who, after skirting the reed clump, so as to be out of sight of his intrepid charge, collapses in stitches in front of us, blurting out in boyish glee - *"Lo baas - yena saba lo crocodile - "* [the boss - is terrified of crocodiles] as an undoubted reference to the whirlwind free style stroke that his charge had executed in mid air before hitting the water.

When I approach the man I greet him with - *"Doctor Livingstone I presume"*, in romantic reference to the famous historical incident, when Welsh explorer and journalist Sir Henry Morton Stanley found David Livingstone somewhere in the Central African bush, during the last century. He is not amused, not at all, keeps our contact short and terse and is soon gone forever. Truth is indeed stranger than fiction, especially in Africa! Had my wife not witnessed this incident I would not dare tell the story.

One late Sunday afternoon we are on our way back to Chiredzi having visited family in Harare some 500 kilometers away. I am in a hurry and driving at speed to get back home as early as possible. We spot one of several roadside curio stalls. Pam asks me to stop. I explain that time is of essence. An argument ensues in which we each lock ourselves into positions. It is an argument that I am guaranteed to lose when she turns to a woman's ultimate weapon.

Tears start to flow.

I am the unfeeling, uncaring, insensitive creature that men are known to be. So I slam on the anchors, execute a U turn and drive back to the stall. After what seems like ages she completes "her shopping", returning to the car with a brown paper packet. For the sake of peace I dare not enquire as to its contents. In my mind I am certain that, if I do, my stance that *"there was nothing worthwhile buying at these stalls"* will be confirmed. Proving myself right will only strain marital relations even more. I might be denied supper and goodness knows what else. So the packet remains on the back seat of the car for the rest of the trip, which is completed in uncomfortable silence. I turn up the volume on a Julio Inglesias tape. Upon arrival home, about an hour later, the contents are revealed. Pam produces two baked mud guinea fowls, emerald green and baby pooh yellow in colour. Each is festooned with a jet-black cravat with crimson polka dots. They are horrible, nasty - well - hideous. But I dare not say a thing let alone complain about the price she has paid for them. In this confrontation between man and woman, woman must win.

My heart sinks further when the horrid creatures are given pride of place on the mantel piece in the lounge. As we retire to bed I have dark thoughts about the matter. What nightmares will overtake our young children tonight. Will they not have bad dreams about these nasty creatures leaving the mantelpiece to seek them out -? The next morning the creatures are gone! They have vanished overnight - to the dark and bad world from whence they came - never to be seen again. No one queries their disappearance. We all know better than to do that. Marital bliss returns.

Twenty-six years later, in 2007, I phone in to Radio 702 hosted by Jenny Crwys-Williams. She has invited contributions from listeners who have had experience of having made regrettable purchasers. I recount my experience with these baked mud guinea fowls. I explain to her that I have had to live with this incident all these years as an unresolved experience in which I was severely traumatized. Phoning her has been a counseling session in which, at last, I have been unburdened. Jenny finds the story so amusing that she spends most of the rest of the program giggling away at *" the emerald green and baby pooh yellow mud guinea fowls with - jet black cravats with crimson coloured polka dots"*.

It is my hope to at last to get revenge on Pam when her colleagues make the connection as I disclose the name of the school where my wife now teaches. I anticipate that her friends and colleagues will tease her or take her to task once they make the connection. All her female friends and colleagues make the connection. They do not take her to task or even just tease her. Instead they all shower her with praise *"for having stood up to a man"*.

You just can't win against the fairer sex.

---

61. And justice must prevail

One day in 1980 that I receive a call from Judge John Pittman. He wants me to be an assessor in the trial of Edgar Zivanai Tekere[1] in a charge for the murder of a White farm manager, Gerald Adams. The other assessor is to be Peter Nemapare, a Black magistrate. It strikes me that the composition of the Court involving a White judge being assisted by one Coloured and one Black assessor is an exercise of "political correctness" undoubtedly on account of the sensitivities of the case and Tekere's importance. I had never

---

[1] **Edgar Zivanai Tekere** [born April 1, 1937] is a Zimbabwean politician. He was a president of the Zimbabwe African National Union who organised the party during the Lancaster House talks.
http://en.wikipedia.org/wiki/Edgar_Tekere#Murder_charge

been an assessor before. I accept the call to the discharge of an onerous but sacred duty.

On 3 November 1981 I re-enter "A" Court, having slunk out of there in 1964 when the great Sir Hugh Beadle put the fear of God in me with the parting admonishment- "Sergeant - take him away - and I hope to never see him in my Court!"

I take my place, sitting on the right side of Judge Pittman, to a jam-packed Courtroom, including journalists from all over the world. Before the hearing a journalist radio-calls home base saying- *"I am outside the Court - and starting to talk to the accused Edgar Tekere - and I am scared shitless - "* Advocate Chris Glaum stands up to announce that he is appearing for the State, followed by Advocate Blom-Cooper QC, from England, who announces his appearance for Tekere and his seven co-accused. So begins a sensational trial.

That the trial was to be sensational was guaranteed firstly on account of the fact that Tekere was the President of ZANU, our victorious ruling party. Secondly was the fact that he had killed a White farm manager. During the only recently ended war such people were routinely targeted by the guerrillas and many lost their lives. Now the killing of such a person was to be visited with a trial in which conviction exposed Tekere to a sentence of death by hanging. On the already known facts Tekere had not behaved as a criminal. He had not killed a man during the course of a robbery or over a woman or for any of the usual criminal motives. The man had been killed by a member of his uniformed platoon as he was embarked on a security sweep of a farm from which gunfire had emanated the night before. Why was Mugabe putting his Commander in Chief on trial in such circumstances? If convicted would Tekere hang? These questions loomed large in the minds of an intrigued new society.

Blom-Cooper was a flamboyant exponent of the art of advocacy. John Pittman was soundly conservative and traditionalist in temperament. Soon there was friction between the two and this subsisted until the end. On several occasions the judge would summon counsel to chambers and the two would have a vociferous verbal confrontation with no holds barred. Pittman needed Blom-Cooper to understand who was in charge in Court and Blom-Cooper needed Pittman to understand who was in charge in defending the accused. Thus they talked "across" each other instead of "to" each other and there was never a winner, let alone a solution. The confrontations were somewhat traumatic for Peter and me given our lack of experience of such situations involving legal giants.

When the trial concluded we met in final discussion guided by Pittman. He was absolutely clear in what was, in effect, a directive. In so far as Tekere had conducted the sweep on the farm he had done so imbued with misplaced revolutionary passion and zeal. The death of Gerald Adams was a foreseen eventuality in respect of which Tekere could not have cared much and had been reckless as leader of the sweep. In law the whole operation had been unlawful and therefore inexcusable. Tekere was therefore guilty of the common law crime of murder.

An important remaining question however was whether or not Tekere was indemnified against conviction in terms of the 1975 Indemnity and Compensation Act, still on statute books. This had been enacted by the previous Ian Smith government despite considerable opposition from the legal profession and human rights groups. This law was typical of laws passed by governments to protect their troops and security agents from conviction for otherwise criminal actions taken on behalf of the state in good faith. By *"good faith"* was meant "utter and genuinely held conviction". Instructive is the infamous Mai Lai[1] massacre as reported.

> "On March 16, 1968 the angry and frustrated men of Charlie Company, 11th Brigade, Americal Division entered the Vietnamese village of My Lai." This is what you've been waiting for -- search and destroy -- and you've got it," said their superior officers. A short time later the killing began. When news of the atrocities surfaced, it sent shockwaves through the U.S. political establishment, the military's chain of command, and an already divided American public."

What happened at My Lai could never have been subject to protection under United States indemnity legislation on account of the total absence of "good faith". The My Lai massacre was an act of pre-meditated, purposeful revenge. The murder of Gerald Adams was the consequence of impetuous, rash and unreasonable conduct by a man who on account of history and circumstance, primarily not of his own making, was inflamed with revolutionary passion and zeal. In particular Tekere undoubtedly believed that the military style sweep was necessary in order to protect the security of the state, especially as there had been gunshots emanating from the farm the night before.

We scarcely debated the issue, as the central issue had been so clearly exposed in evidence and, in particular by Tekere, as a witness. He was utterly convincing for being unreasonable, intemperate and passionate about what he considered his duty to ensure the security of the newly won state of Zimbabwe and its leaders. That this was "good faith", as envisaged under the

---

[1] **Mai Lai** - http://www.pbs.org/wgbh/amex/vietnam/trenches/my_lai.html

1975 Indemnity and Compensation Act, Judge Pittman had absolutely no doubt. Neither had we in accepting his analyses, which, in any event, fully accorded with our view. The meeting did not last long and the judge undertook to write a judgment which he would send to us before resumption, for handing down.

About two weeks before resumption Judge Pittman phoned me to say he had changed his mind and would be sending me a draft judgment to that effect, convicting Tekere of murder. The document never arrived. When we met on the day the judgment was due to be handed down, 08 December 1980, he purported to make a case for rejection of "good faith" on Tekere's part. It was a rambling explanation that failed to answer an important question which I then put to him more than once.

Why had he changed his mind? What had made him to do it? On consideration of the very same facts, issues and assessment of Tekere as a witness he had previously been satisfied beyond doubt that Tekere had acted in *"good faith"* and now he was satisfied on *"a balance of probability"* that Tekere had not acted in good faith. I was a mere magistrate. So was Peter. Magistrates held judges in reverence. The situation was extremely confusing to us and we said so. No clear explanation was proffered by this normally eloquent and clear exponent of the art of setting out law and fact.

Instead he uttered words to the effect that, in any event, he was sure that this was *"what the top guy wants"*, clearly referring to Mugabe, then Prime Minister. I was shocked to the core, even accepting that the statement was simply his opinion and not an indication of political interference. Peter and I refused to relent in our stance, despite Pittman exhibiting annoyance at our intransigence.

What was now a very painful confrontation ended with him ordering me to write a dissenting judgment on the issue of indemnification for Tekere and his men on the basis of *"good faith"*. Having been confused, then numbed, we were shattered when he then said that I was not to be allowed access to Court facilities or use of a Court typewriter. In addition I had just a couple of hours in which to produce the judgment. Given Pittman's stature as a judge, undoubted gifts as a jurist and depth of experience, his conduct was unfortunate, on a number of counts, starting with his treatment of Peter and I, who had accorded him highest respect throughout.

I left Court and went to a florist shop, owned by my cousin Penelope Theunissen, where I borrowed a typewriter and did my best with setting out our reasons. On resumption he handed down a judgment ending with a summary of our view. In an article title "Saved by Ian Smiths law" Time[1] reported the proceedings as follows -

> "Flanked by his lawyer in a Salisbury Courtroom last week, Tekere glowered menacingly as white South African-born Justice John Pittman, wearing the traditional red robe and curly wig, began reading the verdict. Pittman's dry voice droned on for 50 minutes, but his final words rang out like a shot: "All the accused are acquitted."

The chamber erupted in pandemonium. Tekere, barely fighting back his own tears, fell into the arms of his weeping wife. His jubilant supporters hustled him out of the Courtroom and into a cheering throng of well-wishers, many of whom raised their arms in clenched-fist salutes. From upper-story windows of the Courthouse, white civil servants gazed stunned and stony-faced at the impromptu fete."

> "The trial was conducted according to the best traditions of our inherited judicial system," said Prime Minister Robert Mugabe."

On this occasion Mugabe had regarded the loss of the life of a White farmer as sacred, and had insisted that the law take its course, even though the accused was the President of his party. Time Magazine concluded that a test of the new government had been successfully passed.

The inconvenient truth about Mugabe's real nature, regard for all human life, and the life of White farmers in particular, was yet to meet the world, waiting on the near and distant horizon.

Tekere's revolutionary fervour and passion also found expression in a new countrywide phenomenon. All over the country people were hauled before tribunals, summarily set up and manned by ordinary untrained people, and tried for a range of *"political crimes"*. The punishment, routinely metered out by these *"kangaroo Courts"*, was nearly always a public flogging as part of political *"re-education"*.

The Lowveld was visited by Samora Machel, then President of Mozambique. In his speech he stressed the need for unity between ZAPU and ZANU, as had the late Josiah Tongogara at Lancaster. This was well received by a community that was already peaceful and well integrated. Within days the province was invaded by political commissars, sent from ZANU PF headquarters in Harare, and a campaign of the victimization of ZAPU members conducted. My Court interpreter and the matron at the local hospital, both Ndebele, had to be smuggled out of the province until the campaign ended.

---

[1] http://www.time.com/time/magazine/article/0,9171,924606,00.html

The police arrested the senior commissar responsible for the campaign and he was put on trial before me. He was clear, matter-of-fact and unrepentant about his actions, as they had been conducted on orders from Mugabe, communicated via ZANU PF head office, from whence he had come. That was his case. He confidently requested an adjournment so as to be afforded opportunity to produce proof of his mandate. On resumption of the case the man was a picture of pitiable disillusionment. Not only could he not produce the proof of his mandate, it was clear that he was not at liberty to disclose why. He pleaded for mercy saying that I should understand his predicament. I did.

By this time I had formed very strong views about our new leader Robert Gabriel Mugabe. These were informed, in the main, by ZANLA Commanders who would come to see me whenever one of their charges from the local ZANLA Assembly Point was put on trial. Mostly this was for assaulting members of the local populace as part of *"re-education"*. I had never been a fan of ZANLA. However these Commanders were, to a man, brutally frank about just about everything, whether or not it was embarrassing to their cause. They just told the *"whole truth"* with disarming forthrightness and what they had to say "dove-tailed" with the briefing Lieutenant-Colonel Derry MacIntyre had previously made to members of the judiciary. They too were more than suspicious of the real cause of Tongogara's death. I developed a profound respect for them. Not one of these brave fighters, and real heroes, who has since passed on, is buried at "Heroes Acre".

So I already had a very clear impression of the real nature of Mugabe. Bad people make good people do bad things.

I imposed a term of imprisonment on the political commissar, but suspended the whole of the sentence, appealing to him to learn from his experiences and commit to nobler aspirations. It was a heartwarming experience when some three years later he introduced himself to me in the street and was able to assure me that he had delivered fully on this commitment. He was now an upstanding, proud and well respected member of the "ordinary" community.

To the immense credit of the police force *"kangaroo Courts"* were never tolerated and its members routinely prosecuted. Fortunately this unhealthy state of affairs soon petered out and kangaroo Courts confined to history.

62. Resourcefulness

In 1981 I move to take up the post of Provincial Magistrate in Masvingo. As it was so soon after independence we were required to effect *"transformation"*. By this was meant re-aligning the office to reflect the changed order in the country. It was an exciting business in which we made up the rules as we went along. Henceforth certain principles were to be regarded as fundamental and sacrosanct. Foremost of these was that the Magistrates Courts were the "face of justice" for being closest to the people. "Justice delayed is justice denied". "All people are equal before the law". "An accused person is presumed innocent until proved guilty". "An accused person is entitled to a fair trial". In order to give effect to these principles the office was given a complete make-over and staff re-trained to the point of optimal efficiency and effectiveness. In addition workshops were conducted with the police and prosecuting authorities so as to ensure the most seamless administration of justice. In less than three months I had every reason to be proud of our Court for being a well functioning organ of state and center of justice. We also supposed that it was perceived to be so by the public in general.

Our comfort zone received a rude shock on the aspect of public perception. This was on account of the discovery of the actions of a particular individual, who was then arrested and brought up for trial on charges of systematic fraud. What he had done was to set up in business at the doorstep of the Courthouse. His business was to approach members of the public gathered there and enquire as to their presence at Court. Typically a woman would lament the fact that her son was to be tried on some charge or other and she feared that he would be convicted and imprisoned. This rascal would then guarantee that this would not happen if she paid him a fee. To re-assure her that there was no risk for her he would insist that the fee be held by a trusted stakeholder, such as a pastor, until completion of her son's trial. If he failed to deliver on his guarantee, and her son was imprisoned, the stakeholder would return the fee to her and she would have lost nothing. However if her son was not sent to prison the money would be handed to him by the trusted stakeholder as his fee. For obvious reasons many people accepted his services and paid over considerable sums of money. After all there was no risk for them and it was a price well worth paying so as to ensure the continued freedom of themselves or their loved ones.

The problem for my Court in all this was that the general public was being given the assurance that justice was being perverted and freedom purchased at a price. Obviously the public were of the impression that Court staff were in on this corrupt practice to our financial benefit. We were not; and actually knew nothing of it until his fortuitous capture. The criminal genius of his scheme reposed in the fact that, in the ordinary course of Court business and trials, a good percentage of accused persons are never, in any event, sent to prison for a variety of reasons. Some are found not guilty and even those found guilty may receive a non-custodial sentence. Our artful friend was taking advantage of the very nature of the justice system itself. However the public was not to know this, neither were we. The result was that he profited at the expense of our good name and reputation as his clients believed they were buying justice from a corrupt Court. What was intriguing was that this man had virtually no education, and yet was able to think up a scheme of such criminal genius. The criminal mind is ever resourceful. Understandably, upon conviction, I ensured that he received an exemplary custodial sentence and that a press statement was released in attempt to clear our names.

Soon thereafter I lose two people who were part of my life and who I loved dearly. The first is Nicholas Scott. One evening he asks his son-in-law to take him to hospital where he is admitted for observation. Within half an hour he passes peacefully to the surprise of the nursing staff. He is 77 years of age. I really felt that I had lost part of me.

Bruce Radford Abrahams was one of my two closest friends in my latter years in Embakwe. The other was Edmund "Pra-Pra" Ambrose[1]. It was these two that had been with me when I had a fight with the "vrastaag" maniac on a lonely path all those years ago whilst we were still at school. After leaving school Bruce had quite easily obtained Chartered Institute of Secretaries certification by way of private study and set himself up in an extremely successful agency practice. One morning he collapsed with copious amounts of blood issuing from his mouth. It was found that he had bit his tongue in a diabetic attack. Despite treatment he eventually succumbed to the disease. Thus a brilliant young man was cut down so early in a life, at just age 29 years; a life bursting with promise of things to come. He was the first of our generation to leave us.

It was terrible for all of us and his funeral was a momentous occasion with Richard Brown delivering a most stirring eulogy.

63. Foretasting the full fruits of liberation

In 1982 I am selected to head our country's under-19 Basketball team to attend the All Africa Basketball Championships to be held in Maputo, Mozambique. This country had been under Portuguese rule for some 470 years. After a guerrilla war started in 1963 it was handed over to the Black majority on 25 June 1975, under President Samora Machel. During the bush war of liberation for Zimbabwe Mozambique provided staunch support for

---

[1] **Eddie Ambrose** was also recruited by the previous government under its policy of partnership and worked in the Ministry of Health

the ZANLA forces. Obtaining visas proves to be a long and tedious process on account of the amount of detail required. The sojourn to Mozambique is to be some kind of experience indeed. It starts with an audit of the passengers on our Russian built plane before take-off at Harare. No less than six heads counts of all passengers are performed by three different officials.

On arrival at Maputo a two-hour clearance process then occurs. This includes once again filling in forms requiring the same details as previously required in the visa applications. Each one of us is photographed. Before we leave we are each given a plasticized rectangular card which we are sternly instructed must be worn around the neck at all times. The card includes a photo of the wearer and identifies that person as a foreigner. Mine is headed "Chef De La Delegation". When I request that I be housed in the same hotel as my team I am firmly told that as *"as a Chef"* this is not possible. As I am aware that the country's political philosophy is Marxism I try to make out a case about "egalitarianism" supposedly at the heart of this philosophy. I lose the argument when I am threatened with instant deportation.

I find myself booked into the sumptuous Cardozo Hotel. My room is luxurious. As is my habit I go through an exercise routine and build up a healthy sweat in anticipation of a refreshing shower. It is not to be. The taps burble and gurgle but produce no water. After many telephone calls to reception I eventually am imbued with the awful realization that there is simply going to be no *"agua"* [Portuguese for water].

Depressed I sit on the balcony reflecting on my now unhygienic state. Below me a small team of men pulls a wheeled cart into the courtyard, lifts a cover, and starts drawing water from an underground well. Before leaving Zimbabwe we had been advised to carry certain items, such as bully beef, to trade with locals. I call down to the team. A deal is struck. Soon thereafter they throw me a rope with which I draw up three buckets of water in exchange for a tin of bully beef. In this way I assured myself a regular supply of water. It is amazing how much you can do with just three buckets of water per day.

The next morning I go down to a beautifully appointed breakfast restaurant, the tables exquisitely set out with place mats and sterling silver. There is a delicately printed menu offering a "continental breakfast with coffee". Two white uniformed waiters dance around me, the one offering coffee the other offering me breakfast. I am hungry having only had sandwiches the night before on account of our very late arrival. So I order coffee and breakfast. Soon thereafter I receive a cup of espresso coffee, in a tiny cup, all of 200ml.

It gets worse. My breakfast is one croissant - one croissant - that's it! A man sitting in the corner of the restaurant beckons to me as he notices me vainly querying the situation with the waiters. When I walk over to him he says- *"you are new here I see - "* He invites me to share his breakfast whilst he briefs me. Thereafter he and I meet every morning for breakfast sharing what we have purchased from a duty free shop that accepts foreign currency which we have as visitors.

The first order of business the next day is a briefing by a Russian official. Just like Lieutenant-Colonel Derry MacIntyre, of the Rhodesian army, he is also clear and matter-of-fact in his treatment of issues. Extremely revealing is the fact that had Ian Smith [and Bishop Muzorewa] held on for just nine more months Zimbabwe would probably not have been freed. The reason is that within that period RENAMO[1], an insurrectionist organization sponsored by South Africa, have succeeded in overrunning the whole of Mozambique. The government now controls only the cities, towns, ports and most roads. RENAMO controls all rural areas I start to understand the obsession with security and why I am wearing a placard around my neck.

The basketball competitions are run as a model of organizational efficiency. Every game starts on time and ancillary events such as briefings come of with clock-work precision. As a sports event it is undoubtedly an outstanding success on every count. Also good is that we feast daily on fresh prawns even though having to run up 21 flights of stairs to the dining restaurant of the hotel, in which our team was housed, because none of the 5 lifts work.

However that is as far as it goes. I am to become shocked to the bone as regards the overall situation for the ordinary folk of this newly liberated country. Firstly the card around my neck identifies me as a foreigner to whom no citizen is permitted to speak. Social interaction in public is not permitted. So three or more people may not stand on a street corner and have a chat. Although the basketball stadium, that holds 25,000 people, is filled to capacity for every game, within minutes of closing, the stadium and surrounding streets, are completely deserted, as quiet as a church at midnight.

---

[1] **The Mozambican National Resistance** [RENAMO; Portuguese: *Resistência Nacional Moçambicana*] is [was] a conservative political party in led by Afonso Dhlakama. It fought against the FRELIMO in the Mozambican Civil War from 1975 to 1992···. RENAMO also received support from South Africa. In the United States, the Central Intelligence Agency and conservative lobbying was strongly resisted by the State Department, which would "not recognize or negotiate with RENAMO" and convinced President Ronald Reagan and the Congress to support FRELIMO.
http://en.wikipedia.org/wiki/Mozambican_National_Resistance

People simply put their heads down and scurry off to their homes never daring to breach the rule against public gatherings.

Food is a problem and people are issued rations cards to purchase this at markets. The city of Maputo, once the resplendent port city of Lorenzo Marques, is now grubby and run down. All problems are attributed to the machinations of the previous occupiers, the Portuguese colonial settlers. It seems incongruous; the country has been independent since 1975. It is now 1982!

As a Mozambican you have to make written application for permission to buy a bicycle. The purchase of a motor vehicle takes months in a process, where every aspect is scrutinized, particularly how you are able to access the necessary foreign funds. Visits to the residences of political chiefs reveal that, whatever Marx and Engels might have said, egalitarianism is not practiced. Their houses are jam-packed with goodies imported from *"racist apartheid South Africa"*.

When I meet with a contact at a local hotel it takes 17 seconds for the security police to arrive and order us to leave the room and meet in a public area of the hotel. No visitors are allowed in rooms. It is sickening. In Zimbabwe, Mozambique is touted as a wonderful country, its people freed from the yoke of oppression. Whatever this might be, it is certainly not my idea of freedom.

With great difficulty we manage to secure permission for our young players to have a farewell dance function. They have been making contact with local ladies by way of notes surreptitiously passed at games. Biological need has found some porosity in the rigid establishment rules. On the night of the function the mezzanine floor, on which it is held, is screened off by armed soldiers who are also stationed so as to deny access to hotel rooms. Every local girl is required to hand in her identity card for later collection at a "political education center" where I suppose they will be de-contaminated of foreign influence.

I had visited racist apartheid South Africa three times. The situation there had sickened me. Sadly I felt not much better in Mozambique. Instead of an invigorating feeling of freedom, I felt a suffocation of the human spirit, confirmed by the faces and body language of all the povo[1] around me. This was the Mozambique of Samora Machel. It was, and still is, politically incorrect to portray him as anything other than a hero. His widow, Graca

---

[1] **Povo -** means "people" in Portuguese but is usually used to refer to the poorer class of the populace

Machel, is now married to international icon, Nelson Mandela. She does sterling work in the human rights field.

The happy aspect of my visit was that I made contact with the ANC representative Eric Mtshali who was introduced to me by his struggle name Eric Khumalo. We spent a lovely evening together at his home. I returned to Zimbabwe laden with cashew nuts which I had obtained by trading tins of bully beef.

64. Veritas vos liberabit [1]

The Harare show was a prestigious annual event which afforded the whole country to exhibit its productive capacity. It was held at the Harare show grounds and involved the farming and manufacturing sector showing off their products. The show was always a hit with the public who attended in daily droves. Evenings involved entertainment by way of live band competitions and military displays including mock battles between the victorious liberation forces and Ian Smith's army.

There was also a drum majorette competition between all the High Schools. My wife, Palmira, and two of her friends ran a fast food stall called "Crackers" which endeavour was both good fun and provided a useful return for two weeks labour. A high point was a visit by Ian Douglas Smith. Noticeable was that he was always surrounded by a troupe of Black people who treated him with seeming affection, deference and admiration.

Smith: Now did you see those girls, the drum majorettes ...?

Me: Oh yes - and we are all proud as punch

Smith: They should get those girls from Masvingo Girls High to teach the soldiers in our new national army how to march [he adds with a twinkle in his eye]

Me: Yes they won the drum majorette competition with our eldest daughter Shereen Elizabeth - we are so proud

Smith: Was that your daughter? Well congratulations - what are you offering on your menu to celebrate?

Me: Can I take you back a few years - to 1972 - if you don't mind?

Smith: Not at all young man - those were better years for everyone

---

[1] ***Veritas vos liberabit*** - The truth shall set you free (Motto of John Hopkins University)

- 208 -

Me: Do you remember a delegation led by Gerry Raftopolous to ask you about the appointment of a certain Coloured magistrate. It is said you leaned back, made a thumbs up sign and said *"make him a magistrate"*.

Smith: Oh yes, yes - Green - Green something his name was

Me: Greenland, Chris Greenland - Mr. Smith - and I am pleased to meet you at last - and thank you for having appointed me which Minister Lardner Burke found it so hard to do ...

Smith: Well, what a pleasant surprise - I am pleased to meet you too - you deserved it - you see we believed in merit those days

Me: Well some would dispute that

Smith: You mean these chaps now running the country - it is so sad - these chaps were never trained for government - their commie friends only taught them to destroy things - mark my words - as I have repeatedly said - they are going to ruin this country

Me: Why are you so sure of that - after all every government on the day it takes office has no experience of how to run a country?

Smith: The reason - the main reason is that they are only interested in power, to take and hold onto power - that is what communists are really interested in, whatever they might preach - this lot, these chaps have no love of human beings - you will see - you cannot govern if you do not love people - I will be proved right - but it will be too late

Palmira: Mr. Smith - to celebrate I have made you your favourite steak roll ... of really good Gweru ... as I know that, like me, you come from Gweru

Smith: Oh yes, yes, thank you - it is true - only good people come from Gweru

So ends the first and last conversation I have with the man who so adversely influenced events for our country. The fact that he scrapped the Adventure into Citizenship program and the policy of partnership flashes through my mind. Having stopped the recruitment of Black people into the civil service, for some 15 years, guaranteed the very thing he now complains off - that they are supposedly unequipped to govern.

Tragically, however, history is to prove him right about our new government ruining the country; very right indeed. He must be laughing in his grave. What an aberration; what a most grotesque obscene irony? Zimbabweans are still not free ... 30 years after independence!

By 1982 I have ascended through the magisterial ranks and hold the position of Regional Magistrate, which is the highest position attainable.

Whilst on circuit Court at Masvingo I preside over a trial in which a young successful emergent businessman is charged with rape. The complainant is a middle aged woman. She is well known and respected as a community leader and socialite. The two only know each other by sight. They meet in the early afternoon at a local supermarket. As she is laden with goods, and her car has broken down, the young man offers her a lift home in his car, which offer she is grateful to accept. 30 minutes later she arrives at the local police station. She is a mess. Her hair is disheveled, dress torn, panties torn and she has bruising, including bruising to her vagina, that a medical report states is consistent with forcible entry. The police dutifully accept her allegation of rape, set out in blinding detail by a tearfully hysterical and severely traumatized woman.

In Court the accused is represented by one of the best advocates in the country. The complainant is an outstanding witness and the more she is cross-examined the more obvious it becomes to all present that she has been the victim of a brutal rape. The accused then gives evidence. He is almost child-like in his denial, claiming simply that intercourse occurred with her full consent. He is cross-examined -

Prosecutor: You say she consented?

Accused: Yes she did

Prosecutor: You agree that she is a well known respected married woman?

Accused: Yes she is

Prosecutor: And that you only knew each other by sight?

Accused: Yes

Prosecutor: And that you stopped your car at a spot where you may have been seen by members of the public - it is there where you had intercourse - in broad daylight -?

Accused: er - yes

Prosecutor: You are insisting that this respectable married woman agreed to intercourse with a younger man that she hardly knew in broad daylight?

Accused: er - well - er - yes - it is what happened. [There are murmurs from the public gallery]

Prosecutor: You see that her dress, Exhibit "A", is torn - how did that happen?

Accused: Well - er - I do not know - at the time I did not see her dress torn [More murmurs from the public gallery]

Prosecutor: You see that her panty, Exhibit "B", is torn - how did that happen?

Accused: er - er - maybe it got torn when she pulled off her panty

Prosecutor: What do you mean?

Accused: Well - er - I put my hand on her knee - you know - as a man - trying my luck - and she told me to stop and then grabbed me - she was very hot - even her breathing on me was strong ...

[The public gallery starts to go into voice and I have to remind them to be silent or I will have to clear the Court]

Prosecutor: You seem to be suggesting that she raped you '

Accused: No - it is what happened there

Prosecutor: I want to read the medical report to you. It says bruising on the inner thigh and vaginal bruising consistent with forcible entry

Accused: Well - er - I do not know - maybe it is because she was so forceful - the way she wanted me - as a woman wanting a man... [Again I have to warn the public to refrain from voicing anger]

Prosecutor: Your Worship - as the accused seems to be brazenly claiming that he was in fact the victim of the rape I have no further questions

After hearing both counsel make final submissions I am about to deliver my judgment immediately on this case as, on the facts, things appear perfectly clear. There is little doubt in my mind that he raped this respectable married woman and pillar of society. For reasons I cannot explain, (perhaps guided by my ancestral spirits) I call the complainant back to the witness stand and ask her a few innocuous questions about her standing in the community. For the first time she unexpectedly appears uncomfortable.

Court: What is wrong - you appear to be uncomfortable - I just want to be clear about one or two things

Witness: The accused knows very well that, in our custom, if a man has intercourse with a married woman he must pay the woman's husband damages [This statement is a bombshell]

Court: Please explain what you mean when you say "when a man has intercourse with a married woman"

Witness: I do not know what came over me - after he was smoking something in the car

Court: Yes - please explain - this smoking - what about it?

Witness: My worship - it has never happened to me before - it made me mad - this thing that he smoked - as a woman I wanted him - I was like mad - bewitched - mad with desire ... I feel ashamed ...

[The witness starts to weep. A wave of murmuring, whispers and gasps of astonishment washes over the public gallery]

Harare Courts Magistrates - 1973

Back: Colin Ratcliffe. Ivor Waldeck., Mel Purcell.. Mark Stonier. Philip Finch. Doug Palframan. **Front -** Tony Clarke, Tom Smith. Leighton Gale. Des Utting. Ray McKay. Chris Greenland. (Author)

To a stunned Court and gallery she then goes on to confirm the accused's version of the event in all its detail and ends by explaining that she made the report to the police so as to ensure that she had official proof of the event so as to enable the successful award of damages to her husband in later customary law proceedings. I am shaken to the core. It was my intention to summarily convict this young man and send him the prison for seven years.

Rape is a most heinous and pernicious crime in that it comprises the forcible injurious invasion of the body, leaving the victim traumatized, often for life.

Rape victims are doubly traumatized, firstly in the rape itself and then in the subsequent proceedings, where often the victim is made to look like having "asked for it", accused of being a brazen liar, of having loose morals and subjected to other attacks on her name, reputation and personality. There is an extremely low success rate of rape prosecutions in the Courts. Both Human Rights lobbies and feminists in particular, have very understandable concerns around the plight of rape victims. Courts often come under harsh criticism for their handling of rape cases.

However we now know that, even amongst the relatively few that were convicted, many were actually innocent. See the book "Wrongly Convicted" by Saundra Davis Westervelt, John A. Humphrey, which reports on the irrefutable proof of this in terms of DNA technology.

I had always been confident of my ability to asses where the truth lay in these cases and had confidently handed down verdicts and sentences. In addition, because of similar experiences in other cases, I had long since adopted a philosophy of "when most sure, be most careful". In this case however, no amount of care would have saved the destruction of this innocent man's young, promising and productive life had the complainant not so unexpectedly recanted. Why and how she recanted rests purely in the realms of chance. The judicial process had provided no guarantees.

Both State and defense counsel came to see me in my office. We were all shaken in the realization of how close an innocent young man had come to being a victim of injustice predicated on an artfully contrived and monstrous lie. The case was shattering in its implications. It meant that, despite a conscientious adjudicator, full, competent and diligent representation on both sides, terrible injustice was a simple possibility.

I went to my office and penned my resignation from the magistracy. I suspect that the letter was preceded by at least three "Hail Marys".

It was time to move on in the journey of life.

65. Our Zambezi

It was about this time that I have the pleasure of introducing my English brother-in-law Rob Pool to the magic of Africa. He is a born and bred Englishman who has come out to teach under a United Nations sponsored program. His love for what he found included tying the knot with my wife's younger sister. Sojourns to the Zambezi valley provide a wonderful respite from the drudgery of city life. So off we go, traveling in two vehicles with boats in tow.

Entering the Zambezi valley involves driving down an escarpment, that is breathtaking in its magnificence, as the road winds down several kilometers bordered by knife edge drop-offs as it switches and double-switches back on itself. "Oh my - just look at that - " Rob mummers loudly as we survey several scenes of huge multi wheeled articulated vehicles lying at the bottom of deep crevices. *"Yes" I reply " - mostly South African - unused to the conditions - tired and careless in their impatience to get to Zambia and back home again - "*

These scenes are a timeous cue that we are entering a dangerous land where nothing is to be taken for granted. As the sun starts to set we come across huge dark coloured mounds on the road. Our little convoy comes to a halt and we all alight to survey the product of the alimentary canal of Africa's largest pachyderms. Rob is beside himself with excitement at the sight of elephant dung, still fresh, warm and moist. He even wants to collect some of it. We calm him down and assure him that soon he will actually have the greater pleasure of actually meeting the elephants. It is wonderful to witness his reaction of seeming disbelief at the prospect.

Moving on it is not long before we come across wild animals, hyena, impala, kudu, buffalo and elephant. For us Africans it is still an enrapturing experience. For Rob it is quite an unbelievable adventure into a world that he has never known, only imagined. It is his very first encounter with the world's great animals.

Arriving at our camp, at Chirundu, on the banks of the Zambezi, the vehicle lights pick up a lone buffalo as I execute a turn and stop about 100 yards further on. *"What are you doing?"* Rob enquires most anxiously. *"We are at camp"* I reply. "Oh no you can't ... you can't stop here - " Rob splutters " - *did you not see the boofolo* [Yorkshire pronunciation of "buffalo"] - *there is a boofolo right here - "* he goes on in a voice of extreme apprehension. It takes a long while to re-assure our guest that the lone young buffalo is no threat.

After a campfire meal and drinks under a beautiful night sky we retire for the night. No sooner have I fallen asleep when I am shaken awake by Rob who is wide-eyed and anxious as he repeats - *"what is that - what is that - ?"* Our camp has been invaded by a hyena which is boldly circling the boat still attached to our vehicle. It is quite unperturbed at the stones I throw at it and the yelling of *"booger off"* [Yorkshire pronunciation for "bugger off"] that I encourage Rob to do. Finally it dawns on me that the hyena has caught the scent of a dead spring hare that I had unfortunately run over en route. I retrieve it from the well of the boat and throw it to the animal. It grabs the gift and disappears into the night.

Sleep is once again disturbed when Rob wakes me up with another - *"what is that - what is that -?"* referring to a sound emanating from some distance away. My explanation that this signifies the presence of feeding elephants is very bad news for my English friend. It takes some time for me to convince him that the elephants pose no threat to us as they are intelligent animals, fully aware of our presence and doing no more than feeding off surrounding trees.

After a stiff shot of brandy we once again doze off. A very deep sleep is disturbed by a sound that I instantly recognize even though I have never heard it before. However I recognize it as I have been an avid reader of biographies of all the great White hunters such as Frederick Courteney Selous, who visited Africa at the turn of the century. It is the sound of the rumblings of the gut of an elephant. As I open my eyes the whole world is filled with the sight of a huge elephant bull standing above me, no more than a foot or so from our heads. My mind goes into a spin as I lie frozen in terror. I envisage, anticipate being gored by one of those huge tusks or being subjected to what George Anderson used to refer to as "pachyderm foot massage" [definitely not recommended].

I finally decide that the elephant means no harm, because, if he did, he would have long since done us in. This is confirmed by the fact that the animal is in the process of picking up wild fruit that it has shaken off a tree close by. A new terror than takes hold of me. There is every likelihood that my English friend will wake up and jump up, shout scream - or something like that. In my mind the elephant will react, as elephants do, by issuing a warning trumpet. At this distance, so my mind tells me, the trumpeting will be quadraphonic and vaporize both of us. It is not the fear of being gored or trampled on, but the fear of being trumpeted at that now near paralyzes me. All my instincts insist that I crawl into my vehicle which is no more than ten feet away. But I just cannot leave Rob. He will get up sooner or later and then his death is assured. Well that is what my mind tells me. Somehow I contrive to cover his head, whisper to him and then lead him slowly to our vehicle still covered up. Thank God he is obedient throughout and soon we are both in the vehicle with Rob in the front seat with me in the back.

Relief is very short-lived as a nightmare starts for both of us. The elephant turns towards us, in the dim early morning light, and in a moment we are confronted, confronted in all our sensibilities by its huge head swaying to and fro, in front of us - its tusks barely millimeters from the windscreen. It is a terrifying sight. It is only a matter of time before his tusks make contact with the glass. In that event, so my mind repeatedly insists, it will assume that Rob has attacked and it will retaliate - with our gruesome deaths assured thereafter. Rob sinks lower and lower in his seat gasping for air as he struggles to breath. I am paralyzed through and through but grateful to be in the back seat. Fortunately my fears are not realized and, after what seems like an eternity, the great animal turns away and resumes feeding. Brandy has never tasted so good before and soon we are jabbering away in relief having been joined by Jaqi, my wife's sister in law, who also become aware of the elephant. She says that it had actually stepped very close to their two-man tent in which her husband, Mark, is still asleep.

The next day we launch our boats and make off for our final camp some 45 kilometers upstream. It is always a truly hazardous business piloting a boat to the camp. We soon lose sight and contact of each other when I foolishly take a slightly different route on the river. Only my young son is with me on my boat. Concern turns to anxiousness, anxiousness turns to fear when I repeatedly fail to find "the road" [deep and navigable channel] in the river and keep colliding with stumps, rocks and sand banks. The road is either easy or difficult to see depending on the position of the sun and cloud. The Zambezi is an extremely dangerous river. Things are going wrong. Because our fuel is finite there is a limit to how much searching for the channel we can do.

I decide to make for an island from which I will be able to survey the river and detect the road. As I pilot the boat to the sand island our landing spot is occupied by an enormous crocodile which inexplicably declines to move. This is not normal. Crocodiles always shy away from boats. This one stays put. Such brazenness much surely mean it instinctively knows that we represent an impending meal. I am now in a state of panic; a panic that I dare not betray to my son. A coward does indeed die many times. *"Hail Mary, full of grace - "* Panic induces indecision and I fail to implement any avoiding action. Collision with the toothy monster is imminent. However at the last second the crocodile makes off. I try desperately to posture to my son that this result was a consequence of correct action on my part.

From the top of the island I finally make out the road. We resume our trip only to find that what I have assumed to be another island, which borders the road, is actually a huge pod of hippopotami on a submerged sand bank. As our boat approaches they start to peel off making for the deep channel that is our road ahead. I have to make an instant decision. Either I accelerate, and attempt to beat them to the road, or I back off. As regards the first option, there is a chance of collision with fateful consequences. As regards the latter, we will be in shallow water infested with these beasts. As a "born and bred" motor cyclist I instinctively opt to accelerate and beat them to it. I open the throttle wide whilst shouting at my son to look at me and not ahead. My pulse is racing. Nerves are jangling. As we roar past the island, gargantuan reddish brown monsters crash in within feet of the boat. It is hairy and so very, very scary - but we make it through - only just.

We finally make contact with the other boat and continue our trip. As we approach camp we hear the calling of human voices on the Zambian side of the river. They know us well, as we often trade items like coco-cola and bully beef with them for live bait, which they have caught in their traditional nets. Incredibly all the teenage girls pull of their tops and start to clap their hands, sing and dance for us. The impromptu top-less concert they put on for us is an expression of joy by simple people eking out an existence in a most natural environment, seemingly untainted by the modern world. More importantly it is their way of saying "this is your special welcome".

A most astounding phenomena however is that when we finally reach them and engage in conversation they tell us, in clear and confident voice, that Zimbabwe will be one day, not too far off, infinitely worse off than Zambia. It is a most surprising prediction and we are more than bemused especially at how certain these simple folk are about the matter.

But they will brook no argument on the matter. They are as certain of it as one is certain that day follows night.

Nyaumba camp is a bush camp with absolutely no amenities. That fact contributes immensely to its charms. It is situated at the end of the 15 kilometer long snaking river gorge that starts at the Kariba Dam wall. However it is completely inaccessible except by 45 kilometer boat trip from Chirundu, involving running a most perilous gauntlet of submerged rocks, sandbanks, stumps, rapids and hippopotami. After the arduous business of setting up camp we collapse in our camp chairs to take in the view. It is breathtakingly beautiful with the majestic gorge exiting to our left into a wide gushing, gurgling expanse of swirling water, huge and lazy, going past with an air of timelessness and power - so much beauty - so much power.

To our right we see a small group of elephants watering sedately at the river's edge. My eldest son, takes a camera and makes his way towards the group. Suddenly, without warning, as if from nowhere, a huge bull elephant, followed by two other elephants, steps noiselessly into his path, no more than ten meters ahead. Neither he nor us had seen or heard them approach. He freezes, unable to walk thereafter. Mark and I finally go and retrieve the lad as he now has difficulty in walking. Richard Gannaway, the owner of the other boat, hands me a cold beer. I can truly say that I have never in my life tasted anything so delicious. I now fully understand how man must have first fallen in love with beer. From the far bank our friends wave goodnight as the sun starts to sink as a giant golden orb on the water. We wave back. The world seems to be at peace with its quietude now disturbed by new sounds of the night including the happy crackle of our camp fire. Being in the Zambezi valley is always a spiritually uplifting experience.

I spend the evening partly teasing Rob about this equation: - White man + African magic = Coloured folk. He is game in replying that this is hardly surprising, given the welcome we experienced that afternoon. The next day my son catches his first tiger fish - all of 8.2 kgs of electrifying beauty, power and grace. *"Hydrocynus vittatus, striped waterdog - the most beautiful and ferocious freshwater game fish in the world"* I tell him.

He will never forget it. As his father I will never forget the look of sheer joy on his face. I imagined that it was the look we must have had on some of our faces when we were given our first Xmas party by the Toc H Society of Bulawayo so many years ago. Rob goes back to England but to no avail. The magic of Africa has changed him forever. He returns to Zimbabwe and then settles in Botswana after he is refused residency in my country, even though married to a local girl. In Botswana he establishes himself as the local Bill Gates in the IT industry.

We also have something else that is unforgettable - the prophesy of the simple river people of Zambia that our country is going to fail. We are not to know just how well Mugabe is due to ensure its emphatic fulfillment.

---

66. The Advocate

My intention was to join what was then known as "the De Facto Bar" and practice as an advocate. The name *"Bar"* simply means advocates establishing themselves in one building where they share expenses and resources. Earnings however are a private matter. The reason why it was given the pre-fix "de facto" was that it continued to operate in traditional mode. In terms of that mode, only advocates had right of appearance in the superior Courts and acted purely on brief from attorneys [lawyers]. In Zimbabwe the professions was now *"fused";* meaning that attorneys could also appear in the superior Courts and therefore did not need to brief advocates. The Bar now comprised some seven exclusively White advocates who, like me, shared the belief that this mode of the practice of law was essential to the profession of legal representation. Resources at the Bar included the best library in the country and, as a collective, advocates were better resourced than the average lawyer. There is some analogy with the medical profession where you have doctors and specialists. Having been a student of the lives of great English Advocates like Norman Birkett and Marshall Hall, and having received short but inspirational counsel from

Sydney Kentridge, I needed to do this if my life was to be worth what I felt it should be worth.

"Advocacy[1] is the pursuit of influencing outcomes - including public-policy and resource allocation decisions within political, economic, and social systems and institutions - that directly affect people's current lives. [Cohen, 2001]". That is its technical definition. In Court an advocate is one who speaks on behalf of a person involved in a case such as a person on trial.

A Lord Chief Justice of England summed up the requirements for winning a case in Court as- a good case, good evidence, good witnesses, a good judge, a good jury and good luck. A theologian and philosopher Sidney Smith said- "Justice is practiced experimentally to be best promoted by the opposite efforts of practiced and ingenious men, presenting to the selection of an impartial judge the best argument for the establishment and explanation of truth."

Many writers have also agreed that the "hardest thing to establish is the truth". Memories fade, people see things differently and human beings often find it hard to cope with the intimidating atmosphere of a Courtroom. What an advocate does is to use all factors so as to influence the Court to accept his/her client's case as being the truth. Obviously it is often not the truth but something the client has manufactured in order to escape conviction or to win a legal dispute. It is not the advocate's function to believe in his/her client's case. His function is to believe in his argument in "the pursuit of influencing outcomes". That argument is presented by him in an opening address, in leading evidence, in cross-examining witnesses and in final submissions to the Court using all his knowledge, skills and understanding. Its purpose is to ensure that his client's case, however good or bad, is believed or accepted.

The most publicized case in modern times is the 1995 case of the State of California versus O J Simpson charged with the murder of his wife and her friend. O J Simpson was found not guilty. There is no dispute that this was mainly on account of the skillful strategy and tactics of the high powered defense team employed to influence the outcome. A civil Court later had very little difficulty in concluding that Simpson did, in fact, commit the murders.

The reason why the Bar in Zimbabwe was an all White affair was that, before independence, it was extremely difficult for a Black advocate to secure enough briefs to make a living. Lawyers were mostly White. In the general

---

[1] http://en.wikipedia.org/wiki/Advocacy

scheme of things they, and their clients, preferred White advocates. It would be simplistic to attribute this only to racism on their part.

The fact of the matter was that most Black clients also preferred to be represented by White advocates. This is what is occurring in South Africa right now as this text hits my screen. [2010] Because of history White advocates had more proven experience and the Courts were presided over by White judicial officers. For many Black clients it was simply safer to employ White representation when the stakes were so high and the possible consequences of loss so great. An analogy is that if your child is dying you will get the doctor that has the best chance in your view, of preventing death, even if that doctor has red eyes, horns, cloven feet and a tail.

Going to the Bar therefore was daunting for me. I had no track record as I had never practiced law privately. My marketability was therefore, at best, questionable. It was only three years after independence and attitudes may not have changed that much on the part of the White dominated legal profession and their paying clients. I was married with four children. Was leaving the sheltered employment of the office of Regional Magistrate, with its good and guaranteed income, to prove a brave step or a foolish one? In the result I took the prudent step, so I thought, of verbally communicating my intentions to all the Black, Coloured and Indian lawyers in private practice. Their reaction was to express great delight at my proposed move and assurances were given that I would not be able to cope with the deluge of briefs that they were going to send me. That I was to secure financial success looked like a sure thing. I was also greatly encouraged by Advocate Julia Wood, possessed of a brilliant legal mind.

I was welcome by the leader of the Bar, Adrian de Bourbon SC, and its other members, particularly the brilliant Ian Donovan, who gave me much encouragement, help and advice at every turn, without which things would have been undoubtedly disastrous. What I found particularly satisfying was the culture of *"agree, disagree, agree to disagree, in a climate of mutual respect - "* In Court advocates fought with everything at their disposal on behalf of their clients and the fact that we were all members of the same Bar counted for nothing. The interests of the client were always paramount. Conversely, once the case was over, *"win lose or draw"*, collegiality and friendship was immediately resumed once we were back in chambers. It was a highly professional *"sapiential"* environment.

It was a truly wonderful and intellectually stimulating environment. Within a relatively short time both the Supreme Court [Court of Appeal] and the High Court kindly expressed commendation for my efforts in judgments. Such commendations are by no means routine in the Higher Courts. It was a relief that the flow of briefs was difficult to service on account of volume. Surprisingly, despite their previous promises, not one was from a non-white attorney or firm for the first year of my advocacy. As said, they must have had good reason for this considering my lack of experience. But still I felt disappointed. Instead I received briefs from White attorneys, some of whom I had mentally classified as being probably racist, as in the past they would scarcely greet on chance meetings. All this was confusing and bemusing.

It proved that prejudging and stereotyping human beings is extremely dangerous. So one day after I had just finished a conference with Harry Kantor, of the great firm of Kantor and Immerman, I asked Harry if I could speak to him privately. He said he was busy and hoped that it would not take long. He cut me short when I started to express my long overdue gratitude for all the work his firm had given me saying - *"Please understand that I do not brief you because I like you - have a good day!"*

Whatever one may choose to make of this, for me it was and remains the biggest compliment of my life and has helped to shape my professional and political attitude at its very center

---

67. New madness - truth is rarely pure/never simple[1]

From the day of independence in April 1980 Robert Mugabe was obsessed with transforming the country into a socialist model, with a command economy and highly centralized control under a one party state. Most of the political rhetoric was concerned with this issue and the general public was regaled with the advantages of a one party state. Mugabe's heroes were the eastern bloc leaders such as Nicolae Ceaucescu. Irony and pathos accrued when at the very moment that Mugabe, addressing a ZANU congress, was hailing Ceaucescu as a great leader, unbeknown to him, the Romanian people were putting this tyrant to death.

Joining in the clarion call was a certain Professor Shadreck Gutto who ran a televised program titled "Road To Socialism" in which the superiority, virtues and utility of Marx, Engels and Lenin based social systems of the East were trumpeted as superior to the decadent capitalist West. Later, in 1996, I find that Professor Gutto is with The University of Witwatersrand in South Africa. What's more he appears to be the new South African nation's fountain of wisdom and rock of sense as the media consults him almost exclusively on nearly all topical issues. In all the profoundly wise counsel and

---

[1] **Oscar Wilde**, The Importance of Being Ernest, 1895, Act I, Irish dramatist, novelist & poet (1854 – 1900).

commentary he gives the South African nation there is not one hint of the benefits of socialism, the failings and decadence of the capitalist West or reverence for Karl Marx, Lenin or Friedrich Engels. Man is indeed adaptable to his environment. It must be why man survived the dinosaurs.

However Gutto's endeavors on behalf of Mugabe must not go unnoted. Many South Africans today feel that Zimbabweans themselves are largely to blame for the situation they find themselves in for having blindly supported Mugabe. They did; despite many bad signs about the man. What strongly reinforced their belief in him were also the efforts of exciting Black intellectuals like Professor Gutto especially when he would demolish White opponents on the "Road to Socialism" program like A J A Peck, a high profile White lawyer. People like Sam Gozo[1], who tried to take a contrary view to Gutto, were made to look like "Uncle Tom" stooges of the imperialist West.

At a symposium held at the University I tried to debate a point with the good professor. His response was that capitalism was like an upside down triangle standing on its point. Because wealth and assets were concentrated at the top, the capitalistic model was so unstable, for being top-heavy, that it must eventually topple over. On this he appears to have been vindicated by what has recently occurred with the global financial crisis and its capitalist American origins. When Gutto had outlived his usefulness to Mugabe he was ordered out of the country on less than 24 hours notice. Our esteemed Marxist friend has found a most wonderfully warm home in capitalistic South Africa.

Back in Zimbabwe, after independence we now started to understand that by *"reconciliation"*, apparently accepted by Mugabe at independence, Mugabe actually meant acceptance of exclusive control by him under a one party state. In this scenario ZAPU was a most inconvenient partner of which Mugabe started an ill concealed strategy to rid himself. This soon took on the most brutal proportions, involving the genocide of an estimated 20,000 members of the Ndebele tribe, in what has become known as the Gukurahundi saga. Most Zimbabweans were only marginally aware of the full details and implications of this shameful episode at the time it was occurring, as news of it was masterfully suppressed. There are many authoritative accounts of what occurred. Typical is a report by Kevin Engle and Gregory Stanton in which they accept that the specially formed, North

---

[1] **Sam Gozo** – see "A Crisis of Governance" by James Chikuhwa p.236.

[1] http://www.genocidewatch.org/ZimbabweFacingMassMurder12August2005.htm

Korean trained 5th Brigade reporting directly to Mugabe, slaughtered over 20,000 people[1].

Late one evening an army truck rolled slowly past State House. Persons dressed as soldiers in the back of the truck fired shots at the manned gates of the residence. The guards on duty returned the fire. It was soon over as the truck made off.

As a result of this little episode ten members of ZAPU were arrested and charged with having attempted to stage a coup and conspiring to murder Robert Mugabe. I was asked to defend them. For obvious reasons it was an unpopular brief and since the defendants had no money it would have to be accepted on a pro deo basis for which remuneration was nominal. As the head of a family of five it was no small sacrifice for me to accept the brief. However I did. The trial lasted nine months, the longest for any trial in the country's history.

The State relied on the evidence of an accomplice, one Arthur Mtunzi, and confessions allegedly made by the accused. All the confessions had been made whilst the accused were in police custody; denied access to the outside world in terms of the State's own version of its case.

Its case was based on allegations that had all the hallmarks of an event that had been stage- managed, with a bogus attempted coup, to which the accused were then linked and implicated in terms of where they were at the time and what they said under coercion. According to the state the attempted coup involved the coup plotters driving past the residence of the prime minister firing weapons. Upon the fire being returned by the guards at the residence they immediately abandoned the attack. In effect therefore the supposed attempted coup comprised nothing more than what is known as a *"drive by"* shooting.

The whole thing smacked of contrivance. It had all the attributes of a stage managed sham attack as opposed to the actions of persons really bent on affecting a coup. After all the coup plotters would have known that the prime minister's residence was guarded and that the guards would return fire. Their plan would have included a strategy to deal with this expected resistance had this been a genuine attempted coup.

Of course, it was enormously convenient for Robert Mugabe to be able to prove that ZAPU was breaching the terms of the partnership and

---

[1]

http://www.genocidewatch.org/images/AboutGen_Facing_Mass_Murder_in_Zimb abwe.pdf reconciliation in this most pernicious way. It gave him good reason to get rid of ZAPU and install a one party state.

Most experienced lawyers and advocates will tell you that it does not take long for you to be satisfied as to the guilt or innocence of your client whatever the client might say. In the nine months I was with my clients, often for long hours at the prison, often having lunch within earshot of them and overhearing their conversations, not once did any of them utter one word or act in a way that betrayed guilt on their part.

The only one that had a difficulty was Samson Nhari, Accused No.1 and this was because he was actually at the scene of the sham attack. The stage was reached where I had to unfortunately relinquish my brief in respect of him. The whole thing appeared farcical. Symptomatic of this was the state's star witness under cross-examination as I question him about their journey back to Bulawayo after the so called failed coup attempt. I took him through each stage of the trip asking what they did - etc - until arrival backed home, having traveled some 500 kms. This is what follows with me as counsel –

Counsel: I have just taken you through the whole of the trip back to Bulawayo?

Mtunzi: Yes that is so

Counsel: And you and I have agreed on everything that happened on the way back - like where you stopped for food - who you spoke to - what was said?

Mtunzi: Yes that is so

Counsel: Yes you have - you have given us all the details - and have not left anything out?

Mtunzi: Yes that is so - because you have asked all the questions about our trip

Counsel: And we now know everything that you and the accused spoke about on that return trip to Bulawayo which, as you have said, was without any problems? [And then I spring the trap that I have carefully laid for him]

Counsel: And we now know that no one spoke about the attack on the Prime Minister's residence -?

Mtunzi: er - er - yes

Counsel: Thank you for your honesty - we can be sure that from Harare to Bulawayo you did not discuss what had happened in Harare? [The man is now stuck in the trench of his lies]

Mtunzi: er - er - yes - we did not speak about it [He is dead and now needs to be buried]

Counsel: Your group is traveling to Bulawayo, an eight hour or more journey, and not once does anyone mention, lament or say one word about what has just happened, which included the death of a soldier? You want the Court to believe this Mr Mtunzi?

Mtunzi: er - er - yes [His grave needs to be covered up]

Counsel: Yes you are telling the truth … you never spoke one word about the attempted coup … **you would not have - because it never happened!**

Quite obviously the fact that no failed coup attempt was spoken about on their trip back to Bulawayo was only consistent with the fact that they had not been involved in any such affair. People do not talk about what has not happened!

Despite my efforts five of the ten were convicted. Fortunately they were not sentenced to death but to life-long terms of imprisonment. On appeal I managed to get one of the remaining five off.

Since all the judges that dealt with this case, in the trial and on appeal, were persons whose integrity I accepted without question, I concluded that I had failed the four who still remained incarcerated on such a bad state case.

68. Admirable guile - wisdom - and power corrupts

In one case I defend the son of a man whom I will refer to as Old Man Naran, as that is what we all called him. Naran was a very simple man who arrived from India penniless. He spoke what is commonly referred to as "broken English"; very broken. He settled in mid Zimbabwe, renowned for its gold mining. The police soon noticed that this simple almost illiterate man, running no more than a shoe repair shop and then a cycle shop, was gravitating from being poor to being apparently well off in - well - no time at all. They understandably concluded that he must be dealing in gold. Bringing him to book would be a simple matter. They set the standard trap which involves a plain clothes police officer selling the target a nugget of gold which the police then find the target in possession off when the trap is sprung and they rush in. The problem was that when they rushed into Narran's shop, where the trap was conducted, the gold was nowhere to be found. An exhaustive search failed to uncover it. It had disappeared without a trace - in seconds. Without the evidence Naran could not be charged.

Police are resourceful. The BSAP were good. They were going to get their man. In the ensuing months they sent a stream of undercover agents to Naran hoping to trap him again. The message to each of these agents was the same. The old man explained to each of them that he suspected that they were undercover police officers out to trap him and the size of the gold on offer confirmed this. The police always used gold of moderate size and value in these traps. The Chief Superintendent, ever resourceful, realized that he needed "to think out of the box"; to employ now fashionable terminology.

Things were now desperate. Naran was gravitating from well off to fabulously rich - right under their noses. He now lived in fancy big house and owned other properties. Their "out of the box thinking" bore fruit. Well doesn't it just. The good superintendent obtained special permission to use a really large nugget of gold of extremely great value in order to tempt Naran. Naran would settle for nothing less. The police concluded it was well worth it considering how much their man had apparently already profited illicitly in the gold business. Naran took the bait. He was breathless with excitement. He told the agent to meet him on the center spot of the local school soccer pitch at midnight. This was to ensure that they were truly alone. The police were happy to agree knowing that even if Naran had the head-start of the length of soccer pitch, when they sprung the trap, they would easily overhaul him.

At midnight, as arranged the deal was done and money and the valuable gold exchanged in relative darkness. Within no time at all the scene, much to the audible distress of the old man, was invaded by a platoon of police officers. They had got him at last.

It was only when they had actually started shaking hands and patting each other's backs in self-congratulation that someone announced that there was a problem - a big problem - a very big problem. The gold was missing; it could not be found. Concern turned to disbelief, disbelieve turned to panic, panic turned to catatonic disillusionment when they had to finally accept that the gold, their precious large lump of gold, of great value - was gone. It had apparently vanished into the thin dark air of the night.

The old man's mournful bleating that this was how they treated a poor old man was just so much salt being rubbed into a shared and festering wound. But they had no option. They had to release him. Without the gold they had no case. The matter ended for the police with a high level official enquiry. It was generally accepted that this incident cost the superintendent his promotion to Commissioner of Police. Naran was never caught and lived to a ripe old age.

For us the story of how he did it still occupies many a happy social gatherings. It is also has its pride of place in conversations within the police and Courts. In the first trap Naran had secreted the gold nugget in a half-loaf of bread he "just happened to be selling" to a disheveled old man who then walked out of his shop disdainfully ignored by the police. In the second incident he placed the juicy lump of gold into a pouch attached to a five hundred yard long fishing line which was immediately reeled in, using a Penn Jigmaster reel, by a faithful servant concealed in the darkness at that distance. The police, poor buggers, had come against the guru of gurus of the now fashionable concept of "thinking out of the box".

As said choosing your lawyer or counsel is important, and a matter of intense personal choice for a client, who is paying and has to bear the consequences. At the time of independence it would appear that the newly formed government understandably did not know the full range of its immoveable assets. This included developed plots in neighboring Francistown, Botswana. According to the State a syndicate of three decided to exploit the situation. They engineered a situation where they were able to have the plots sold to their immense financial benefit.

Regrettable one of the three was my erstwhile colleague, Peter Nemapare, who had sat with me as an assessor in the Tekere trial. The other accused was a certain Mr. Moresby-White. This man was a very successful White farmer and businessman renowned as a "professional litigant". He had won famous victories in the Courts particularly as regards the emotive and vexed issue of land appropriation by government. Despite strenuous advice and counsel by his lawyers Moresby-White insisted that he wanted Greenland as his defense counsel. The lawyers pointed out to them that they had always briefed another counsel who had many more years experience than Greenland and had always given exemplary service. In giving this advice they were not being racist. They were acting entirely in the interests of their client.

Peter Nemapare and the other accused accepted this very good advice and elected to have the other counsel as their advocate. Moresby-White, on the other hand, was adamant saying that, as a person, with considerable experience in the Courts, he was satisfied that Greenland would best protect his interests especially as the stakes were so high and upon conviction a long term of imprisonment was certain. Coming from an experienced litigant like Moresby-White, and a White man at that, his stance on me was a very pleasant surprise. So we had a politically intriguing situation of the Black accused persons choosing White counsel and a White accused choosing "Black" counsel. This has yet to occur in South Africa.

He was fully vindicated. The trial was a very tricky affair but I got him acquitted at the end of the state case. Peter and the other accused were unfortunately, for them, convicted and sent to prison for five years. When I asked Moresby-White as to why he had insisted on having me he said- *"The other counsel may well be more experienced than you are, but in my reading of the situation you have the understanding"* as he handed me a bottle of expensive whisky as an additional token of his appreciation.

A White Canadian female doctor was attending to a childbirth. Unfortunately, as so often happens in Africa, the poor mother died in the process. The newborn infant was in such a bad state as to require constant care and attention. In the end the good doctor decided that this was best assured by taking the child home with her. This she did and the child's life was saved. However the baby had no traceable relatives.

The doctor felt she had little option but to keep the child until the authorities could trace her family. They never did. White doctor and Black baby bonded. The social welfare authorities agreed to formalize the situation under a statute titled the Childrens Protection and Adoption Act. By the time I saw them she had been the official foster mother of a now 6 year old beautiful little girl since her birth. As the doctor now wished to return to Canada and probably enter into marriage with her fiancé, also a doctor, she needed to put her relationship with the child on a permanent basis.

It was at this point that things went badly wrong. The social welfare officials refused to support her application to adopt. In fact they actively opposed it; vigorously. The matter was escalated to the Permanent Secretary of Home Affairs, Ernest Tsomondo, without success. I told her not to worry as I knew Ernest. He had been appointed as the first Black magistrate in the late 70s and had come under my guidance and mentorship. A more reasonable and gentle spirited individual you simply could not find in this world I went on. I made an appointment and we went to see Ernest imbued with quiet confidence.

The interview proves to be a shocking experience. Ernest is no longer the quiet, gentle spirited individual I had known. He is now a powerful bureaucrat and we should know it. We should also understand that, as a Black person, he is in a better position to determine the issue as we were not capable of *"thinking like a Black person."* I simply could not believe that this was the same Ernest I had known for years and who, to his knowledge, I recommended for the very post he was holding after Herbert Ushewekunze, the then Minister for Home Affairs had offered me the post. This offer by the then Minister even resulted in a question being put in the United States Congress[1]. Our meeting took on something of the following -

---

[1]

http://www.unhcr.org/refworld/country,,,QUERYRESPONSE,ZWE,456d621e2,3df4bed0c,0.htm. The question insinuated that I had been offered the post as a reward for having acquitted Tekere.

- 228 -

Me: Ernest. When you look at my client and this child ... what do you see?

Ernest: I see a White woman - a privileged White woman

Me: Do you not see the child?

Ernest: Of course I see the child - she is a Black child

Me: So you only see white and black - nothing else - ?

Ernest: That is what they are - I am not blind - and this is the issue here - this is a White doctor and this is a Black child - join the real world my friend

Me: Do you see anything else - ?

Ernest: Like what - she is Canadian - a rich Canadian - this child is African - a poor African

Me: What else do you see?

Ernest: I do not know what games you want to play here - I am a busy man - what is your point?

Me: Do you not see a mother and her child?

Ernest: It is not her child - that is nonsense - utter nonsense - just because we allowed her to keep this child - now you want to say it is her child; you cannot see that it is nonsense

Me: Ernest - with respect - it is her child - and she is the child's mother

Ernest: It's what I mean - when I say you people are incapable of thinking like an African - a White woman can never be a mother to a Black child - that is pure nonsense

[Apparently this has all changed in recent times with none other than Angelina Jolie adopting a Black Malawian child. Madonna has followed suit]

Me: who is the mother of this child - where is the mother -?

Ernest: She has no mother - the mother died as you well know

Me: You are wrong my friend - and to prove it let us ask the child - what do you think she will say - if you ask her who is her mother -?

Ernest: er - well of course she will say that the doctor is her mother - but you need to think more deeply - like an African - she does not know better because she is only a child - if you give a child a sweet she will say anything

Me: Do you not understand also that, to this child, it matters not one jot what colour or ethnicity her mother is - what is important is the love and security the mother gives her - and that if you force them apart you will be doing terrible damage to the child - as you were a magistrate you are well aware that to a child love and security are the most important and precious needs?

Ernest: These psychologists' reports in the Courts are always by White doctors and so called White experts - they are not Africans and cannot know an African

Soon thereafter we are told that he is tired of listening to nonsense and that we should leave.

I make application to Court under the Childrens Protection and Adoption Act for the Regional Court to overrule the government bureaucrats and permit the adoption. The application is hotly opposed in arguments littered with emotive statements predicated upon racist, ethnic and xenophobic considerations. The Court, so it is argued, should never allow a poor Black child to be victimized by sanctioning a situation where a rich White person can come to Africa and snatch a poor Black child who will then grow up in a racist White country. The child should not be denied its Black heritage is the cornerstone of their case.

The learned Regional Magistrate [Dave Bartlett] has little difficulty in holding that, as the upper guardian of all children, he is satisfied beyond a shadow of doubt that it would be most tragic and cruel for child and mother to be now torn apart and that as my client had been the *de facto* [as a matter of fact] mother of this beautiful little girl for all her life it was already long overdue that she become the *de jure* [legal] mother. He is also happy to agree that, although my client did not give birth to the child, without her the child would not have lived. She was the child's mother. That is what fate decreed. It was an undeniable reality. He rules that the adoption must go through without any delay.

My client bursts into tears, holding her child to her in an embrace that only mothers are capable of. Ernest is incensed and makes an impromptu speech about the necessity to transform the Courts as the magistrate is White.

To me the result was most satisfying. Perhaps it was easier for me to see the "fundamental truths" of the situation as I too had been "mothered" by foreign White German nuns as a child in need. At that time the accusation of not being able to think like a Black person presented as something of an irritation. Later, in 1994, this same White magistrate was appointed by the Black government as a judge of the High Court. Perhaps Ernest turned in his grave as by this time sadly he had passed on.

He however got his revenge by refusing my sister in law's English husband, Rob Pool, the right to settle in Zimbabwe. They had met in Zimbabwe when he was teaching under a government sponsored aid program. When I pointed out to Ernest that it seemed to be the case that a Black male could import any foreign woman, even a prostitute, and have no problems about securing rights of residency, I was once again regaled with a lecture on my lack of understanding about Black culture in which the male species was paramount. The result was that my sister in law and her husband were forced, very fortunately for them as it turned out, to leave Zimbabwe and settle in Botswana.

What struck me then is how good people change once infused with power; change as human beings. The cliché; that "power tends to corrupt, and absolute power corrupts absolutely[1]" is a cliché precisely because it is so true. History and society are replete with examples of this on a never ending basis. Another good example was Patrick Chinamasa. We, his compatriots in the legal profession, were all so happy when he went into the Mugabe government in the early 80s. A more sensible, gentle and reasonable person was hard to find.

Chinamasa has long since metamorphosized to being Mugabe's right hand man and architect in turning a wonderful country into one of the most cruel and repressive regimes of the modern world.

69. Duty of advocacy

As said an advocate is required to present the best possible case for his client. Whether he believes in the innocence or guilt of his client is quite irrelevant. He or she must simply put the client's case to the opposing witnesses and the Court, as instructed, using all his or her skills to make that case as acceptable as is possible. The White dominated legal profession of Rhodesia generally carried out this sacred duty to an exemplary standard when representing Black nationalists in a cause that threatened their very own way of life.

In 2004, whilst in Namibia the media published a story that persons on treason charges were being dumped by their advocates for the reason that the advocate did not share their view that Namibia had no jurisdiction over the Caprivi Strip, which the accused were claiming as their own sovereign state. To me this was totally unacceptable. It matters not one jot whether or not you share your client's political views or ideas about sovereignty. It should be remembered that people were once executed for advancing the then "unbelievable", objectionable and intolerable heresy that the earth was not flat, but round. Your duty as counsel is to take your client's case and put it as best you can, telling the Court that you have been "instructed" to do so.

---

[1] Quotation by John Emerich Edward Dalberg Acton, first Baron Acton [1834–1902].

In 1995, in Botswana, an acquaintance came to me in a very distressed state. He was in danger of losing his livelihood permanently as the local committee regulating his profession, accountancy, had unfairly struck him off the professional register. The implication of this was that he would be unable to practice his profession for the rest of his life. He needed the intervention of the High Court.

Part of his problem, he said, was that he could not get a single lawyer to represent him. His problems included a dispute he had with his previous landlord. The reason why lawyers were shying off him, so it seemed on his version, was that his adversary in the tenancy dispute was the registrar of the High Court, a powerful person in the legal world and whose antipathy lawyers felt they dared not risk In the circumstances I was forced to arrange that an advocate friend of mine, Tim Cherry, travel down from Zimbabwe to represent the man. This Tim successfully did and the man's career was saved.

I should add that, personally, I had always found nearly all lawyers in Botswana to be perfectly proper in their professional approach.

I had occasion to represent a White game warden who was charged with having corruptly issued hunting licenses. Interesting was that before we started the trial the whole family formed a circle and prayed loudly for God's help in my defense of their loved one. The man was most senior in the department and had all the appearances of rectitude. I had little reason but to believe that he was innocent especially as his family presented as being religious.

The State was relying, as is the position in all such cases, mainly on the evidence of the person who allegedly paid the bribes to my client. He gave his evidence well. If I did not break him in cross-examination my client was dead in the water. It was not too long before the man was in trouble on his story as I set to work on him. Soon thereafter he was visibly shaken; stammering and having to apologize to the Court for contradictions and other problems I managed to force him to make for himself. The stage was reached where he started making statements like " - *you are just too clever for me - I am not used to Court - it is all so confusing - honestly I don't know what else I can say ...* " as he feverishly wiped his brow and looked pleadingly at the presiding magistrate to save him.

He asks for an adjournment as he feels he cannot carry on. I oppose it. The magistrate grants a 15 minute adjournment. I feel more than satisfied with progress. Outside the Court the wife of the accused, my client, approaches me.

Me: There are no guarantees but it is my view that the magistrate will find that he cannot convict on the evidence of this man and your husband will be free. It appears that your prayers will be answered.

She: Mr. Greenland - do you enjoy your work -?

Me: Yes I do - I would say it is satisfying rather than enjoyable - especially when it goes like this case is going and injustice prevented

She: Do you enjoy destroying innocent people -? [I am stunned]

Me: No - I believe in justice

She: You said you feel satisfied - does it give you satisfaction to publicly humiliate an honest and good person who has had the courage to come to Court and tell the truth -? [she adds testily - I am numbed in shock - this is my client's wife telling me that the witness is speaking the truth about her husband]

Me: I did not hear what you just said - this conversation is over

She: Are you really not ashamed of what you do - ..? [I walk away]

I am now a repository of inner conflict. I believe her. I now believe that my client is guilty and that the witness is telling the truth. But *belief* is not enough. Unless I *know* that he is guilty I do not have a problem as his advocate. She is not my client. He is. My duty is to him.

I go to him and ask him- *"are you guilty of the offences charged?"* He replies indignantly - *"Certainly not!"* When I then ask him if the witness is telling the truth he responds by saying that the man is *"lying through his teeth"*. I go back into Court and finish off the witness who leaves the witness stand in tears. The magistrate finds that the evidence of the main witness cannot be accepted as "credible and reliable". My client is found not guilty and discharged.

His wife embraces him, her face awash with sheer joy and relief. They leave Court holding hands.

Well - they say truth is stranger than fiction.

---

70. A daughter of the soil

It was around this time that I met Judy Todd for the first time. She had always existed in my imagination from the first time I saw a picture of her in a press report during Rhodesian days.

There was this lone attractive White girl standing side by side with Black people in open defiance of the Smith regime. Thereafter there were many reports about how she and her father, Sir Garfield Todd in particular, were hounded, persecuted and arrested by the regime. She never wavered and kept up activist resistance until the country was freed. In my mind she presented as a truly extraordinary person with principles and courage that I could never have. She came to see about Alibaba Dlodlo, one of the accused I had defended on charges of having attempted a coup and conspired to murder Robert Mugabe. Like Sydney Kentridge had, she made me feel so important. Inwardly I was somewhat shameful considering how precious little I had contributed to the struggle for freedom. Thereafter I had the honour of being invited to her home for a social evening. A conversational piece was that behind her toilet door was a picture of a man with Ian Smith in the sights of his rifle.

A point was reached when she made an utterly astounding suggestion to me. She said - "You know Chris - I think it would be good if you could visit my parents - and develop a relationship with my dad - my father never had a son - I am sure he would appreciate you - won't you consider it - he would dearly love to have a son … ". Judy and I did not become close and I rarely saw thereafter. In her book she goes on to say that she then received a phone call from Masinga the head of ANC intelligence, now known by the whole world as Jacob Zuma, President of South Africa.

Judith Garfield Todd is an extraordinary human being by any standards. Amongst other things she has devoted her life to always putting herself in harm's way so that others can be free. She was and is on first name terms with all the regional struggle heroes and leaders such as Joshua Nkomo, Nelson Mandela, Oliver Tambo, Kenneth Kaunda, Jacob Zuma, Thabo Mbeki -. the list is endless. For her to have demonstrated the regard that she had for me, including mooting possible adoption by her great father is an honour beyond description.

Also see chapter 73 below.

---

71. Hidden agendas

There is a saying in the Courts that one should never ask a question of a witness unless one is sure of the answer. One of the advocates at the Bar represented a lady who was seeking divorce on the grounds of her husband's adultery with her best friend who was the wife of a neighboring farmer. There was no dispute that adultery had been indeed committed and that she was entitled to her divorce. She was being led by her counsel purely as a formality required by procedural law. This meant that even if the other party was consenting to the divorce the Court must hear what happened and also that the person seeking the divorce was innocent of similar conduct. Proceedings then went along the following lines –

Counsel: Understand that this is just a formality - so that you confirm your case, which is not disputed by your husband, on oath. Your husband has accepted that he committed adultery

Witness: Yes - it seems they were very busy - and for a long time

Counsel: Yes ... yes - it is in your papers - we just need to confirm this to the Court

Witness: Ok - I understand

Counsel: How did you find out about the adultery?

Witness: I got a tip off and followed my husband to their farm. They have always been our close friends. Her husband was not in the main house. They had locked themselves in the guest cottage, closed the curtains and were in there for an hour. My sister and I could hear the sounds of them having sex - you know the sounds people make - well - during sex. When we knocked on the door they refused to open. When they did open the bed was in a mess - .

Counsel: And did he admit it?

Witness: Oh yes - she was crying and saying she was sorry - and they both admitted that this had been going on for a long time. I had noticed that he used to disappear and then tell me funny stories about where he had been.

Counsel: So can you confirm to the Court that you seek divorce on grounds of adultery and that you have never condoned his adultery?

Witness: Yes my Lord - I confirm that - I want the divorce - I have not forgiven him

Counsel: And can you confirm that you, yourself, have not committed adultery? [There is a long pause before the witness answers]

Witness: My Lord - I am a Christian - I do not want to lie

Counsel: [sensing a problem] My lord can I have a short adjournment so as to consult with my client?

Judge: Well - what is the problem - can she not just answer the question? [Her advocate is still very worried - very worried - the answer is not what he expected]

Counsel: suppose so - but would respectfully request just a short adjournment

Judge: [to the witness] Will you please answer the question - as a Christian you know you are on oath and must simply tell the truth

Witness: My Lord - it is true - I have committed adultery. [This is a bombshell - there is a wave of tittering in the Court]

Counsel: My Lord I really must urge you to grant me and adjournment

Judge: And I must really urge your client to tell us more [and turning to her] with whom have you committed adultery?

Witness: With her husband, Roy - our neighbour. [A wave of gasps, tittering and other sounds of astonishment sweeps through the Court - the judge struggles to conceal a smile]

Judge: For how long has this been going on?

Witness: For about - I would say - about a year. [More tittering -]

Judge: Does your husband know about this?

Witness: No - it is the first time it is being mentioned - I am sorry

Judge: You should know that I cannot grant you a divorce as you did not disclose your own adultery in your papers and your husband has therefore not condoned your conduct. Counsel you may now have your adjournment.

Her red faced advocate is severely embarrassed. Everyone else in Court however has been marvelously entertained. His client explains that she never disclosed her adultery before as she was never asked. Her whole legal team had simply presumed that only her husband had been adulterous. This was understandable but a legally fatal mistake as the proceedings proved.

Fortunately the story had a seemingly happy ending. About a month later the Court was able to grant her divorce and a divorce to her best friend and neighbour on the grounds of the adulterous relationships that had been in progress between these neighbors and friends. The news paper splashed the story and picture of the happy couples leaving Court having exchanged spouses. Smiling broadly they promised to remain friends. By all accounts they did!

News of a suicide never fails to numb the mind. The reason is that we are all so aware of our own instinct of self preservation. So we cannot imagine taking our own life. And yet people commit suicide very day. It is commonplace.

One day I traveled with a client to a magistrate's Court in a country town which I think was Shamva. My client was a very good looking, educated, personable, well dressed White male. He had been found in possession of dagga at a police road block. Since he had admitted his possession to me I could only help him as regards pleading with the Court for a lenient sentence. I had a nagging concern in this regard. In terms of the quantity of dagga he had been found in possession of, the magistrate would have been able to justifiably impose a custodial sentence.

Regrettably I held suspicion in mind that race politics may come into play. There was a good chance, so I mooted in my mind, that the magistrate, being a Black person, would find it all too easy to seize the opportunity to wreak revenge on this White male in satisfaction of long held deep-seated aggrievement against White folk. After all historically Black folk had much to be angry about.

The young man handed me a sealed envelope which he requested that I open, only once the case was finished. In Court he pleaded guilty and we threw ourselves at the mercy of the Court in pleading in mitigation. In reasoning that represented the very best in exercise of judicial discretion the learned magistrate sentenced my client to a stiff fine and a suspended term of imprisonment. Provided he paid the fine and behaved himself he was a free man.

Immediately Court was adjourned the young man pulled a pistol from the inside pocket of his jacket. He then told me, in cold matter-of-fact tones, that had the magistrate imposed a sentence of imprisonment he would have shot himself there and then in Court. He explained that he was acutely aware of the fact that White males like him were certain of being extensively sodomized in prison as *"pay-back"* for what Whites had done to Blacks in Rhodesia. It was for this reason that he had prepared a Will which was contained in the envelope he had handed me.

All this had a chilling effect on me as we stood outside the Court in the bright morning sun. I asked for an audience with the magistrate and we were soon in his chambers where I expressed appreciation for his mercy on my client and told him what I had just learnt. He was greatly relieved that he had opted for a non custodial sentence and, with disarming generosity, told my client that he was fortunate to have been represented by Advocate Greenland, a person he had always wanted to meet. I thanked God and the ancestral spirits for all our good fortune.

Law is not an exact science. Many jurists agree that it is really an art in the pursuit of justice. The result of a trial can be envisaged as a painting. It has been painted using all the rules of law. However it is only beautiful if justice has prevailed. The acquittal of O J Simpson is quite ugly in many people's minds.

I represented an insurance company that had repudiated a claim for the replacement of a truck under an insurance policy covering loss by accident, fire or theft. The truck had indeed been destroyed after it caught fire as it was being driven along a country road. Understandably their client wanted it replaced under the "loss by fire" section of the policy.

The problem was that, examination of the truck proved beyond doubt, that it had no working brakes at the time and was therefore in a seriously dangerous condition. Obviously a truck without brakes was a very serious road hazard and all too likely to be involved in an accident resulting in its loss. This had exposed my client, the insurance company, to the risk of having to replace the truck had an accident occurred because of the truck having no brakes. The owner's criminal negligence in driving without brakes was a fundamental breach of the policy. My clients were fully entitled to repudiate.

The owner was a young Black emergent businessman. In a conference with his legal team he was told the bad news about the law by me and by his own advocate. The man was stubborn. The bad brakes did not cause the accident he argued. It was a bush fire for which he was not to blame. My clients, the insurance company, he went on, were only interested in accepting payment of premiums but not interested in meeting claims. Despite strong advice he insisted on carrying on with his case even when we offered to pay all his legal fees incurred to date as a compromise. I confidently went into Court and presented our case. The advocate on the other side presented his case as best he could, as an advocate should, even though he did not believe in it. In law we had to win.

We lost! The judge was not going to let law frustrate justice. She found a good legal basis for saying so. We took the case on appeal. I was supremely confident that we would win. Before the hearing we had another conference with the plaintiff. Again he was advised at great length by his own counsel to "abandon" the judgment in exchange for us meeting all his legal costs. The man was really stubborn. He declined all offers. In the Supreme Court I confidently made our case pointing to law that had been established over many decades starting in England.

Again we lost! We lawyers and advocates on both sides were proved wrong. An ordinary man who believed he was being treated unjustly was proved right. The Supreme Court of three judges was able to find a way to apply the law in a way that would not frustrate the justice that an ordinary man was demanding.

As said, the practice of law is not a science; it is an art and like all art, its beauty is in the eye of the beholder.

One day I received an urgent call. My cousin, Willie Blumears, had disappeared, taken off a flight to Europe by the Central Intelligence Organization, "the CIO". Attorneys acting for his family could not find him anywhere. The police were a wall of silence. I had some experience of the

CIO. I had dealings with them in connection with their harassment of ANC operatives. The Mugabe government was no friend to the ANC. It was aligned to the PAC. Using the good links I had developed over many years with members of the police force I was able to find Blumears, who has been secreted in a cell at police headquarters. We then had a meeting in the CIO offices along the following lines -

CIO Officer: What do you want My Greenland - we have this man in our custody

Me: On what charge

CIO Officer: We decide such things - we are an intelligence organization - we report directly to the Prime Minister, Robert Mugabe ... that is where we take our orders

Me: I respect that - but what is the charge

CIO Officer: It is not about charging - intelligence is not about charging

Me: My client has informed me that you took him off the plane and removed a gold necklace that he had around his neck

CIO Officer: That is true

Me: You then took him into the bush and showed him a mineshaft

CIO Officer: That is true

Me: And you told him- "Dogs like you, we throw down these shafts"

CIO Officer: And we will do that - we will throw dogs like him down a hole - if he does not understand what we want

Me: What is it that you want?

CIO Officer: This man is a rich business man. He deals in diamonds. We know that. He is mixing with members of cabinet. We know that. We want him to tell us what is happening with some of these people - what they do - what is the problem - is the PM not to know what his ministers are doing?

Me: You mean you want him to be an informer - to inform on ministers?

CIO Officer: What is wrong with that - is the PM not to be told if his ministers are doing bad things -?

I fully related to what I was hearing and understood the implications perfectly. I had previous experience of this. An Ndebele Court interpreter I knew had endured two weeks of being in the clutches of the CIO. During his time with them they had shown him mineshafts in which there were human remains. On being released he had said that all he wanted was to go home to his family and never breathe a word about his totally illegal ordeal. Going to the police to report would have only ensured that his body would also end up down a mineshaft.

Me: I want to talk to my client - so I will take him to the lift and talk to him in the lift

CIO Officer: You can talk to him wherever you want - you can take him anywhere - it does not matter - because if he does not return you know that we will find him - and you - and you know what we do with dogs - dogs who are disloyal to our country. [I withdraw to one of the lifts with my client]

Me: Willie - what is it that goffals [Coloureds] are very good at and are renowned for?

Blumears: Well - er - oh - talking bull - "eating you in the ear" as we say [he says with a knowing smile]

Me: Well - these people are now above the law - they are Mugabe's people - they are extremely dangerous and do exactly as they like - I do not think that going to Court with this will help

Blumears: Yes I agree - from what they showed and told me last night - and what the police, who were trying to be nice, confirmed to me about the CIO - I was dead in the hands of this lot …

Me: So - we are going back - and we will agree to you becoming their informer - on Mugabe's ministers - you know what to do after that - when they come for information

Blumears: [laughs - his face a picture of mischief]

Blumears: Leave it to me - they are going to get long stories - long - long stories - that say nothing …

We go back and tell the CIO officers that my client will become an informer on Mugabe's ministers. They are ecstatic. Blumears is immediately given the best of treatment, his gold neck-chain returned and he is put back on a flight to Europe, with some other passenger being kicked off the plane, so as to ensure he has a seat.

After two years of visiting Willie, and listening to his *"long stories, say nothing"*, they finally give up and the man is left to live free of further harassment.

---

72. Better things

During this period I had always had a particular problem with the press media. On numerous occasions the press miss-reported matters causing inconvenience, embarrassment, even great damage to human beings. Apologizing afterwards had limited effect on the damage already done. In my conversation with editors I insisted that they should always first check their story with the persons being reported on. Such a precaution was consistent with the otherwise sacred duty of the media to serve and protect human rights. It would have ensured that the editor is alerted to possible errors before irretrievable damage was done. This they steadfastly refused to do in many cases.

I received a brief to represent Minister Edson Jonasi Zvobgo, one of Mugabe's most senior ministers and a struggle hero. We were successful in securing a judgment in which the press was ordered to pay him substantial damages for having defamed him in falsely reporting that he had misused his ministerial powers. The very same newspaper then carried the report of the trial and the judgment the next day, and faithfully reported the facts - with one critical mistake.

The report read that - "...the Honourable Judge held that Minister Zvobgo had misused his ministerial powers -." leaving out the word "not" before the word "misused" - thereby defaming him once again. They did not mean to defame him again. It was simply a case of what is known as "a typo", inadvertent leaving out of a word. Regrettably because of this "typo" great damage was done once again to my client and we had no difficulty in getting the paper to agree to pay almost double what the Court had just awarded Zvobgo. Had they checked the story with me or Zvobgo before going to print this would have been all avoided.

A notable public service that the legal profession performed was voluntary participation in a legal aid project run under the auspices of the University College of Zimbabwe. The driving force behind this was Denis Robinson also famed as a Springbok[1]. Lawyers and advocates gave their time freely to the clinic on Saturday mornings to review cases compiled by university students involving people too poor to pay for legal representation. If a case had merit a lawyer (and/or advocate) would be assigned to act for the client without fee.

---

[1] **Hard as granite and graceful as a Springbok.** So was Denis Robinson, the Rhodesian Springbok full back. We played him at fly half for Trinity. He could run, swerve, dummy, side-step and feed our three quarters with unflappable grace under pressure. But our secret weapon lay in his right boot.
http://www.timesonline.co.uk/tol/sport/rugby_union/article614217.ece?token=null&offset=12

A case that came to my attention was one in which a mature man had walked into a hospital on a Saturday afternoon, reeking of alcohol, clutching his midriff and shouting that "my fucking guts were killing me". Taking offence at his lack of sobriety and foul language the medical staff at the casualty department turned him away. He went home. Within a matter of hours his appendix burst causing the onset of septicemia from which he nearly died during a three month long struggle for his life. He was no longer capable of working.

The students at the legal aid clinic had done their best to see if the hospital could be held liable in a claim for damages. When I joined them they were very despondent especially as during earlier sessions senior lawyers had opined that there was little hope of success. Civil cases are very much "adversarial". As so often depicted in television programs about Courtroom battles, these case nearly always depend on the quantity and quality of the medical experts a person can amass on his/her side. The team had understandable already concluded despondently that we had no hope as the medical profession in Zimbabwe was very much a small affair, with everyone knowing everyone else. There was no hope of getting any expert to help our case. They were not inclined to give evidence against their peers. This had already been confirmed to the students.

I told them the story about old man Naran and said we needed to "think differently" (now fashionably called "thinking out of the box").

We devised a new and unique plan and then implemented it. The hospital administrator was contacted by letter and phone. He was told that in Court we were going to admit all the bad things they were saying about our client, i.e., his inebriation and swearing. We were then going to subpoena and call the hospital administrator, i.e., the defendant himself, as well as his senior specialists on his hospital staff to the stand in Court. They were going to be questioned only as follows-

```
"In terms of your medical qualifications, knowledge, skills
and expertise, are you of the professional opinion that kicking
a man out of casualty on a Sunday afternoon who has walked in
screaming that his "fucking guts are killing" him indicates
that a proper diagnosis of his condition has been made and that
he has received the indicated treatment?"
```

We also informed him that they should be pleased to know that we were going to make sure that representatives of international medical journals, such as Lancet, were going to be in Court, waiting with bated breath, to hear their answers so that the whole medical world could be enlightened on how such a patient was to be dealt with.

Within two hours of the meeting the hospital's lawyers contacted us and made an offer of settlement. Quite obviously their medical experts were not at all interested in having to answer such a question on oath in front of the whole world. After negotiations our client's case was settled on reasonable terms. It was an extremely satisfying result indeed and one that Denis and I were very proud of. Denis was later appointed a judge but very sadly succumbed to cancer in 1995. The country lost a legendary sportsman, a great tutor and a wonderful human being.

One evening we heard the sound of a road crash. Investigation revealed that a sedan vehicle had left the road, outside our residence, and overturned. The lady driver was unconscious. Her passenger had facial lacerations and was quite hysterical. Soon thereafter they were conveyed from the scene by ambulance that we had summoned. The police were of the opinion that the driver had simply lost control on account of being unable to cope with the misty, wet and slippery conditions.

Two weeks later the driver came to see me. She was being sued for a very substantial amount of money by her erstwhile passenger friend. She felt nauseated by the fact that, on the night in question, she had acted as "an angel of mercy", for her friend. She had very kindly decided to give her friend a lift to the home of the friend's mother to save her from a beating she was receiving from her abusive husband. Now this was her reward - to be sued for a sum of money that would ruin her family for life. Things appeared bad for her as she had no recollection of the accident and could not explain why she had lost control.

However the subsequent conference with the passenger's lawyers was very gratifying indeed. I was able to inform them that we had fortuitously located a security guard who had seen the whole accident on the night in question. He was able to say that the driver had been faced with a situation of extreme sudden emergency when the driver of another car had recklessly jumped a stop sign and driven into her path. My client had lost control in trying to avoid the car that had jumped the "Stop Sign". That was the end of the case for the ungrateful greedy passenger and great relief for our client.

I enjoyed practicing as an advocate. They were the happiest days of my life. Kentridge was right when he said that it is an honourable profession. Not once was it the case that my efforts were not appreciated by a client even when I had clearly been in error as was the case when I gave a client urgent advice on copyright law. The client returned and queried my advice. When I discovered my error and rectified it their response [a company] was to, not only pay my fee, but also present me with a case of expensive whiskey as a show of gratitude.

So as an advocate your work is appreciated and you are routinely honoured by fellow men. It is very difficult to describe the feeling that infuses you when faces turn to you in desperation, when human beings place all their hope and faith in you, when they cry tears of unmitigated joy upon a loved one being released from the talons of injustice.

When Bishop Schmidt smacked my cheek and said "Pax Tecum" he anointed me as a soldier of Christ. That soldier, to my mind, was also very much a soldier of justice. My efforts do not go unrecorded. Over the relatively short period that I practiced as an advocate the South African Law Reports record the following cases in which I appeared receiving commendations from the Court as regards the first two -

```
CROW V DETAINED PATIENTS BOARD 1985[4] SA 83 [ZH]. S V BENNET-
COHEN 1985[2] SA 465 ZS. ORION INVESTMENTS [PVT] LTD v UJAMAA
INVESTMENTS [PVT] LTD AND OTHERS 1988 [1] SA 583 [ZS]. J PAAR &
CO [PVT] LTD v FAWCETT SECURITY ORGANISATION [BULAWAYO] [PVT]
LTD 1987 [2] SA 140 [ZS]. MOYO v JANI 1985 [3] SA 362 [ZH] ; S v
MPOFU 1985 [4] SA 322 [ZH].
```

73. A judge

We are visited by my aunt Mamquebu, sister-in-law to my mother. Mamquebu is a spiritualist. She goes into an impromptu trance when the spirits take hold of her and emits strange sounds in strange voices. It is the first time she has visited alone. Previously she always came with Uncle Willie, her husband. She has traveled over 500 kms.

She has a message - a very important message - from the ancestral spirits. They are pleased. However henceforth I need added guidance and protection as my work will became so much more important. This is to be invoked using a "ntebe". The Western equivalent of this would be a lucky charm such as a rabbit's foot. However this is much more than a lucky charm as firstly it has been made up on the instructions of the ancestral spirits. Secondly it is to be handled only when invoking the spirits. In appearance it is a slightly curved object about 28cms long and about a centimeter diameter; firm and wrapped in cloth material. The innards are a secret and could even include noble ingredients like lion's fat. It has been with me ever since.

Within weeks Pam has conducted a very successful campaign against the bookies at Borrowdale racecourse using *"the tail"*, as she calls it, in picking winners. I retrieve it; admonishing her that the ancestral spirits are likely to became very angry to find that we are only interested in the easy acquisition of wealth.

Soon thereafter, on his invitation, I attend in audience with the Honourable Mr. Justice Enoch Dumbutshena , Chief Justice of Zimbabwe. I tell him that I am very happy as an advocate but will consider his request which is incredibly disarming in its implications. He assures me that his view is shared by all his judges. I am shattered. Minister Zvobgo follows up on the same issue with me. I finally agree to what my country is putting to me, the call it has made. On the eve of 18 May 1987 Pam sits me down and asks me to tell her the story about my life. I start with Walmer Estates, England.

The next day I am sworn in at State House by Reverend Canaan Banana, the President of the Republic of Zimbabwe, as a judge of the High Court. He asks me to raise my right hand and swear to uphold the Constitution and the laws of the country "without fear, force or prejudice.[1] " The fact that I am the first Coloured judge is a total irrelevancy in our new Zimbabwe. As my dear wife Pam hugs me in congratulatory embrace she looks at me through proud moist eyes and says - *"fear, force and prejudice - it has been our lives - we know that you will be a good judge".*

Her view may well have been shared by others, as evidenced by the kind mention of me Judy Todd makes in her 2007 book "Through the Darkness[2]" .

> "I went to see Chris Greenland, who Bryant Elliot told me, might soon be made a judge. I hoped so. He was impressive. I contacted him because we had been requested by Alibaba Dlodlo, imprisoned in 1982, to help him study O-Levels by correspondence. He - and others had been found guilty of having attempted to attack the prime minister's residence in June 1982.
>
> I found him a very troubled man. Greenland was convinced that Dlodlo and two of the other member of the group of about five were totally innocent. They had also been tortured. He said that the failure of the appeal was something he would have to live with for the rest of his life, and kept wondering if there was something better he could have done for the prisoners."

It is quite difficult to point to some other example of how your country can honour you as it does on appointment as a judge. On *"elevation to bench",* as it is called, I joined a judiciary of then internationally respected judges. Such appointment implies that your personal and functional integrity is beyond question. It means also that you can be implicitly trusted. Typically we have the following "Qualities of a Judge" published by the Canadian Judges association[3] -

---

[1] in South Africa —"without fear, favour or prejudice"

[2] **Through the Darkness** by Judith Garfield Todd at p. 194

[3] **Qualities of a Judge** - http://www.cscja-acjcs.ca/qualities_required-en.asp?l=5

The judge is "the pillar of our entire justice system," the Supreme Court of Canada has said, and the public has a right to demand "virtually irreproachable conduct from anyone performing a judicial function." Judges must strive for the highest standards of integrity in both their professional and personal lives. They should be knowledgeable about the law, willing to undertake in-depth legal research, and able to write decisions that are clear and cogent. Their judgment should be sound and they should be able to make informed decisions that will stand up to close scrutiny. Judges should be fair and open-minded, and should appear to be fair and open-minded. They should be good listeners but should be able, when required, to ask questions that get to the heart of the issue before the Court. They should be Courteous in the Courtroom but firm when it is necessary to rein in a rambling lawyer, a disrespectful litigant or an unruly spectator.

Also as appears on a blog website under the title "What are the qualities of a good judge[1]?" -

The judiciary, especially in a democratic state, is well known for its impartiality. In numerous cases it has taken decisions even against the state for the achievement of the ends of justice. This impartiality of the judicial system in a democratic state can be attributed to the good qualities of judges who have always asserted their independence from executive control.

The qualities of a good judge include patience, wisdom, courage, firmness, alertness, incorruptibility and the gifts of sympathy and insight. In a democracy, a judge is accorded great respect by the state as well as its citizens. He is not only permitted to assert his freedom and impartiality but also expected to use all his forensic skill to protect the rights of the individual against arbitrariness. Though such a state of affairs makes it easy for the judge to exercise his functions, he still requires many qualities to perform his duties effectively.

What I have also learnt from many years in the Courts is that when "you are most sure, be most careful". The rape trial in which I nearly sent an innocent young man to prison was an example of this.

One day after I have finished practicing golf on my front lawn I notice that my Omega Seamaster watch is missing. In order to have my insurer replace it I have to report the loss to the police. When they arrive they quickly establish that the only other person present at the time of the loss was a young lad who we gave casual employment to so that he could earn extra cash to fund his education. I am unable to counter their argument that he must have stolen it. As the watch vanished in his presence the inference that he stole it

---

[1] http://language123.blogspot.com/2008/06/qualities-of-good-judge.html

is inescapable. They take him into custody and bring him back the next day. He is a mess. He has obviously been severely beaten as there are bruises, marks, weals and swellings all over his face and body.

He looks at me, tears of disillusionment and hurt streaming down his face. *"Just give me my money..."* he says repeatedly. I remonstrate with the police about their conduct. It is clear that my words are regarded as the ranting of a fool. I pay the lad what we owe him and they start to leave. As I re-start my golf practice I find the watch in my shoe. I had simply forgotten that I had secreted it in the shoe the previous day as I started practice by changing from everyday shoes to golf spikes[1].

As I call the police back and report the find a nauseous feeling overtakes me. They are unrepentant. I am sick. The young lad is inconsolable. He refuses to return to work despite an offer of a substantial increase in pay. A decent young life has now been forever brutalized - and I was part of it. I must never forget it.

One of my first duties is to preside over circuit Court at Mutare[2]. The opening of the circuit is a grand affair to which dignitaries from all sectors are invited. It starts with a parade by uniformed forces which the judge then inspects. Thereafter the judge presides over an opening hearing in which he/she makes a speech. Proceedings are rounded off with cocktails for the guests.

In my speech I pick up on the theme that, in a democracy, the judiciary must function without fear, favour or prejudice and that it is implicit in the rule of law that even the lowliest among us must be protected as equals before the Courts, particularly as regards abuse by those with power. *"In this scenario - "* I say *" - there may well be tensions between the executive arm of government and the judiciary - but never confrontation, if we are to sustain a democracy "*.

Immediately after the opening session CIO officers, now regarded as Mugabe's Gestapo, demand a copy of my address. When I query this I am told that it is their function to check on *"political speeches"*.

This is a portend of both the existing situation and much more sinister things to come. On the horizon was a day when the judges' chambers would be invaded by gun wielding Mugabe acolytes who would threaten the judges in order to intimidate them into handing down "on side" judgments. One Judge, Fergis Blackie, was arrested and brutalized for having handed down a

---

[1] **Golf spikes** – special shoes worn when playing golf

[2] **Mutare** - formerly Umtali - city in north-eastern part of Zimbabwe.

judgment that was not to the liking of the Mugabe regime.

74. Dispensing death

A case I had to deal with on the Mutare circuit involved an accused who the assessors and I had little difficulty in finding guilty of the premeditated, planned and viciously executed murder of an elderly defenseless woman in the sanctity of her home, to which the accused had gained access through the roof tiles. He had thereafter subjected his victim to a long, slow and lingering death by torture. This involved slicing her all over her body whilst playing a "cat and mouse" game with her and then leaving her to die of blood loss, cold and exposure.

Under Zimbabwean law murder is punishable by death unless there are *"extenuating circumstances"*, i.e. special features mitigating the crime. There were simply no extenuating circumstances, only aggravating features. This was a case of the cold blooded and ruthless putting to death of a human being by an arrogant and unrepentant killer. There was little his counsel could advance on his behalf.

Any normal person will baulk at sending another human being to death. It is hardly surprising. When a person is hanged he is placed on a trap door with his hands handcuffed behind his back and his feet manacled together. His head is covered with a black hood. The noose is then placed around his neck with the knot under the left side of the chin.

Upon the hangman pulling a lever the trap doors spring open and the man falls a distance that has been especially calculated taking into account his weight and height. Once the man has fallen the length of the rope the noose snaps tight and the knot jerks his head backwards dislocating the vertebrae at the axis bone of the neck which severs the spinal cord. This induces an instant loss of blood pressure and unconsciousness with brain death occurring within minutes. As the central nervous system is shut down, on severance of the spinal cord, all muscles instantly relax, including the sphincter muscle, often leading to the release of faeces and urine down the legs of the deceased.

Correctly executed it is a most effective and humane way of putting a human being to death. This scientific fact however brings little comfort to the mind of any normal human being involved with the execution of a human being. There is something terribly disturbing to one's innermost self about the whole business of consciously, purposefully and cold heartedly killing another human being.

As I proceed to pronounce on sentence there is a particular expression of expectancy etched in the faces of the relatives of the deceased, seated in Court awaiting justice for their loved one. I hear the voice of the judge, in his red robes, black sash and white wig, set out the reasons for sentence, the words falling like the deft strokes of an artist painting a picture that is disquieting, chilling, disturbing to the senses.

> "You took it upon yourself to decide that this defenseless fellow human being should be put to death, to die even though in the sanctity of her own home ..."

That voice is mine, but it is not me, it is the voice of a judge, the voice of justice. This phenomenon of disassociation in which I have an impression of having a dual personality occurred when I first walked into Court as a judge and was to remain with me for all the years I served. When I first walked into "A" Court, some 10 years after Sir Hugh Beadle said- *"Sergeant - take him away - and I hope to never see him in my Court"*, the fear for a Court that then gripped me as a private individual was still with me and was to never leave me every time I entered Court. This fear, however, did not infuse the mind or heart of me as the presiding judge. Therein lay only a deep sense of solemnity and reverence for the age old business at hand. I am conscious also of the faces of all those in Court, solemn and expectant, that the wheels of justice must now make their final turn. The voice of justice goes on-

> "The manner of her death, at your hands, was to be cruel and sadistic. After so many years of living, interacting with others, including her most loved ones, her life was to be prematurely terminated in a process involving prolonged torture; with death coming as a blessed relief after slow, lingering, terrible suffering.
>
> Stand up. Because there are no extenuating circumstances as envisaged by law in your case, the Court is obliged to impose the following sentence. You are to be taken to a place of execution and there hanged by the neck until you are dead. Do you understand?"

Court was then adjourned. Although dealing with the issues regarding sentence and imposing the death sentence was an extremely solemn and serious business indeed, at no stage did I feel any discomfort, only a deep sense of solemn exaltation at this final turn of the wheels of justice.

Having exited the Courtroom I reached a point where I had to step down in order to enter a passage leading to my chambers. It was only a small step. I tried to take the step and failed. Try as I might I could not manage the simple business of stepping down into the passage. I was not paralyzed but my legs would not respond.

I had only experienced this once before when our boat bumped onto a submerged hippopotamus in the Zambezi. The animal rose up behind the boat bellowing at nerve vaporizing sound decibel levels whilst advancing on the boat. A terrible fate for us was just nano seconds away when fortunately the boat started and we sped away in the nick of time to a safe distance.

When I then tried to stand up in the boat I found that I could not. I had lost the use of my lower limbs. I had also lost control of my arms, as when I tried to pick up an object in the boat, I found that I ended up throwing the object high into the air instead of simply bringing it up to where I wanted it. All my movements were jerky and uncontrolled. Undoubtedly the boat experience was due to shock. Being that close to such an animal in that state of rage made my blood curdle, my body freeze and all my nerves jangle. I was shaking like a leaf.

However I had not been aware of any effect whatsoever impacting my person in sentencing the accused to death. Other than feeling very sombre, I felt as normal as could be. But I was not. I could not take the step and was only able to finally do so, and walk to my chambers, when the Court interpreter arrived and physically assisted me. Obviously imposing the death sentence on another human being affected me profoundly even though I was not conscious of this.

There has always been much debate about the imposition of the death sentence and most countries have now stopped the practice, urged on by the abolitionist lobby. Personally I have never wholly accepted the abolitionist's central arguments that it is immoral and that executing murderers has no deterrent effect. There cannot be the slightest doubt that it will deter some. The deterrent effect however is greatly diluted by the legal pantomime that plays out in most western countries after a Court imposes the sentence. In many instances execution takes place, if at all, up to 20 years after the event. An example is the case of the State of California versus three time killer Donald Beardslee[1]. Beardslee, who in 1981 brutally murdered two young San Francisco-area women after he was paroled from a Missouri prison on another murder conviction, waited 21 years for his day of reckoning. He was 61 and had been on death row longer than the entire life span of one of his victims.

Obviously the message that is conveyed to would-be killers, by such cases, is that in sentencing a person to death the Court neither really means what it says or says what it means. At that point deterrence becomes something of a

---

[1] **Donald Beardslee** - http://articles.latimes.com/2005/mar/06/local/me-deathpen6

lottery. Conversely that deterrence has effect is quite unarguable as regards certain Islamic countries where execution, sometimes in public, takes place with minimum delay.

As regards the moral argument, this to my mind, must also fall down once one has to concede that the killing of another is perfectly justified in certain circumstances. An example is when a father finds his child being raped and strangled. No one will blame the father if he there and then puts the attacker to death. Starting at that point it then becomes somewhat artificial to attempt to draw a line in the sand and say that a point has been reached where killing is now immoral. If armed men arrive at your home at night must you wait until they kill first? If you have failed to stop an intruder from shooting your wife, who is now lying in a pool of blood, must you leave the attacker to escape and not fire on him? As said the moral argument must fail for being, in effect, artificial in its parameters.

And regrettably there are some who do not share the noble ideas espoused by the abolitionist school regarding the sanctity of human life. There are some incredibly evil people who will plan, rape, torture and strangle even a five year old child. To my mind it is logical to say that such people forfeit the right to their own lives apart from being a danger to others. In these circumstances the ancient biblical adage of *"eye for and eye and a tooth for a tooth"* has merit and resonates in the hearts of most human beings.

In categorizing such ancient counsel as barbaric, instead of respecting it as ancient wisdom; we arrogantly accord ourselves, as supposedly modern civilized beings, a standard that is simply untrue.

The truth is that man is more barbaric than ever. Proof reposes in the fact that, despite having the so called United Nations, at unbelievable public expense, rape, torture and genocide is flourishing and so is the insidious killing of humans by way of needless deprivation, exposure and starvation. Obscene is the fact that more people have been killed in the name of religion, i.e., moral grounds, than for any other reason in history. Despots, tyrants and killers are routinely lauded, revered and lionized as great leaders. We are as "uncivilized" and as "barbaric' as ever, and should not hypocritically presume to be otherwise.

We certainly appear to have little basis for disdainfully rejecting the ancient wisdom of our forefathers who to my mind were saying, in their "eye for and eye - " statement, no more than we now profess to say –

`"Justice must not only be done, it must also be seen to be done".`

Despite this personal view I however do **not** support capital punishment. My reason is quite simple. Given the vagaries of human nature it is just too dangerous to have this extreme, and **irreversible**, form of punishment available as it **will** undoubtedly be abused intentionally and also unwittingly. Even the best judges will make a mistake.

The rape trial that I have recounted proves how the judicial system can be manipulated, even by an ordinary individual, to convict an innocent man. Juries are even more prone to making decisions on account of the theatrical impact of the trial than on evidence. 12 Angry Men is a 1957 American drama film[1] adapted from a play. Directed by Sidney Lumet, the film tells the story of a jury made up of 12 men as they deliberate the guilt or innocence of a defendant on the basis of reasonable doubt. It is absolutely brilliant in illustrating how fickle human perception of evidence is and there is simply no guarantee that a jury of perfectly reasonable men will arrive at the right decision.

DNA technology is now proving that many innocent persons have been wrongly convicted.[2]

In Zimbabwe I always sat with two assessors. These were laymen who helped me, as the judge, in deciding the facts. My assessors were African elders and one was a Chief. Each always presented as a fountain of wisdom and rock of sense in the often difficult business of separating fact from fiction and assessment of witnesses. They were persons of complete personal integrity. Without them I would have been seriously hampered in doing justice.

However a problem became manifest once we had a case involving competition between the rights, including the right to be believed, of a woman and a man. Suddenly everything would change in their approach, attitude and resolution of the evidence. Tangible bias against the woman would become manifest. It was absolutely clear to me that such bias was unconscious and that they were not in the least bit aware of it. However it was the reality. In this way, highly principled, decent and otherwise extremely wise human beings routinely failed on account of subconscious gender bias.

To a greater or lesser extent, subconscious bias will impact most human beings, especially in context involving race, gender and political undercurrents. The O J Simpson trial was undoubtedly so impacted. So too as regards the trial of White officers, videotaped brutally assaulting a Black youth, Rodney King. Their wrongfully acquittal led to the 1992 Los Angeles

---

[1] **12 Angry Men** - http://en.wikipedia.org/wiki/12_Angry_Men

[2] See The Innocence Project - http://www.innocenceproject.org/

riots. There is also a problem in some instances, which I too experienced, where a person will confess to a crime that he/she never committed.

The problem is further compounded in terms of the prerogative of mercy that reposes with heads of states. In terms thereof a monarch, or a president, has a prerogative to pardon a convicted person or commute his/her sentence to a lesser sentence. Since heads of state are politically, not judicially orientated, there can be no guarantee that an even handed approach will subsist.

In Zimbabwe, Robert Mugabe did not overtly interfere with the judiciary. However he routinely pardoned his lackeys, after they had been rightfully convicted and sentenced to death. In one case one of his henchmen arrived at a police station, dragged a man out of the cells and executed him in cold blood. Mugabe freed him in a matter of days after he had been convicted and sentenced to death.

As said it is my respectful view that, given the vagaries of human nature, man simply cannot be trusted to decide whether or not another human being should live or die.

Because death is irreversible, its imposition is simply impractical.

75. Do I love my child

At about this time the country experienced an extremely unusual phenomenon. All over the country women were either killing their newborn babies or abandoning them in drains, in toilets, on streets, at doorsteps and a range of other places where they would often die.

The scale and extent of "baby dumping", as the phenomenon became known, remains unexplained. The phenomenon presented as a problem for the Courts. What were the Courts to do with these offenders where death of the child was involved? In sentencing an accused during a circuit Court at Masvingo my words approximated the following-

"Stand up. In this case you have been convicted of murder, the murder of your new born child. This child did not ask to be conceived. That was your decision. The child did not ask to be born. At birth a child is entirely dependent on its mother. Having carried the child in her womb for so long, all of nine months, the bond that a mother feels for her child at the moment of birth is unique. There is no other bond that it can be likened to. It comprises feelings of incredible love and protection ... that protection is needed. A human baby is one of the most helpless at birth needing its mother for everything. We know how animals behave as regards their offspring. Most will give their lives in defense of their young. The lion, the leopard, the hyena, the wild dog - will kill or be killed in defense of its young. These are but animals. They do not have the power of reason. A human being has the gift of reason - and of understanding. A mother therefore understands how helpless her baby is - that this little person cannot - will not survive - unless she gives of her love and protection.

Having not asked to be conceived or borne, but having been given life, the baby has a right to life - the right to grow and develop - to realize its potential as a human being. That is how the world has been blessed with great human beings like Mahatma Gandhi and Nelson Mandela. It is because at birth their mothers loved and protected them.

In your case, not only did you fail to protect your child; you took it upon yourself to end his life. As a sentient human being, and even though you were his mother, you strangled him with a cord and disposed of his body in a drain. Your actions were heartless, cold and calculated. It can be argued also that your actions were also motivated purely by self interest. In terms of what you have said you appear to have been very much concerned throughout with yourself.

Murder is the most serious crime that a person can commit. That much is accepted by all. For that reason societies over the years have often visited this crime with execution of the offender as the punishment. There are many in society that believe that such a punishment is richly deserved. That is how serious the offence you have committed is. In this country we have the death sentence as the primary punishment for murder.

In sentencing, a Court is required to weigh up all factors in the scales of justice. Sentencing is not about revenge. It is about justice. The Court puts all interests in the scales - the interests of the victim - the interests of society - and your interests as well, even though you are the guilty party.

You have pleaded guilty. From the time of your arrest you were remorseful and fully cooperated with the police. In Court it was obvious that your remorse was genuine. I do not think that the tears you shed when you explained what happened were crocodile tears of hypocrisy. As a human being I was able to feel deeply the terrible loss that you have endured as a human being. You have lost nearly everything - your sense of self-worth - your dignity, name and reputation as a human being - and your child who was with you for all of nine months inside your womb. You have explained, and State Counsel has accepted this, that when you got pregnant your parents condemned you, chased you from home and would not give you any love and support. You were regarded as a failure and a disgrace especially as the father of the child disappeared.

When you went to your granny she too rejected you. This is something that rarely happens in African custom where every child is welcomed. You were alone in the world with no one to give you love and support. As a result you contemplated suicide. Had it not been that just one friend gave you refuge we have no way of knowing what might have happened. As a person I have some idea what it is to be alienated and marginalized. What you went through was complete rejection of which I have no experience or understanding. I can only imagine it.

What I also have no experience of is childbirth. As a man it is simply impossible for me to have even an idea what having another human being in your body is like and what given birth to that person is like. Most importantly I have no idea what effect it had on you as the mother. What I do know is that many mothers are affected in a way that sometimes leads to a mother even being a danger to her own child. It is a phenomenon called "postpartum blues". In your case you had the terrible added pressure of rejection by your family. You were alone in the world, abandoned, rejected, and unloved. The future was completely hopeless. I can be satisfied, at the very least; that you concluded that there was little chance of a meaningful existence for you and the baby.

Given the lack of support and condemnation that your own family subjected you to I can understand why you came to such a conclusion. The rest of what was going on in your mind and in your heart is simply beyond my comprehension as a man. In the result I must accept, in all humility, that I am only partially qualified to judge you. So I must be very careful in condemning you.

I have thought very carefully about the sentence. Your plea that I should understand and give you a chance has struck a chord with me. The sentence is merciful. At the same time it must not trivialize what you have done. In return I want you to promise me that you will learn from this terrible experience and do something positive with your life. Your baby's death will, to at least this extent, not have been in vain if, in return, you take this chance to make a better life for yourself and others. Life is only worth something if what you do is also good for other human beings. That is a debt that you, in particular, now owe humanity.

You are sentenced to five years imprisonment with labour. The whole of the sentence is suspended on condition that you are not again convicted of committing, during that period, any offence involving injury or death to another, for which you are sentenced to imprisonment without option. You are now free to start again. Do you understand?"

My approach in passing sentence in the *"baby dumping"* [infanticide]cases was shaped, not only by what is revealed about my thinking above, but also as a consequence of sterling work that was done by female activists who felt that the plight of woman in this situation required a new understanding.

It is pertinent to point out that this group of activists was almost exclusively White even though nearly all accused persons involved in the phenomenon were Black. They were dead against imprisonment as a punishment for their counterparts who they believed were still largely disadvantaged. Such was the level of inter-racial understanding and sympathy in our new Zimbabwe. Fortunately the *"baby dumping"* phenomenon, still unexplained as a social phenomenon, did not last long and such cases became comparatively rare once again.

It came as a wonderful surprise when, years later, in 2006, a smartly dressed and attractive lady, face brimming with pride, approached me at a conference in Accra, Ghana. *"Judge Greenland - "* she said, taking my hand in both of hers - *"you should understand that because of the chance you gave me - I am now able to help in saving so many lives - especially those of babies ... "*

She was the girl I had given a chance. She had taken the chance. She was now working for the United Nations in the mother/child care field under an HIV/AIDS prevention program.

---

76. Silence is not golden

In its desperate fight to prevent the advent of majority rule the previous White government had decided to increase its chances of securing convictions by seriously encroaching on an accused person's so called "right to silence" or more correctly termed "right to protection against self-incrimination". This right has been with "civilized" western societies for a very long time and is generally regarded by jurists and human rights activists as hallowed, even sacred. In America the right is protected under the 5th Amendment based on English common law going back to the Magna Carta of 1215. This is understandable. History is replete with examples of oppressive governments using all kinds of means, including torture, to force incriminatory statements and confessions out of innocent people. Under pressure people will often say anything.

Under security legislation of the previous government, all kind of otherwise normal human activity such as being in a gathering, or holding meetings without permission was an offence. In such a situation the Rhodesian government needed people to talk; not assert a right to silence. The security agencies need to know what people were up to. The right to silence was a serious impediment to the effective enforcement of security laws and to securing convictions for persons engaged in the struggle, which was necessarily subversive of the *status quo*. So what the government did was to amend this ancient sacrosanct law. An accused person no longer had a blanket right to silence. After arrest he/she was obliged to explain accusations put and evidence presented. Failure to do so incurred the risk of a Court, subsequently trying the person, drawing adverse inferences about the conduct of the person as an accused, greatly increasing the chances of conviction.

Certainly this amendment to the law had been brought in for bad or flawed motives. But was the law itself bad? Is the so called right to silence still to be regarded as sacrosanct? In my view the answer is perhaps a surprising **"No"**. In over 24 years of practicing in the Courts as a prosecutor, magistrate, advocate and judge it was rare for me to find a case where the obligation in itself, now cast on an accused person, to explain his conduct or evidence, could have be considered unjust or resulted in a wrong conviction. As said Zimbabwe was, at the time, served by judges of impeccable personal and functional integrity before whom exceptional counsel practiced. Not once did I detect any meaningful discomfort with the procedural practice. There was certainly no expressed view that this serious erosion of the so called "right to silence" was leading to injustice in the Zimbabwean Courts.

The reason is that actual experience in the Courts has shown that silence, for the sake of silence alone, without exception, benefits only the guilty. Provided that no force or any form of coercion is employed there is simply no good reason why a person should not be obliged to explain, without delay, **incriminatory evidence uncovered at public expense.** An innocent person has nothing to fear in saying why his/her car was seen at the scene of the crime, or why stolen goods have been found in his/her house or why his/her fingerprints are on the murder weapon - etc.

Obviously police cannot be allowed to simply go around arresting people and interrogate them in the hope of finding incriminatory evidence. Such "fishing for evidence" certainly must be protected against; not in terms of a so called right to silence but in terms of a right to privacy, personal security and freedom from harassment.

However once society, via its investigative agencies, has found incriminatory evidence, in my respectful view, society is entitled to an explanation. Only the guilty, or those seeking to protect the guilty, benefit from an entitlement to keep mum, consult with clever lawyers and then tailor their explanations to later explain away the state case.

To my mind the blanket right to silence, as presently conceived, is in all probability founded on an understandable but convenient untruth; convenient to criminals, that the public is being protected. It is criminals and criminal conduct that are being protected.

77. Talking shop - judicially

Around about 1988 I had the privilege of attending an All Africa Judicial Conference held in Livingstone, Zambia. It was opened by Dr Kenneth Kaunda, then President of Zambia, who led a sing-song in our honour. He was warm, approachable and seemingly unassuming; a personification of the spirit of humanism, a philosophy he so passionately espoused. It was a very well run conference and meeting with so many of our counterparts from the rest of Africa proved both interesting and enlightening. What emerged as the central theme was remuneration for the judiciary. There was a consensus that, apart for Namibia, the judiciary was universally underpaid in Africa. The irony was that Africa was replete with revolutionary leaders whose campaigns for liberation, power and emancipation were founded on the call for justice. South Africa was yet to be freed. Once power was secured however, sadly it appeared to be the case that all this was quickly forgotten and the norm was to accord justice little priority.

A Commonwealth Judicial Conference, which the Chief Justice selected me to attend in 1990, in Sydney, Australia was a much more ostentatious affair. As the flight there was packed with African refugees, none of whom appeared to be able to speak English, I could not help reflecting on the incident that occurred in 1963 when the Australian representative told me in Bulawayo that *"we don't want no kaffirs in Oz."* The biggest delegation to the conference was from one African country which I do not propose to name. Apart from seeing them at the registration process on the first day we never saw more than one of them at any session thereafter, during the week long conference, except at the gala farewell dinner which they all attended.

There are two sessions that stick out in my mind. In the first one we were addressing the issue of the need to protect prisoners from violence on arrest and whilst in police custody and that a statement should not be forced out of a human being. Several delegates stood up to understandably make strong submissions on the issue which was of concern in many parts of the world where prisoners were routinely abused. It was all very serious and there was little doubt that a strongly worded resolution was in the offing. Human rights imperatives demanded this. The holding of conferences that produce sanctimonious resolutions is now an international pandemic.

It is just then that a delegate from the South Sea or Pacific islands asks for permission to go on stage and address us. He is a very dignified man, whose flawed English accent and stilted command of the language, only serves to enhance his natural stature and dignity. When he stands on the stage, now changed into his traditional island reed skirted attire, he is an imposing figure indeed, who really holds our attention. What he has to say is -[1]

"Good morning to all the honourable guests and the friends we have made from all over the world. I am very honoured that you have given me permission to address you. I am humbled. [A ripple of appreciative handclaps is heard]

My country is made up of islands. We are a very peaceful people. In my country I am Chief Constable. The people they elect me every year to be the chief constable ... it is democracy. [He has our full attention - you can hear a pin drop]

When someone report to me that there is a problem I go and investigate. A police officer must investigate - without delay - it is his duty. When I investigate I always carry rod - to help with investigations - in England policeman have baton - on my island I have rod - it is the same thing. When I meet suspect I ask him- "did you steal the pig?" - and to help him - to help him bring out the truth - I use rod. [An audible uneasy tension ripples through the conference hall]

Rod always makes sure that truth comes out. When he tells me that he has stolen the pig I stop - I arrest him - and I put him in the holding cells - so that he can be tried on charge of theft.

Afternoon time I am Chief Magistrate. [a tangible uneasiness washes over the room]

The people on the islands - every year - they elect me as the Chief Magistrate. I am very honoured - honoured because my people they trust me.

Prisoner who steal pig - he is brought before me for trial. We have no delay. Justice delayed is justice denied. Prisoner - he never gives any trouble. I ask him- "Did you steal pig?" He admit that he steal pig - he never deny ... he only speak truth. [Audible gasps, whispers, even giggling can now be heard running through the hall of delegates]

You see rod makes sure that truth come out in Court. Rod is friend of the truth - very big friend - we have very little theft on our islands - everyone happy and live in peace …"

At this point whispers amongst our audience have graduated to audible murmurs and loud giggles. It becomes quite impossible to maintain the

---

[1] Reconstructed

solemn decorum required for the conduct of the serious business at hand. The convener of the session jumps up and announces that it would appear to be an opportune time to adjourn. She thanks our speaker and he proudly waves to everyone as he makes off the stage. It is simply hilarious.

A high point was being addressed on Human Rights by The Hon Justice Michael Donald Kirby AC CMG and President of the Australian Human rights Commission. It is somewhat surreal that the world has so many great advocates of Human Rights and a United Nations espousing these rights in its Universal Declaration of Human Rights with countless other supporting protocols; and yet the abuse of human rights is rampant as ever. Sickening and shameful is the fact that the abusers, such as Robert Mugabe, are routinely lauded and supported by leaders whose countries are signatories to the Declaration and supporting protocols.

The other session that sticks in my mind concerned domestic violence and abuse. This was chaired by a female and led by an all female panel. Speaker after speaker lamented the plight of women in the domestic setting and the widespread abuse experienced at the hands of men. This undoubtedly was, and remains, a very bad worldwide problem.

I stood up and posed a question. What I wanted however, was an explanation of why, almost without exception, in my experience over some 25 years in the Courts; a wife would turn a blind eye to, or even cover up, the sexual abuse of her daughter by her husband? Only some of these cases were explicable on the basis of financial dependency. Many were not. The Gwelo case, where a mother was more concerned about saving her husband, than for her 14 month old baby whom he had raped, was a graphic example. As judges are the upper guardian of all minors I was understandably concerned that in these situations little girls appeared to be unprotected. I wondered whether or not studies had been done as regards this phenomenon.

As it was clear that this phenomenon had never been addressed, so the convener somewhat irritably ruled, we would not be able to meaningfully discuss it. She was simply not going to let the focus be shifted from the misconduct of men. This was disappointing.

Apart from this one small blip the conference was an outstanding success in every respect. Highlights were a visit to the Sydney Opera House, a day trip to Old Sydney Town and a day trip to an island up the Hawkesbury River. I also succumbed to an invitation by a magistrate named John Sebury to spend a very enjoyable week with his family in Wollongong.

What struck me was how developed, clean and orderly Australia was. There were certainly no inner city slums and shack townships in which thousands of human beings struggle for survival. Widespread poverty was absent.

The question, that no one could answer, was how had Australia done so much better than South Africa, given that it was colonized on roughly the same time scale, less well resourced and without the benefit of cheap Black labour.

The answer could be that, apart from the evil apartheid system, South Africa also had an incredibly corrupt "asset stripping" clique as it's government.

Has this systemic deviance not been inherited by our new "free" South Africa? It think it has.

---

78. A wind of change

During an interview in 1989 Mikhail Gorbachev is quoted as saying "I detest lies". It was this yearning for the truth that led him to introduce the policy of glasnost, literally "openness" in English. The liberal press exploited this leeway and continuously challenged its boundaries. Whole periods of recorded Soviet history were changed by glasnost. Stalin, Brezhnev and Cherenko, previously great leaders, were unmasked as the brutal oppressive murderers they really were. From 1986 he had initiated a structural reform of social and economic policies under a concept named perestroika[1].

On 10 November 1989 East Berliners walked through the Berlin Wall at Checkpoint Charlie, which event effectively marked the collapse of the Eastern Bloc and the end of the Cold War. Nicolae Ceausescu, an Eastern bloc captain as head of Romania was put to death by his own people on Xmas day, 25 December 1989.

The rest of the world was moving on. Mugabe was posed with a problem. The political philosophy, that founded his whole approach to life, stood quite comprehensively discredited in the international arena. His problem was seriously elevated when, in 1990, proof emerged that his own people had become infected with a need to have real change when they voted against his constitutional reforms. These reforms where designed to further entrench his position and that of his party. It was the first time the public, who had gave him 97% support in the first 1980 elections, broke faith with Mugabe. There was undoubtedly a wind of change blowing.

It was also the year that the then Chief Justice, Anthony Gubbay, had selected me to attend the Commonwealth Judicial Conference in Sydney, Australia. At the last moment Ministry advised that there were insufficient funds but the delegation would include a relatively junior member of Ministry staff. As a result Tony Gubbay solicited funding for my trip from the Canadian High

---

[1] http://www.historyorb.com/russia/glasnost.shtml

Commission. There was now a clear climate of antipathy towards the judiciary and in many instances our judgments granting damages to citizens brutalized by State agents, such as CIO, were simply being ignored.

In addition it was now routine for Mugabe to grant a free pardon to his agents after conviction and sentence by the High Court regardless of how heinous the crime committed was. In a case that I presided over, the accused waylaid a young man simply because a girl had preferred his company to that of the accused in a night club. The killing was by way of pumping a hail of bullets into the victim after stopping him on the road. It was a cold blooded ruthless execution of a human being motivated by puerile jealousy. In Court he wept as he pleaded with me for mercy. He need not have bothered with the tears, because within a day of me sentencing him to death he was back at Court smugly showing off to staff that Mugabe had granted him a free pardon.

We were now an "animal farm" and the rule that "no animal shall kill another animal" had been changed to "no animal shall kill another animal – without good reason"[1]. It was also clear that "all animals were equal – but some animals were more equal than others".

With Mugabe having succeeded in entrenching himself as executive president, a new mood set in characterized by routine aggrandizement of the leader and his clique. So if you attended a State function a badge was pinned to you as you entered denoting your status as either a "guest" or a VIP (very important person) or a VVIP (a very, very important person). So much for the philosophy of egalitarianism that is supposedly sacred to Marxist philosophy.

The business sector organized a gala dinner at which Clem Sunter was the guest speaker. Clem was CEO of Anglo American and already recognized as an outstanding human being and technocrat. Amongst other things he has written 14 books, some of which have been best sellers. At that stage he was renowned for a talk titled "The Attributes of a Winning Nation" which he delivered with electrifying impact. At the dinner it was no different. The man came across as a rock of sense and stunning source of wisdom. It was to no avail. Mugabe acolytes reacted with disdainful bemusement; ears deafened by arrogance and power. It was so very disheartening.

The whole climate towards the judiciary turned to one of antipathy. It was therefore not at all surprising when all efforts to have our salaries adjusted were routinely turned down. The net effect of this was that, whereas at the time of independence in 1980, judges' salaries were on a par with their

---

[1] See summary on Gerge Orwells classic story –**"Animal Farm"** - http://www.k-1.com/Orwell/site/work/summaries/animf.html

counterparts in Namibia and South Africa, by 1991 we were earning less than half in real terms.

For my family and I it distilled down to simple arithmetic. With four children requiring education the remuneration I was on was woefully inadequate. I had no option but to voluntarily relinquish my judgeship as precious as it was to me, my family and my community in particular. The decision was also influenced by advice from the ancestral spirits, via Mamquebu, that starting with the "baby dumping" phenomenon, the portends as regards the country's future were very bad indeed.

At the end of 1991 I submitted a written tender of my resignation from the bench. In my letter I expressed my sincerest appreciation of the great honour that had been bestowed upon me stating that *"this is something that can never be taken away"*. Leaving the Zimbabwean bench was a heart wrenching act for me. However it was unavoidable. Because I had been a judge for more than three years I was entitled to attach the prefix "The Honourable" to my name under Zimbabwean law. Once again it was time to move on.

At the time my family and friends thought that I was mad to move. However, by 2009, over 3.5 million of my country folk had come to the same decision on account of Mugabe's madness and were now in the Zimbabwean Diaspora[1], stripped of our inherent dignity, wallowing in a need for acceptance.

---

79. Dumela

"Dumela" is the standard greeting in Setswana the majority dialect of Botswana. On 2 February 1992 I reported for duty at the Ministry Of Finance in Gaborone, Botswana. Pam had already started work mid-January as a teacher at Thornhill Primary School, Gaborone serving under a wonderful Head Mistress named Mrs. Helen Mathole and her Deputy, Pam Muller. The net effect of this was that on arrival we had Pam's pay check as her January salary even though she had worked scarcely two weeks. It was a happy start to the five years we were destined to spend in Botswana. Leaving our beloved country had been heartbreaking. It is true that, apart from bereavement, relocation is the most traumatic experience for a family.

---

[1] **The Zimbabwean diaspora** refers to the diaspora of immigrants from the nation of Zimbabwe. Countries, in the main, are South Africa, Botswana, Namibia, The United Kingdom, Australia, Canada and the United States.http://en.wikipedia.org/wiki/Zimbabwean_diaspora

```
"In the time you have taken to read these words - metal will
have met flesh ... skin split open ... blood spilt ... muscles
torn ...limbs ripped apart - bones broken - mothers widowed
- children orphaned and - then - left - left alone to contend
with the often tragic after effects of this most unequal
encounter - - "
```
[from one of my presentations]

Henry Hale Bliss (June 13, 1830 - September 14, 1899) was the first person killed in a motor vehicle accident in the United States. On September 13, 1899 he was disembarking from a streetcar at West 74th Street and Central Park West in New York City, when an electric-powered taxicab (Automobile No. 43) struck him and crushed his head and chest. He died from his injuries the next morning. Arthur Smith, the driver of the taxicab, was arrested and charged with manslaughter but was acquitted on the grounds that it was unintentional.

Most people have never heard of Bridget Driscoll. She's not exactly a household name. Her claim to fame is that she was the first person to be killed by a motor car. The 44-year-old married woman and her teenage daughter were visiting London on August 17, 1896, to watch a dancing display on the grounds of the Crystal Palace. While they were walking along the terrace, she was hit by a car that was offering demonstration rides to the public. The car was moving at only four miles an hour when it hit Ms. Driscoll, but the impact proved fatal. At the inquest, the coroner delivered a verdict of "accidental death," and warned "that this must never happen again". To-day this type of "accident" has reached into the multi- millions.

So although the advent of the motor car was finally accepted as a boon for mankind Governments have understandably been concerned that it was also a menace to the well being of its citizens. So it is standard practice in most countries that drivers are required by law to purchase what is known as 3rd party insurance so as to ensure that road crash victims receive compensation for the loss and suffering occasioned by death and injury on the roads.

Whatever might have been intended originally in this regard, has long since been overtaken by a system that is entirely hostile and inimical to road crash victims in that, after any road crash, they are forced to "find" the driver of the vehicle involved and do battle with his/her insurer for compensation. It is nearly always an awful struggle for victims as they try to take on well resourced insurance companies motivated to protect profits. What renders the whole business obscene is that over 94% of victims, being passengers, pedestrians or the innocent "other driver", are blameless. In this way societies, all over the world, routinely acquiesce in systemic social injustice of gargantuan proportions. Road crash victims present as second only to HIV/AIDS as an international pandemic.

Botswana was attempting to implement a compensatory system that was fair and just. It involved imposing a fuel levy on every liter of fuel sold. The funds were used to compensate road crash victims. In this way no driver could not be uninsured and no victim uncompensated. Note that in recent times it was found that one fifth of drivers in one region of the United Kingdom were uninsured[1]. Just before leaving Zimbabwe my in-laws were involved in a horrific road crash in which both nearly lost their lives. The driver was uninsured. The financial consequences for them were disastrous. Botswana's fuel levy model was conceptually brilliant and unmatchable in terms of a "cost/benefit' test in that there were no profits to fund.

The problem was that this wonderful model had long since become dysfunctional and corrupt in all five countries in which it presented. In the result all the MVA [Motor Vehicle Accident Funds in the region were in serious financial deficit. South Africa was many Rand billions in deficit. On my arrival in Botswana that Fund was in the region of Pula 20 million in deficit. Hence my recruitment. I was soon summoned to a meeting with the permanent secretary to the President. He was an impressive individual with a mind like a steel trap. To him the Fund was dysfunctional, riddled with fraud and now increasingly embarrassing to Government. As it was, in effect, a replica of the South African Fund and that country had continually failed to rectify the thing, despite many judicial commissions of enquiry, it seemed to him that prudence and good governance required that it be sold off to the private sector from whence it had been wrenched in the first place. Since his stance had huge validity it was with considerable difficulty that fortunately I was able to entreat him to give me three years to rectify things. He was by no means convinced but agreed.

For a person of my background, training and experience it was relatively easy to acquire the expertise revolving around the MVA system. The fuel levy system as a concept was simple enough. The challenge was to find out why it was not working. Surprisingly this too proved relatively simple. The main problem was that the system was completely fault based. By this is meant that a victim received no compensation for losses suffered unless he/she first proved that the driver in question was at fault. Issues of fault are steeped in sometimes extremely complicated legal concepts of which ordinary members of the public have no clue. In the result the legal profession spawned a new type of lawyer, the MVA practitioner. In South Africa this segment of law has developed into a multi billion Rand business. Their business is to secure road crash victims as clients. Their target is the MVA Fund. Their remuneration is mainly represented by sharing in whatever compensation can

---

[1] Close to 2m' uninsured drivers - http://news.bbc.co.uk/2/hi/8272054.stm

be wrested from the Fund. The standard rate is around 33% regardless of how much work is involved.

In Botswana four legal firms had decided to "specialize" in this highly lucrative business. Since nothing was payable until fault was proved the system was inherently contentious, often resulting in complicated and expensive legal battles. Certainly there was very little chance of claims being settled timeously. Even upon proof of fault there was the added hurdle, for the victim, of proving the extent and value of loss. What is a broken arm worth? What is a tibia fracture worth? There are at least nine recognized types of tibia fractures with significant difference in their effects. The loss of a hand to a bricklayer is catastrophic. To a lawyer it may have little effect if that is not the hand he uses in his work. Should the bricklayer and the lawyer be paid the same compensation for loss of a hand? Everyone will agree that a sprained finger is an extremely minor injury. To Tiger Woods however, a sprained finger could result in him being unable to play in the British Open with the financial loss implications running into tens of millions.

It is said that there was a bad road crash. When a police officer arrived he found a man lying on the ground. He enquired of the victim - *"are you hurt? are you injured? how bad are you feeling ?"* The reply was - *"Look - I am only a doctor - if you want the answers to those questions you will have to ask my lawyer - "*

This little story graphically illustrates the central problem with these funds in that the industry concern became a culture to convert injury and death to as much money as possible. So all the Funds were riddled with operational problems. These ranged from genuine disputes involving complex issues of law to downright criminal fraud. A striking example was a Namibian case where a claimant, represented by a lawyer, was about to receive a substantial amount as compensation only for the Fund to discover that the man had lost his arm, not in a road crash, but as a result of snake bite. Another example was a person who claimed on the Fund even though his injury was due to being stabbed in a fight. A woman would falsely claim that a man killed in a road crash was the father of her child so as to receive maintenance for her child. A claimant would feign being unable to work for the rest of his life so as to secure a lifelong pension. The list of nonsense, deviance and fraud that permeated the systems was endless. Unsurprisingly a highly adversarial climate subsisted with Funds being ultra careful, if not downright sceptical, of just about every claim.

One morning an advocate arrives from Johannesburg accompanied by a lawyer and secretary. We go into a scheduled conference with my deputy, Ms Vaka, and I representing the Fund.

Lawyer: Good morning, may I extend our appreciation for this conference, this is Advocate Udian[1] who has been retained by us on brief [he finishes with a flourish]

Advocate: Good morning - yes thank you - hopefully this will not take too long - we are planning to take the opportunity of flying up to the Delta[2] on an excursion this afternoon

Ms Vaka: Good morning gentlemen, we hope you had a good flight - and welcome to our country Botswana - you will love the Delta - the jewel of Africa [she adds coquettishly]

Lawyer: And you Mr. Greenland - how are you? - I heard that you are from Zimbabwe - which does not have MVA ... [he adds quite pointedly]

Me: Good morning, and welcome to this scheduled conference. I find MVA incredibly interesting - this business of converting injury and death into money - into as much money as possible [Advocate and lawyer try to hide the reproachful look in their eyes]

Advocate: Well compensation is a right, a constitutional right and at common law has been with mankind from the time of Justinian [said with combative emphasis]

Me: As is our practice proceedings will be recorded - are we agreed on this ground rule?

Advocate: You certainly have our agreement - provided, of course - as is our practice, you furnish us with a copy of the record [he says keenly eyeing Ms Vaka who has a note pad in front of her]

Ms Vaka: Good then we can proceed

Advocate: As said this should not take long. The merits [whether or not a claimant is entitled to compensation] are obviously in our client's favour so we can go onto settling the quantum [the amount of compensation payable]. So as to save time we have prepared a proposal of settlement which, as always, is open to negotiation

Ms Vaka: We would prefer that you finish your submissions first and then we will respond

Advocate: In round figures we propose a cash payment of [mentioning a substantial sum] as a reasonable settlement even though, as you are

---

[1] Name is fictitious

[2] Referring to the world-famous Okavango Delta in Botswana

undoubtedly aware, a Court would probably grant a much higher sum as an award [the Courts are indeed notoriously and understandably pro-claimant]

Ms Vaka: Why cash, his loss is mostly loss of earnings which the Fund can pay annually as if the accident had not occurred? That way he will not be tempted to spend the money and then be dependent on the State when he has no income

Advocate: Yes but if the Fund were to pay annually; you will see from the actuarial report, that we filed, that your Fund will end up paying a sum totaling many millions until he reaches retirement age of 65. So our proposal is greatly to your advantage

Ms Vaka: We can debate that one for a long time - is there anything else that you have?

Advocate: No, I think what we have proposed is fair and reasonable for a man who has suffered such terrible injury

Me: Except that his injuries were self inflicted. As you are undoubtedly aware no compensation is payable to a person who actually caused the accident.

Advocate: Now wait a minute - what are you getting at? - the merits have been conceded. It was the first thing we agreed in this conference - only quantum is now on the agenda!

Ms Vaka: No - with respect - that is not so - we have never conceded the merits

Advocate: [now visibly agitated] - look we agreed first thing in this conference which you undertook to record [he adds looking at her note pad] - and my instructing attorney here has also kept notes on what has been agreed

Me: Mr. Udian, it is simply not the position that the merits were conceded - you were requested to complete your submissions

Advocate: I beg your pardon Sir - I don't know what you are playing at - [raising his voice] but we have a record of the concession which you cannot unilaterally withdraw - and I am prepared to put my instructing attorney in the witness stand to give evidence of that fact

Me: You will recall that we agreed a ground rule that the proceedings be recorded?

Advocate: Yes - and my instructing attorney has also been keeping an accurate record - [he says emphatically]

Me: I am glad we have agreement on that. Now if you look above you; you will see a tiny black spot on the ceiling. That is a microphone. The proceedings have been recorded with absolute accuracy as is electronic recordings. So we don't have to rely on notes that may be inaccurate. Do you want the recording played back?

Advocate: This is outrageous. [in a now very raised and agitated voice] You have recorded us without our knowledge or permission! Bugging is unconstitutional! It is against the law! In over 30 years of practice I have never come across such unethical conduct.

Me: I thought we had just agreed - not even a minute ago - that there was a consensus that the proceeding were to be recorded - that is precisely what has happened - utilizing the most accurate means known to man -

It is soon over after we produce evidence that their client caused the accident and take the stance that he cannot be compensated under the law. The advocate demands that we send them a copy of a transcript of the electronic recording and vows to institute legal action on the basis of invasion of their rights to privacy. They do not go on the trip to the Okavango Delta. We send them a transcript. We hear no more of the matter. They had no case. We had never conceded the merits, i.e., agreed that their client was entitled to compensation. They had agreed to the proceedings being recorded.

Finding out that the recording method was electronic and therefore unarguable was an inconvenient and unpalatable truth.

In another case I was just about to sign a settlement agreement with the lawyer acting for a claimant, in terms of which the Fund would pay over some P600,000 as loss of support to an Irish lady, married to a Black Zimbabwean doctor, who died after a road crash that occurred in Francistown, when our Investigations Manager, Mr. Vincent Butale walks in.

Butale: Sir, I am sorry to disturb you, but I am not happy about this case.

Lawyer: Now come on Mr. Butale, don't be so harsh - this woman is suffering and this is an open and shut case

Butale: I need two weeks - I am begging you - just give me two weeks - I want to investigate something

Me: Mr. Butale - it is indeed an open and shut case –

we have the police report, with plans and photos showing that the deceased was killed when the other driver crossed onto his side of the road and collided head-on with him we have the death certificate, signed by the superintendent of the hospital in Harare, certifying that he died three weeks later as a result of head injuries sustained in the accident

we have full proof of what he earned as doctor so we know exactly how much this woman has lost in financial support

it is one of the best presented cases we have seen in this Fund and you know that justice delayed is justice denied! [I finish irritably]

Butale: Please - please I am begging you - just give me two weeks

We finally and very reluctantly agree to give our Investigations Manager two weeks. I am heavily influenced by two things. Firstly Butale is an exceptional investigator. Secondly from my judicial experiences I hold to the view that - "when most sure - be most careful".

After two weeks the conference is resumed.

Lawyer: Well - is the Fund now ready to pay my client - this poor woman?

Butale: No. You see the truth is that the deceased was the cause of his own death and you know that, in such case, the Fund is precluded from paying compensation

Lawyer: What nonsense, with respect - you have the police report, photos and plans showing -

Me: - wrongly showing that the other driver came onto the deceased's side of the road. The accident was witnessed by two "ladies of the night" who actually refused to jump into the car of the deceased because he was weaving all over the road - the truth is that he actually drove onto the wrong side and collided with the other car - he was the one at fault

Lawyer: But are you saying the police officer's report and plans are false - why would she have done such a thing?

Butale: Yes - you see she might have been a police officer - but she was also the girlfriend of this doctor – the deceased - many witnesses have confirmed this in affidavits

Me: And your client's husband did not die from accident injuries. As you know - if he died from other causes the Fund cannot pay.

Lawyer: What do you mean? The death certificate says he died from head injuries caused in the accident - it is signed by the medical superintendent of the hospital in Harare!

Butale: Yes - that superintendent is having an affair with the widow - your client who is claiming

Me: Here is the original death certificate by the pathologist who conducted the post mortem the day after death. It clearly states that the deceased died on account of pneumonia induced by HIV/AIDS

Butale: And the hospital superintended withdrew that certificate and made another one because he is having this love affair with your client – the widow - all a plan to get money

Me: And it may interest you to know that the female police officer who made the false report in the first place - and who was having an affair with the deceased - has also recently died of HIV/AIDS - no doubt contracted from the deceased or maybe vice versa.

Despite this evidence of artful attempted fraud the lawyer sued the Fund. After many years of protracted legal battle the case was finally withdrawn.

In another case the Fund declined to compensate a claimant. I was visited by Minister Kwelagobe, a fire brand personality. He was able to show that we had made a mistake. The claimant was nearly denied some P70, 000 that she was entitled to by law.

The above incidents dramatically illustrate how the MVA Funds were severely challenged for being fault based. Another fundamental problem was that the Funds were all completely under-funded in relation to their potential liabilities. By this is meant that the Fund was required to cover the value of loss in full even if this ran into many millions. At that time Botswana was a world leader in the business of road carnage. On average Europe was killing 2.5 persons per annum for every 100,000 vehicles on the road. Botswana was killing 40. A motorist was paying about Pula 250 per annum by way of fuel levy instead of the thousands of Pula he/she would have had to pay if forced to purchase similar cover privately. This gross mismatch between income and liability guaranteed the financial deficit that all of the Funds accrued. As Ms Vaka would often say - `"these Funds provide Rolls Royce cover on an ox-wagon levy income."`

I was fortunate to be at first mentored and tutored by a highly professional Englishman named Alan Norrie who was the insurance advisor to the Botswana Government. Our boss was John Stoneham who was also Permanent Secretary in the Ministry of Finance. He was far sighted in his approach and a risk taker by disposition. Our joint approach under Stoneham was to be innovative, imaginative and, of course, always sapiential. Expertise and skills were augmented by visits to international experts in London, Munich and New York.

Notable was the kind and collegial way I was always treated by members of cabinet whom I sometimes had to address in the reform process. Death, injury and money constitute a volatile cocktail and issues can become extremely emotive. Disagreement, strong disagreement, was inevitable. On one occasion a Minister Merafe (now Deputy President) expressed his anger at my stance on an issue. However once the debate was over he accorded me complete collegiality. On one memorable occasion we were locked in discussion on what constitutes reasonable compensation in payment for a funeral of a person killed in a road crash. This was an emotive issue. Batswana take funerals very seriously and routinely spend considerable amounts of money on them. Alan Norrie was not impressed and ventured the otherwise imprudent/insensitive statement that - *some people want to be reimbursed after they have killed half the national herd for consumption in the funeral feast - "* The President, The Hon Quet Masire, declined offence being taken and immediately starting chortling in amusement - *" - killing half the national herd - killing half the national herd - "* all but collapsing in laughter. Everyone joined in and a potentially ugly moment was avoided.

Our Minister was Festus Mogae, Deputy President of the country and later to become President. In our meetings he would always make me feel that, if there was any importance in the room, it attached only to me. It was humbling. Notable was the fact that, despite my entreaties that they should address me as *"Mr. Greenland"* or *"Chris",* the President and all his ministers always addressed me as *"Judge".*

When we had configured the reform model it had to be legislated after a consultative process. This included defending the model to the House of Chiefs, where all leaders meet, chaired by the President. He was completely disarming in his attitude to me and made me sit right next to him saying that I would need him *"when the jackals wanted to eat me up".* On commencement of proceedings he introduced me by saying, grinning broadly - *"well here is the good man who is responsible for this draft Bill, if you think you can eat him up, now is your chance".* Change is nearly always problematical. So there were some who felt strongly, even resentful, about what I was proposing. They did not mince their words. At every stage the President supported and protected me insisting that the ball be played and never the man. At the end he congratulated me and insisted that others acknowledge my brave defense of the draft Bill.

Given this level of support it proved a relatively easy matter to substantially reform the MVI Fund of Botswana. By the end of the third year it was no longer in deficit and was processing claims almost seamlessly. The turn-around time for the processing of a claim had been reduced from an average of 18 - 36 months to an average of just three. It had been transformed from a dysfunctional wasteful entity to one in which levy income was spent on road crash victims whose needs were being serviced with minimum delay. An important player in this process was a young, bright, personable female lawyer, Regina Dumilana Vaka, who I had the privilege to guide and mentor. Later she was to go on to become the General Manager of the Fund and quickly succeed in making it the best in the region.

We spent five happy years in Botswana. For me this included two return trips to the world famous Okavango Delta and Kazangula which I had first visited in September 1975 when the country was one of the poorest in the world, but the richest in number and diversity of game. On the first of these two trips I arranged a reunion with a school friend, George Wicket, whom I had not seen for some 30 years. The much anticipated reunion did not take place. George was killed in a plane crash in the Delta on the morning of my arrival there. My second trip was a most memorable week long fishing trip to the Delta where we lodged at Guma Camp run by ex Zimbabwean, Jeff Randall.

It is a clear bright hot morning. The road stretches out in front of me in slow lazy curves as our vehicle glides along steadily, eating up the road with ease and grace, scarcely emitting a sound. It is an executive model, supplied as a company car, and has all the mod cons such as sound system and air-conditioning. The latter has been on some time now giving comfort to my family who have been up since 4 am when we left Gaborone to sojourn home to Harare, Zimbabwe. Our three youngest children, David, Christopher and Nicola are now back asleep after the rigours of the Botswana/Zimbabwe border crossing.

There was a five hour long queue with hundreds of people milling around like ants clutching immigration forms - asking for a pen - wondering from one counter to the next. Every few minutes a stranger would approach and insistently propose a deal in foreign currency. There were vendors displaying their wares including food items like roasted mealies [corn] and fruit. This organized chaos never ceased to amaze. It also never ceased to infuriate. Politicians make all kinds of promises at election time. When in power the needs of ordinary people count for nothing. The chaotic state of this border post has subsisted for over fifteen years. More and more people were now working in Botswana as it was the fastest growing economy in the world. Zimbabwe's economy was starting in a downward spiral. We had jumped the queue on account of good relations built up because of so many crossings on our part.

The vehicle crests the high ground and as I turn slowly to the right the road starts to dip into a valley below. Soon we will be crossing the Shangani River, another milestone in our trip. As I drive towards the bridge there are stirrings in the car as the children wake each other up. Excited whispers replace the sound of the radio whose volume I turn down. Something is about to happen.

The air is charged with expectancy. As the front wheels of the vehicle make it onto the bridge my window goes down as I tap the control button. Turning to the river below I call out in loud reverent tone -

```
Siya tsela ku hlula oba bantu be dala - salibonani - linjani - ?
[We are begging for leave to pass this way - from you - our
people from so long ago - Greetings - How are you ...?]
Siya hamba ekhaya - siya funa ku bona u mama lo baba
[We are going home - we want to see our mother and our father]
```

and I go on in plea and supplication to the ancestral spirits asking for their protection and, thanking them, bid " - hlala kahle" [remain well]

The children are absolutely enthralled. They do not speak or understand isiNdebele. To them it just all sounds so great and mysterious as their father addresses unseen beings with such intensity and reverence. It is always the high point of the 1200 km trip home. I have to once again explain to them that Shangani has great significance for the Ndebele people. It is regarded by many as our ancestral home. It is also where an Ndebele impi defeated and wiped out the colonial Allan Wilson patrol but still honoured the vanquished with those famous words -"they were men and their fathers were men before them". As I was ethnically half Ndebele, it was incumbent of me to accord due respect, seek protection and give thanks to our ancestral spirits. They love it and we have a talking point for most of the rest of the trip as I am peppered with a plethora of questions about who we are. This nearly always leads to me having to recount experiences from my childhood, with my granny, at Sacred Heart Home and at Embakwe.

We had a good life in Botswana. A high point was when I received word from the Catholic Diocese that, after many years of careful scrutiny and consideration, Rome had ruled to annul my first marriage.

Pam and I were able to re-marry in a quaint little chapel of the local Catholic Church with Patrick Muir, with whom I had served mass all those years in Embakwe, acting as my best man. Sadly our life in Botswana had to come to an end. Under Botswana law we were not eligible for citizenship or permanent residence.

Our eldest son was turning 18, making him an adult, and no longer entitled to residency as our minor child. As a family we were at a cross-road as to what do next. Returning to our beloved Zimbabwe was, however, not an option.

The problem was that by the end of 1996 it was all too clear that Robert Mugabe was purposefully ruining our country and reducing its populace to poverty. It is unnecessary to expand on this as it is well documented in many books such as "Through the Darkness" by Judith Garfield Todd, "Cry Zimbabwe" by Peter Stiff, "Zimbabwe; The Land That Weeps" by Charles W. Duke, "Our Votes, Our Guns: Robert Mugabe and the Tragedy of Zimbabwe" by Martin Meredith; and now "Mugabe and the White African", a documentary film by Lucy Bailey and Andrew Thompson. So going back home was out of the question.

Like millions of other Zimbabweans, soon to follow, we were condemned to doing our best in what has become known as the Zimbabwe Diaspora[1].

80. Whither Thou Goest[2]

It was just then that I receive an offer.

Pam and I travel to Pretoria, South Africa in mid 1996 to consult on the offer and check with immigration authorities. The latter assures us with a beaming smile that " ... *people like you are most welcome in South Africa ...*" On leaving we stop on the banks of the Hartbeespoort Dam, just outside Pretoria and say a prayer asking Almighty God for guidance. Strange as it may seem it is a far more difficult decision to make than the one we made about me giving up my judgeship, so precious to me, and leaving Zimbabwe.

The panoramic view from the edge of the section near the spillway is beautiful with a mass expanse of water stretching to the horizon on which sailing craft serenely ply their way. Wispy clouds hang in a true blue sky.

---

[1] **The Zimbabwean diaspora** refers to the diaspora of immigrants from the nation of Zimbabwe··· estimated that there are millions of residents outside of Zimbabwe's borders who were either born in the country or are descended from immigrants; Many recent emigrants are illegally residing in other countries because of the fall of the standard of living and economic conditions in Zimbabwe.The Zimbabwean diaspora has a 95% literacy rate in English and a very highly educated adult population. The main languages spoken are English, Shona, and Ndebele. http://en.wikipedia.org/wiki/Zimbabwean_diaspora

[2] **Whither Thou Goest** is a popular song written by Guy Singer. The song was published in 1954. The words are adapted from the Bible (Ruth 1:16-17) (King James Version). Also see John 13:36: 'Simon Peter said to him, Lord, whither goest thou? Jesus answered him, Whither I go, thou canst not follow me now; but thou shalt follow me afterward.'"

The far side border of the spillway gorge, known as Kosmos, is a rising hillside festooned with beautiful villas of every description.

However the waters before us are murky, turgid and tainted by dark green algae bloom, unlike the crystal clear waters of the Okavango or the lively sparkle of the Zambezi. Perhaps it is this impurity in the middle of so much beauty that gives me a twinge of inner foreboding.

Pam: My husband - why do you look a bit worried - God has opened another door - we must have faith - and walk through it - and you know how we have always just loved Cape Town

Me: Maybe you are right - we can't stay in Botswana - we can't go back to Zimbabwe with the situation there - but I should tell you that I am entitled to claim British citizenship by right of descent

Pam: True - but, do you want to go to England - after your trips there you have always said how lucky we are to live in Africa - and Rob and Bridgett [her brother-in-law and sister] couldn't wait to get back here -

Me: True

Pam: and our son Manuel phoned to say that you must be mad to be in doubt ... he has been at UCT [University of Cape Town] for the last three years

Me: Yes, and how our sons love the Springboks - David went mad last year when they beat the mighty All Blacks in the world cup

Pam: ... and phoned us from the stadium ranting like a lunatic - screaming like a mad thing on the phone about Madiba - Madiba wearing a Springbok jersey ... [very few people referred to Nelson Mandela as Madiba in 1995]

Me: - but in my heart I feel that when you look at it - at who I am - and where I come from - you realize that despite my pedigree - half English/half Ndebele - there has been nothing English about me to this day ...

On 08 May 1996 Deputy President Thabo Mbeki had made a stirring speech starting with the words –

"I am an African.

I owe my being to the hills and the valleys, the mountains and the glades, the rivers, the deserts, the trees, the flowers, the seas and the ever-changing seasons that define the face of our native land.

My body has frozen in our frosts and in our latter day snows. It has thawed in the warmth of our sunshine and melted in the heat of the midday sun. The crack and the rumble of the summer thunders, lashed by startling lightening, have been a cause both of trembling and of hope - - - -

Today, as a country, we keep an audible silence about these ancestors of the generations that live, fearful to admit the horror of a former deed, seeking to obliterate from our memories a cruel occurrence which, in its remembering, should teach us not and never to be inhuman again.

I am formed of the migrants who left Europe to find a new home on our native land. Whatever their own actions, they remain still, part of me".

This speech is reassuring at a number of levels. We are able to identify ourselves in it - as being African - with a place of welcome and protection in South Africa.

By way of this admixture of mind, heart and reality, the issue resolves itself. I decide to accept the offer and forget about emigrating to England, the land of my forefathers.

81. The fair Cape of Good Hope

At a grand farewell dinner Freddy Modise, Undersecretary in the Ministry of Finance, expresses the gratitude of the Batswana for my humble efforts. He curiously adds - "and when those people in South Africa have no use for you - please remember you can come back to us". In my response to the speeches made I adopt hope as my theme. Because of the sanctuary that their country gave our family, and the exposure it gave me, I was well equipped to go forward with real hope for our futures. The next day the Deputy President, the Hon Festus Mogae, disarmingly says thank you and *"God-speed"* in a telephonic farewell conversation.

As a child I was enraptured reading about the Cape of Good Hope in the book I was given that Xmas titled "Under Drake's Flag". That fascination still reposed deep in my psyche as we set off from Gaborone. It all seemed just a little bit unreal; the anticipation of going to the historically magic place, on the one hand, and the tug we feel in our hearts at having to move further away from home. Nearing Cape Town my family marvels at the endless expanse of verdant green and gold that comprises the Paarl wine producing lands. There is a rich admixture of beauty and majesty about, that permeates all the senses. After the long featureless landscape that is the Karoo, with its searing heat, we are infused with a sense of deliverance; deliverance into a fabled land, a promised land.

Then one of our children asks an awkward question. We are soon chastened by the realization that, amidst all this beauty, are hundreds of squalid edifices, there for all to see, in which human beings are living "like rats" as our children observe. They are referring to the appalling box edifices, in shanty groupings, in which the farm workers have to live.

It gets worse. *"Are they not Coloureds?"* is the question, and then *"Why - why - ?"* so many questions about the unfairness, the injustice - which we just cannot answer to the satisfaction of young minds, unencumbered by convenient untruths and obfuscation. *"I am sure that Madiba is going to fix it - "* observes 15 year old David, with a tone of assurance and faith, *" ... otherwise we would not be coming here".* Right there all our hopes and dreams as a family, coalesce around Nelson Rolihlahla Mandela and everything he represents.

On the radio we hear about a new concept, called *ubuntu*, that will replace the viciousness of apartheid. As said by Archbishop Desmond Tutu -

> "You can't be human all by yourself, and when you have this quality - Ubuntu - you are known for your generosity."

After a fourteen hour drive we arrive in Cape Town, to be met by our eldest son, beaming from ear to ear. He has been alone for a long three years in Cape Town. The next day he takes us to visit his *"foster father and mother"*, Mohammed and Shirley Omar who live in Woodstock. This wonderful couple have gone out of their way, for three whole years, to ensure that they were there for our son in all his needs. We remain forever indebted to them. On the way back we make a tour of the now world famous Waterfront. Pam buys me a Springbok jacket *"for luck"*.

Cape Town, in late December, is a wonderful city. At that time the radio programs inevitably passed on subliminal messages of the Mandela influence and we heard much about *ubuntu*. I could immediately identify with this concept as kindness, consideration and respect for others were at the very core of everything I experienced as a child at my grandmother's village and at the villages I was given sanctuary when I ran away from home.

The next day I was introduced to the staff of the Cape Town office by Mr. Johann van Oudtshoorn, Claims Executive of the Road Accident Fund. They numbered some 146, comprising an admixture of Coloured and White, with just one or two Blacks. Their reaction to me was tangibly positive, completely welcoming and tinged with intrigue at the arrival of this brown Zimbabwean judge. I was immediately forgiven for my rotten Afrikaans and assured that I had been *"adopted"* with open hearts by all. The hope I had spoken of in saying farewell to the Batswana started to change to faith.

That faith received its first dent on the morning of my first day at work. I was in conference with the managers when a call came through. It was from the High Court where the Fund was locked in a legal battle. The Fund's advocate told me that he did not mind me speaking directly to counsel for the other side, as he was aware that I had been a judge. When the claimant's advocate came on line he introduced himself as a Senior Counsel from the Cape Town

Bar. In the legal profession attaining the rank of senior counsel, or SC, is the highest that one can rise to as an advocate. Whilst all lawyers and advocates are regarded as officers of the Court, judges accord Senior Counsel unquestioning regard. Personally I held Senior Counsel in esteem approaching reverence. This was on account of the incredible personal and functional integrity they had hitherto displayed in my life in Zimbabwe. Much earlier I had met Kentridge SC, seen him in action, and been personally inspired by the great man. I had seen Chaskalson SC, who then became South Africa's Chief Justice, in action. So too as regards Zulman SC, against whom I had appeared in Zimbabwe, who now serves as a judge. I had never attained the rank of SC, as I was an advocate for a mere five years. All these men radiated integrity. So it felt good to be on the phone to one of this special breed on my first day at work.

We engage in a formal telephonic conference in order to see whether or not the Court dispute could be settled, or at the very least curtailed, by way of agreeing some of the matters hitherto in dispute.

[Picture of Minister Maharaj (middle) Hermann Karberg (his right) and me - 2002]

It goes well and at the end of the conference I dictate to him *"the Fund's final position"* and ask him to read it back to me as I write it down on my desk pad in the presence of my managers. Ten minutes later I receive a call from the judge's clerk. He reads out what the advocate had conveyed to the Court as the Fund's final position. It is exactly the opposite of what I had said. This news comes as a shock which will never really leave me. I am also unaware of just how bad a portend it is as regards my future in South Africa, especially the events of 19 October 2008 on the distant horizon. To be fair I am still to meet many Senior Counsel who are of diamond hard integrity.

Three other experiences are somewhat negative. On attempting to open a bank account with ABSA we come against the "what I have I done to deserve this" attitude as our Zimbabwean pedigree strikes a bad chord with the relevant White manager. So we try our luck with First National Bank and there we are welcomed, accorded "royal treatment" and have to resist being laden with every kind of card and bank product on offer. This bank has always provided exceptional considerations and service.

At Home Affairs, where we go to regulate the issue of residency in the country, we come against a Scottish lady, just three years in the country, whose disdain for us is so bad that she pointedly says - *"there is nothing that you two have to offer this country"*. A Coloured lady comes to our rescue and includes an apology.

The third incident was when we accepted an invitation to dinner by a prominent MVA lawyer. He opened the discussion by proudly announcing that he had just "banged" the RAF with seven summonses. In the subsequent conversation it became clear that he saw nothing wrong/sad about a situation where a public entity was continually under siege, whatever the reasons were, at expense to the public running into Rand millions. This same lawyer is to one day give me a long lecture that there were only two things people understand - *"greed and fear"*.

So what should have been a good start is tainted with not insignificant problems. I am not to know what they portend for the future.

Pam had little difficulty securing a teaching post at Rondebosch, on account of her exceptional references as a teacher even though, at that very time, the teaching sector was shedding thousands of jobs. I settled down well with my staff in the Cape Town office of the RAF. With little exception, all the staff responded positively to my efforts.

It was obvious that I was different, acted differently and had a different mindset to that they were accustomed to. All this they seemed to find invigorating. So there was a climate of mutual curiosity and positive appreciation. Many were more than bemused and intrigued that I traveled by train to and from Bergvleit, where we lived. The train was clearly for lesser mortals, not Fund managers. The managers were fully supportive throughout, particularly, Phillip Simpson who, with over 22 years experience would have undoubtedly secured the post I was in had South Africa now not been going through "transformation". He harboured no resentment; only fierce loyalty.

My duties are augmented with the honour of serving on a committee of experts, appointed by Minister Mac Maharaj, concerned with advising government of how to reform the RAF system. For that purpose I periodically travel up to Gauteng. Leading the process is a Dr Izak Fourie. There is much merit in what he proposes and it helps to refine my own ideas, which are already well formulated, on account of my involvement with reform in Botswana.

This is when I meet George Maluleke It is easy to be taken with this man who speaks 14 languages fluently. He is far more passionate about MVA then I am. He has an incredibly interesting past and deserves admiration for his achievements. There is also a judge serving on the panel.

Sadly the committee appears to be, in effect, primarily divided in terms of sectoral interests. One school, led by George, a lawyer, wants the thing kept intact apart from a few relatively minor changes, but funding increased so as to match liabilities. The other wants it radically changed so as to be wrested from the legal profession and transferred to dominance by the medical sector.

I, and the judge, think that the system should be transformed so as to serve only the public interest. We are a very small minority indeed.

82. A snake pit

In 1998 I am transferred to Head Office in Pretoria to take up the post of Claims Executive, previously held by Johann van Oudtshoorn. He is re-assigned to investigations.

A Deputy CEO has been recruited to understudy the CEO, Willem Swanepoel. His name is Humphrey Kgomongwe, whose background is finance. Ms "X" a Black female lawyer, has also been recruited. She has worked for George Maluleke who runs one of the biggest MVA practices in South Africa. There is also Sipho Mkizhe appointed to head Human Resources. Virtually overnight RAF top management is changed from being exclusively White to a nice admixture of Black, White and brown. The Board, chaired by Piet Botbyl, but dominated by a personable lawyer named George Negota, described in the press as an ANC "hitman", are effecting "transformation", a new dogma in a country badly in need of normalization after decades of apartheid.

It is not long before I realize that I have moved from the serene beauty and grace of Cape Town to a snake pit. When Willem Swanepoel assembles the staff in order to introduce us, Black and White staff openly display their antipathy towards each other and take their places in racially divided format.

There is a clique of Black staff, led by one Morris Mokase, who immediately start revolutionary verbal posturing about the need for immediate racial transformation of the Fund and that *"it must be an event - not a process"*. This draws reaction from some White members of staff who respond with comments like *"why don't you just sit down"* and *"oh just shut up"*. Eventually some of White members of staff simply walk out.

Soon thereafter, Swanepoel subjects us to a course of "the Six Thinking Hats" which is one of the latest management fads internationally[1]. It seems to induce some new found bonding. Immediately after the meeting Annamie Roux, (a senior manager with many years of experience) Ms "X" and I, seek an audience with Swanepoel. We are fired up with enthusiasm to work together to effect the change so badly needed by the Fund in all its attributes. I draw Swanepoel's attention to the symbolism in him now being in audience with a management team comprising Black, White and Coloured members of management.

Kgomongwe entreats me to accompany him to see Swanepoel for the purpose of conveying and pledging our loyalty to him. Kgomongwe insists that this is important. I accept that he is being sincere. Swanepoel is visibly touched, says so, and invites us both for a lunch at a Portuguese restaurant where he confides in us details of how he has hitherto survived politically inspired attempts to have him removed simply on account of his ethnicity.

Within a day or so Ms "X" and Kgomongwe invite me to an evening meeting to discuss "real transformation" of the Fund. I decline, pointing out that there appears no reason why this needs to be discussed in secret. When Ms "X" then puts the word out that I have reported their meeting to Johann van Oudtshoorn I realize that they have had their secret meeting anyway. Whatever bonding there was between us instantly dissipates.

Within a matter of days we are summoned by Piet Botbyl, Chairperson of the Board, and informed that Swanepoel is to be relieved of his position as CEO with immediate effect. He has accepted a severance package. In a short speech Swanepoel quietly states that it *"is a shame that things have come to*

---

[1] **The de Bono Hats system** (also known as "Six Hats" or "Six Thinking Hats") is a thinking tool for group discussion and individual thinking. Combined with the idea of parallel thinking which is associated with it, it provides a means for groups to think together more effectively, and a means to plan thinking processes in a detailed and cohesive way. The method is attributed to Dr. Edward de Bono and is the subject of his book, Six Thinking Hats.
http://en.wikipedia.org/wiki/Six_Thinking_Hats

be done in this way". By next morning he is gone. Overnight the Fund has no CEO and the hunt for a new CEO is on. Kgomongwe and Ms "X" are brimming with satisfaction at developments.

I feel sickened by the prevailing climate, by the attitudinal viciousness, by the lack of kindness and consideration permeating everything. Surely this is not Mandela's new South Africa? Surely this is not the *ubuntu* that the nation is hearing about from quality leaders like Dr Mamphela Aletta Ramphele?

Will preoccupation with race and ethnicity once again dictate what happens in and to our lives?

83. Terminal illness

But it is, certainly for now anyway. To the management team the issue of racial transformation becomes an obsession with scant regard for service delivery.

Claims take anything up to 10 or even 15 years to be processed. The main reason for this is that the system in inherently contentious. It is guaranteed to be so, given that the objective, at all times, is to convert injury and death into as much money as can be possibly extracted from the Fund.

Most road crash victims are from the poorer sector of society, i.e., passengers and pedestrians. Because the whole system is fault based it is neither understandable nor accessible to them. Assistance by MVA lawyers is unavoidable. This comes at enormous cost to the claimant, i.e., usually around 33% of any compensation secured. The sheer injustice of mostly poor people having to sacrifice about one third of their compensation, to which they are entitled to by law, secured from an entity run by their own government, is lost on everyone.

Claims staff are seriously out-gunned. Every claim has to be resolved according to law, often complex law. 97% of claimants are represented by qualified lawyers. Most claims staff, including claims managers are not lawyers. The most experienced ones have received their training in the offices of short term insurance firms who previously processed the Fund's claims under what was then known as the agency system. At the heart of the system is the insurance sector concept of "3rd party cover". This simply means that unlike other insurance, where a person buys insurance cover for himself/herself, in this case the driver (the 1st party) pays for insurance to the insurer (the 2nd party) so that when the driver has an accident the loss accruing to the victim (the 3rd part) will be met. When I ask claims managers what is meant by 3rd party cover, only Annamie Roux and Hermann Karberg are able to say. In addition the operational culture of a private sector insurer is fundamentally different from a public sector entity. The former, as with all business, is concerned worth maximizing profit; the latter is concerned with serving the public interest.

The real problem for claims staff however is that they are hamstrung on account of the reactive operational mode of the Fund. They only become aware of the facts of an accident once a claim is filed. They really have no way of knowing whether what is being put to them is fact, fiction or an admixture of both. The Fund has very little capacity to verify information submitted. As already pointed out deviance and fraud is rampant. In addition the prevailing law is understandably weighted heavily in favour of a claimant. The law, of course, presumes that a claim is genuine. The reality is that many are not, wholly or in part. Often the process is just unmanageable through no shortcomings on the part of claims staff.

Regrettably we also appear to have a serious internal problem as regards systemic fraud. This is evidenced by the issue regarding claims for whiplash. Throughout the western world, particularly America, whiplash claims are notorious for being fraudulent. What happens is that there is a minor "bumper-bashing" road crash. The occasion is then used to found a claim for "whiplash" by one or more of the occupants. Whiplash comprises the physiological and neurological effects that, on rare occasion, accrue in consequence of the snapping of the neck during a collision.

In my many consultations with the captains of the insurance industry in London, Munich and New York I learnt that probably 97% of such claims are fraudulent. However, because some may be genuine, any person claiming whiplash presents as an incredibly difficult problem to medical experts on account of difficulty in distinguishing genuine whiplash cases from malingerers. Later, in 1999, I am to be engaged in an interview with a local Jewish lawyer who tells me frankly that he is a millionaire on account of a very successful whiplash practice. He however believes that over 97% of such cases are fraudulent. As a lawyer he can do nothing about this. He is obliged to present his client's case as best he can. I refer him to Judge Satchwell who is chairing a commission of enquiry into the MVA system. As regards the RAF we find that, of some 400 odd employees, approximately half have themselves successfully claimed for whiplash on the very Fund they are administering. One manager has done so three times.

In a report to be handed down in 2002 the Commission of Enquiry is to conclude that the Fund is an inefficient and ineffective vehicle for the delivery of compensation and to recommend that the whole system and the Fund be replaced. In 1998 however our management team's obsession is racial transformation. Efficiency, effectiveness and service delivery receive scant consideration.

In 1999 Minister Maharaj appoints me Acting CEO of the Fund to serve for two years. In a meeting with George Negota, in the presence of Kgomongwe, I had given him the assurance that I was not interested in being appointed as CEO and that I would prefer to provide support for Humphrey Kgomongwe who had, in any event, been appointed Deputy CEO under Swanepoel. I accept that it is important, in terms of transformation polemics, that a Black person be appointed. This mini-plan is comprehensively subverted when Botbyl produces proof that Kgomongwe has been convicted for driving under the influence of alcohol. To my mind that fact trumps everything else. I accept that such a conviction effectively disqualifies a person from appointment as head of the RAF, given the appalling road crash rate in South Africa, with alcohol abuse being a prime contributor. The reason that the appointment is for two years, at my request, is that Government is in the process of appointing a commission of enquiry into the system, to report in one year, and a new system to be implemented thereafter.

My post as Claims Executive is filled by Ashraf Ebrahim, an advocate from Cape Town. Ms "X" is incensed and thereafter openly hostile to me even though I have had nothing to do with the selection. In writing I had asked Dr van der Merwe, of the Board, to chair the selection panel, openly disclosing that as I was too close to all of the candidates, I could not be involved in the selection in any way.

It is not surprising that Asraf is selected. He is easily one of the most intelligent, imaginative, skilled and articulate human beings I have ever met. The Fund desperately needs functionaries of his calibre and intellect at this particular time.

---

84. Yes! we can – No! you cannot

Kgomongwe is understandably deeply aggrieved. In reality he had been the CEO designate and, on Swanepoel's departure, should have been elevated. He is technically correct in holding to the view that his conviction for drunken driving cannot be now used against him when it was not used on his appointment to Deputy CEO. The Mokase clique rally around him and they come to see me. They make it clear that, unless the Fund is racially transformed with no delay, so as ensure Black dominance, they will ensure it becomes "ungovernable". In that stance they are fully supported by Ms "X" who insists that she wants only Black managers at the branch that she heads.

The staff composition is over 90% White. We are four years into independence. The racial grievance is valid and impatience understandable. The problem is enormous as one cannot just fire "experienced" White staff and replace them with "inexperienced" Black entrants. The present "competent/experienced" complement is already not coping. Compensation is a sacred right for persons injured or for the dependents of those killed in road crashes. The claimants have an absolute right to expect that their claims will be processed at the requisite level of competence.

Because of apartheid we simply don't have a pool of competent Black candidates to recruit from. And yet racial transformation is a non-negotiable imperative on all counts. So for the years 1999 - 2002 our preoccupation is the incredibly difficult business of tackling racial transformation of the Fund with Sipho Mkizhe providing the lead; which role he has been especially assigned to by Minister Maharaj as an adjunct to my letter of appointment. His life is made especially difficult as the Mokasa clique, supported, by Kgomongwe and Ms "X", push a new concept of "demographics".

In terms of this new found concept there will be no peace until the staff of the Fund mirrors the racial composition of the country. So, if Indians represent 2.5% of the general population, staff must not comprise more than 2.5% Indian. The fact that Indians and Coloureds are defined, for employment purposes, as Black in our labour statutes, under an infamous "extended definition of Black," is completely immaterial. In terms of "Employment Equity", a new legislated dogma, Whites, Coloureds and Indians are not to be "over-represented" in the Fund.

Things heat up as regards our Cape Town office. Coloured folk are a huge majority in the Western Cape Province. What does the doctrine of "demographics" say about this? The answer is that application of the doctrine is to be national, not provincial. So Black domination that is countrywide must also apply to Cape Town! My entreaties that this approach simply perpetuates the central culture of the apartheid regime, to determine and ascribe human rights and privileges in terms of ethnicity, are vociferously rejected and condemned. The letter and spirit of Martin Luther King's "I have a dream" speech is met with disdain as is Mandela's reconciliatory philosophy. Our new president Thabo Mbeki and his "I am an African" attitude is king. It becomes incredibly difficult to distinguish "transformation" from a form of localized "Pan-Africanism".

The Fund was already a repository of racial tension. This escalates as we proceed with our exercise to "pack" it with Black faces. I had foreseen this and had made it a condition of my appointment that I have the facility to conduct "team building" workshops for the purpose of effecting racial reconciliation, closure on the past and adopting a new found philosophy under the concept of *ubuntu,* in which acceptance of difference and merit are the two sides of the new currency in which we deal. As the workshops start their noble purpose is immediately subverted and they are turned into bitter occasions for the escalation of race hatred and division. Eventually we are forced to abandon the whole program.

Ashraf Ebrahim, our brilliant Claim Executive, resigns for the second and final time. On the first occasion the Board had entreated him to return. When he did, Ms "X" made this an issue in an executive management meeting, implying that he must be some sort of stooge. With chilling emphasis, Ashraf subjected her to a lecture that she was out of line on any number of counts and that, if her machinations were intended to be intimidatory, she should never forget that, not for a moment was he afraid of her and her kind. However he has now had enough. Whatever it may have been that Thabo Mbeki meant, in his speech "I am an African", it now all seems so glib and divorced from reality. The Fund has just lost a huge chunk of its intellectual capacity at executive management level and in terms of what is required in the public interest.

Despite the climate I doggedly pursue small but important reform. The first of these is to conceive, devise and implement what we call "Patient Outreach". Under the system the Fund, instead of paying out cash to a crash victim to fund future medical costs, had been providing written guarantees (called "undertakings") to pay for such costs as and when they occur. The new unit soon confirms that there are many victims who, on account of poverty and ignorance, are not utilizing their undertakings. Some are wasting away and dying as a result, even though entitled to full first rate medical treatment. Patient Outreach, staffed by qualified nurses and social workers goes out to help these people use their guarantees.

Secondly I continue a pilot project, that I started whilst still branch manager of the Cape Town office. The project is designed to test the efficacy of mediation/arbitration, as an alternative dispute resolving mechanism, to replace the present highly adversarial, protracted and expensive litigation mode.

Thirdly, I formed a litigation department, comprising the most talented legal staff, dedicated to arresting the dreadful situation regarding litigation, in which the Fund was awfully immersed at incredible cost to the country and routine wastage of the time of the superior Courts. The unit was headed by Lyndsey Steel whom I recruited for her exception abilities and skill in MVA law.

Fourthly I replace the White dominated panel of attorneys who represent the Fund in the now innumerable Court cases the Fund is involved in. This issue is a "hot potato" and I receive representations from Maluleke who heads the Black Lawyers Association (BLA) and an Indian female executive of the National Association of Democratic Lawyers (NADEL) based in Durban. The latter is extremely emotive in advancing the point that I need to understand that *"not all Blacks are real Blacks"*.

My stance is that the issue is resolved in terms of Black empowerment. Black empowerment only occurs if those who are still disadvantaged on account of the historical effects on their ethnicity are now empowered. It simply cannot mean that those who have overcome that disadvantage must be further "empowered", i.e., enriched. So the panel I appoint comprises, in the main, Black lawyers who show good potential but are still struggling.

Fifthly, I appoint customer service officers whose role is to assist victims who want to institute and pursue their claims on the Fund without having to resort to legal representation.

I also implement a policy that English is the *lingua franca* of the RAF. This is immediately resented by some White members of staff. A spokesman emerges. His name is Marius.

Marius: Mr. Greenland, this policy of yours is nothing more than yet another measure to demean, degrade and devalue the Afrikaner, his culture and his worth as a human being.

Me: Look - let us not see scorpions, snakes and spiders where there are none. It is really very simple. We have 14 official languages in this country. We cannot use all 14. We have to choose one of them as our working language.

Marius: But under the Constitution we are all equal.

Me: True. But we can't use all 14 languages. It is just impractical. I am sure you know that Botswana has a Black government - and the majority of people are Black - and that their language and culture is Tswana.

Marius: Yes - yes - so what?

Me: Guess what. English is the official language in Botswana. They have done this simply because it is convenient and practical.

Marius: Well if the Botswana people have agreed to that, it is their right. We Afrikaners have not agreed to English! [to him lack of consent is the checkmate]

Me: Well how do you think it should to work?

Marius: Each person should have the right to use his or her own language.

Me: You know that Ms "X" is a senior manager. She is Tswana. If she is going to insist on speaking Setswana, how is it going to work?

Marius: She can speak her language - and I can speak mine [he finishes strongly]

I am forced to terminate the pantomime that our conference has become. The great sadness about all this is that this young South African graduate and his constituency, are utterly convinced about the righteousness of the stance he is representing. What compounds the problem terribly is that this type of attitude helps fuel Black anger, resentment and need for urgent revolutionary change.

Faced with this type of attitude Black militancy is absolutely guaranteed.

---

85. National reform

On 19 November 1999 I lead a presentation to the Road Accident Fund Commission of Enquiry that has been set up to once again look into the road crash compensatory system. The main body of the presentation has been prepared by Advocate Asraf Ebrahim and Ms Lyndsey Steel. Ebrahim is no longer a Fund employee. The reason I have had to secure his help is the dearth of any meaningful internal contribution from the plethora of Fund managers, some of whom submit what can only be characterized as "wish lists". Kgomongwe can be excused. He knows virtually nothing about the issues at hand. Annamie Roux has been seconded to the Commission, so I don't have the benefit of her counsel.

Our presentation commences at 08h00 and ends at 17h40 hours with a 20 minute break for lunch. It is marked by searching debate on every aspect of the Fund, as a concept, as an entity, as a public service vehicle, its operational culture and mode - conducted mostly at the instigation of the Chairperson of the Commission, Judge Kathleen Satchwell. George Maluleke is in attendance. He is there as Chairperson of the MVA Committee of the Law Society. We had established a relationship characterized by friendship and collegial frankness.

At about 11h00 hours, Judge Satchwell passes a mini-judgment. In her view the presentation is the best that the Commission has received from any sector. Not long thereafter Maluleke leaves. This observation on her part comes as both a surprise and relief in what is a difficult forum of hard debate. The Fund is a mess, on every test, and present management, led by me, is accountable! *"The buck stops with you"* she insists. Technically she is right, on every count, even though the mess has been created over a period of some

47 years (the Fund started in 1942) and has defied the attentions of numerous previous Commissions of Enquiry.

In articulating the solution, I obviously put forward the essential characteristics of what is now, in effect, the Botswana model, which I helped devise over some five years. In this model the system is rid of its obviously objectionable weaknesses and transformed into a system in which its income is applied primarily for the benefit of crash victims. At present the ratio of transaction costs (costs of delivery) is about 45%, i.e., expenditure on lawyers, actuaries and other experts is almost the same as what is being spent on crash victims. What is more I issue a guarantee that in return for an income of no more than 19 -21 cents per liter of fuel the Fund will be fully functional within a reasonable time and rid itself of the multi billion Rand deficit in just 9 years.

The Commission is openly approving of the mediation/arbitration pilot project in that 95% of disputes are resolved in weeks rather than months/years, without the need for formal adjudication, and there is a saving of at least R80 million per annum guaranteed. The Commission members are later visibly touched when Advocate Mathipa Theledi, who heads the Patient Outreach unit, makes a presentation on what we have found and the utter human misery we have been able to alleviate.

Judge Kathleen Satchwell visited the Botswana Fund. She was impressed. This included publicly suggesting that Regina Vaka, whom I had groomed, trained and mentored, then General Manager of the Botswana Fund, should be recruited as CEO of the RAF. When her Commission finally produced its report in 2002 there was a huge convergence between its recommendations and what I, with the able assistance of Asraf Ebrahim and Lyndsey Steele, had proposed on behalf of the Fund on 19 November 1999.

86. The firm[1]

However, the intervening period is to prove traumatic. A new Board is appointed. It includes Christine Qunta, who at her interview before the Parliamentary selection committee, chaired by Advocate Kgomotso Moroka

---

[1] *The Firm* is a 1993 legal thriller film directed by Sydney Pollack, and starring Tom Cruise,··· http://en.wikipedia.org/wiki/The_Firm_(1993_film)

SC[1], stated words to the effect - " ... *look I know nothing about the MVA Fund and MVA - but I am here because I was asked - "*

Qunta, and two other members, are to go on and later take out a full page advert in the Sunday Times, in praise of Thabo Mbeki, our new President, at personal cost estimated at R14, 000 each. In his book, "Architects of Poverty", published later in 2009, Moeletsi Mbeki[2], brother to the President, is to comprehensively make out the case that South Africa is failing on account of becoming encumbered with a new *"elite"* class of Black people. The new Board also includes George Maluleke, head of one of the biggest MVA law firms in the country.

Carte Blanche, a program screened weekly, broadcasts an exposé of the obvious gross conflict of interest situation that Maluleke is in. It is to no avail, as the new chairman of the Board, Advocate Kessie Naidu SC, against truth and good conscience, brazenly defends the indefensible and insults the intelligence of a whole nation in saying that Maluleke's verbal disclosure of the conflict of interest was sufficient compliance with good governance and functional integrity imperatives.

At its very first meeting, Minister Abdulla Omar arrives and, among other things, appeals to the Board to work with the Acting CEO (me). He pointedly laments the fact that, it is now well known, that there are board members who take seats on boards to serve sectarian and other interests instead of the public interest.

At the very next meeting the minutes of what he, the Hon Minister had said, are rejected out of hand as being incorrect in a resolution led by Qunta and Naidu. The Board secretary, Hermann Karberg (White), a person of exceptional conscientiousness is summarily replaced with Lawrence Mafolo (Black). In this small but brutal way Naidu is there to start delivering on a passionate promise he made in lobbying support for his appointment as Chair in the first meeting. He articulated his credentials as an agent for *"Black Empowerment"*.

---

[1] **"It must be in the genes. Moroka**, a mainstay at SA's new businesswomen's elite, is the daughter of empowerment pioneer Nthato Motlana. She is also married to a descendant of one of the founding fathers of the ANC". Per SA's MOST POWERFUL WOMEN IN BUSINESS. Financial Mail.
http://secure.financialmail.co.za/04/0430/cover/coverstorybl.htm

[2] **Moeletsi Mbeki** is a journalist, businessman, political commentator and brother to Thabo Mbeki, President of South Africa after Nelson Mandela.

The agenda I had prepared, designed to focus the Board's attention on a program of reform, is disregarded in its entirety and Naidu announces that the Board is proceeding, in secret session, from which all management, including me as the Acting CEO and accounting officer of the Fund, is excluded. He then issues a press statement lamenting the parlous state of affairs at the Fund advancing generalized details which he largely ascribes to deficiencies on the part of management. His Board goes on to be interventionist and fix things up. Statements of support for his agenda are elicited and published from various spokespersons in the legal fraternity. The Naidu firm has arrived and it means business.

From that moment my role as Acting CEO of the Fund effectively ceases as Naidu takes over, in a program of micro managing, just about everything. This starts with the commissioning of a *"forensic audit report"* by an obviously onside Black audit firm selected, in effect, by Qunta. Its auditor, one Barend Peterson, who is due to write the final report, is patently uncomfortable in the role assigned to him.

There is a subtle but important difference between auditing and fault finding. So he wants to know all about the "soft issues", regarding disunity at management level. I point out to him that there is a difference between lack of cohesiveness and disunity. Lack of cohesiveness was unavoidable given the historical facts, including the bad business of Kgomongwe having been at first promised, then denied, the CEO post, the specialist nature of the Fund and the wide differences in perceptions of what it is as an entity and what it should be doing. To that end Kgomongwe, Mkizhe and I subscribe a substantive statement making this clear. Kgomongwe is then secretly flown to Cape Town, as part of forensic report brief, where he secretly recants on the issue of unity. It is all very amateurish; but pernicious in its nefarious intent.

In addition, *ad hoc* contracts are entered into with exclusively Black advocates to *"assess the situation"* in the Fund. This lucky group includes one of Naidu's colleagues from the Durban Bar and, surprise, surprise, Advocate Moroka who had chaired the committee that selected the Board members. Each walks off with a contract fee of about R90, 000. The forensic report is presented to management at a special Saturday morning meeting held at a Midrand hotel. It contains nothing that is not already known and which management would have quite enthusiastically particularized to the Board had it asked. Absent is any evidence of what contribution the group of advocates had made, even though Naidu claims that this is included in the report. However it does include an important finding that has nothing to do with forensic science - Greenland has failed to unite Executive management".

Prefacing my stance with the statement credited to George III –

> "the role the King is required to play is not a post but a predicament"

it is all too easy for me to rubbish the report. In a written reply I characterize a good chunk of the contents as fatuous rubbish and quite easily prove it. It is so susceptible to scorn being poured over it that that I am able compile a nine page table of innumerable typos, bad grammar, syntax errors, repetitiveness and mistreatment/confusion of issues. I write a letter of protest to the Minister. He calls me in and assures me, in a voice of great passion, that he will not allow unfairness. The letter is reproduced –

Thursday, 01 March 2001

(delivery by hand)

Dear Minister

Forensic Audit Report

Post of CEO - Road Accident Fund

Enclosed is my response to a forensic audit report compiled by a Mr. Barend Peterson of Skonki Sizwe Ntsaluba Inc. It is respectfully submitted to you on account of the extreme importance of the matter in principle and on account of the consequences.

1. The report is remarkable for presenting with the following components:

a) An ill disguised but hopelessly flawed attempt to discredit me.

At the core of this is a strategy of "divide and rule". It had been correctly realized that if executive management stood by me on the central issues the agenda must fail. In the result the report is preoccupied with demonstrating a divided executive management with me, as Acting CEO, being pilloried with responsibility for mismanagement. (However see 3 below.)

b) A total absence of revelations on fraud, corruption and poor controls other than melodramatics of what was already known to and being addressed by management. This despite extensions having been afforded to the auditor.

In fact, the Board was compelled to insist that the auditor be sent away and return with "concrete" findings on the issue of fraud.

2. In short, the report presents as a rather naïve "hatchet job" and largely fails on its own stated mandate.

3. The strategy to discredit has failed in that you will note, in particular, that the Human Resources Executive, displaying exceptional adherence to principle and integrity, has emphatically given the lie to the adverse findings on me in the report, describing the ploy as "mischievous and misplaced". (see Annexure 6 of my response.)

4. A question that necessarily arises is why this perverse attempt to discredit and mislead? It is patent that Peterson is seeking to purposefully influence the process of selecting a CEO, which process is in its final phase.

5. In the circumstances you will excuse me for advancing the observation that if the Board were to be adversely influenced by this fatuous nonsense, and this should present as highly improbable, it will destroy the uberrima fides required of the Board in its recommendation to you required by section 12 (1) (a) of the Road Accident Fund Act No: 56 of 1996.

6. I take the opportunity to advise you with the clearest of conscience that the Fund has not been mismanaged under my tenureship. See Annexure 1 of my response, jointly subscribed by executive management, in setting out the realities of the situation. Certainly, as consistently advised before, there have been significant problems presenting in a climate of continuing crisis. However by the time the present Board took office a plateau of reasonable calm and stability had been achieved.

7. In particular there can be no doubt that if important operational processes that I have initiated are carried through the Fund will, in the foreseeable future, shed its crisis mantle and present as existing for the public benefit on both a subjective and objective test. All that is required is support organizationally and legislatively. As regards the latter Judge Satchwell observed that our submissions were the best and most intellectually stimulating of all the submissions received.

8. You should also forgive me for observing further that it will necessarily be the position that in the process of putting integrity and the public interest first I will have fallen foul of those whose personal interests were affected. It is not being melodramatic to proffer this as a possible explanation for the Peterson report. I respectfully request an audience with you at your earliest convenience.

Yours truly,

C N Greenland

Acting CEO

Naidu is quite unable to take issue with me on the merits, so in the meeting, he resorts to taking extreme objection to my 9 page rubbishing of the report for its bad grammar, typos etc. He unashamedly tries to stir up racial passions by characterizing my stance as being in contempt of a previously disadvantaged Black whose first language was not English. Peterson is not Black, he is Coloured and speaks English fluently. This pathetic product of fertile mischievous minds is never published, even though it costs the public over R1.3 million as a fee to the auditors.

I am soon completely marginalized. I am never consulted even though I am the accounting officer for the Fund, under rules of governance. Naidu holds secret meetings, at undisclosed venues, even though the Fund has its own board room. Then he issues directives. These are mostly concerned to ensure the awarding of contracts under what is called "affirmative procurement". He is incensed with the hitherto lack of Black empowerment and, coming out of yet another closed meeting, he dresses Mkizhe and I down saying - *"You would never believe Black people have been running this Fund."* When we produce the year on year record of the credible transformation of the racial composition of the Fund, as "charity begins at home", he is disdainful in according us no credit whatsoever.

He quickly demonstrates what he means by Black Empowerment. In an open Board meeting, he issues the following directive -*"Mr. Secretary - please approach Advocate Dukada and request him to furnish a written quotation as to how much he will charge the Fund to provide a feasibility report on the Fund opening an office in the Eastern Cape".* The Advocate is a colleague of Naidu's from the Durban Bar. He is also a Board member, sitting and present in the meeting Naidu is addressing! This brazen example of insidious corruption, at worst, and clear breach of good governance, at the very least, is serenely accepted by all present as perfectly proper. It is hardly surprising. At an earlier meeting Qunta had undertaken to produce a paper on corporate governance. What she then produced was remarkable only for its utter superficiality.

Naidu is aware that the Commission is approving of the mediation/arbitration project. So it is agreed that it be rolled out nationally, after appropriate refinement, in the light of experience. A tender is put out. However, an award is vetoed by Naidu, as he is dissatisfied with the short listed candidates, despite the fact that they have past mustered the stringent criteria set. The tender is published again. Again he vetoes it. In the result a tender is never awarded. This; despite the Minister writing on 13 Sep 2000 –

```
"Thank you for your letter of 11 September 2000 enclosing
copy of presentation referred to.

I fully support the use of alternative dispute resolution
mechanisms in an endeavour to finalise long outstanding third
party claims.

I look forward with interest to hear the views of the Board."
```

To this day [2010] mediation/arbitration presents only in the Western Cape as a continuation of the *"pilot project"* I initiated in 1998. A national model remains outstanding. It becomes an entrenched practice to log-jam superior Court rolls with RAF matters and then settle them at the very last moment, usually on the day of scheduled hearing. In nearly all instance the RAF pays for the accumulated fees of both legal representatives and their experts. The financial cost to the country sounds in Rand billions.

The day-to-day situation in the Fund becomes an intolerable hot-bed of division, intrigue and dismal work ethic. When I institute a system to measure performance the reaction is bad as almost all the managers, pressured by the staff they lead, take a non supportive stance. In this exercise I find that there is an incredible wide divergence in performance. The best performing branch, by a long way is Cape Town. The worst, is the branch headed by Ms "X". Sylvia Griebenauw, a claims handler in Cape Town, assesses about 15 claims cases per month on average. The average for Ms X's branch is just 1.5 claims per month. The Fund is being infected by the agents of dysfunction, propagating a culture of entitlement without a corresponding service delivery ethic. I feel like an outsider speaking in a foreign tongue, conveying a foreign message - regarded as false.

The stage is reached where the Mokasa camp follow through on their threat to render the Fund ungovernable. One morning everything is brought to a halt as the Black staff conducts an "anti Greenland" demonstration, chanting, singing and toyi- toying in the manner that South Africa is notorious for.

Ms "X" smugly informs me that I should understand that they do not understand why Swanepoel and van Oudtshoorn *went all the way to Botswana to go and carry you on their backs to South Africa*. *"Maybe - "* I reply *"they felt the same as the lot who must have carried Gary Teichmann, our Zimbabwean born Springbok rugby captain"*.

Minister Omar calls me in and informs me that he has spoken to Naidu, a person for whom he has a high regard on a account of his contributions during the struggle. He has intimated that Naidu and I should have a good relationship. He is pleased when I later inform him that, in consequence of his approach, Naidu has invited my wife and I on a cordial visit to Durban.

Later I simply cannot bring myself to report to him that, on our arrival in Durban, Naidu gave us a telephonic "run-a-round" and finally stated that he was too busy to meet with us. Pam and I believed that Omar should be spared this display of "yet again" contempt.

In the meantime, Judge Satchwell bombards the Fund with requests for explanations on every aspect of its composition, operational culture and mode. Later her attentions shift to questions about the Board. Naidu is concerned. He engages a law firm to respond to the questions so as to ensure, as many accused persons also seek to ensure, that he has his lawyer.

It is notable that this supposed stalwart of Black Empowerment chooses a White law firm, Wertheim Becker Attorneys, when his own neck may be on the block.

The firm is the employer of his son.

---

87. The beginning of the end

My acting term comes to an end. A selection process for the appointment of a CEO is run. Naidu chairs the Committee. However, on the day Kgomongwe and I are interviewed, he is absent and the committee is chaired by Maluleke. Maluleke is Kgomongwe's attorney. He has recently acted for him in a failed attempt to make a case against the Fund, based on how Kgomongwe had been treated in being promised and then denied the post of CEO.

The whole thing is a sham. It is a complete and brazen sham of a process if only for the reason that Maluleke is in a complete conflict of interest situation. Despite the fact that Kgomongwe's profile has little that matches the requirements of the post, his criminal conviction for drunken driving and the excellent credentials of other candidates, including senior advocates, Kgomongwe is confirmed as the new CEO. Again Carte Blanche's lamentations are to no avail. The Minister writes me the following letter –

Dear Judge Greenland,

19 April 2001

Now that the two year period of your acting appointment as CEO of the RAf has come to an end, I would like to record my appreciation for the services which you rendered as Acting CEO, both during the period of office of my predecessor, Mr. Mac Maharaj and myself.

You rendered valuable services in you capacity as acting CEO under very difficult circumstances. I express appreciation for this.

I also enjoyed your respect and co-operation at all times and for this also I would like to thank you.

I know you will always be available to render assistance to the Fund.

With your experience and dedication, you will continue to be of great help and your service is appreciated.

With best wishes to you.

Yours sincerely,

Abdulah Omar MP

Minister of Transport.

Picture of Chris Greenland, Farieda Omar, Palmira Greenland,
Minister Dullah Omar. 2001

I revert to my post of Claims Executive. A Finance executive, Duncan Anderson, is recruited. An Information Technology executive, Sello Mokale, is also recruited. Other senior posts are created and filled exclusively by Blacks.

Just as Kgomongwe had been an inconvenient inheritance to me as Acting CEO, I am now an inconvenient inheritance to Kgomongwe. In our executive management meetings there is a very clear division.

Mkizhe and I stoically stand our ground to be faithfully to that which is true, right, proper and in the public interest. The others, led by Anderson, vie with each other for Kgomongwe's favour. It is a truly nauseating business, as we go through the motions of managing the Fund when, in effect, we are grossly mismanaging it as a completely disunited team

I now head a department called Corporate Legal Services. I am doing my best to support Kgomongwe in his role as CEO.

To my mind what may be of assistance is a broadening of perspective and a *"think big, start small"* component to his emotional intelligence. So I convince him that what is also needed is a regional forum of Fund CEOs. The road crash problem is now a pandemic in the region. In every accident it is still human flesh that splits, human muscles that tear, human bones that shatter - whether the accident happens in South Africa, Botswana or Swaziland. All the countries in the regions have the fuel levy compensatory system. All are experiencing the same problems. It makes sense that a cooperative, consultative approach is adapted to reform. Kgomongwe is quite enthusiastic about the concept and I am given the green light to proceed.

The inaugural meeting of regional CEOs takes place at the Waterfront in Cape Town. It is attended by Botswana, Swaziland, Lesotho and South Africa. South Africa, as host, is required to take the lead. Moreover all the problems stem from a compensatory model that is a South African invention. Things become quite embarrassing. Eventually I am challenged to bring proceedings to an acceptable end when delegates intimate that *"being in Cape Town is wonderful - but there appears to be a lack of "discernible skills"* in our camp.

In May 2002 the RAF hosts a symposium at a hotel in Vereeniging on the Vaal River. It is intended to be consultative on the way forward for the Fund. It turns out to be a failure as representatives of the legal profession seize the opportunity to point out the RAF's many sins, real and imagined. The only high point is an address by Regina Vaka from Botswana, which proves captivating. Kgomongwe goes around mooting the idea that she "should be poached".

Maluleke contacts me and we meet for dinner at a beef house in Sandton. He sounds completely sincere in voicing an apology to me personally and saying *"we have made a very big mistake in appointing Kgomongwe"*. In lamenting the decision he expresses frustration that he will be unable to garner sufficient support from *"Kessie's Board"* to do anything about it. We also discuss the issue of reformation. He pointedly asks me what advice would I give the Minister if I were asked what to do about the Fund. I reiterate my commitment to what I had submitted to the Satchwell Commission. He is quite emotional in his response that - *"in that case we might as well scrap the Fund and adopt the American system of private insurance!"* He appears sincere in his stance. I am quite unable to agree. The American system is so bad that even George Bush made it a second term election promise to address the litigious environment in that country. He would have probably done so had he not become immersed in Iraq.

In such a situation those who are vulnerable will be got rid of. This is made absolutely clear by Qunta when we make a presentation to the Parliamentary Portfolio Committee. She openly says words to the effect that *"we will get rid of"* those in the Fund who are deemed to be unacceptable. After the meeting Maluleke comes to me and in lamenting tones says - "This women - Qunta - where does she get all this power from?" I take this as an oblique warning.

It is therefore hardly surprising when, in early October 2001 City Press, publishes a prominent article "Legal head of RAF in deep trouble". The article is structured to include words like "deep trouble", "could face possible deportation", "dubious", "mysterious" and a litany of inaccuracies all calculated to invite the reader to conclude impropriety on the part of my wife and I in having secured residency in South Africa.

It is obvious that the editor is in possession of correct information that we were indeed refused permanent residency. What they appear not to know, is that we subsequently succeeded in an application to be accorded citizenship instead, on the basis of right of descent as both my wife's father and my father were South African. The reporter, Elias Maluleke, had first phoned Botswana and put it to the General Manager, Regina Vaka, that I was known to be an agent for the apartheid regime; had been brought to South Africa to oppress Black people; was never a judge in Zimbabwe and had falsified my degree certificates. Her response was to assure him that Botswana does background checks on all ex-patriot employees and that *"we Batswana are very proud to be associated with Judge Greenland".*

In the next Board meeting Naidu makes sure that the matter is tabled as an agenda item. He could have, and should have, first asked me for an explanation before making it an issue before the Board. That the media publishes nonsense is nothing new. Qunta is smug in her stance *"that this is a very serious matter".* Led by her and Naidu the Board resolves that the matter must be investigated and the result reported o the Board.

After the next Board meeting, in which I presented a letter from the Director of Home Affairs, my family is in sombre discussion.

Pam: So how did the meeting with the Board go to-day?

Me: Not good

Pam: But surely you showed them the letter from Home Affairs. It states clearly that our citizenship was processed according to the laws of the country and that there was no impropriety.

Me: I certainly did that

Child: Did you ask them to issue a media statement correcting these lies?

Me: Oh yes - I certainly did that.

Pam: And - ..

Me: The reaction was not good. Naidu seemed disappointed. Qunta was incensed.

Child: What do you mean?

Me: Well she made out a case that it was well known that Home Affairs could not be trusted, that she doubted the authenticity of the document and would be having the thing checked out by her own contacts.

Pam: What are you saying? Is she saying that the clearance, signed by the Director of Home Affairs is lies?

Child: Yes mum - that is what dad is saying.

Child: So they are saying that you, as a judge, and mum, as a teacher, got our papers by fraud?

Me: They are saying more than that. They are saying that we are such criminals as to have the brazenness to falsify the evidence and cover it up.

Pam: Is Kessie Naidu not an advocate? Is it not the law that people are presumed to be innocent?

Me: Yes - Naidu is a senior advocate ... and the Board has another senior Advocate ... Dukada ... and Qunta is a lawyer

Child: So they want us to prove that we are innocent and when we do so they say we are liars as well - who is Kessie Naidu - who does he think he is?

Me: Kessie Naidu has an exceptional record for having acted for people who were being persecuted under apartheid and for championing the cause of people being victimized.

Child: So that is why he is now a big cheese ...

Child: And the other Board members - were they happy with this - surely not?

Me: Well they said nothing and Qunta, as usual, had her preach.

Child: Dad - why are they doing this - they already got rid of you as CEO and appointed a person who knows little MVA and has been convicted for drunk driving - what are they up to?

Me: I really don't know - it is impossible to work it out

Child: Dad - you should know that you are at risk - real risk - there is obviously an agenda - to get you out of the way.

Me: It certainly seems so. I cannot understand how lawyers like Naidu and Dukada can just tear up the presumption of innocence and insist that we must be real criminals.

Child: And you have the other Board members, all professionals saying nothing, doing nothing - whilst you are abused?

Me: Yes - they must have all experienced gratuitous abuse of human beings during apartheid. They know what it is like - and they sit there apparently comfortable with it - while Naidu and Qunta - who were once champions for victims - are now busy …

Child: Well they now have power - and in Africa power is everything

Child: And the Minister - where is he in all this?

Me: You read his letter thanking me and making it clear that he wants me to stay on at the Fund. He has also said, with some passion I might say, that he will never stand by and let unfairness take place.

Child: Well then you are OK.

Me: I would not bet on it. This lot has shown little regard for the Minister. He asked them to work with me. They flatly refused to do so. They even went so far as to resolve to increase their Board stipends whether the Minister likes it or not. I wouldn't be surprised if they have.

Pam: This is so bad - why you my husband - why us - what have you done to these people - ?

Child: Dad I think you are not wanted here - you were born in Zimbabwe - Naidu and gang don't like you - maybe they want their own mates sitting on top of the pile of money

Child: What I know is that people will always act to serve their own interests - it is not in their interests to have you around

Child: It is just like that Tom Cruise movie "The Firm". These people have power. You are the outsider and don't fit in their plans.

Pam: Well, Naidu showed us what regard he holds us and Minister Omar in when he snubbed us on our arrival in Durban on his invitation

Me: You know - it is strange - long ago a sangoma predicted all this … it would be my life he said - it would be the story of my life.

My family was right. In effect my wife and I were put on trial before a Board comprising professionals who presumably rely on Naidu (senior counsel), Qunta (lawyer) and Dukada (senior counsel) for guidance.

The culture of these "legal eagles" should have induced them to lead a stance that innocence is presumed until guilt is proved. It was patent; however, that such a noble principle as a presumption of innocence was furthest from their minds. I was required to prove our innocence. When I did, it was then openly postured by Qunta that the evidence I was producing was false. So not only had my wife and I obtained citizenship fraudulently, in Qunta's view, we were such resourceful criminals as to have the brazenness to falsify evidence. A supine timid Board, led by an unprincipled chairperson, allowed her to get away with this grossly insulting behaviour. The obvious question is - why? Board members comprised a cross-section of seemingly very good human beings. Most of the members were Black. Undoubtedly, to the man, they had fought to have the abuse of human beings stopped forever. Why were they comfortable with the open abuse of another human being?

The answer appears to be, at least in part, of being infected with a good dose of a malady soon to become manifest in South Africa - xenophobia.

One must compare this with the conduct of the NBFIRA Board[1] of Botswana on which I sit. It is chaired by Ken Matambo with Mmatlala Dube as Deputy. The Sunday Standard of Botswana published a sensational article that one of the executive managers, a Namibian citizen, had misrepresented her profile, was wanted in Namibia for nefarious conduct (providing salacious detail of dubious transactions) and that her employment stood to subvert the good relations between Botswana and Namibia. Without hesitation, or prompting, the whole of the NBFIRA Board took the stance that she was to be fully supported and protected until such time as evidence was produced to support the accusations. When proof of her innocence was produced the relief on the part of all members was tangible.

So I have won the first round. The Minister obviously senses something is afoot. He summons Kgomongwe and me to an audience with him in his office in Cape Town. He is quite clear in his message that he appreciates the fact that we are working together and expects this to subsist. Just as his appeal to the Board that it work with me was in vain; so too is this wish to prove a wishful hope on the part of a wonderful man, "who fought tirelessly for justice in an unjust legal system"[2] in the very twilight months of his life. Abdulah Omar MP is to die of cancer just one year later on 13 March 2004.

Things come to head when Naidu, Kgomongwe and I visit London in order to settle the Fund's reinsurance cover with the international market. The only reason that I am on the trip is that I am the only one of the three who has familiarity with this highly specialized business and has an association with the market going back many years.

---

[1] **Non Bank Financial Institutions Authority** – same as Financial Services Board in other countries

[2] See - http://wn.com/Dullah and http://www.communitylawcentre.org.za/omar-memorial-lecture

I have consistently taken a stance against the employment of Company "X" as RAF agents in the settlement of fees to the medical sector claiming for having treated crash victims. To my mind the arrangement constitutes a form of racketeering, at prejudice to the public, running into Rand millions. Naidu has been ambivalent saying nothing. It is known that Cyril Ramaphosa, senior member of the ANC and contender for the presidency is involved with the holding company. On our arrival in London, Naidu pointedly informs me that he has just been contacted by Ramaphosa. He does not say why. However I fully understand the message intended. I need to realize that powerful interests are in the mix and I better back off.[1]

The reality however is that years later, in 2007, my stance is to be vindicated when the High Court rules that the contract with Company "X" is irregular and it orders the company to pay back over R57 million plus interest. That however is on the distant horizon. Soon thereafter Naidu introduces me to a friend of his, now doing business in London. He then subjects me to a fatherly lecture on why and how we should "use our people", and that this man could be involved with our reinsurance. His fatherly lecture is returned with a polite lecture of my own. What he is proposing is simply not on. When the Fund pays for reinsurance, in this case R3.9 million, it has to be sure that the reinsurer, that it is paying, will be around for the next 30 or so years to meet any claim that may arise on account of an accident occurring this year. It cannot run the risk of having the reinsurer disappearing, or going under, in that time. For that reason the Fund was necessarily constrained to only dealing with the old established reinsurance houses under the auspices of world renowned Lloyds of London. Those houses will simply not deal with persons like Naidu's friend as the precious commodity of *"confidence"*, on which the market trades, is non-existent with this person whom they do not know. He looks at me in resigned frustration.

That evening Naidu invites Kgomongwe and me to another session with *"his friend Glen[2]"* on his RAF Fund expense account in the hotel bar. The happy evening ends after the following exchange -

Naidu: You know you chaps; it was such a pity that you both competed for the post of CEO

Me: Please don't dignify the thing. It was a sham in terms of a predetermined agenda. Merit was never the criteria.

---

[1] Note - There was nothing to indicate that Ramaphosa had anything to do with it

[2] **Glen** = Glenfiddich whisky

He accompanies me into London City. *En route* I elaborate on what I have said. I leave him in no doubt that, whatever his motives are, what he has done and is doing, simply fails a public interest test. We part company in London. It is the last time I am to have a face-to-face conversation with this man. I am not to know that he is intent on fulfillment, not abandonment, of what is a pernicious agenda that will soon rock me and my family in a truly shattering way.

On the morning of 16 April 2003 I reiterate, in writing, my stance on the Company "X" contract. Within an hour I receive a letter from Kgomongwe. That evening I phone Naidu and raise the contents of the letter with him. I put him on speakerphone, so my family is able to hear him. He flatly denies any knowledge about the matter. By the next day I am escorted out of the building on the written authority of Naidu.

In subsequent Court papers, Naidu is forced to reveal on oath that, after the London trip, he conducted a meeting at a secret venue where my personal and functional integrity were put in issue without my knowledge. He admits that he gave specific authority for what occurred on 16 and 17 April.

So ends my employment with the RAF of South Africa on the basis - not of misconduct - not of incompetence - not of dereliction of duty - not of breach of duty or contract - but on account of *"incompatibility"* - for being different - for being *the other*.

As with Cyril Ndbele, hounded out of office all those years ago in racist Rhodesia, for being a *"dangerous munt"*, I too was perceived as dangerous.

In the process the express wishes of Minister Dullah Omar, a struggle hero, were trampled on with complete disdain; and the general public was being visited with a mortgage sounding in Rand billions ... and escalating.

88. Murder for hire

By the end of May 2003 Minister Omar, on account of terminal illness, has been replaced by Minister Jeff Radebe. I learn on the grapevine that he has requested Kgomongwe to explain my departure from the Fund.

This induces a premonition in my eldest son. His premonition is not misplaced. On the morning of Wednesday 18 June 2003, I am sitting in my study when our domestic worker, Katrina, happens to see two armed intruders scaling our wall. She warns me. As I look through the window, I see them running past the two front doors to make their way around the house to the back door. These are professionals. They have done their homework. That is how they know that the front doors are locked and only the back door open, so as to afford Katrina access to the laundry. In my mind I do not have the slightest doubt what this is about.

Everything goes into slow motion. I rush to the bedroom, close the door, grab the gun-safe key, open the gun-safe, retrieve a pistol and re-open the door, just as the first of the intruders is turning from our kitchen into the passage leading to where I am. He is a young ever so good-looking adult. His facial expression starts to register surprise at seeing me drop the holster to the floor and lifting a pistol to point it at him. He is still bringing his armed hand around from behind the kitchen door post from whence he is turning. We both know that I have the advantage.

There is now enormous conflict between heart and mind. My heart says I cannot shoot this young man. But my mind tells me incessantly "if you don't wake up Greenland - you are gonna be dead - life is cheap in South Africa - they are going to kill you - and to society it will be just another killing - of so many ... " Analogous is what Andy McNab says at page 135 of his book "SEVEN TROOP" -

> "But the loudest sound of all was the hollering in my head:"
> I don't like this! But I know I have got to do it!"

In my mind's eye I even see an ever so small story relegated to an inside page of a newspaper titled "ex Zimbabwean judge shot dead in Pretoria suburb". No one will care tuppence!

So I lift and point the weapon only to then realize I had not cocked it. "You idiot!" I murmur to myself and cock the weapon as it remains pointed.

Now there is a huge problem. Katrina is making her way to escape via the main door, screaming with such intensity as to wake the dead. The problem is that she is in the line of fire. The first bullet in the weapon is hardnosed. At ten paces it will go through and through my assailant and hit Katrina. The nano seconds are ticking as I hesitate momentarily. I cannot baulk at shooting this young man or in another nano second he will have brought his weapon round and will undoubtedly shoot me.

Thank God I have the presence of mind to lower the weapon and fire at his lower torso. The sound of the shot is greatly amplified by the enclosed passage and there is an earth-shattering bang, as my assailant falls back into the kitchen, leaving only his feet exposed as a target.

The bang jolts me out of all my ambivalence. I am back at Llewellyn Barracks - I am an armed soldier - I have a gun - and I am going to kill these two goons stone dead. Without hesitation I rush to the study, half way down the passage, so as to close the gap in anticipation of the other assailant charging around the same bend that his friend has just fallen back in. It he does he will be "double tapped" (shot twice) in head and chest before he can even blink, as the range is now just three paces. He does not. Instead I see the feet of the first assailant pull back into the kitchen. I decide to wait.

A few moments later I see my second eldest son David, dressed only in his underpants, through the window. He is waving two hammers and shouting out *"come you bastards"*. He has thrown his wife, Irena, into their wardrobe, locked it and come out to take on evil. I am mad with panic and scream at him *"David - they will shoot you"*. Our son is in world where he will lay down his life for me.

As I leave my post I hear the sound of a distant shot. When I get to the front door I find Katrina standing at the open door, beckoning to armed neighbors who are arriving. When she sees me she collapses saying *"but - but - you are alive"*. She has assumed that the shot (she says she heard two shots) signified my execution. She had not been aware that, in terms of the premonition, my eldest son had ensured that his father had access to a weapon.

She explains that the intruders had forced the door open as she was attempting to lock it. The first one pushed her aside, paying scant attention to her screams, and had not even attempted to tell her to shut up. The second was being detained by our young bull terrier who he did not shoot so as not to alert me to their presence. It was clear to her that I was their target.

The bang created by the shot has traumatized our two dogs and we cannot find them anywhere. Eventually we find them hiding in the laundry. When the police arrive they inform us that the intruders escaped over our wall and chanced upon a neighbour, about to leave in his car with two young children. One of them shot our neighbour in the upper thigh. They made good their escape in the vehicle. The children noticed that one of the two was bleeding from the groin area. The car was recovered an hour later in Pretoria. It had blood on the seat and floor.

On 29 July 2003, I faxed Naidu the following letter.

```
Adv. H. K. Naidu S.C.
702 Salmon Grove Chambers
407 Smith Street Durban 4001
Tuesday, 29 July 2003
By Fax: 031 3011103
Advocate Kessie Naidu SC,
Re: Common Decency, Professionalism and Ethics
Humphrey Kgomongwe's Answering affidavit, as confirmed on
oath by you, constitutes a revelation setting out a saga in
which, despite the imperatives of common decency,
professionalism and ethics, you were apparently prepared to
oversee secret meetings at which I was made the subject of
```

discussion and agreement was reached impugning my personal and professional persona.

Central to this admission is the fact that the saga was superintended by you and, despite the professional imperatives attaching to you, personally and professionally, you were prepared to do this without the slightest regard for rules of natural justice, professionalism and common decency that would have enabled me to defend myself.

It is apparent that this saga culminated in a plot, then brazenly executed by Kgomongwe, in complete contempt of my rights and the imperatives of the Constitution and the Labour Relations Act with their insistence on substantive and procedural fairness. The intended outcome was to hurt my family and me, which result was achieved.

his whole business was/is unbelievably shameful, underhanded and pernicious in the extreme - assuming it is all true - which appears to be the claim.

Surprising is that apparently, such is your commitment to this unprincipled, unprofessional, unethical conduct, and having hitherto kept it all a secret, you are now prepared to admit the plot/agenda in a brazen attempt to defeat rectification by a Court of justice - or are we wrong on this?

In the circumstances we are entitled to an explanation of your conduct. Explain to us plainly and simply why: -

a) despite the fact that you had never known me you adopted a vindictive and hostile attitude towards me from the start?

b) you made every effort to discredit me and devalue my worth?

c) having made the City Press article, impugning the integrity of my wife and I a Board concern, you failed to issue a corrective statement once furnished with a letter from the Director of Home Affairs dispelling any questions about our integrity?

d) you denied me an increment for matters for which I was not responsible, knew nothing about, without affording me any opportunity to deal with your alleged concerns?

e) you failed to so much as acknowledge letters communicated to you in which I properly raised the issue of substantive and procedural unfairness on the salary issue?

f) you were prepared to superintend this plot to hurt my family and me?

In considering your reaction to our request I would refer you to the professional and ethical standards attaching to the calling of advocacy, those attaching to a Board and the standards required in terms of the particular rules governing conduct of members of the General Bar Council.

In addition I would refer you to the Constitution, which reads: -

Basic values and principles governing public administration

195. (1) Public administration must be governed by the democratic values and principles enshrined in the Constitution, including the following principles:

1. A high standard of professional ethics must be promoted and maintained.

2. - - - ..

3. Good human-resource management and career-development practices, to maximize human potential, must be cultivated.
"

You should consider also that such gratuitous victimization of other human beings cannot remain un-redressed.

I bring to your attention also the fact that very recently an attempt on my life was made by two armed intruders. Regrettably a neighbour was shot and seriously injured by the intruders when affecting their escape.

Since you are the only person I know who is apparently so ill disposed towards me as to be prepared to actually occasion me and my family real harm I am compelled to ask you whether you were in any way party to this attempt?

The Hon C N Greenland.

He never replies.

89. Animal farm

On Monday, 19 November 2003 thereafter, on invitation, I make a presentation to the Parliamentary Portfolio Committee on Transport.

In summary the evidence given included the following shocking revelations —

· So bad is the risk profile of the RAF that the international reinsurers, based on London, have upgraded the premium from R3.6 million to R100 million [in simple language, that is what Naidu has just cost the SA public by shedding Greenland]

· Having failed to attend to the matter, the Fund was actually uninsured at a time in history when it was most exposed and vulnerable - during the African Union Conference in Durban and the World Summit on Sustainable Development

· Fund is now a completely dysfunctional bloated bureaucracy with the general public having the pay twice as much for a one third of service with the claim backlog having trebled

· Over the past two years the backlog of unprocessed claims trebled from 120 000 odd to over +- 350 000

· this deterioration includes a doubling of internal capacity and administrative expenses - from R125 million in 1999 to R237 million in 2002

· in 1999 the reinsurance premium was R3.6 million odd. By mid 2002 it had escalated to R100 million, an increase of some 2.7 thousand percent! This is not explained by an increase in the accident rate, which was only 7% per annum. Neither is it explicable in terms of deterioration in the value of the rand. It is explicable only in terms of what an incredibly bad risk international experts now agree the Fund represents

· despite approval by this very Committee, Judge Satchwell and a directive from the Minister nothing has been done to roll out mediation/arbitration with wasted costs to the public sounding in hundreds of millions

· new unworkable systems costing in excess of R39 million have been indulged in

· illegal practices have been employed

· an audit report lists 34 pages of problems sounding in actual financial prejudice of at least R93 million

· with R56 million irregularly paid over to Alexander Forbes

· at least R53 million wasted in incompetent handling of disciplinary matters

· Executive management is non-existent in that Kgomongwe has rid himself of the HR and Legal execs, the IT exec has been fired for corruption and the Finance Exec is on suspension for incompetence and corruption - leaving him only with a newly recruited Medical Exec.

By any test, this shocking situation represents a total collapse of an entity, in itself, and in its ability to deliver on its mandate.

The members of the Committee are extremely concerned and ask me what should be done. I remind them that it is their duty, as a national oversight authority, to start with commissioning a high-level investigation.

Jeremy Cronin, as chairperson, rules that the RAF has a right of reply. The RAF's spin doctor, head of corporate communications, concentrates on telling the Committee that Greenland's contract was terminated with the approval of the Board.

In such a situation, where the man is being played, and not the ball, human beings instinctively start to decide which side they should be on, and forget what their duty is. Although human beings are born as unique individuals, they spend much of their life wanting to be accepted by, and fit in with, others. Sight is soon lost of the smelly issue that needs to be addressed. People instinctively want to avoid smelly issues, especially if it may involve incongruence on their part with those who are powerful and connected, like the Board of the RAF. These are the dynamics that have forced societies to introduce legislation to protect whistle blowers.

The exercise soon deteriorates, losing focus on what duty demands. So when Jeremy Cronin, as chairperson says the magic words - *"we don't want to bring things like investigation into the equation - nobody wants the Fund to fail ... "*, committee members accept the invitation to adopt a herd mentality and drop, not open, the Pandora's box that is now before them.

The informant is simply not important enough. He lacks the currency that the exercise is now trading in. The RAF's spin doctor has made that clear. Cronin has endorsed it. Committee members are off the hook. They need do nothing. In this situation I am "the other", just as John Dean and Archibald Cox were, when Nixon fired them during the period that the cover up of Watergate was in full swing.

The Fund has already failed; completely by any test. It is functionally corrupt and needs massive intervention. This is the mess guaranteed as a result of the actions of the Naidu led board. These people are the new elite. Nothing happens, and the Fund fumbles to the prejudice of hundreds of thousands of road crash victims and at extreme prejudice to public funds sounding in the Rand billions.

Naidu and Kgomongwe go on a trip to New Zealand and Australia to supposedly garner information to help in the reform of the RAF. I receive a message, via the international reinsurance sector, that as regards their New Zealand visit *"it is quite difficult to decide whether or not their lack of interest in reform surpasses their ignorance of the system they are supposedly leading"*. On their return Naidu treats the Board to a 10-minute report. When the media complains, that a 10-minute report hardly justifies the expenditure of the trip, it is fobbed off.

Within two years Kgomongwe, and most of his gang are to be shed, as the Ministry struggles to cope with the mess started by Naidu, Qunta *et al.* Some members of Kgomongwe's firebrand supporters club, that organized the demonstration against me, are arrested for fraud on the Fund after they set up their own MVA law firm to exploit the results of their handiwork. The Minister fires the entire new Board, apparently for having failed to clean up the mess. In 2006 the High Court will set aside the whole Company "X" deal that was the final trigger for Naidu having me removed from the Fund. Judge Satchwell's sterling recommendations, handed down in 2002, are to remain on the shelf until 2009 when an attempt at some form of implementation is to occur. The reforms are challenged by the MVA sector of the legal profession at every turn, through 2010, and it takes a serious of Superior Court decisions to frustrate the challenges.

By October 2003, the country is awash with media coverage about statements allegedly made by ex Minister Mac Maharaj that National Director of Prosecutions, Bulelani Ngcuka, had been an apartheid spy. A commission of enquiry, headed by retired judge Jools Hefer, is instituted by President Mbeki. Naidu gets the plum job to lead the commission. Many voices question his suitability for this important and extremely sensitive duty. Obviously the implications are very far reaching for all concerned. It is to state the obvious that the commission must comprise persons of impeccable integrity - persons who can be trusted implicitly to be fair, reasonable and principled.

I fax through a submission on Naidu and Elias Maluleke, who is due to be called as a witness to the commission. I set out the conduct of both in regard to what occurred when I was employed at the RAF. As regards Naidu the sting of my attack is –

> "d) That Naidu can and will act unfairly and prosecute a secret agenda against a public official is established by his own admission on oath."

> The implications of State resources being expended in secret to victimize a subject in brazen disregard of the most elementary rules of common decency, fairness and other imperatives are self-evident and offensive in the extreme. Such conduct can be described as improper, unprincipled, under-handed, mala fide, disgraceful - the list is seemingly endless. I remain numbed at Naidu's admission on oath.

> In considering the temptation to dismiss my concerns, which are necessarily founded on subjective experience, I believe that one would have to be dismissive also of the following exhortation by Martin Luther King - "Injustice anywhere threatens justice everywhere"."

Nothing happens. I do not receive so much as an acknowledgment. I am the outsider – "the other". The new elite, "the firm", has little time, it would seem, for trivialities such as public interest, truth and justice. They have business to do, big fish to fry, as big as legendary struggle hero and co-liberator of this country - Mac Maharaj. In the ensuing proceedings, all witnesses who give evidence for Maharaj receive a savaging. Those against the man get sweetheart treatment. Mac Maharaj is to lament why he is being treated in this way. He should realize that on this farm he has been now cast in the role of Snowball. George Orwell[1] is smirking smugly in his grave.

On Friday 21 November 2003, the Mail and Guardian newspaper publishes an article titled "Road Fund in Disrepair" on its page 8.

90. Uncle Chris

As I leave the city, the road is bush and scrub with a high mountain range in the near distance. This topography changes rapidly as altitude decreases. A beautiful morning is soon transformed into a cauldron of searing heat. Outside an ocean of sand, pitted with some rocky outcrops, stretches to the far horizon. The air-conditioning system of the vehicle we are traveling in works hard to combat the heat. The road ahead is continually unmasked by a shimmering haze. This is the Namib Desert. I breathe a sigh of relief as a sign comes up - "Swakopmund - 15 kms". Just five minutes later, as I drive into this little coastal town everything changes. The transformation is incredible as the Namib Desert and its searing heat is instantly replaced by a cool, dank, grey blanket of a sunless sky. Swakopmund has all the appearances, smell, look and taste of many an old European town. The houses are all quaint, neat and seem to say - *"No - we are not old - not old really - we are just historical"*.

In no time at all I am through the town, and on the coastal road to Walvis Bay. Again there is an instant transformation as the whole scene becomes bathed in glorious sunshine. To the right is an endless expanse of the steel blue waters of the Atlantic, just meters away. I cannot resist the urge. After stopping I strip down and plunge in. The water is cold, very cold, but not the cold that numbs the body, freezes the mind and disheartens the spirit. It feels pure, uplifting, invigorating. As I drive on I am taken by the enrapturing presence of now world famous dunes on my left. They are majestic; they are

---

[1] ***Animal Farm*** is a dystopian allegorical novella by George Orwell.. The novel addresses not only the corruption of the revolution by its leaders but also how wickedness, indifference, ignorance, greed and myopia destroy any possibility of a Utopia. While this novel portrays corrupt leadership as the flaw in revolution (and not the act of revolution itself), it also shows how potential ignorance and indifference to problems within a revolution could allow horrors to happen if smooth transition to a people's government isn't satisfied.
http://en.wikipedia.org/wiki/Animal_Farm
Note - Maharaj was to regain favour with the advent of the Zuma government

timeless; they are simply sensational works of art in their composition, coloring and endless blend of intricacies and subtlety. To think that, but tiny grains of sand, have combined to present with such overpowering beauty. If only man realized how puny he actually is in the greater scheme of things.

Unable to work in my own new found country, South Africa, I spend the next four years in Namibia, as a technical advisor primarily concerned with reformation of that country's MVA system. This is at the instigation of Philip Amunyela, a former SWAPO cadre who saw action to liberate his people. Here I find a CEO, a Board, a Minister and Cabinet that are truly intent on ensuring that their MVA model will exist for the sole benefit of the general public and road crash victims in particular. My ideas find fertile ground to grow in the mind of a young somewhat overactive CEO, Jeremiah Lukas Muadinohamba, imbued with imagination, innovation and passion for the advancement of his people. Despite having to start from scratch, urged on and inspired by the Deputy Minister of Finance in particular, Hon. Tjekero Tweya, we attain the goal of developing a model that the technical advisor to the New Zealand Fund, industry leader to date, describes as unmatchable. He is South Africa born Professor Graham Hukins. When I present the draft reform Bill to him he says - *"Chris - I must tell you - apart from further small refinements - you cannot get it better than this"*. That Hukins is right is soon proved.

One morning in 2006 Namibia experiences the worst road crash in its history. 29 people are killed. Within 6 hours MVA Fund investigators (certified) are on the scene. Telephonically they communicate their findings. A decision is made and communicated to all concerned. From that moment the relatives of deceased receive help to redress the social harm that has accrued. Loss of support is provided from day one as if the breadwinner had not been killed. Funeral parlours are contracted by the Fund. The army is enlisted to provide air transport to ferry relatives on account of the vast distances involved. At an agreed date thereafter, all the dead victims are laid to rest. Not a single family member has suffered financial prejudice. Not one has had to seek or enlist help to alleviate their plight let alone claim on the Fund. The Fund, led by its passionate CEO, has addressed all the social harm that has accrued to survivors of the victims - seamlessly! We all feel so proud. Innovation, imagination and passion for the public interest has endured and conquered all!

Jerry organizes an all inclusive symposium so as to moot our reform ideas to all sectors consultatively. It is also attended by a Board member from the RAF, accompanied by the new Acting CEO, as Kgomongwe has been shed. I make our presentation, articulating the reform we imagine is now an imperative. Regina Vaka, from the Botswana Fund is outstanding in improving on it. All this is appreciatively received and endorsed by delegates except the chairperson of the local law society who condemns the proposals as no more than an attempt on the part of the Fund to save money at the expense of the road crash victims. This is, and continues to be, central to arguments advanced in opposition to reform by MVA lawyers in the region.

After the symposium, Namibia hosts a second meeting for the purposes of reviving the concept of a regional CEOs forum. Delegates are strongly supportive but the CEO of Swaziland, whose Fund I had visited on consultation, makes it clear that her Fund's support is conditional on *"Judge Greenland chairing the forum"*. She gives her reasons. If reform is central to the objectives then Greenland is naturally indicated on any test. She is supported by Botswana. Many nice things are said and commitment expressed. However that is the last time the issue receives any attention. On leaving, the acting CEO of the beleaguered RAF tells me that I will be hearing from him. That is the last I see, or hear from, this man. Events in South Africa take a revolutionary turn when the Minister fires the whole Board and appoints Jacob Modise as the RAF's substantive CEO. Now, some five years later, Modise regularly laments to the media the parlous state the RAF continues to find itself in. The more things have changed, the more they have not stayed the same, but gotten worse in our country.

In 2004 we were invited to a symposium hosted by the South African Fund, at a resort in Magaliesburg and led by Marissa Du Toit, for the purpose of implementing now overdue reform of the RAF. At the end attendees were asked to make closing remarks. A Dr Giba, who had been closely involved with the RAF, under the tenureship of Kgomongwe, in providing medical services, made an impassioned plea that my services be garnered urgently in assistance of their endeavours. In doing so she was simply, in effect, echoing the wishes of the late Minister Omar. Delegates from the ACC and Victoria, Australia, nodded approvingly. We had paid them a visit so as to inform our Namibia reform program, led by the Hon Tjekero Tweya. Senior Ministry officials asked for my business card. I never heard from anyone in South Africa.

Today the Namibia road crash compensatory model is unmatchable except perhaps as regards the very rich countries that can afford full blown social security. Even then the proactive nature of the Namibia Fund probably renders it superior. How was this achieved considering that it had a replica of the South African model and suffered from the same ills? In a nutshell, there was the political will to commit solely to the public interest. Then the expertise required was dispassionately garnered. It is also a critical reality that xenophobia is virtually nonexistent in Namibia amongst ordinary folk. A Namibian can speak four languages on average. Such folk have long since crossed the block of acceptance of the culture of others. This is despite the stoic insistence of the Basters, with their enclave town of Rehoboth, run as something of a bastion against all and sundry.

So in Namibia, and in the Fund, ethnic diversity was appreciated, not resented. A high point is when I attend an occasion to officially honour Frankie Frederick Namibia's legendary Olympic sprinter. The program includes a poem by a tribesman reciting the poem in Nàmá (Damara) a Khoekhoe language. It is spell binding and captivating as the poet strings together an incredible range of clicks in a milieu of sound that is always seductive, always soothing, always propositioning the soul itself. I cannot understand one word of it but have never heard anything more beautiful.

In Rundu I meet a local King. He radiates immense dignity. He sits me down and spends time making me feel welcome and appreciated. He explains that *"you should always be good to a stranger as there was a time when you too were a stranger"*. I later find this noble adage emblazoned on a mounted plaque in a small historical site near Walvis Bay. A high point is when I address the council of traditional leaders. To the man and woman they radiate a certain power; unpretentious but reverend and tangible to the senses. A warm wave of appreciative response meets my opening statement that - *"Today I am truly honoured - and my ancestral spirits are truly pleased - that their child is in the presence of the spiritual leaders and custodians of all that is the people of Namibia"*.

To the good folk of Namibia I am referred to as "Uncle Chris" in a spirit of affection and endearment. Typical is John Sindano, a young man of quiet disposition that masks a refreshingly clear and unencumbered intellect.

Sindano: Uncle Chris - what is on your mind?

Me: There are things that worry me.

Sindano: Well as long as it does not have to do with the way people think, those things will be less dangerous to mankind than even HIV/AIDS

Me: Well actually it is about the way we seem to think in this region. The reason why the journey of life brought me here to Namibia had much to do with exactly this issue.

Sindano: What do you mean?

Me: You see at a certain point I was seen as being different to what was required of a leader because it was concluded by the empowered camp in South Africa that I did not think like a Black

Sindano: I will never know what that means. Do Black people perhaps think in binary code? [he says in amusement] But what is important is that, if people are going to be classified on the basis of their thinking, it means that we already have thought policing and thought police[1].

Those who go around labeling others like that must be thought police. Such people propagate new tyrannies.

Me: Hmnnn - organically induced thought policing. And what about incompatibility as a reason for shedding a member of staff? I think it is just a convenient way of getting rid of a person whose personal and functional integrity you cannot fault.

Sindano: It is more serious than that. Such nonsense will be natural to a system of categorizing people because of their thinking. The fact that you are competent, skilled and performing becomes irrelevant. Thought policing gets you labeled as a threat to a herd mentality. That is how victimization starts. Incompatibility, like patriotism, is a refuge for a new breed of scoundrels[2]. They operate in terms of corrupt patronage. Incompatibility simply means you do not qualify for patronage.

Me: Ah - here comes Jerry [We put the big man in the picture]

Jerry: The problem is people need peace of mind - peace of mind is the key.

Me: You may have a point Jerry - my hostel master, Richard Brown, used to say that "violence is the last resort of a frustrated mind". He included non physical violence in this statement.

Jerry: Look here my brother - In Namibia we say to you - "we are together - we are the same - aah - but we are from each other!"[3]

I also meet a young man, brown like me, who sits me down and tells me a story. This story, like so many great stories, is essentially romantic at its core. It is about a Greek man who arrived in then South West Africa about 35 years ago. He settled down in the small but developing town of Otjiwarongo, situated in the Central Northern district. Like early Rhodesia the country was

---

[1] **The Thought Police** (*thinkpol* in Newspeak) is the secret police of Oceania in George Orwell's dystopian novel *Nineteen Eighty-Four*.
http://en.wikipedia.org/wiki/Thought_Police

[2] **"Patriotism** is the last refuge of a scoundrel." Boswell tells us that Samuel Johnson made this famous pronouncement that patriotism is the last refuge of a scoundrel on the evening of April 7, 1775. Johnson was indicting false patriotism
http://www.samueljohnson.com/refuge.html

[3] This statement is credited to **Sam Nujoma**, Founding Father of SWAPO who liberated Namibia

undeveloped but full of promise. And like so many White settlers in Rhodesia, he fell in love with, and took unto himself a Black woman with whom he settled down as man and wife. This White man and the Black woman had four very brown children. The young man, now facing me, is Franco the eldest.

Franco: You know Uncle Chris, we were a very happy family.

Me: And quite a beautiful one too; judging from your sister. She is absolutely stunning.

Franco: One moment we were one family - happy - with everything; the next moment it was all gone - and we had nothing.

Me: Well you know a business can fail. I must say it is rare that a Greek business goes under. They tend to support each other in hard times. It is their way. But I suppose there were not many Greeks in Otjiwarongo those days.

Franco: No Uncle Chris, it was not about the failure of the business. Our father made a lot of money when he sold the business. He was, and still is, a very rich man.

Me: Oh - then I don't understand '

Franco: [his eyes glaze over, veiled in sadness] Our father left us. He just disappeared one day. No goodbye. No nothing. I was about 11 years old. The man left us to starve.

Me: Left you - left his whole family - ?

Franco: Yes - with the youngest still a baby .. the man just abandoned us - left his Black wife and his children - and went back to Cape Town - as if we never existed. We suffered terribly.

Me: And did you not ever see him again?

Franco: Of the children only I have seen him. I went to Cape Town to attend University. So I went to see him - to see if he could at least help me. University is very expensive. He is a very wealthy man.

Me: and - - ..

Franco: Uncle Chris, the man told me straight - straight to my face that he could only help me a little bit - just a little bit - but that he could not help me more as that would mean that he was helping me more than his own son, who had not even made University.

Me: What do you mean - help you more than his own son - are you not his son?

Franco: He explained that he has a White wife and children. We are his "other children. I am his other son".

Franco certainly made a huge impression on me. He radiated goodness. When he smiled his whole face lit up and made you feel that man is indeed a beautiful species. A quite unassuming disposition belied an intellect of diamond hard integrity. This was proved at one of the now innumerable management "workshops" that are conducted in our region. When it was his turn to make a presentation he ended it by saying, in voice and tone that had no hint of preachiness –

```
"  - if it is not right - do not do it
   -   if it is not true - do not say it"
```

Those words, and the manner of their saying, like true genius, were so telling in their simplicity as to strike a chord in the heart and mind of every delegate, displacing everything else that had been mouthed, trotted out and prescribed before. Delegates could talk of nothing else. For all of us it was a defining moment, never to be forgotten. Franco is now a magistrate in Namibia. I am more than certain that, whatever else, Franco is a repository of justice.

A summarized explanation of the Namibian road crash compensatory model is set out below. Its motto is "Peace of Mind", as Jerry had so passionately insisted on. In simple terms the model is configured to perform on a logical functional continuum represented as follows –

a) Road crash and injury prevention. The TAC and ACC experiences have shown that annual investment in this in terms of a consensually agreed plan, based on experience, is the "smartest investment" such a Fund can make in terms of the returns achieved as a value of the reduction in costs of claims.

b) Road crash response. Victims are picked up from the crash site without avoidable delay under a Muadinohamba concept named *"Kwik Response"*.

c) Treatment. This is then timeously given. Trauma victims are treated in accordance with a "Treatment Plan" consensually arrived at. So too as regards those requiring rehabilitation. Loss of income plan is implemented immediately as if the accident had not occurred. Dependents are also picked up and supported as if the breadwinner were still alive.

d) Those permanently disabled receive lifelong "quality of life enhancement" in their own homes, with family members being trained as care givers.

Hon Chris Navavie Greenland

A journey ...

A journey that started over three years ago has just come to an end
and the Fund enters into a harvest season of what you have sowed. The wisdom
you have instilled in its people is the seed for the future of the Fund as the
journey continues.

As you take a walk in the journey of life, remember to pick the flowers amongst
the thorns. It is your endurance through the thorns that will determine whether
you will get to pick the flowers.

May your new journey take along the flowers that will always
bring laughter and joy into your life and that of others.

May the dawn of a new day make a difference
in the lives of people you meet along your journey.
As for the Fund you were part of the difference.

The MVA Fund Board, CEO, Management and
the entire MVA Fund Team wishes you a great journey.

Keep walking, the future is now!

MVA Fund

The Motor Vehicle Accident Fund of Namibia
Driven to lend a helping hand!

CEO   Chairman

Plaque presented to me on leaving Namibia

---

91. The angel of death v Fuyane

It is Good Friday 2007. I am on my way home from Namibia to spend the
Easter weekend with my family. I have had a very bad night and decide to
have the problem attended to at Windhoek

private hospital before boarding the plane home. My throat is painful. The
doctor on duty asks me, as all doctors do as regards sore throats, to open wide

and say *"aah"*. He prescribes and intravenous antibiotic and lozenges to be sucked. *"In an hour or so you should be just fine"* he says confidently.

He is wrong - deadly wrong. His diagnosis is wrong. The prescribed treatment is inappropriate. In an hour, as I board the plane, I am in a very bad state, suffering anaphylactic shock, with breathing becoming increasingly impaired. I push the seat back, say my *"Hail Marys"* and keep myself alive for the one and half hour flight to Oliver Thambo airport, South Africa.

On being picked up, by my dear wife, I am barely able to speak. Somehow I convey to her that she get me to the hospital at once. The situation goes from bad to terrifying as I feel my air supply suddenly cut off - as surely as one cuts off water draining from a sink by inserting the plug.

It is quite impossible to describe what I feel, on realizing that I have just taken my last breath, - that my access to air has just been cut off - gone forever - that I will never breath again - and that this means death - certain death. I start my *"Hail Mary ..."*

Just as panic starts to well up inside me I am overtaken by a wave of calmness. It envelopes me from deep within and a silent voice seems to say *"do not fear my child - I am with you - you are safe - do not fight for air - trust in Me - "*

All panic and fear leaves me, and I relax and wait. I simply wait without seeking air - without seeking to breath. Then I feel the air making its way, forcing its way, past the obstruction that is in my throat. As it does so, a sound is produced, best described as an admixture of a death rattle and a church organ, as my chest reverberates and amplifies the sound of air squeezing past the obstruction, down my wind pipe and into my chest. Pam's eyes go as wide as saucers and she floors the peddle, breaking the speed limit and jumping red lights. With my eyes I try to convey the message to my dear wife that it is all right - that I am safe. I feel detached as I too listen in wondrous amazement at the sound of what is now my breathing.

Within an hour I am on the operating table at Pretoria East Hospital being tended to by a medical team hastily assembled by a Dr Wilken. The anesthetist puts the mask over my face and commands me to inhale. This time I make the effort. Soon I have drifted off into another world in which I am once again in the custody of the Sergeant at Arms and being escorted into a huge Courtroom. In panic I recall that Sir Hugh Beadle had said - *"Sergeant - take him away - and I hope to never again see him in my Court!"*

However as I look up I see that this time it is not presided over by Sir High Beadle, as had happened all those years ago, not by any judge, but by a lady. She is standing tall and imposing, scales of justice in her left hand and a sword held high in her outstretched right hand. Her exquisitely beautiful face has a blindfold across her eyes. It is Lady Justice, international symbol of justice. I see her lips move and the words she utters come like rose petals, caught in bright sunlight, floating across a vast valley, to fall onto my eardrums, infuse themselves and permeate through to my brain.

Lady Justice: Who stands before this Court of eternal truth and justice?

Me: - er - er - [I am surprised, confused and overawed. A voice booms out and reverberates around the Courtroom. I realize it is that of her counsel]

Counsel: Can you not answer a simple question? [he asks in a tone of high insistence] Identify yourself. Truth cannot start without knowing who you are; and admitting it [he commands]

Me: I am Christopher Navavie Greenland [I blurt out trying to sound brave and confident.]

Counsel: Christopher Navavie Greenland - you are on trial - you must now account ... account for the gift of life that you were given. Do you understand?

Me: I do. [So it is not to be St Peter at the pearly gates, but Lady Justice, that will decide where I am to be for eternity]

Counsel: What is love?

Me: Love is God [I say without hesitation, confident that I have just scored a huge point. However the comeback by counsel is equally quick and quite shattering]

Counsel: Come on now. Please don't trot out hackneyed statements. We are not in the school of sloganeering here. We want truth [he says sternly]

Me: I think it means acceptance - unconditional acceptance - of others.

Counsel: Even if what they do is bad? You just "unconditionally" accept them - is that what you are saying? [he says with a hint of sarcasm]

Me: Uhmm - well - No - - [my mind is racing] I mean Yes - Yes I accept them - I accept the person "unconditionally' - but condemn bad conduct. [I finish strongly]

Counsel: So you want to posture that you have condemned no one - only their actions.

Me: I have tried to adhere to the statement in the Lord's Prayer ' "Forgive us our trespasses, as we forgive those who trespass against us." [If I am ever going to get to heaven I need to drag Jesus Christ onto my side sooner rather than later. Name dropping is a well practiced art amongst humans]

Counsel: What is justice?

Me: I suppose, in essence, it means love thy neighbor as thyself and treat others as you would have them treat you [again dragging in Jesus Christ and His central admonishment to mankind]

The trial proceeds but proceedings are interrupted when I come to in the Intensive Care Unit. Tended to by a completely multi-racial staff of quite exceptional work ethic I make a full recovery.

During this period I become quite addicted to being bed bathed, a duty the nurses carry out with care and tenderness that a mother imparts to her own child. My wife is happy and relieved at my obvious satisfaction at how I am being nursed. However things go badly wrong for just a moment or two as I land in big trouble with my dear wife. Nurses are dumb. Well so it would seem. One of them tells my wife that it is so good to see that I am experiencing *"spontaneous erections"*. Medically this is undoubtedly a very good sign of recovery to full health. But it is not the news a wife wants to hear about her husband who is enthusing about nurses who are tending to all his needs. What planet these on?????

On the day of my discharge a young lady comes to take copious notes, explaining to me that my case is to be reported to the international medical fraternity. Medical history has been made. My problem had not been a sore throat, influenza, laryngitis, common cold or any of the other ailments that routinely inflict humanity. I had suffered an upper respiratory obstruction due to epiglotitis, i.e., swelling of the epiglottis. This had gone to the size of a golf ball and had all but cut off my air supply. In the history of medical science the condition often presents in children - but never in an adult. My case is unprecedented. That I survived was a miracle, due firstly to the fact that neither of the examining doctors, at Windhoek and on being admitted, had placed a spatula on my tongue as is the custom with doctors in such situations. Secondly I had not panicked and actually tried to breath at any stage. Had either occurred the golf ball, that was now my epiglottis, would have jammed itself into the wind pipe rendering the obstruction complete with death following within moments thereafter, i.e. vagal inhibition.

Dr Wilken was quite taken that neither had occurred. In my mind I recalled miraculously also escaping death, on account of diphtheria, all those years ago. I also recalled the sangoma telling me that Fuyane would always be with me and that I was destined to have a long life - all be it a troublesome one.

I was quietly smug about the power of saying that truly beautiful prayer that starts - *"Hail Mary - blessed art thou amongst women -."* and ends *" - Holy Mary, mother of God, pray for us sinners, now and at the hour of our death - Amen"* .

92. And the frog is being boiled alive

Fourteen years after independence, and the shedding of one of the most evil systems the world has known, South Africa is in a mess despite the great promise that came with Nelson Rolihlahla Mandela in 1994.

Infrastructure and public service are in a parlous state. The Public health system is so bad that the investigative journalism sector, such as Carte Blanche, now almost routinely report that some hospitals are death traps, especially for babies. When the Health Minister Manto Tshabalala-Msimang, is exposed for having a alcoholic liver cirrhosis - - a disease synonymous with chronic alcoholism, and for having a conviction for having stolen a patient's watch, hospital blankets, linen, and heaters, and for having been declared a "prohibited immigrant" in Botswana, President Thabo Mbeki stubbornly refuses to recognize her inherent unsuitability for the post, despite having challenged the media to provide evidence of this.

Schools are under-resourced, teaching levels poor and the national Matric results in a downward spiral. The roads are now overcrowded, on account of a really bad transportation policy, leading to the country now being a world leader in road carnage. An under-resourced demoralized police force, led by a Commissioner who openly consorts with a drug lord, tries vainly to contend with rampant crime in which at least 22 people are killed a day and a woman or child raped virtually every few seconds. Nearly everyone has experienced serious crime such as hi-jacking, rape or robbery or has a friend or family member who has.

I have survived attempted murder in the sanctity of my own home. My wife has been hijacked at gun point and her car taken.

We have lost our 25 year old second son, our beloved David Sigidi, after complications in his injuries sustained in a road crash.

The power grid fails to cope with demand and wholesale electricity black-outs are now routine. This is the legacy of years of bad government. The ministers involved, like Alec Erwin, are not held to account. They strut about obfuscating simple truth.

Glossy magazines extol the success of South African wine vineries. The wine farms stretch out on both sides of the N2 Highway, confirming such success, and the fabulous wealth of the owners. However the shacks and ramshackle squalid housing of the farm workers, there for all to see, like a cancerous infection on a landscape of perfection, is ignored by a supposedly people centered government. Thabo Mbeki makes little attempt to conceal his

Life is not measured by the number of breathes we take, but by the number of moments that take our breath away.

Our beloved son David Sigidi Greenland
06 June 1979 – 16 February 2006

affection, admiration and support for the despot that Robert Mugabe has long since become. He makes the earth shattering statement that *"there is no crisis in Zimbabwe"* and then he, and the acolytes in the constituency of the elite, trot out so much more obfuscation in defense of both his statement and stance. For this constituency, power, amassing and consumption of assets is the preoccupation. For the masses it has become survival.

The list comprising clear evidence of failed government and a nation en route "over the precipice, eyes wide open[1]" is everywhere. Despite a vibrant media "crying wolf", at every turn, society proceeds serenely on its way, neither

---

[1] "In Nigeria we live in terrible times. We are a nation heading for the precipice with our eyes wide open expecting a bridge to appear miraculously to prevent us from falling down a yawning valley." Terrible Times by Imohimi Uduigwome Airenevboise

admitting nor denying that this could never have been what so many made great sacrifice for in the struggle for liberation.

It is said that if a frog is thrown into hot water it will immediately jump out. However if it is put in a pot of cold water, which is then brought to the boil, the frog will remain in the pot until it is boiled alive.

There is scant evidence of a national realization that this "boiled frog" syndrome is at play. There is still a plethora of sycophantic chants about a *"rainbow nation"* and *"being proudly South African"*. The gap between rich and poor has widened considerably since independence and more people than ever now live in cardboard boxes and under plastic sheeting and corrugated iron. Under Black Empowerment deals and affirmative action agendas, a new Black elite has emerged, in obscene partnership with the previous dominant White minority, leaving the people enmeshed in the *"dark brown taste of being poor"*.

The Minister of Health, Manto Tshabalala-Msimang, leads a South African delegation to an international HIV/AIDS conference, and puts on a stand exhibiting garlic, ginger and lemon as the answer to the pandemic. The whole world is appalled and a plethora of articles are published pointing out that "garlic", for instance, will do nothing to "HIV/AIDS or vampires". In the end, of these poor people, over 320, 000 have to die on account of being denied anti-retroviral drugs to combat the effects of HIV[1].

Under the veneer of seeming acceptance of this appalling situation, within the "boiled frog syndrome", a time bomb ticks away. It then explodes. Almost overnight, the whole country is engulfed in widespread attacks on foreigners. The world is treated to filmed footage, screened almost daily, of Black foreigners, particularly Zimbabweans and Mozambicans, being attacked, beaten and burnt alive. These people are now "the other"; needing to be exorcised from society. A people who once gave their lives in order to remove a culture of race hatred now openly displays such hatred, and victimizes the hated, with enthusiasm and energy that chills the heart and numbs the brain. Xenophobia, an inconvenient truth, has reared its ugly head and is everywhere. By the time the attacks end, at least 62 lives have been lost and many thousands displaced.

---

[1] In 2006, an estimated 350 000 South Africans died of HIV/Aids - nearly half of all deaths for that year, and the leading cause of death for the country's adult population.http://www.mediaclubsouthafrica.com/index.php?
option=com_content&view=article&id=103:hivaids-in-south-
africa&catid=34:developmentbg

There will be no commemoration of this bloody saga in which people were killed and maimed for just being different. There will be no reparation.

By the time South Africa stages the World Cup in June 2010, great pathos will be played out as BBC screens video footage of "Volvo" Ndaye Mulamba, one of Africa's legendary football stars, who helped Zaire to qualify for the World Cup back in 1974, and who still holds the record for scoring most goals in a single African Cup of Nations tournament - scoring nine times in 1974. He is shown shuffling around in the poorest area of the Cape Flats, impoverished, unnoticed, unacknowledged by the local organizing committee. BBC will also show footage of the poor and disadvantaged against a backdrop of one of our multi billion Rand new stadiums[1].

In a program, yet to be screened in August 2010, Carte Blanche will expose xenophobia yet again in revealing the plight of residents from Bangladesh, in particular. Moreover, by 11 February 2010, the 20th anniversary of the release of Nelson Mandela from years of imprisonment, the Sunday Times Newspaper of South Africa will be littered with reports that the country is in serious failure. A banner headline will scream out - "Long walk remains - as South Africans remain imprisoned in many respects despite the momentous events that led to the release of Nelson Mandela 20 years ago and the subsequent birth of democracy - with true freedom still under lock and key". The editorial will lament failure of leadership and state that it appears "unconcerned that they convey an image of South Africa as just another banana republic - and on a slippery slope". Lead articles by Thabo Makgoba, Archbishop of Cape Town, and Warren Goldstein, Chief Rabbi, will plead for realization of the awful plight of ordinary human beings in the country, brought about by a lack of a moral conscience on the part of leadership. Typical will be a statement by the good Archbishop - *"The greatest moral problem of our society is that millions experience unbearable suffering daily"*.

A Black intellectual, Xolela Mangcu, publishes a book titled "To the Brink" lamenting the creation of a new intolerant elite, and the absence of a non-

---

[1] [229] By 14 September 2009 (even before the World Cup) the country has a new Jacob Zuma led government. When he institutes a President's hot line to afford citizens and avenue to raise concerns over 40 operators are unable to cope with the deluge of calls raising issues of poor service delivery, denial of rights, corruption and bad governance.

racial nationalism in South Africa, in which the interests of all of the people are paramount.[1]

So I am uncomfortable with all of it. After the great promise that permeated everything, under Nelson Mandela on our arrival in South Africa in December 1996, the picture is now bleak. Despite having been accorded citizenship in 1998, I have never felt comfortable in South Africa. Botswana and Namibia have been far more accepting and appreciative of who and what I am. I have felt far less of a stranger in those countries. It is no surprise when a website appears titled "bruin ou.com" as South Africa's Coloured Community site. Also on line is "goffal.com" which Wikipedia explains as

> "Goffal is a term used for people of <u>mixed race</u> from <u>Zimbabwe</u>, particularly white people of British & Dutch descent with black people. It cannot be pinpointed exactly when Coloureds started referring to one another as Goffals but it is widely accepted that it evolved in the late 1980s to early 1990s in goffal communities around the country."

The site goes on to explain that "goffal" communities have sprung up in cities around the world. This means that, in going into the Diaspora, my community has insisted on carrying its identity with it. There are no "White" or "Black" websites. These groups do not feel alienated and have no need to express their identity. We Coloured people do. We are "the other".

My family feels somewhat differently. Whereas we all agree that apartheid was damaging to members of all race groups, leaving them with permanent unresolved issues, my family thinks that there is hope. South Africa has aligned itself to the first world. In that world, a young senator is due to contest the presidency of the United States in just a month's time. He is the Democratic candidate. He is ethnic brown, having been elected by ethnic Whites. He is Barrack Obama, a Euro-African, just like me.

We do not have the slightest doubt that the White dominated electorate in the America will vote him President. An important bridge will have been crossed. At a stroke, the whole world will be led in taking a significant step for one man and a giant leap for humanity, with all its hitherto racial, ethnic, tribal and other prejudices. Surely South Africa will not miss or fail to appreciate this and the enormous symbolism involved. Surely the incredible message being sent around the world by the American people must start to take hold especially as it has been confirmed by the election of Ian Khama

---

[1] Also see book "Architects of Poverty", by Moeletsi Mbeki published by Pan MacMillan

as President of neighboring Botswana. He too, like me, is ethnically Euro-African, and has been elected by a Black populace.

So my family has hope that these important events will have effect on South African mindset, preoccupied with ethnicity; a nuanced effect but an effect all the same. I am not so sure. I point out that Trevor Manuel, a Coloured, is undoubtedly recognized as the most competent Minister, but not for a nano second, would he be considered for presidency in South Africa.

I deliver the *coup de grace* by reminding them of how a brother to a minister, a Mr. Stofile, had publicly lamented that *"there was no place for blacks in rugby in South Africa"* simply on account of having been beaten, in competition for a post, by a Coloured in a democratically conducted vote[1]. Not one government minister called him to order.

---

93. Cogito, ergo sum -

As I sit on the pavilion of the Twelve Apostles Hotel, looking out onto the Atlantic, and having looked down the corridor of my life, it is these and other thoughts that now occupy my mind. I am in deep and quiet reflection. I reflect on what I have been doing for the last year, sitting in Court, hearing cases as an Acting Judge in the Eastern Cape. Mthatha, East London, Port Elizabeth, Bisho, Queenstown - all step in and out of mind in jumbled sequences. I am preparing myself just as an athlete prepares before an event.

To test myself I close my eyes and recreate the scene in which the great Judge Hugh Beadle glared at me accusatorily. However the scene immediately reverts to my trial that started whilst under anesthetic at Pretoria East Hospital on Good Friday 2007. Judge Beadle is substituted by Lady Justice, the international symbol of justice.

---

[1] In the aftermath of his failure to become the president of the South African Rugby Union (SARU), Mike Stofile said the elections at the annual general meeting held on Friday proved there was no place for black people in South African rugby. ⋯."I've been saying for four years now there is no place for black people in South African rugby and this is the final nail for black people in this country. http://www.mg.co.za/article/2008-03-28-stofile-there-is-no-place-for-black-people-in-sa-rugby

In my mind I tabulate the meaning of this symbol. Lady Justice is tall, regal and beautiful to symbolize that true justice stands out, universally appealing and inoffensive, in all its attributes. She is blindfolded. This indicates that justice is blind to the inequalities of man. No notice is taken of position, status or wealth. All are equal before her. The scales she holds in one hand signify that, at all times, she will balance individual interests against collective interests to ensure that they remain in balance. The sword in the other hand signifies that at a certain point justice must not be compromising in redressing evil.

As I stand before her, preoccupied with her beauty and what she means to all humanity, her counsel's voice once again fills the Courtroom –

Counsel: You will recall that in this Court we are concerned with truth and justice?

Me: Yes, I certainly recall that [I reply feigning confidence]

Counsel: Why have you been masquerading as a judge in the Eastern Cape?

Me: I have not been masquerading. I have been discharging my duties as an Acting Judge.

Counsel: But on Face Book you stated that you were masquerading?

Me: Yes ... well ... you see I was just trying to show that I was only acting ... it was a play on words.

Counsel: Well what is the difference between a Judge and an Acting Judge? Were you only acting, pretending, to be dispensing justice?

Me: No ... oh no ... [then I am at a loss for more words ... the sword in the hand of Lady Justice quivers almost imperceptibly ... I realize I am on a test that I must not fail]

Counsel: You were a Judge in Zimbabwe and now a Judge in South Africa? Where did you learn about justice?

Me: Like others I learnt about it from books, and at University, and from judgments by Courts ... but my understanding of what it means I learnt from life experiences, my own and the experiences of others. To me, understanding is by far the most important ingredient. There are some brilliant legal scholars who cannot be good judges. Justice is a noble abstract thing that needs life breathed into it.

Counsel: What do you mean?

Me: You see when four and half year old Ronny Miller threw his parcel onto the roof he was taking a stand against injustice. He put a stop to it. When Solomon Dlodlo broke ranks with his friend, and told the police the truth about the fight on the bush path I had with his friend, he was taking a stand for truth and justice. When Sipho Mkhize told the Naidu Board that their forensic report was mischievous he was taking a stand for truth and justice.

Counsel: Why do you link justice to truth?

Me: It seems to me that they are completely linked. Injustice is founded on one or more lies. The apartheid system was founded on some big lies, like Black folk are deemed inferior in terms of Biblical authority. Hitler started the Holocaust by blaming the Jews for all the ills of the State. World history is littered with examples. In my case there was a need to contrive an adverse audit report to justify unjust treatment. The pernicious City Press report needed acceptance so as to justify an unjust agenda. So truth is non-negotiable if there is to be justice.

Counsel: You appear somewhat pontifical. Who are you to point fingers, having served the Ian Smith regime as a prosecutor and a magistrate? [the sword quivers ...]

Me: I was not recruited by that regime. They inherited me from the United Federal Party government.

Counsel: But you served them ... you did not resign? Me: [This is embarrassing - the sword quivers again ...] I had little option, once the British Government declined to remove the regime. And please note that none other than the great judge Fieldsend, first Chief Justice of independent Zimbabwe, ruled accordingly ... that the Smith Government had legitimacy, there being no other authority.

Counsel: Well you could have gone for training and joined in the armed struggle like so many others?

Me: I was never brave enough and I do not support violence as a means to achieve justice. I know of no examples where violence has led to justice. France struggled for decades to recover from the French Revolution. I am in the Mahatma Gandhi camp on this one.

Counsel: So you opposed the armed struggle in Zimbabwe?

Me: No, I just did not actively involve myself in it. I respected the choice of those who did.

Counsel: To change the subject; you seem to imply that Black people are just as racist as Whites?

Me: That is not so. I go no further than to say that all people are predisposed to prejudice. Racists act out these prejudices to the detriment of others. You find such people in all communities.

Counsel: What about your grandmother's attitude towards other ethnic groups.

Me: She was simply forthright about her prejudices ... and yes she was discriminatory as to who she would regard as an equal ... however she was dead against willfully causing harm.

Counsel: You also seem to have an enormous chip on your shoulder about your ethnicity?

Me: I do not. I have a strong objection to a government artificially classifying who and what I am. That is unjust. We know about the "Stolen Generation" of Australia. There White people sought to resolve the "Coloured problem" by breeding out our Black blood. In South Africa a Black government imagines that it is resolving the problem by simply passing laws that say we are Black[1].

Counsel: But classifying you as Black redresses the disadvantages suffered under apartheid?

Me: I have a great problem in accepting that an untruth can be used in the name of justice. I am not Black. That is a simple truth; incidentally also drummed into me by my Black grandmother and her people.

---

[1] **The Stolen Generations** (also Stolen children) is a term used to describe those children of Australian Aboriginal and Torres Strait Islander descent who were removed from their families by the Australian Federal and State government agencies and church missions, under acts of their respective parliaments.
http://en.wikipedia.org/wiki/Stolen_Generations

Counsel: But that is not what the law says in South Africa ... that you are Black. It merely says that you are so under "an extended definition" for the purposes of employment and empowerment.

Me: With respect that is a difference of form not of substance. The fact is that we are creating a climate where whole generations of children are being imbued with false impressions of what they are. A child knows when you are lying. Any psychologist will tell you that confusion as to self-identity is bad, very bad. Criminologists will tell you that acceptance and pride in who you are militates against deviance and, by extension, militates against criminality. Conversely problems about self-image and worth are a huge precipitant of deviance and behavioral problems. That is now beyond dispute. We already have a massive problem of deviance and crime in this country. We need to get away from propagating convenient untruths and denying inconvenient truths.

Counsel: Elaborate?

Me: Coloured people are just that ... of many colours ... ranging from almost snow white to quite black. They should not be forced to accept that the only way they will be able to rid themselves of disadvantage is to accept the convenient untruth that they are all Black. The goal cannot be advantage/disadvantage. It must be equality on all counts and freedom to choose what we want to be.

Counsel: So you are against affirmative action?

Me: Not against affirmative action but against it's race based approach. I am in good company. Judge Clarence Thomas, a Black judge appointed to the Supreme Court of the United States, and actually a beneficiary of affirmative action, is also totally against it. The same outcomes could be achieved under "corrective action", which is unobjectionable. In my life I have never been affirmed on racial lines. I have demanded only that I have the same opportunities. Our affirmative action process is demeaning of human beings. To imagine that Mkaya Ntini and Herchel Gibbs were in the South Africa cricket team because they are Black is demeaning of them ... and that is unjust. We had incredible problems at the RAF because of an obsession with race. So before we knew it a person could not be appointed or promoted because this would violate "demographic" imperatives. This effectively gave the lie to the notion that classifying Coloureds or Indians as Black redresses disadvantage. In reality all that is happening is that they continue to suffer the disadvantage of being a minority.

Counsel: So how should you be classified if justice is to be achieved?

- 333 -

Me: As a human being and accorded the same rights and privileges as all others. What is happening has led to a situation where an educated Indian lady insisted that I need *"to understand that some people are not real blacks"*. It is an absolute tragedy that a University graduate like her did not even start to realize that her statement actually applied to her as an anthropological reality. One of my problems at the RAF was that I was classified as *"not thinking like a Black"*. This is vomitus stuff. It reminds me of when, as an advocate, I had to fight tooth and nail for a White doctor to remain united with a Black child who knew no other mother. Race based intellectualism is false and demeans us as Homo sapiens. It worries me that we may be appointing people as judges who are proud *"to think like a Black"*.

Counsel: Surely all they mean is that you have to have understanding of Black problems.

Me: I was nurtured by a Black grandmother, given refuge by White German nuns ... counseled by Fuyane, a Black spiritualist ... educated by White Irish nuns ... appointed as a magistrate by an undoubtedly a racist White prime minster ... appointed as a judge by a Black liberator, now a despot ... my son was saved by a Black guerrilla doctor ... my other son was saved after a burst appendix by a White surgeon ... and sometimes I have been soundly abused by Whites, Blacks and an Indian.

There are no Back problems. There are no White problems. There only human problems. I do not need to *"think like a Black"* to work that out. *"Cogito, ergo sum"* tells me that.

Counsel: So you disrespect the right of others to think differently?

Me: Not at all ... provided that thinking does not lead to injustice. The nation is preoccupied with skin colour and ethnicity, the very things that underpinned the evils of apartheid. My daughter was told by Black lady, interviewing her for a job, that she would have to go the Home Affairs and return with proof that she was indeed Coloured. A certain Stofile complained bitterly *"that there was no place for a Black in Rugby"* after he was beaten fairly and squarely in a democratically conducted vote by a Coloured. Such nonsense is guaranteed if you make ethnicity the criteria for the according of rights and privileges. So I must insist that as long as we have this type of ethnic based obsessions I, and others like me, stand to be treated unjustly. It is guaranteed as surely as the Titanic was going to sink once it had hit the iceberg. It is that blindingly obvious.

Counsel: What then should be the criteria to drive transformation?

Me: <u>Subsisting apartheid induced disadvantage.</u> It really is as simple as that in truth and justice. That way affirmation and empowerment would accrue to those who are actually still in need; and not used for enrichment of the corrupt elite to the further disadvantage of the still dispossessed majority.

Counsel: Are you saying there is no justice in South Africa?

Me: What I am insisting on with all the passion I can muster is that racial/ethnic classification as criteria for rights and privileges is fundamentally inconsistent with justice. If colour, that is being white or black, of which I am neither, is at all relevant to justice, why is Lady Justice blindfolded ... why is she blind folded? [The great Lady dips her head and slowly raises it in an assenting nod]

Counsel: I see ....

Me: And there is an incredible deficit ... starting with the gap between rich and poor ... with people still living in cardboard boxes and under plastic ... and the over 300, 000 that have died of HIV/AIDS on account of being denied available medication. Note that this happened because of a denial of truth. The analogy is to agree with Beverly Tatham that if you want to know if there is racism you simply look at who is benefiting and who is not. So too as regards injustice. You cannot say there is justice if you have this type of disparity between rich and poor. Simply put, there can be no justice without social justice. We need to be all concerned at the evidence before our very eyes.

Counsel: You are writing a book?

Me: Yes. God gave me the gift of articulation. When I tell my story it may start a conversation for others who will see their own stories as part of mine. I believe that one's life has little meaning if it does not confer a benefit on humanity. Injustice founded on convenient untruths needs to be confronted. I imagine that what I have to say will make a difference ... howsoever small.

Counsel: What about the Courts?

Me: Again there are huge deficits, most of which judges have little control over. It starts with the fact that the police simply cannot cope with the *anomie* in which this country is gripped.

Counsel: What do you mean ... *anomie?*

Me: It means that, particularly in revolutionary times, a society will experience a situation where people re-identify their goals and the means of achieving such goals with deviance and crime become endemic. In Zimbabwe, murderers I dealt with were, to put it simply, just bad people. In South Africa young fresh faced kids from decent families, perpetrate crimes of utter depravity, even on young children and elders. Their parents sit in Court disbelieving and numbed at the behaviour of their children. I realize that when I was a teenager the culture in Zimbabwe was blue jeans, rock-and-roll and fun. Here we have a widespread culture of 9mm parabellums, BMWs, rape and murder. With *anomie* there will also be social norm confusion with little agreement amongst the populace on what is right or wrong and therefore systemic blurring of these fundamental issues. In the absence of a common value set, this is guaranteed. So we have a pandemic of all types of deviance, and at every level, petty theft, murders, robbery, hijackings, embezzlement, crooked dealers and business as exposed weekly by Carte Blanche and ... wait for it ... the so called cream of society cooking national food prices. Until government leads the nation to accept that we have this problem of *anomie*, and to address it collectively at every level starting in the schools, in communities, in business forums ... in marriage with *ubuntu* ... we are doomed. We are doomed in our efforts to mould into the society that our world beating constitution envisages. We are doomed in our efforts to eradicate crime.

Counsel: And the Courts?

Me: There is an imperative that justice be brought closer to the people. This cannot happen if people do not have access. Poor people are condemned to non-access in civil matters. Also cases take far too long even though we say that justice delayed is justice denied. I think the Courts *"should think big and start small"*. The judiciary should be in active participation with leadership and others on what needs to be done.

Counsel: Meaning?

Me: In my case I have done some things. For instance, I try to turn around my judgments as quickly as possible. The case of Dikana v S, since reported in the SA Law Reports[1], was turned around in just a day. Also I will not sit in any case involving rape or sexual abuse involving a female without a female assessor. In addition, regardless of complexity, my judgments are couched and formatted as to be understandable to the persons affected. Also law and justice are not necessarily the same thing. So I also took the opportunity in Grahamstown, when admitting seven lawyers to the profession, to encourage them to use their youthful energies to re-examine laws to see if existing laws actually serve justice. This is critically important.

Counsel: Like what?

Me: In the reported case of S v F[2], as a judge I raised the issue of the appropriateness of whipping as a punishment. It was still on the statue books

---

[1] Dikana v S [2008] 2 All SA 182

[2] S v F 1989 (1) SA 460

in Zimbabwe. Later the Supreme Courts in the region cited my judgment with approval and outlawed whipping which now only occurs in Botswana. Here again it was life experience that had given me understanding as I had witnessed the traumatizing by whipping of just one boy of many whipped at school.

Counsel: Anything else?

Me: I feel strongly that the so called *right to silence* needs to be comprehensively reviewed. Zimbabwean experience shows that it is largely a *"false right"*. It works against the interest of justice.

Counsel: Why a female assessor?

Me: Actual experience has shown me beyond any doubt that, as a man, my understanding of how a woman sees things, reacts and behaves in particular situation, is quite defective. I have also been somewhat horrified at the stance taken by some experienced judges, not only here but also in the United Kingdom on these issues.

Counsel: What did you hope to achieve at the RAF?

Me: In a nutshell, social justice.

Counsel: Meaning?

Me: The reality is that over 95% of road crash victims are from the poorer sector. They are the passengers and pedestrians. Right now they forfeit about 33%, in legal fees, of their compensation which they may or may not receive after waiting up to five years sometimes. It is in the highest degree unjust that this should be the case when victims are claiming for what they are entitled to from their own government. The other problem is that the obsession is to convert injury and death into as much money as possible. It should be to redress social harm accruing as Botswana and Namibia have now taken a stance on.

Counsel: Strange, those other countries, but not your own adopted country?

Me: Yes, an indicator that something is wrong. You should know that as early as 1994 South Africa committed to a United Nations resolution to immediately take steps to treat the plight of road cash victims as an issue of health. It is now 2008 and we have done nothing. But then again "But Jesus said to them, 'A prophet is not without honor except in his own country, among his own relatives, and in his own house.' ... He marveled because of their unbelief." (Mark 6:4-6a)

Counsel: So you are blaming the lawyers?

Me: Not at all. The fault based system guarantees that lawyers have to play the role of representing claimants. What do poor people know about *delict,* *quantum, res ipsa loquitur* etc. Lawyers have to be paid. Because South Africa is a world leader in the business of road carnage, MVA work has become big business.

Counsel: So lawyers have much to lose if your ideas are accepted.

Me: Not just my ideas. They coincide with the official recommendations of the Satchwell Commission of enquiry into the system, handed down in 2002. It is now 2008. That is why Mac Maharaj made an impassioned appeal, at the first MVA conference at a hotel in Centurion in 1995, that the reform process includes weaning MVA lawyers off the current system. More importantly the public has much to gain. There would be an annual saving of Rand billions that can be invested in the public health sector once the issue is managed as a public health issue.

Counsel: What do you think is the main attribute a judge should have?

Me: Humility and understanding. Both are products of life experience. It is experience that has given me the humility to now know that *"when I am most sure I should be most careful"* The Masvingo rape case was only one of many lessons on this count. Experience teaches you, for instance, that the fact that an accused person lies does not necessarily indicate guilt. I wrote a full bench judgment reversing an otherwise good decision of a judge on this basis.

Counsel: What about the death penalty? You actually sentenced at least five accused to death.

Me: Yes and each richly deserved it. But I do not support the death penalty. It is simply impractical to think that, in this climate of *anomie*, the risk of undeserving executions is avoidable. In a recent case involving a person's body being fed to crocodiles there was more concern with issues fuelling race hatred than with the fact the sitting judge had approached the matter in quite an objectionable way.

Counsel: So you are insisting that you do have an understanding of justice.

Me: I can never do more than insist that you look for truth on the evidence of my record. You are aware that all systems of justice in the free world are founded on the sacred proposition that *"Justice must not only be done but also be seen to be done"* As a judge I was reversed on appeal only once. However South African judges have followed my judgment which was reported. Also reported were four other judgments[1]. This is an unmatchable record for a Zimbabwean judge over a period as short as five years. Then, as

---

[1] Malaba v Takangovada 1990 (3) SA 413 Washaya v Washaya 1990 (4) SA 41.
Masawi v Chabata 1991(4) SA 764. Fawcett Security v Omar Ent 1991 (2) SA 441.

regards the year I have now spent as an Acting Judge in South Africa, two of my judgments have been reported[1]. Retired Judge Beck, one of the great judicial sons of South Africa, sent me this message on New Years Day *"I wish that the year will be filled with Greenland judgments"*. It would seem that there is a perception that I am concerned to do justice.

Counsel: You are very forthright in your views. Should a judge not be constrained to be temperate and restrained?

Me: True ... however more, a judge is required to think and act without fear, favour of prejudice.

As I notice the faintest of smiles on the face of Lady Justice my daydreaming is interrupted by the seagull which has now been joined by another. I am impressed as to the thinness of their legs. After surrendering the last of my sandwich, which they immediately squabble over, I extract my cell phone from my pocket and phone my wife. She is encouraging as only a wife can be. *"Just be yourself, my husband - you are a good man - I love you - "* she ends.

"Judge Greenland". It is the voice of a young lady who has approached from behind. Soon thereafter she politely shoos me into a large room, whispering as to where I should take my place. I walk in and sit down. As I look up I am met by a vacant space in front of me around which a sea of sombre faces appear. These are the faces of the members of the Judicial Service Commission of South Africa ("JSC"). It is a Constitutional organ of State charged with responsibility of selecting the country's judges and chaired by none other than the Chief Justice ("the CJ"). It is this test that I have been preparing for.

---

94. Some are good, even the bad - some are bad, even the good

The atmosphere is decidedly chilly. I see nothing but sombre faces. The Judge President from the Eastern Cape asks me to deal with three concerns that had been submitted by the White dominated Eastern Cape Society of Advocates.

It is the practice of the JSC to circulate a list of short listed candidates, prior to interviewing such candidates, so as to enable the general public to submit any concerns. In my case the Eastern Cape Society of Advocates had submitted a comment that it appeared that I "was not ready" for appointment as a judge. In support of this self evidently spurious statement they adverted

---

[1] [236] Dikana v S [2008] 2 All SA 182   (E); Gobe v S [2008] 2 All SA 188 (E)

to three incidents. In one instance a case was made around the fact that I do not speak Afrikaans. Considering that there are 11 official languages, and Afrikaans is certainly not a prerequisite for judicial appointment, the inherent temerity of this concern was - well - intolerable. The other was that I had supported the Taxing Mistress of the Grahamstown High Court in her disallowance of the costs of one of their members in a matter. The third was a comment I had made in Court which appeared to indicate that I had not fully appreciated the nature of the issues. I had responded in writing to all three concerns and effectively temperately put them to bed. Only the last of the three had any possibility of merit, but certainly not an indicator of judicial incompetence, having regard to the fact that I had been a judge, in effect, for some seven years and had an exemplary record.

The CJ, the Hon Pius Langa, somberly asks me to particularize the history of my work in law. I do so making the submission that –

" - it seems to me, with respect, that the Commission is required
to appoint a judge only if it can be satisfied that such person
can be trusted to ensure that justice will be done according to
law without fear, force or prejudice - and that I believe that,
on my record, the Commission can be so satisfied - "

Langa then asks me to confirm that the work I do and have done in Namibia and Botswana (I serve on two Boards in Botswana) are at the request of the governments of those countries. I say yes.

Then Commissioner von Klemperer, in a voice tinged with hostility, states –

"Mr. Chairman, we are going to oppose the confirmation of this
candidate as a judge!"

I am shocked. The interview has hardly commenced. The purpose of interviewing a shortlisted candidate is to make a personal assessment of the candidate. This has simply not happened! He has not interviewed me. It is trite law, custom and practice that he first must do that, apply his mind to my performance and then make a decision. None of this has happened. This is the JSC. Surely the most basic rules involved in selection procedure are practiced here. I am astounded at his statement and astounded that no one else steps in to make the point that it is grossly improper to prejudge a candidate. The Commission includes all the most senior judges in the country, as judicial provincial heads, and senior advocates. Apart from the fact that such basic rules are common practice they also accord with their own pronouncements in Court on rules of fairness.

I become even more shocked when von Klemperer tells me that he proposes to quote from a transcript, which I have not seen, as *"this is an ambush"* (his words). My mind is now reeling. Ambush! Why? Why am I being ambushed? Why is an ambush being permitted? The JSC always requires that early notice be given to candidates of anything they are to be confronted with.

Right here I start to conclude that something is afoot - something nefarious - something unholy and sinister - and it is being allowed to happen. I experience déjà vu about being back before the Kessie Naidu Board facing a dog's vomit tendered as a "forensic report". Von Klemperer then serves up his own dog's vomit starting with a <u>completely false</u> statement that - "that during motion proceedings held in East London a Mr. Mark Nettleton had appeared before you to have a client admitted as a legal practitioner".

I feel sick through and through. He goes on to serve up a monstrous lie that in those proceedings I had demonstrated such incompetence, without using the term, as to have wanted to conduct the admission of candidates to the profession in my chambers as opposed to in Court. An unhappy dance between heart and mind starts. My mind tells me that this is a diabolical setup. My heart says, "No, it cannot be - this is the JSC, these are judges - " Never in my life have I felt so utterly bad. The notable confrontations I have had - with that "vrastaag" man from Joburg on a bush path so many years ago; with a howling mob when I arrived in the army; with two armed goons intent on killing me in the sanctity of my own home - all cannot match the deepest sense of confusion, revulsion, anger, disappointment and betrayal that floods through every fibre of my person.

I now vividly recall being taken to dinner a week ago by a judge from the Eastern Cape who pointedly made statements to the effect that - *"Chris - xenophobia is alive and kicking in South Africa - you are not from here - you could well find that you are resented just for who you are - your profile - your competence ..."* At the time I was absolutely disinclined to even start believing that a body, as august as the JSC, could ever have such culture. I also now recall a phone call received at O R Thambo airport, just yesterday, in which an advocate identifying himself as Blume, told me he wished to distance himself from the Eastern Cape Society of Advocates.

I lose all interest in the interview as a process. I know beyond doubt that the whole thing is a sham. I am up against the "firm". It is extremely difficult to stop myself from getting up and walking out. What then happens is that confrontation on the monstrous lie is played out. The media is to report it as follows (carried on the internet)-

[EXTRACT FROM PRETORIA NEWS of 17 October 2008-11-12]

"The next applicant, former Zimbabwean judge Chris Greenland, was grilled over a claim by the Eastern Cape Society of Advocates that he had appeared to be unfamiliar with basic

Court procedure when he presided as an acting judge over a motion Court in Grahamstown earlier this month.

Among other things, said Commissioner Julian von Klemperer, Greenland had reportedly been uncertain whether newly-admitted advocates should take their oath in open Court, or in the judge's chambers.

"That is absolutely untrue," Greenland shot back.

However, Von Klemperer then read out extracts from the transcript of those Court proceedings, in which Grahamstown attorney Mark Nettleton presented Neliswa Dinge for admission as an advocate.

The transcript recorded Greenland as saying: "Yes she's not required to take an oath."

"Yes m'lord, it's customary for the applicant to come before your lordship's registrar [in Court] who administers an oath m'lord," said Nettleton.

"It's not done in Court," said Greenland. "It is m'lord, in submission, madam registrar has the oath before her m'lord," said Nettleton doggedly. Greenland eventually agreed to Dinge taking the oath in Court, and she was admitted. Greenland told the commission he had certainly not implied that the oath should not be administered in open Court, and that he had already before that day presided over numerous admissions. He could only think that there had been a "misrecording", or that the transcript did not contain everything that was said on that occasion. The notion that oaths should be administered in chambers was "preposterous", he said. According to the transcript Dinge was one of six people admitted as advocates or attorneys that day. When they had all taken the oath, Greenland made them all stand up and invited them to "tell me the definition of justice". "Are you not going to make a submission on the day of your appearance, admission?" he asked. He told them being a lawyer was "not about law, it's about justice, and the two are not necessarily the same - even though you are qualified as a lawyer your first duty and allegiance must be to justice"."

All the judges and advocates on the Commission know that, having been a judge for some seven years, I must have admitted perhaps a few hundred candidates into the profession in Court. Nevertheless, the obscene confrontation is allowed, despite its patently vexatious and spurious premise.

The rest of the time is taken up by panel members "going through the motions". I repeat my assertion that, on my record, it is safe that I be appointed. I am not taken up on my record. I am not tested for judicial thinking and approach. No one picks on the unprecedented step I had taken when admitting the candidates Von Klemperer adverted to that they should use their youthful energies to bring justice closer to the people by first scrutinizing our laws to see if they served justice. From the questions put onlookers have not the slightest inkling of whether I am the type of person that should be a judge. In no way whatsoever does it even approximate the proceedings that played out in my mind before Lady Justice just before my interview.

What they hear is that I am originally from Zimbabwe, that Mugabe probably appointed me "out of reconciliation", that I was not skilled in MVA on my arrival in Botswana and other banter that has marginal relevance. I am exposed for not having been a political activist. I try to minimize the damage by pointing out, that in 1982, I made it my business to go and spend time with Eric Mtshali, then ANC representative in Maputo, so as to sensitize him to my availability. I insist that my record is the best evidence and that even my "extra judicial" work in the MVA field, which serves a social justice test, confirms my suitability. I point to the modest innovations I have practiced to improve justice for the people such as delivering judgments without delay and always having a female as an assessor in rape cases. There are no takers.

One Commissioner attacks me for having said that Mugabe would not have appointed me if I was considered a danger to the cause of justice. He immediately imputes to me the stance that judicial appointments should be political. There is an expression of visible disdain when I explain that I meant no more than that a person must be appointment only if, on his profile, it is safe to do so. I advert to an unsolicited statement made about my obvious commitment to the cause of justice in a book by Judy Garfield Todd titled "Through the Darkness". The only light moment occurs when a Coloured Commissioner asks me if I am interested in serving of the disciplinary Committee during the coming Soccer World Cup. I said I would be.

My family and I subsequently file written complaints to the Human Rights Commission and the Chief Justice.

We provided the Chief Justice with written proof, in terms of a signed certificate from the Court transcriber, that the transcript produced and read from by Von Klemperer to the JSC <u>had been false</u> in the section he was relying on. We pointed out that what this all obviously added up to was that the Eastern Cape Society of Advocates had realized that I had effectively dealt with their rather spurious "fault finding' written concerns and therefore they had a problem. This had been compounded by the fact I had received the written support of the Black Lawyers Association, of whom I have never been a member and the Association of Advocates, of whom I have never been a member. Most embarrassing to their cause was the following endorsement submitted by the Black dominated Society of Advocates of the Transkie about me –

"A distinguished jurist. Quite incisive and pragmatic in his approach in issues before him for adjudication. Not being a

member of our Bar and not originating from our area we met
him for the first time upon his acting appointment to our
Bench. He obviously has a wealth of experience on the Bench
and it clearly shows. He is of amiable disposition and is
very able on the Bench; his judgments are impeccable. The
general feeling is that he would be quite an asset to our
Bench and he would strengthen it enormously. We are not aware
of any negative points against him. His integrity, as far as
we are aware, is unquestionable."

Desperate times need desperate measures. So the agenda was conceived and played out as follows –

a) I was ambushed at my interview at the JSC;

b) to that end I was thereafter given no notice of the new and
false concerns, even though I was staying in the same Hotel as
all other candidates and members of the JSC; even though I was
not interviewed first and waited on the hotel pavilion, in excess
of an hour, to be interviewed; even though I could have been
given whatever time Von Klemperer had to study the new-found
transcript with its false information;

c) and in the ambush the false allegations were presented as
being the truth, even though not one of the members of the Eastern
Cape Society of Advocates, as officers of the Court, had ever
heard me say any such thing.

The real reason for the opposition was confirmed soon thereafter; having been first betrayed in the concern expressed about me upholding the decision of the Taxing Mistress about RAF fees in the written complaint. In the case of Malibongwe v RAF, heard thereafter in Mthatha High Court, counsel stood up and made application for my recusal on the basis of perceived bias. In my judgment it was easy to show the absolutely spurious basis of this application on the simple premise that whether I am the CEO of the RAF, or counsel representing the RAF, or counsel representing the claimant, or the presiding judge, the interest I have in any claim on the RAF is that it be paid or denied according to law - no more - no less. In addition, I was able to point out that no such application had ever been made as regards other judges who had been involved in practices doing RAF work and certainly no such application had been made as regards Judge Maluleke who had the second biggest MVA practice in the country.

The irresistible inference, of which we have little doubt, is that MVA dominated members of the profession had a fear that their interests would be prejudiced on RAF matters if I were appointed as a judge. RAF matters dominate the Courts rolls and provide an incredibly lucrative income to some/many of their members. That I am persona *non grata* with many members of the profession because of my MVA reform stance is no secret.

The circumstances in which I was forced out of the RAF, despite the then Minister Abdulah Omar's preferences, confirm this.

Also blog statements made by one of their senior MVA practitioners, Michael di Broglio, on the internet have made it clear that the reforms I affected in Namibia and Botswana are resented. At this blog[1] the following appears –

> Hi Michael, I am adverting to your report of June - July 2006 which includes the following text - 'I see former RAF CEO here Chris Greenland has turned up at the Namibian Fund. He seems to want to help change that system too. One wonders if the let's change it approach, no matter what country we are in, is the right one. Each country can hardly be the same, but anyway, that seems to be the approach -." I don't think we should wonder about changing the systems. As sentient beings we should know, even instinctively, that constitutional democracies are incompatible with a model that was designed at a time and place that was characterized by a diabolical trampling on human rights including the right to have the effect of a wrong undone. It is therefore no small wonder that the MVA Funds in the five countries that adopted the model all experienced dysfunction. None were/are sustainable in the original format if the criteria of serving the public interest efficiently and effectively is employed. My three-year stint in Namibia was an enormous privilege and source of profound satisfaction. The Fund in that country is poised to become probably the best public sector road crash compensation model in the world apart from those relatively few countries that can afford full blown social security. That much is already being certified by independent international expertise. The reason is that Namibia will ensure that most innocent accident victims, over 90% of whom are from the poorer sector of society, will proactively and timeously, have the social harm accruing fully compensated for. This will be achieved at a fraction of the cost of covering loss of equivalent value in analogous private sector schemes. True each country is not the same. However what is the same is what happens when steel meets flesh and bone. The resultant human suffering is the same. When this is not properly addressed, but dealt with in terms of a system that is something of a lottery, then those in a position of leadership, and that includes members of our profession, need to seriously reconsider their positions in terms of moral and ethical tests. Most accident victims are passengers and pedestrians. They have this status on account of being relatively disadvantaged. So George Bernard Shaw would properly opine that it is a case of the rich killing and maiming the poor and small wonder proper compensation is not that much of a priority. The Namibian model redresses this paradigm. It will have functional integrity whatever the test be it jurisprudential, human rights,

---

[1] http://www.lawblog.co.za/blog/month/?year=2007&month=6...

financial, or macro management. It is tragic and somewhat incongruous that the South African Fund continues to flounder in a morass of dysfunction when the remedies have long since been indicated and most of which were properly tabulated in a report of a credible Commission that sat for three years. Regrettably, as a remedy, the amendment Act is badly flawed and probably unworkable if the efficient and effective serving of the public interest is to be the test. In ending I must repeat what I have said ad nauseam before, and seemingly to my cost. It is an indictment against our noble profession that the RAF continues to experience dysfunction in that compensation to victims is something of a lottery and delivered at an internationally unprecedented cost ratio. The profession is the primary service delivery partner of the RAF in terms of organic reality. Whatever the reason we have failed to lead society to reform a badly flawed system that, at a fundamental level, is concerned with human rights. The harsh reality is that at present victims are not timeously compensated and not at full value. Some however do profit in terms of the prevailing operational culture to convert injury and death into as much cash as possible. Regardless of how good management is it will continue to be completely hamstrung in terms of an efficient and effective delivery test. That these aberrations need to be excised is long overdue. A way of engaging Government in a way that is objectively credible for the purpose of properly reforming the system has to be found. "Blame storming" is useless and results in the type of product that the amendment Act is. If Government has confidence in our profession it will listen. But is cannot start to listen until what we say objectively passes a public interest test. On account of my reform modeling those Funds are financially viable to the complete benefit of crash prevention, crash response, crash victims and no one else. Namibia now has an internationally unmatchable victims' orientated model. It appears somewhat shamefully ironical that, despite the plea of Minister Omar, it is only the citizens of neighbouring countries that are benefiting from my expertise. Christopher Navavie Greenland."

To my family it is not being too melodramatic to say, as did Judge Clarence Thomas, a black judge appointed to the US Supreme Court, that what happened at the JSC "was the hi-tech lynching of an uppity nigger" bearing in mind the black/white split on support for my candidature.

We had made out our case to the CJ that the deliberate misleading of the JSC, the Constitutional organ of State, charged with responsibility to conduct the sacred duty of selecting judges for appointment, in the circumstances and tactics employed, was an extremely serious matter. We also needed to know why the JSC had allowed this to happen particularly in the light of my protests that it simply could not be true. The second letter had been a respectful request for information as to how this had occurred and who was responsible for such heinous conduct.

As at 19 August 2009, nine months later we had received no response from the Chief Justice, as chairperson of the Judicial Service Commission, or from Jody Kollapen, as chairperson of the Human Rights Commission.

The senior judges who sit on the Judicial Service Commission are the guardians of our Constitution. It is lauded and acknowledged as probably the best in the world. However, it is not worth the paper it is written on unless and until the judges uphold its provisions. The right to fair and equal treatment is entrenched. **It was comprehensively breached.** This breach occurred in an agenda played out in the very presence of our judges and senior advocates, who are officers of our Courts. Also played out in their very presence was a premeditated, purposeful subversion of our Constitution, by the artful presentation of a monstrous falsehood in order to mislead the Judicial Service Commission in its sacred duty to select a judge. Despite incontrovertible evidence, protestations, requests and appeal, no response or explanation is proffered. The matter, like the person involved, is treated with apparent disdainful disregard, unworthy of an answer.

Our Constitution is the cornerstone of a State that was hard won in one of the most terrible saga's known in the history of man. That Constitution, and the rights that accrue under it, cannot be more precious. When they are breached it is always serious. When they are breached in witting or unwitting complicity with the most senior judges the nation needs to stand up and take notice. In the absence of an explanation such complicity stands to be inferred.

There was unequal treatment. There was unfairness. There was downright lies. The selection process was vitiated firstly by Von Klemperer making it clear that he and others, as this is what was meant by him saying *"we"*, were going to oppose my confirmation even before hearing me. Secondly it has now been established that the JSC was brazenly lied to, as to what happened in my Court. Our Constitution was subverted. Officers of the Court conceived and prosecuted all this as an agenda for nefarious motive. All this is now known by all involved.

Refusal to answer fair, reasonable and legitimate questions and concerns is a most certain indicator of something rotten. If the reason is that the citizen asking is considered unworthy of response the injury to that individual is greatly compounded and rendered grievous to all. The South African Congress of Trade Unions was undoubtedly right in adopting Martin Luther King's telling statement that *"an injury to one is an injury to all"*.

Over all this looms the immense question of why? Why was the JSC comfortable with the ambush of one candidate? What was it about him that made him deserving of this? Why, as regards this candidate, were they prepared to ignore their own rule of fairness that timeous notice of concerns be given? When he protested that this *"is preposterous"* why no intervention or amelioration of the situation. Why? Why has absolutely nothing been done since?

We have come through an era which has given rise to many questions; the gap between rich and poor; those who died needlessly of HIV/AIDS; failure of service delivery; systemic corruption; persecution of individuals and - questions about the culture within the judiciary. Questions of inconvenient truths and convenient untruths are being raised.

Our new President, Jacob Zuma, was severely lambasted by the media and commentators for, in effect, implying that the culture within the judiciary needs to be looked at. The judges who sat on the JSC at my interview were comfortable with the unequal, unfair treatment meted out to me in terms of the ambush. They were comfortable with Von Klemperer saying - *"Mr. Chairman - we are going to oppose confirmation of this candidate - "* even before having interviewed me. By "we" reference was being made to Von Klemperer and at least one other on the Commission. The implication is serious. It means that the operational culture and mode of the JSC is that its members are in lobby camps who predetermine who should and who should not be appointed as a judge. **The selection interviews are therefore, to that extent, just a sham.**

If by "we" Von Klemperer was referring to persons who were not commissioners the implications are frightening. What it means is that commissioners routinely arrive to push for or oppose a candidate in terms of a sectarian mandate. There can be no other interpretation. The necessary consequence of this is that the JSC selects judges accordingly. The frightening conclusion is that judges have been selected, not on the basis that they can be trusted to serve the public interest, but because they can be trusted to serve and protect sectarian interests. Right there the independence of the judiciary, so precious a commodity and essential component of a constitutional democracy, disappears into a puff of very smelly smoke, only the pungency of which needs to be established.

The country was in the grip of what was called the Hlophe saga for a very long time. Mr. Justice John Mandlakayise Hlophe, Judge-President of the Cape High Court, stood accused of having attempted to subvert the Constitution. His accusers were the Constitutional Court judges headed by Langa who also headed the JSC when I was interviewed. The allegation was that his conduct, in attempting to influence two ConCourt judges to decide a case in Zuma's favour, had the inevitable effect of subverting our Constitution, even though, it must be said, the likelihood of the two judges succumbing to such influence was negligible. Note the allegations against Judge Hlophe remained unproved.

By employing the same reasoning approach; misleading the JSC in order to influence it in the selection of a judge must also be subversive of the constitution and, it must be said, with a higher probability of success. Note that the fact that misleading actually took place is an indisputable reality.

So why the incredible enthusiasm, as regards Judge Hlophe, but paralysis as regards the perpetrators of falsehood to the JSC? Why the deafening silence about this matter but an immediate media statement, in which Judge Hlophe's name and reputation were unavoidably, and probably irretrievably, impugned. The justification for going public on Hlophe was that it was in the public interest as the matter was that serious. Lying to the JSC does not, it would appear; even deserve an acknowledgement of the concerns raised by my family.

The inaction and deafening silence speaks volumes. It says that one of us, and some of us, are being betrayed. It says, there are some who are not important enough, not deserving enough - of fair and equal treatment.

It says this man is one of those. It says - We, as guardians and custodians of our Constitution, reputedly the best in the world, appointed to be arbiters of all rights and status, charged to act without fear, force or prejudice - say that

Lady Justice may be blind but we are not.

We see for who he is. He is ---- **the other …..**

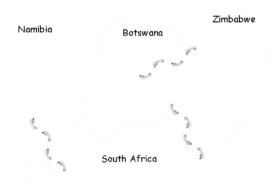

PostScript

- Over 3.6 million Zimbabweans remain scattered around the world
- Our family is now spread over South Africa, Europe, Canada, Australia and Brazil.
- Robert Gabriel Mugabe remains firmly entrenched (for 30 years) in Zimbabwe despite having lost the last elections.
- The Human Rights Commission of South Africa has displayed little interest in the issues raised at the end of this story.
- The Constitutional Court has handed down a decision upholding reforms as regards the Road Accident Fund of South Africa vindicating, in essence, the stance I had taken as early as 1999 with the reform commission.
- By September 2011 the RAF is over R42 billion in deficit. However management continues to collect hefty annual bonuses in addition to their Rand multimillion salaries.
- BBC has screened video footage showing the poor, the hungry; against a backdrop of one of the multi billion Rand stadiums being shown off in the World Cup being staged.
- It has also screened footage of "Volvo" Ndaye Mulamba shuffling around the Cape flats during the course of the World Cup.
- No one has suggested reparation for the victims of the so-called xenophobic violence that occurred in 2008.
- In his televised program, "Judge For Yourself", screened early 2010, Judge Dennis Davies and his panel agreed that the issues of race and ethnicity are treated with incredible superficiality in South Africa and need to be urgently addressed.
- Charles Ash valiantly continues the conversation about the plight of Coloured people in South Africa on his web site bruin-ou.com.
- On 3 July 2010 the German and Argentinean teams were made to hold up a banner stating "Say No To Racism" before their quarter final clash in the FIFA World cup in South Africa, a country in which a human being, even if in dire need of help, will be discriminated against under affirmative action and Black empowerment protocols, unless that person is able to prove that he/she is Black.
- On the morning of Wednesday 07 June 2010, Redi Direko, of Radio 702, tells the nation that the issue of xenophobia cannot remain unattended, after a Zimbabwean is thrown off a train, and interviews a lady, called Molly Blank, who has compiled a documentary on the issue.
- Days later, the Star newspaper carries reports over two full pages, and is then joined by a Bishop Desmond Tutu broadcast, lamenting

xenophobia at the very moment the country is celebrating its successful hosting of the 2010 World Cup.

- A few days later government calls in the army to help ...
- The waters at Hartbeespoort Dam are even more murky, turgid and tainted by dark green algae bloom ...
- Sadly on 23 September 2010 the Sowetan carries the following headline – "ROTTEN JUSTICE" (It's the most CORRUPT government department the country) about the Department of Justice and Constitutional Affairs".
- On 30 June 2010 I addressed members of the medical sector in Swakopmund, Namibia and asked for a definition of "justice'. A young Coloured nurse answered ..."it is simple – *love thy neighbour as thyself; and do unto others as you would have them do unto you"*.
- On 17 December 2010, twenty-six-year-old, *ordinary Tunisian citizen*, Mohamed Bouazizi, performs immolation, in protest against injustice. In response, other *ordinary* people rise up and *set their faces against 23 years of deception, lies and injustice*. By the end of January 2011, their dictator has fled the country and they are free.[1]
- A similar stance is then taken by the ordinary people of Jordan. In response, their King immediately fires their government and institutes social justice reforms. Similar "people driven" reform occurs in the Yemen.
- In early February the whole world is mesmerized by scenes of millions of ordinary Egyptians, who also decide to set their faces against 30 years of deception, lies and injustice, demonstrate in their Freedom Square for the removal of Hosni Mubarak, dictatorial president.[2] At 6pm on 11 February 2011 he steps down.
- Jimmy Manyi, Chief government spokesman, and president of the Black Management Forum, makes a statement on 9 March 2010 that – it is "very important for Coloured people to understand that there was an over concentration of them in the Western Cape" ... and that "they should stop this over – concentration situation as they are in an oversupply situation" where they are, and should move out to other Provinces. He finishes by stating the Employment Equity Act is a very good Act. Government then drafts and signs off a Bill designed to ensure that an estimated one (1) million Coloured workers in the Western Cape would lose their jobs and thus be forced to move to other Provinces. This

---

[1] http://en.wikipedia.org/wiki/2010%E2%80%932011_Tunisian_uprising

[2] http://articles.cnn.com/2011-01-28/world/egypt.press.club_1_saad-eddin-ibrahim-egyptian-american-egyptian-people?_s=PM:WORLD

diabolical scheme is shelved when exposed for being a contemptible piece of social engineering.

- In May, 2011 a film is screened titled "I'm Not Black, I'm Coloured", Identity Crisis at the Cape of Good Hope" by Mondé World Films depicting the plight of Coloured folk in the new South Africa, on account of the inherently racist Affirmative Action transformational model.

- In September 2011 political analyst, Professor Adam Habib, and others agree that the JSC does not appear to have any idea what its role is when assessing a candidate for a judgeship when it approves Judge Mogoeng, as the President's choice for Chief Justice, despite a disturbing record and objections from human rights groups

- However, the stage is reached when, in 2016, Mogoeng subjects President Zuma to a tongue lashing for being in breach of the Constitution.

- ……. 2016 … South Africa is accorded junk status ………

- By April 2016 the deficit accrued to the Road Accident Fund of South Africa had risen to R100 billion … as a really terrible consequence of the machinations of Advocate Kessie Naidoo, Christine Qunta and gang..

I'm for truth, no matter who tells it.

I'm for justice,

no matter who it's for or against.

Malcolm X